PETER GRILL
AND THE PHILOSOPHER'S TIME

09

Story & Art by
DAISUKE HIYAMA

CONTENTS

Chapter **38** Peter Grill and the
Dragon's Contract 003

Chapter **39** Peter Grill and the
**Strongest Property
in the World** 045

Chapter **40** Peter Grill and the
Walking Nightmare 079

Chapter **41** Peter Grill and the
Door to Tomorrow 111

Chapter **42** Peter Grill and the
**Fearsome Tiger's
Attack** 149

Previously, on *Peter Grill*...

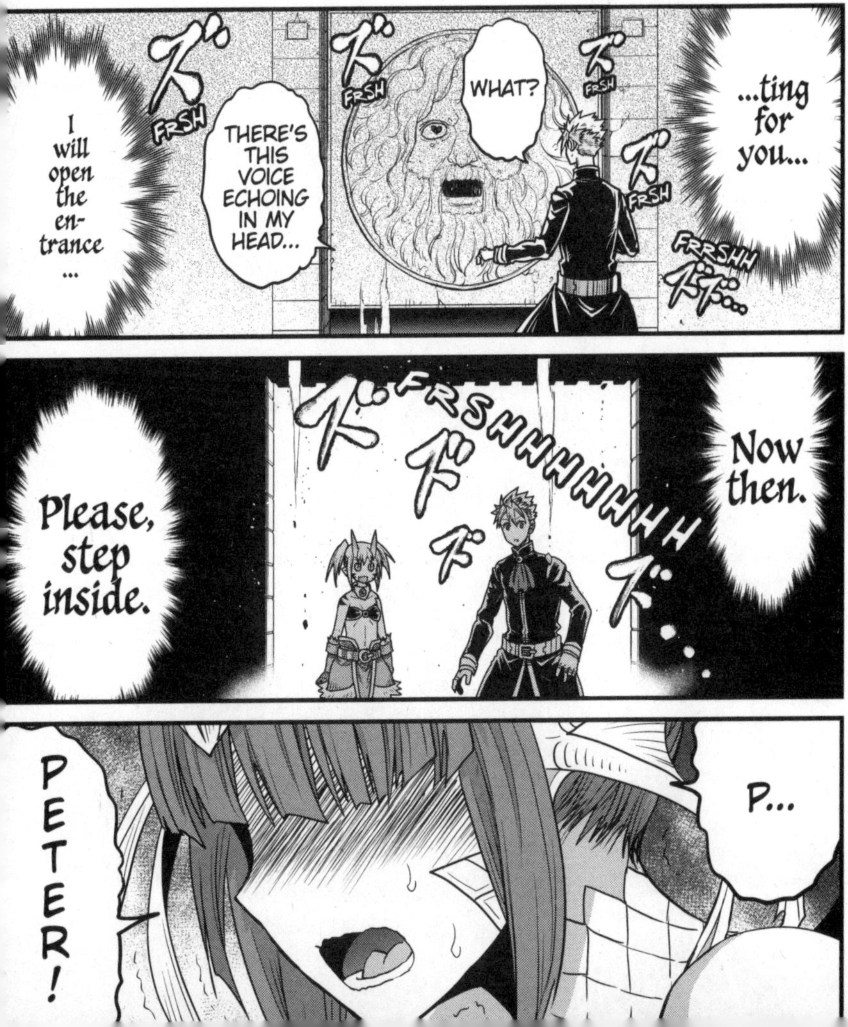
...ting for you...
FRRSHH
FRSH
WHAT?
FRSH
FRSH
THERE'S THIS VOICE ECHOING IN MY HEAD...
FRSH
I will open the entrance...
Now then.
FRSHHHHHHHHHHH
Please, step inside.
P...
PETER!

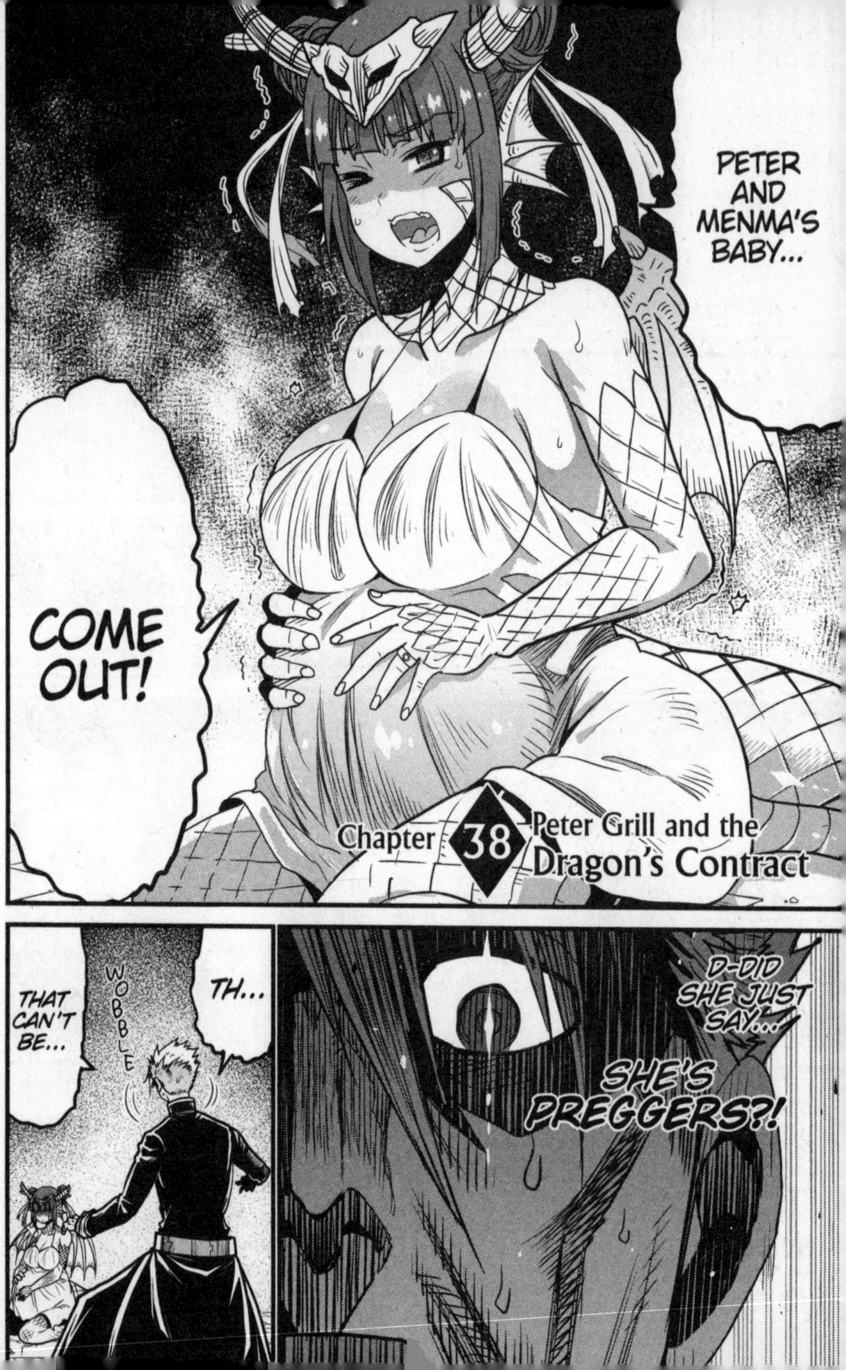
PETER AND MENMA'S BABY...
COME OUT!
Chapter 38 Peter Grill and the Dragon's Contract
D-DID SHE JUST SAY...
SHE'S PREGGERS?!
TH...
WOBBLE
THAT CAN'T BE...

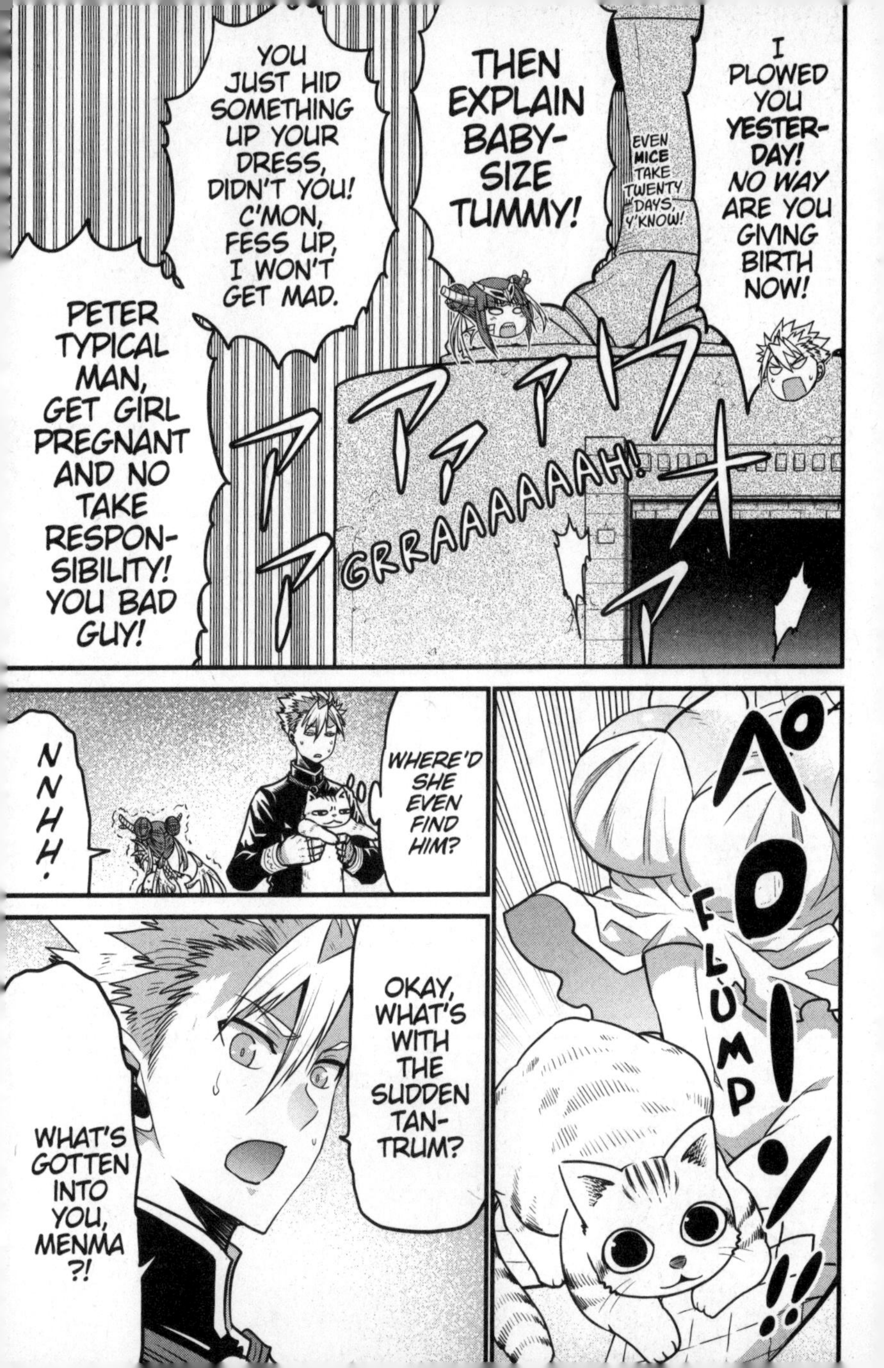
I PLOWED YOU YESTER-DAY! NO WAY ARE YOU GIVING BIRTH NOW!
EVEN MICE TAKE TWENTY DAYS, Y'KNOW!
THEN EXPLAIN BABY-SIZE TUMMY!
YOU JUST HID SOMETHING UP YOUR DRESS, DIDN'T YOU! C'MON, FESS UP, I WON'T GET MAD.
PETER TYPICAL MAN, GET GIRL PREGNANT AND NO TAKE RESPON-SIBILITY! YOU BAD GUY!
GRRAAAAAAAH!
FLUMP
WHERE'D SHE EVEN FIND HIM?
NNHH!
OKAY, WHAT'S WITH THE SUDDEN TAN-TRUM?
WHAT'S GOTTEN INTO YOU, MENMA?!

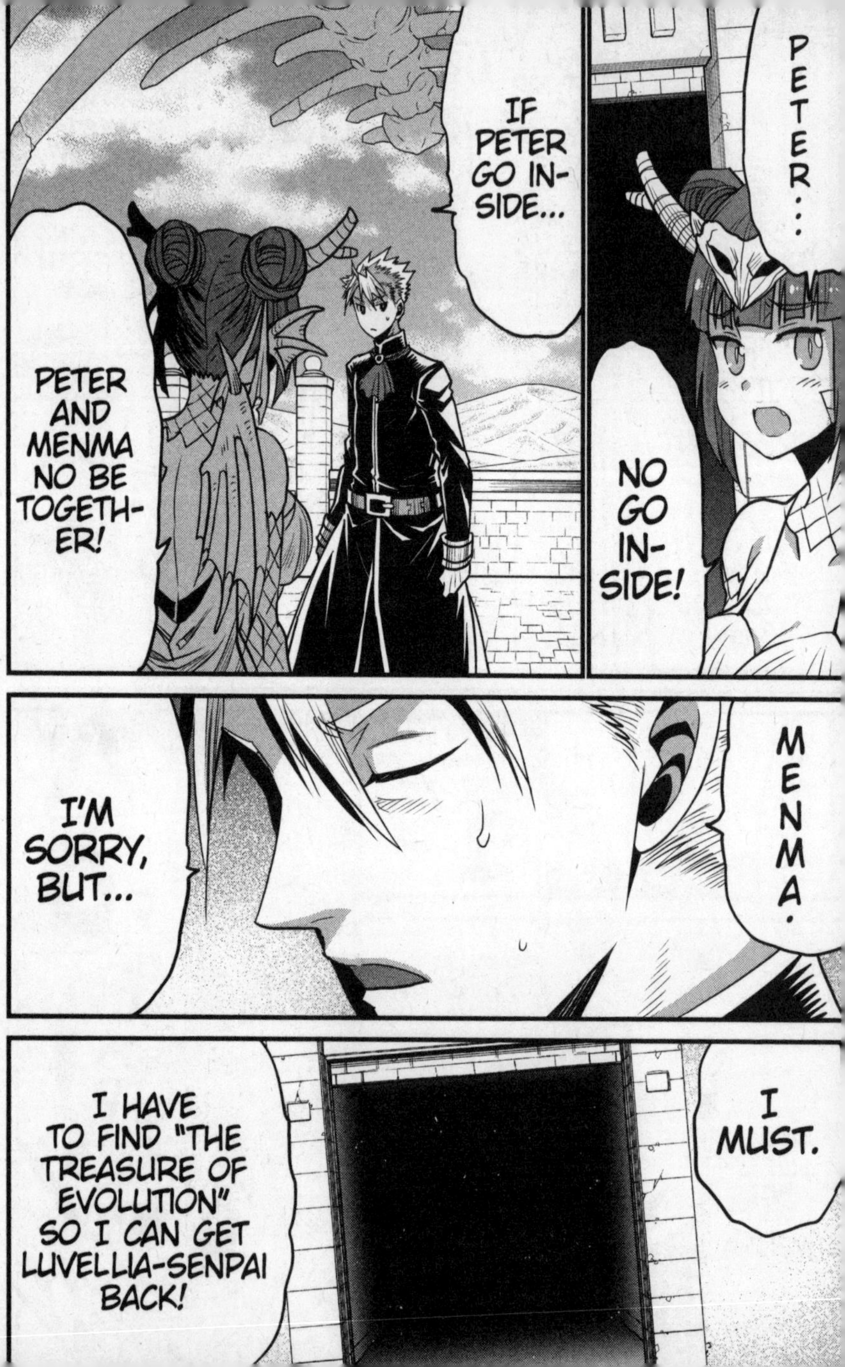
PETER...
NO GO INSIDE!
IF PETER GO INSIDE...
PETER AND MENMA NO BE TOGETHER!
MENMA.
I'M SORRY, BUT...
I MUST.
I HAVE TO FIND "THE TREASURE OF EVOLUTION" SO I CAN GET LUVELLIA-SENPAI BACK!

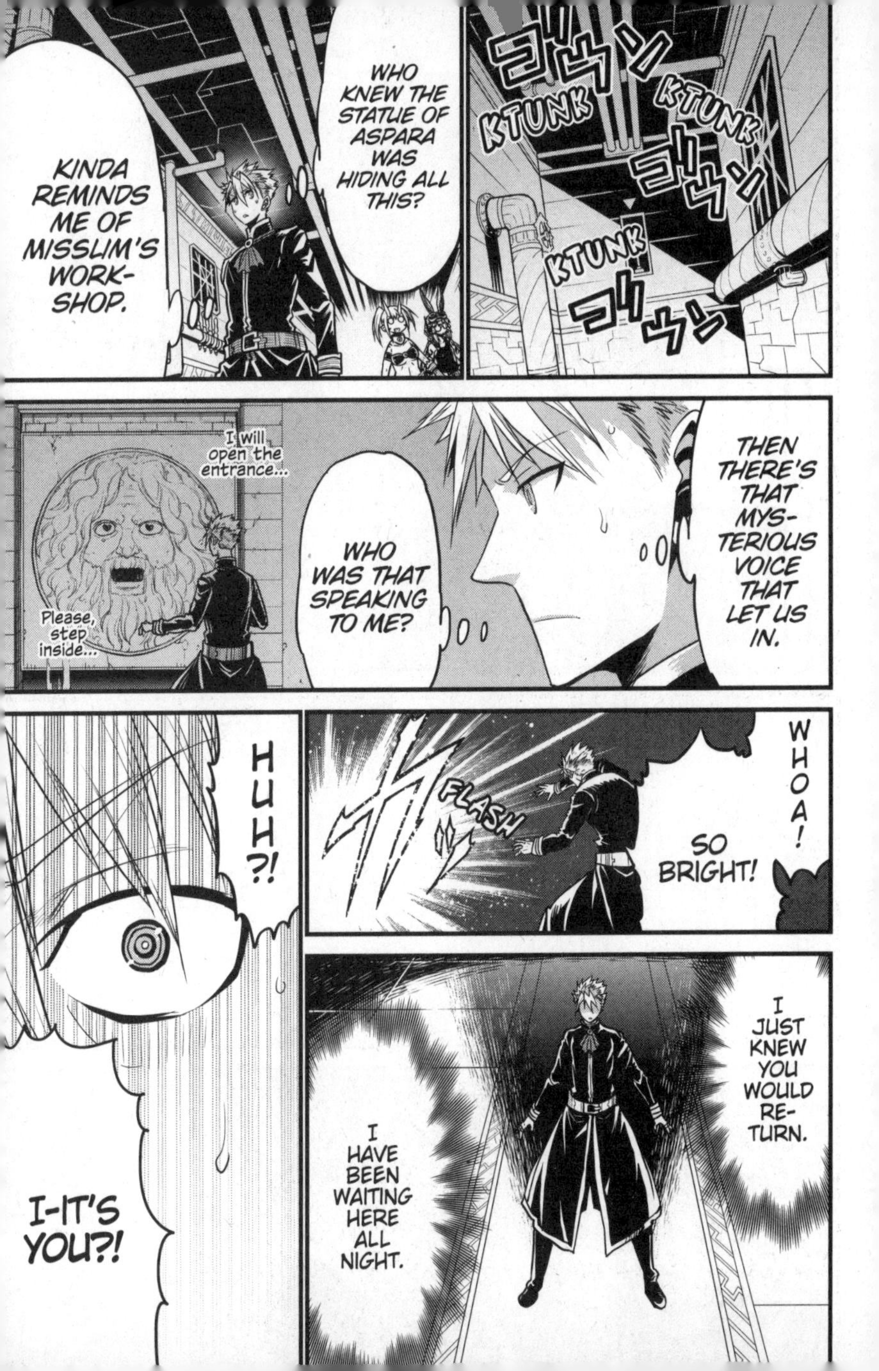
KTUNK
KTUNK
KTUNK
WHO KNEW THE STATUE OF ASPARA WAS HIDING ALL THIS?
KINDA REMINDS ME OF MISSLIM'S WORKSHOP.
THEN THERE'S THAT MYSTERIOUS VOICE THAT LET US IN.
WHO WAS THAT SPEAKING TO ME?
I will open the entrance...
Please, step inside...
WHOA!
SO BRIGHT!
FLASH
I JUST KNEW YOU WOULD RETURN.
I HAVE BEEN WAITING HERE ALL NIGHT.
HUH?!
I-IT'S YOU?!

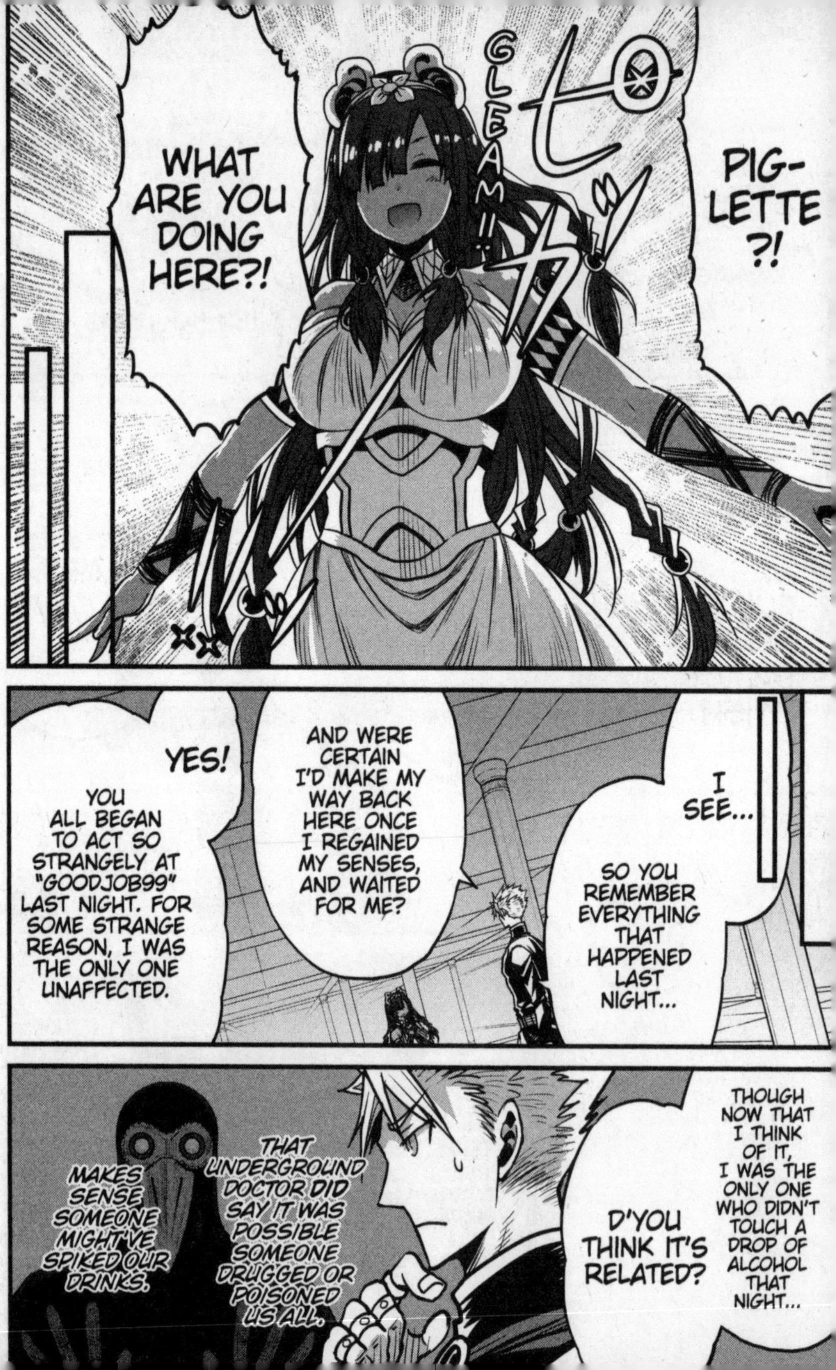
PIG-LETTE?!
GLEAM!!
WHAT ARE YOU DOING HERE?!
I SEE...
SO YOU REMEMBER EVERYTHING THAT HAPPENED LAST NIGHT...
AND WERE CERTAIN I'D MAKE MY WAY BACK HERE ONCE I REGAINED MY SENSES, AND WAITED FOR ME?
YES!
YOU ALL BEGAN TO ACT SO STRANGELY AT "GOODJOB99" LAST NIGHT. FOR SOME STRANGE REASON, I WAS THE ONLY ONE UNAFFECTED.
THOUGH NOW THAT I THINK OF IT, I WAS THE ONLY ONE WHO DIDN'T TOUCH A DROP OF ALCOHOL THAT NIGHT...
D'YOU THINK IT'S RELATED?
THAT UNDERGROUND DOCTOR DID SAY IT WAS POSSIBLE SOMEONE DRUGGED OR POISONED US ALL.
MAKES SENSE SOMEONE MIGHT'VE SPIKED OUR DRINKS.

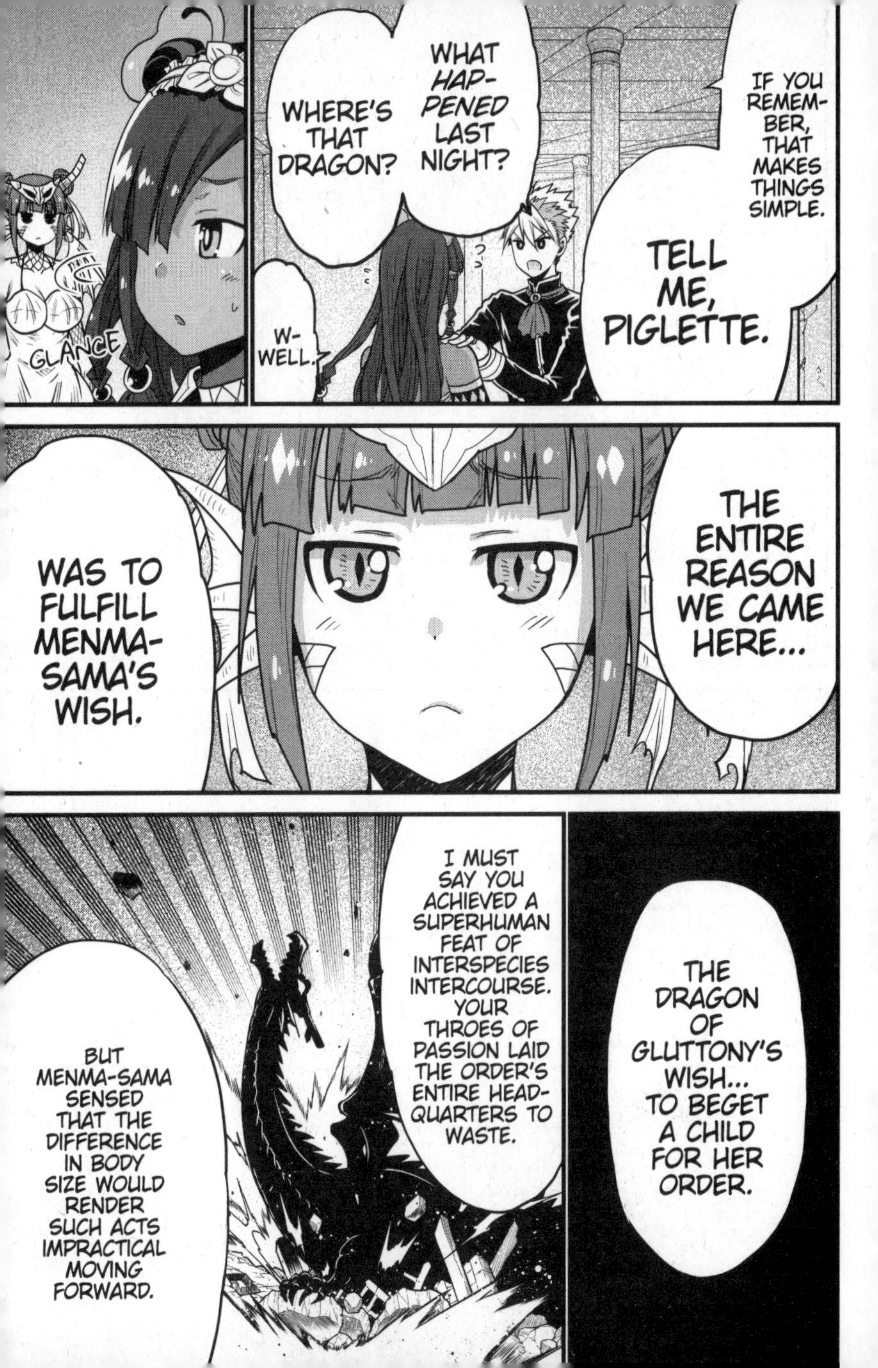
IF YOU REMEMBER, THAT MAKES THINGS SIMPLE.
TELL ME, PIGLETTE.
WHAT HAPPENED LAST NIGHT?
WHERE'S THAT DRAGON?
W-WELL...
GLANCE
THE ENTIRE REASON WE CAME HERE...
WAS TO FULFILL MENMA-SAMA'S WISH.
THE DRAGON OF GLUTTONY'S WISH... TO BEGET A CHILD FOR HER ORDER.
I MUST SAY YOU ACHIEVED A SUPERHUMAN FEAT OF INTERSPECIES INTERCOURSE. YOUR THROES OF PASSION LAID THE ORDER'S ENTIRE HEAD-QUARTERS TO WASTE.
BUT MENMA-SAMA SENSED THAT THE DIFFERENCE IN BODY SIZE WOULD RENDER SUCH ACTS IMPRACTICAL MOVING FORWARD.

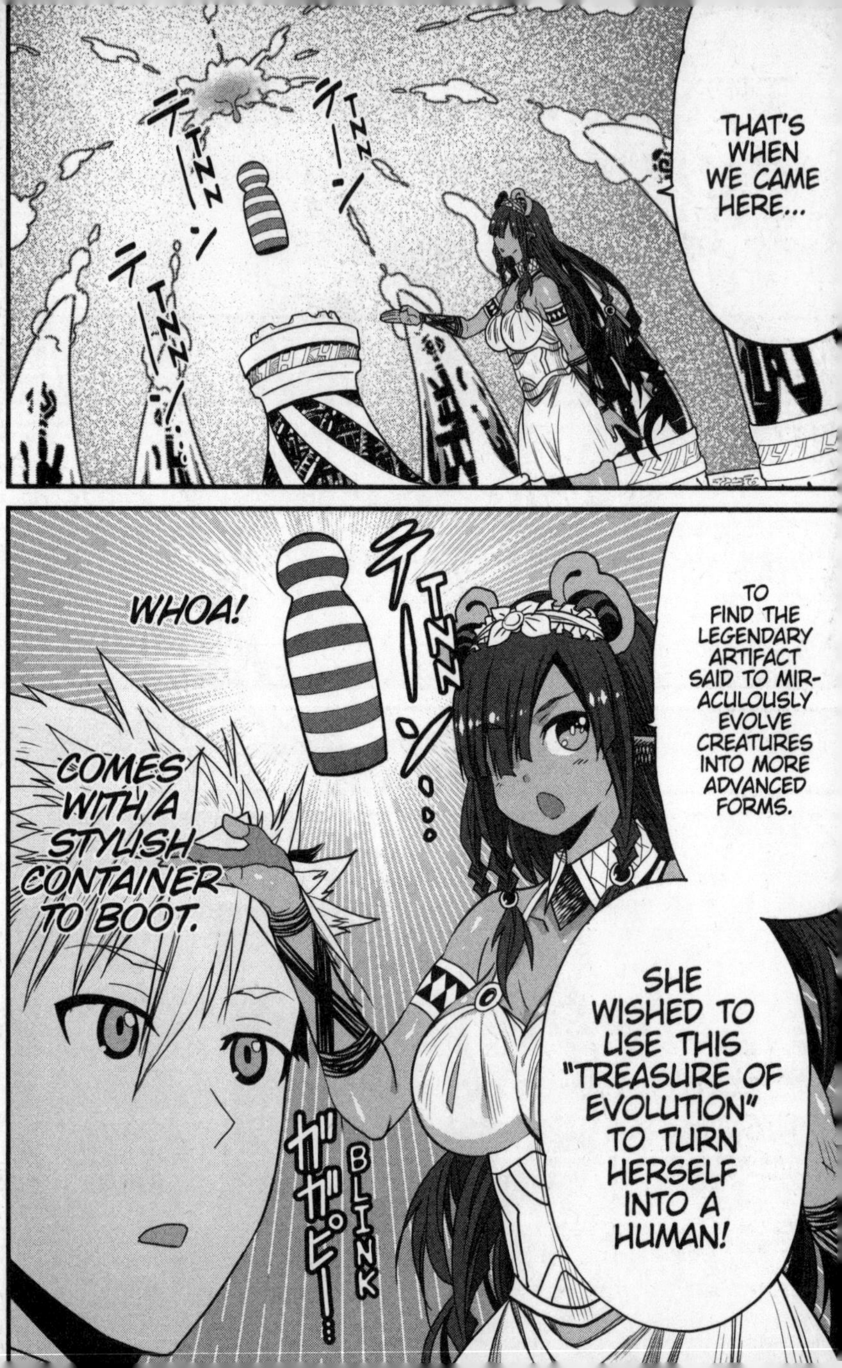
THAT'S WHEN WE CAME HERE...
TNN
TNN
TNN
TO FIND THE LEGENDARY ARTIFACT SAID TO MIR-ACULOUSLY EVOLVE CREATURES INTO MORE ADVANCED FORMS.
SHE WISHED TO USE THIS "TREASURE OF EVOLUTION" TO TURN HERSELF INTO A HUMAN!
TNN
WHOA!
COMES WITH A STYLISH CONTAINER TO BOOT.
BLINK

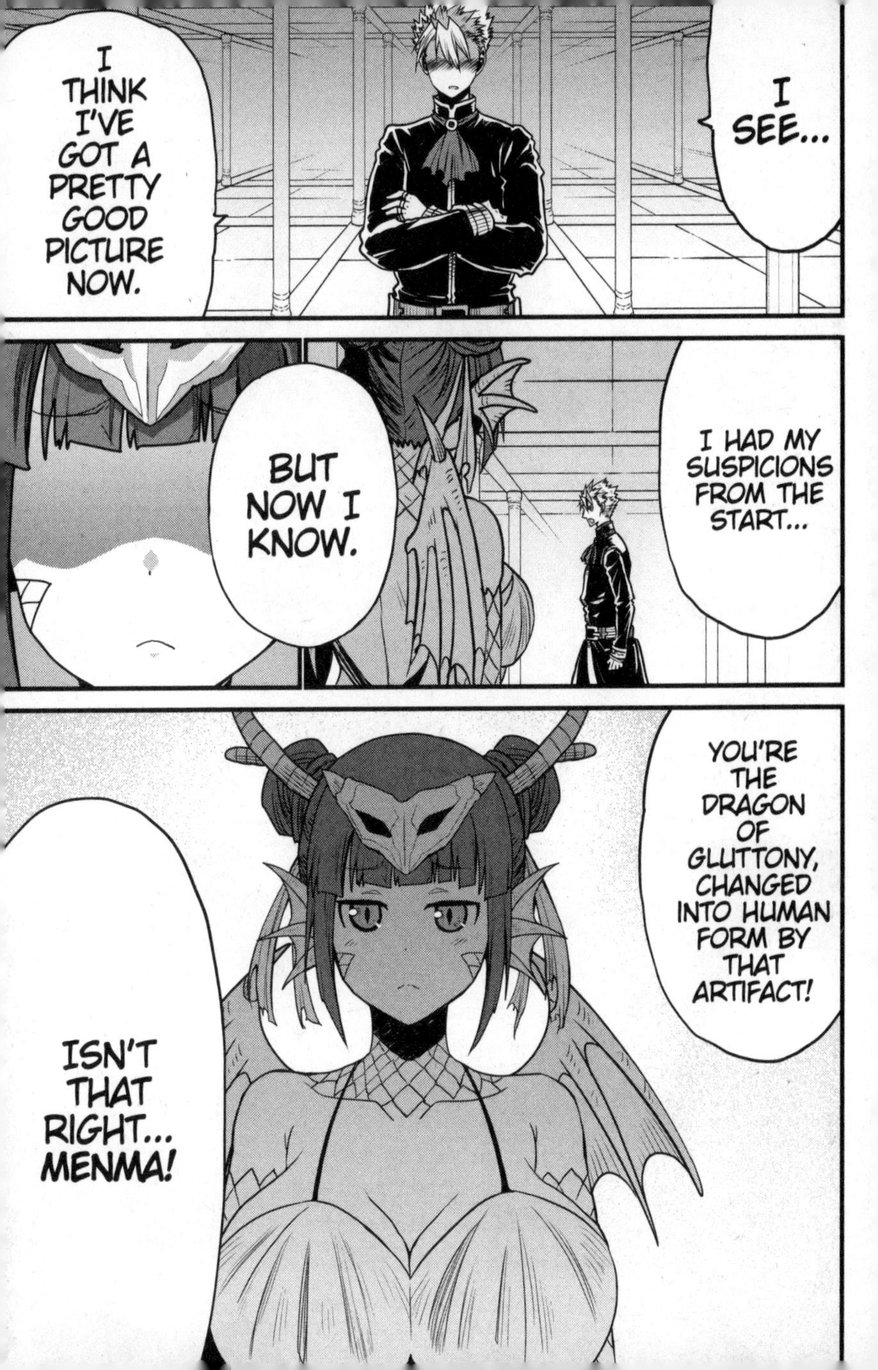
I SEE...
I THINK I'VE GOT A PRETTY GOOD PICTURE NOW.
I HAD MY SUSPICIONS FROM THE START...
BUT NOW I KNOW.
YOU'RE THE DRAGON OF GLUTTONY, CHANGED INTO HUMAN FORM BY THAT ARTIFACT!
ISN'T THAT RIGHT... MENMA!

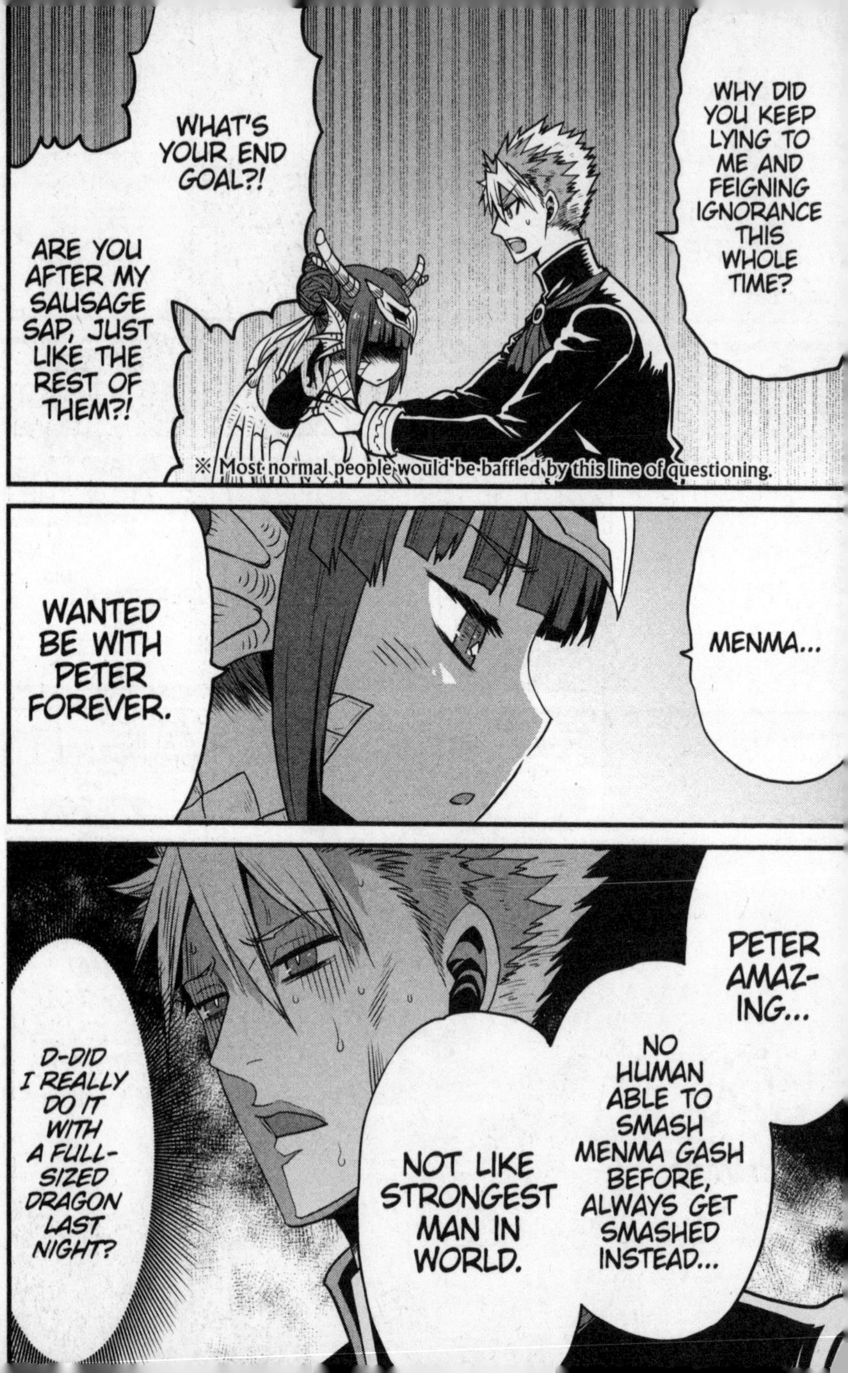
WHY DID YOU KEEP LYING TO ME AND FEIGNING IGNORANCE THIS WHOLE TIME?
WHAT'S YOUR END GOAL?!
ARE YOU AFTER MY SAUSAGE SAP, JUST LIKE THE REST OF THEM?!
※ Most normal people would be baffled by this line of questioning.
MENMA...
WANTED BE WITH PETER FOREVER.
PETER AMAZ-ING...
NO HUMAN ABLE TO SMASH MENMA GASH BEFORE, ALWAYS GET SMASHED INSTEAD...
NOT LIKE STRONGEST MAN IN WORLD.
D-DID I REALLY DO IT WITH A FULL-SIZED DRAGON LAST NIGHT?

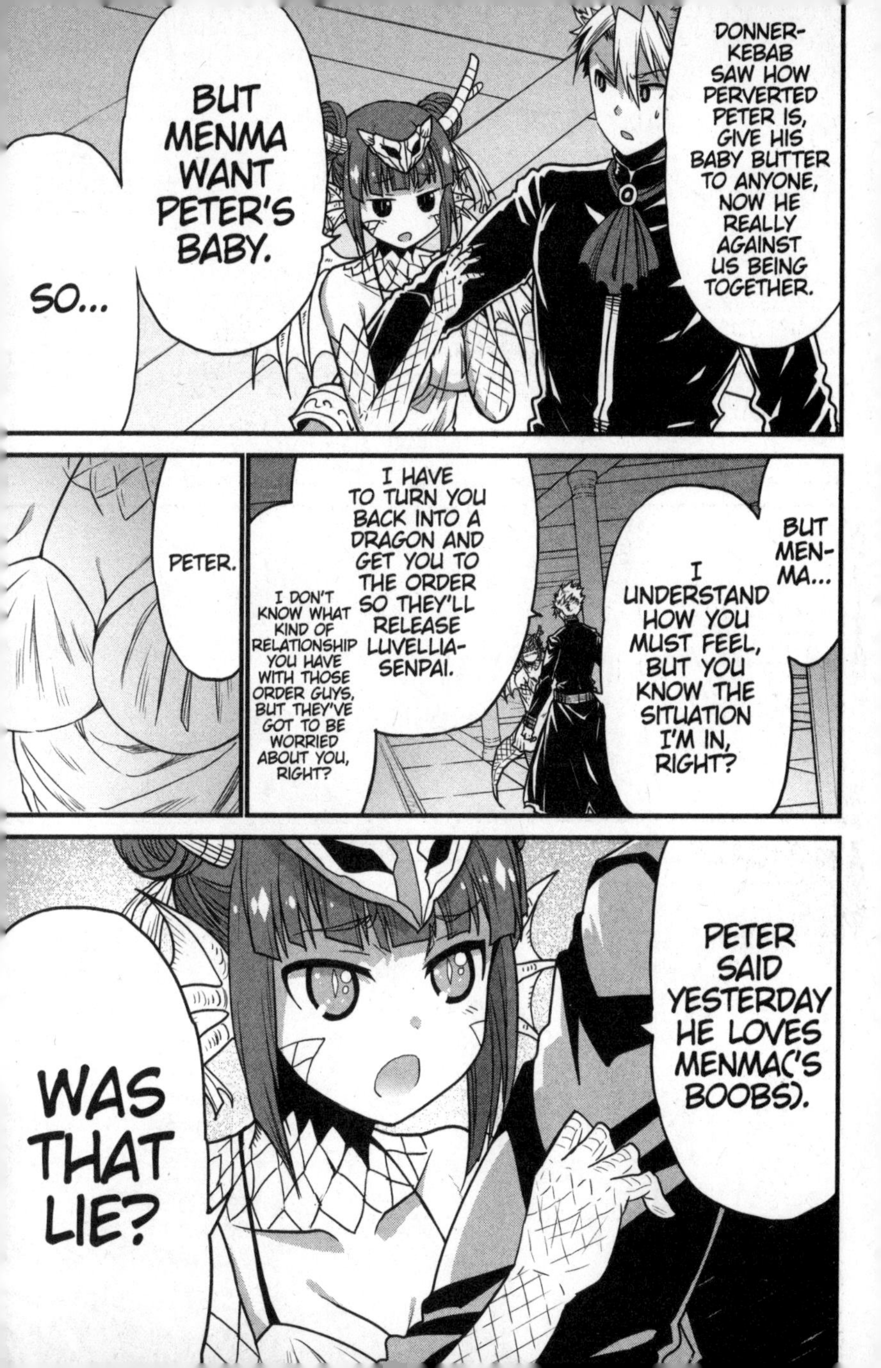
DONNER-KEBAB SAW HOW PERVERTED PETER IS, GIVE HIS BABY BUTTER TO ANYONE, NOW HE REALLY AGAINST US BEING TOGETHER.
BUT MENMA WANT PETER'S BABY.
SO...
BUT MENMA...
I UNDERSTAND HOW YOU MUST FEEL, BUT YOU KNOW THE SITUATION I'M IN, RIGHT?
I HAVE TO TURN YOU BACK INTO A DRAGON AND GET YOU TO THE ORDER SO THEY'LL RELEASE LUVELLIA-SENPAI.
I DON'T KNOW WHAT KIND OF RELATIONSHIP YOU HAVE WITH THOSE ORDER GUYS, BUT THEY'VE GOT TO BE WORRIED ABOUT YOU, RIGHT?
PETER.
PETER SAID YESTERDAY HE LOVES MENMA('S BOOBS).
WAS THAT LIE?

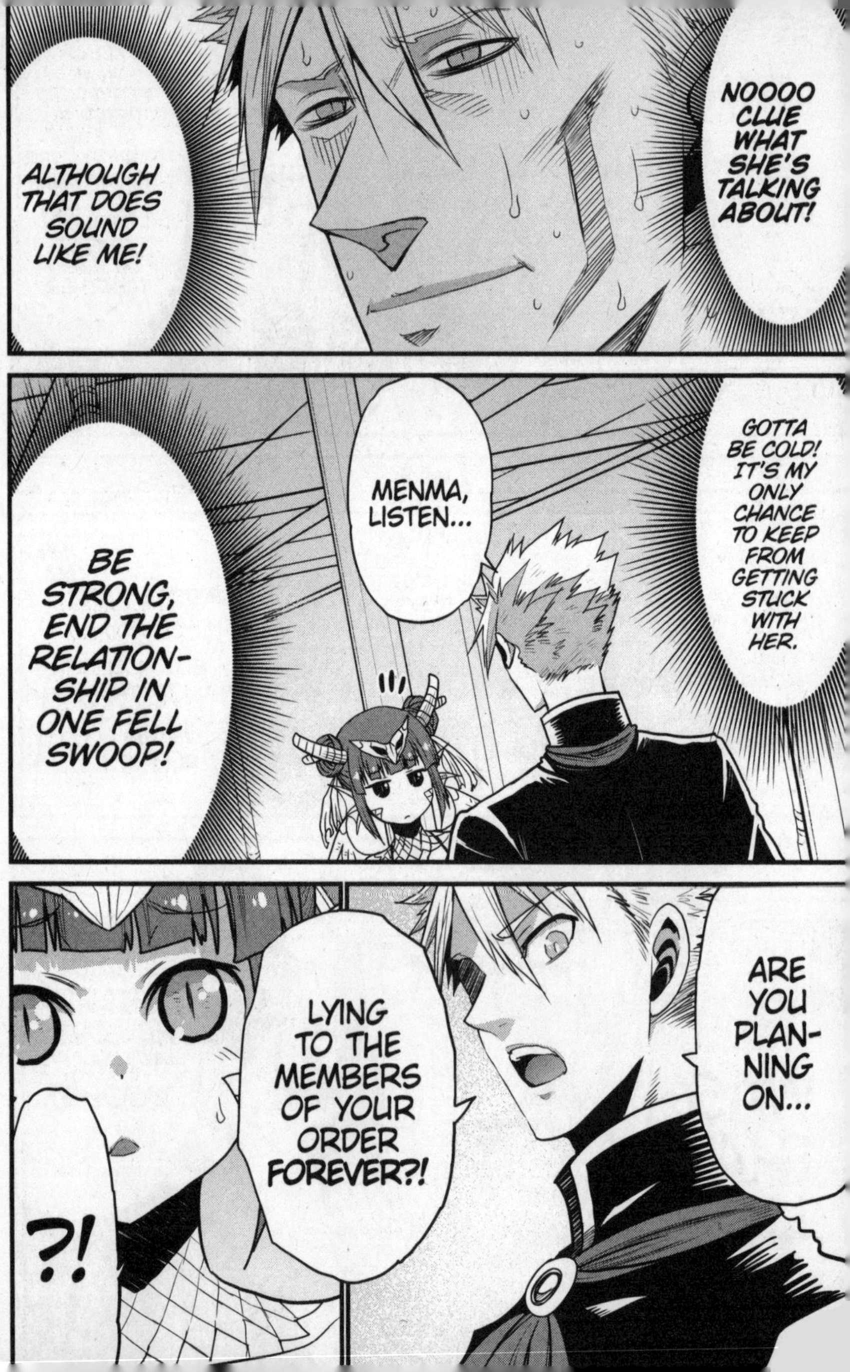
NOOOO CLUE WHAT SHE'S TALKING ABOUT!
ALTHOUGH THAT DOES SOUND LIKE ME!
GOTTA BE COLD! IT'S MY ONLY CHANCE TO KEEP FROM GETTING STUCK WITH HER.
MENMA, LISTEN...
BE STRONG, END THE RELATION-SHIP IN ONE FELL SWOOP!
ARE YOU PLAN-NING ON...
LYING TO THE MEMBERS OF YOUR ORDER FOREVER?!
?!

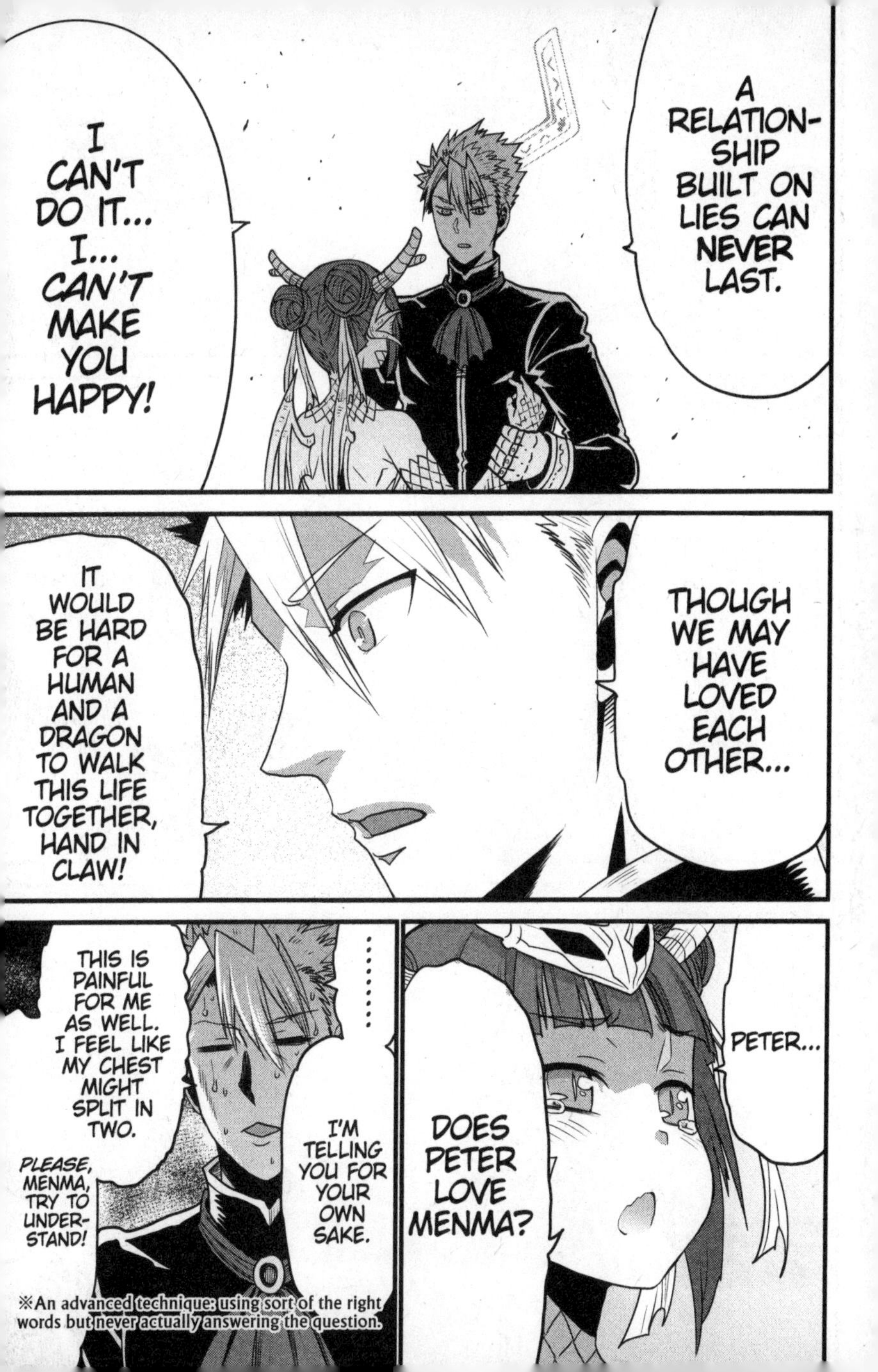
A RELATIONSHIP BUILT ON LIES CAN NEVER LAST.
I CAN'T DO IT... I... CAN'T MAKE YOU HAPPY!
THOUGH WE MAY HAVE LOVED EACH OTHER...
IT WOULD BE HARD FOR A HUMAN AND A DRAGON TO WALK THIS LIFE TOGETHER, HAND IN CLAW!
PETER...
DOES PETER LOVE MENMA?
....
I'M TELLING YOU FOR YOUR OWN SAKE.
THIS IS PAINFUL FOR ME AS WELL. I FEEL LIKE MY CHEST MIGHT SPLIT IN TWO.
PLEASE, MENMA, TRY TO UNDERSTAND!
※An advanced technique: using sort of the right words but never actually answering the question.

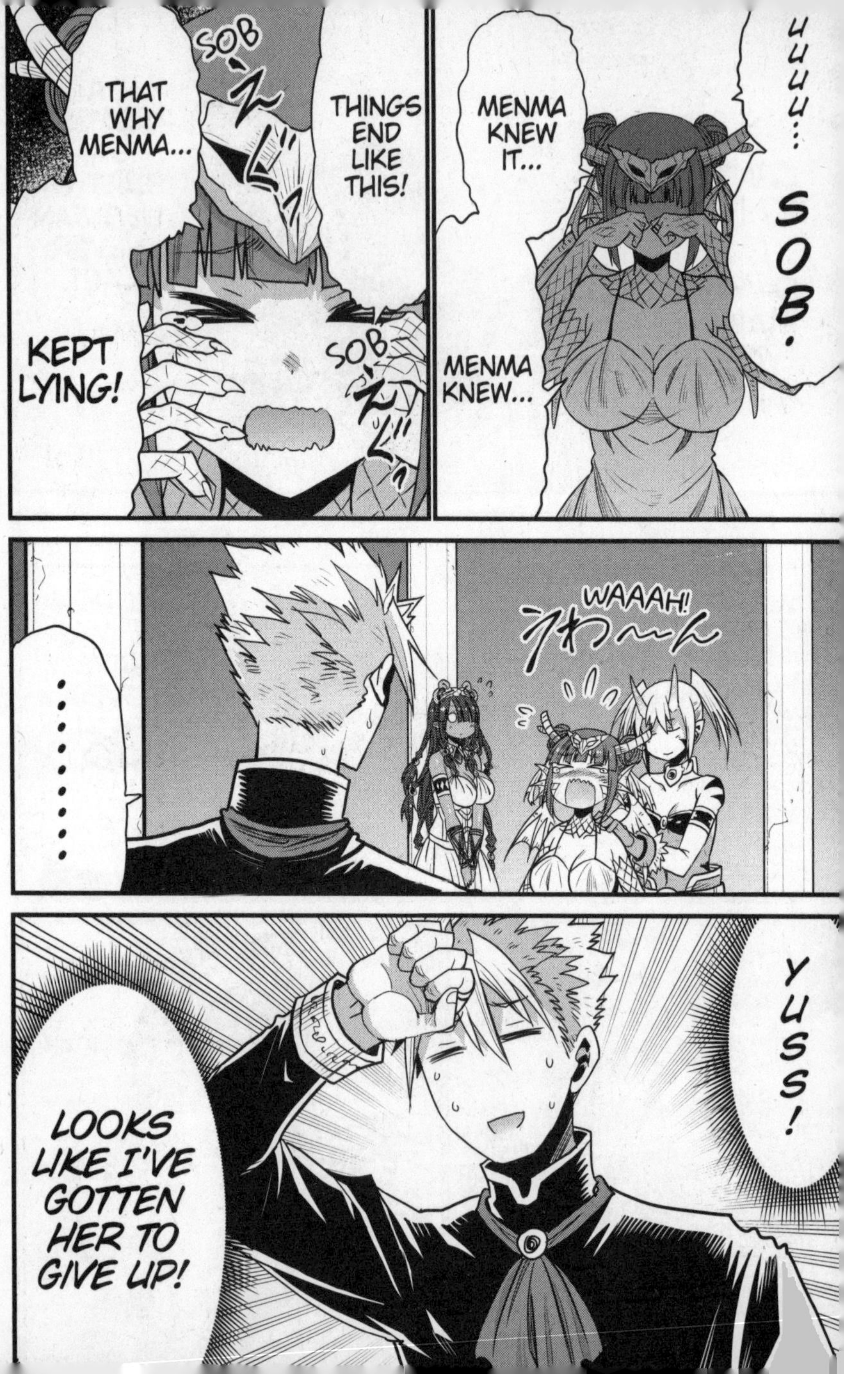
UUUU...
SOB.
MENMA KNEW IT...
MENMA KNEW...
THINGS END LIKE THIS!
SOB
THAT WHY MENMA...
SOB
KEPT LYING!
WAAAH!
うわ〜ん
......
YUSS!
LOOKS LIKE I'VE GOTTEN HER TO GIVE UP!

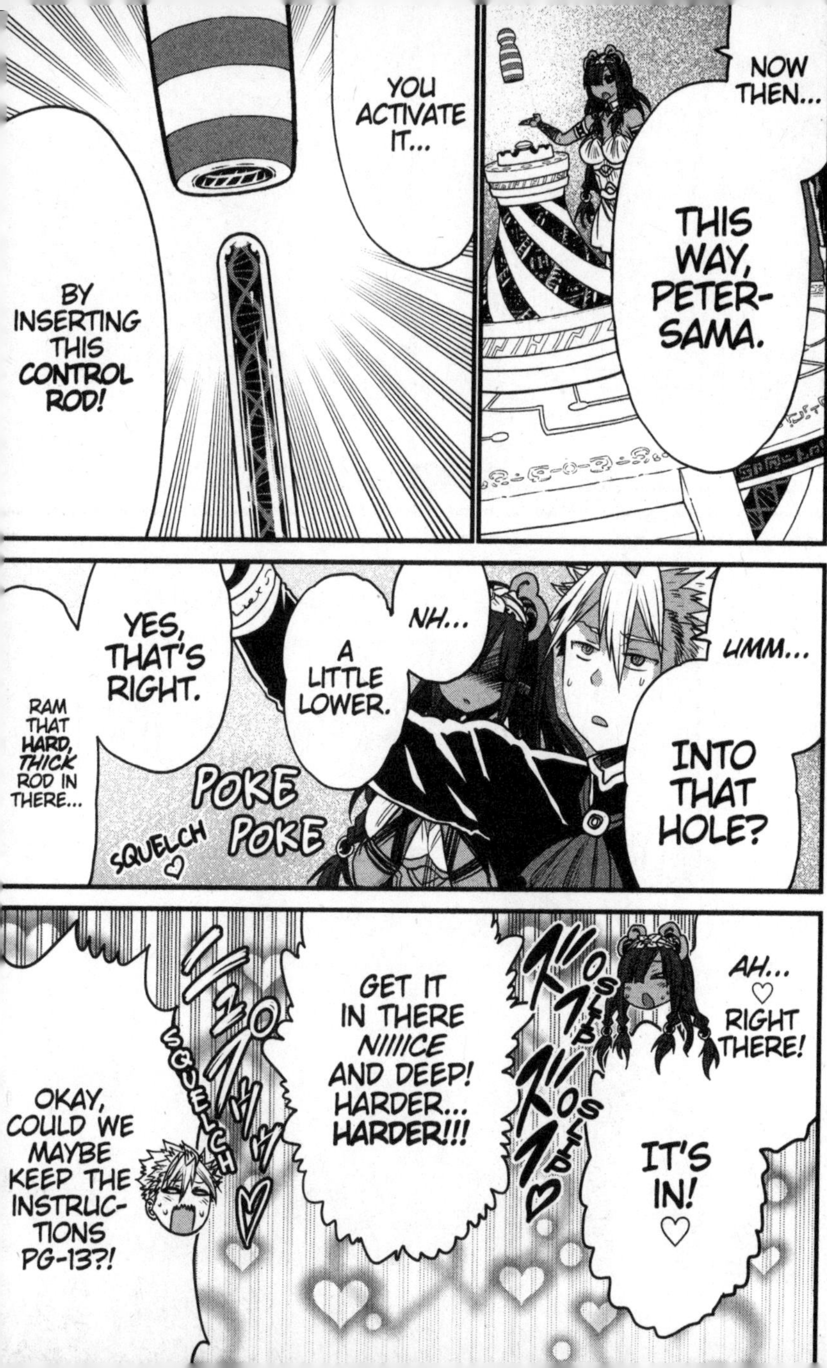
NOW THEN...
THIS WAY, PETER-SAMA.
YOU ACTIVATE IT...
BY INSERTING THIS CONTROL ROD!
UMM...
INTO THAT HOLE?
NH...
A LITTLE LOWER.
YES, THAT'S RIGHT.
RAM THAT HARD, THICK ROD IN THERE...
POKE POKE
SQUELCH ♡
AH... ♡ RIGHT THERE!
IT'S IN! ♡
SLIP
SLIP ♡
GET IT IN THERE NIIIICE AND DEEP! HARDER... HARDER!!!
SQUELCH ♡
OKAY, COULD WE MAYBE KEEP THE INSTRUCTIONS PG-13?!

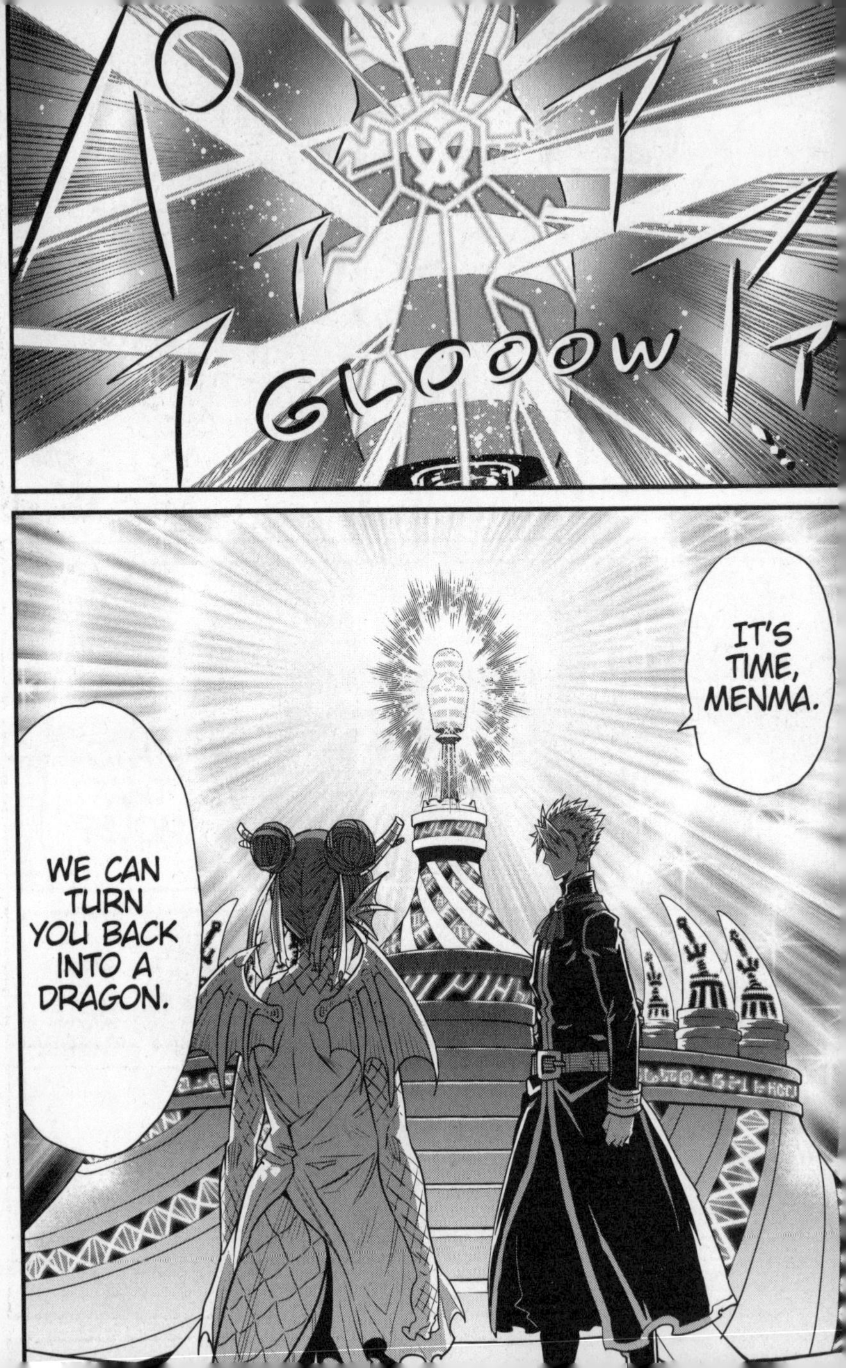
GLOOOOW
IT'S TIME, MENMA.
WE CAN TURN YOU BACK INTO A DRAGON.

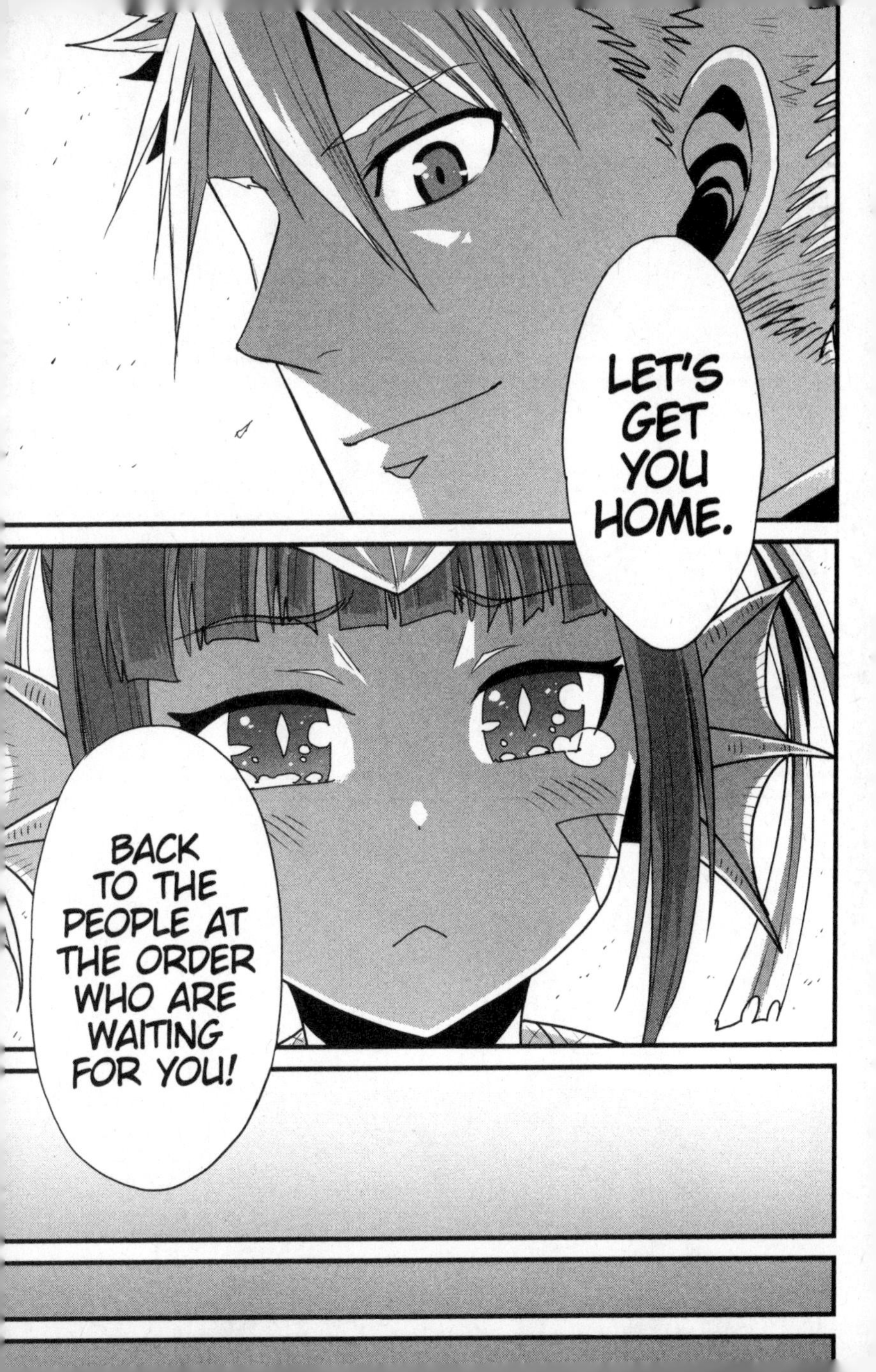
LET'S GET YOU HOME.
BACK TO THE PEOPLE AT THE ORDER WHO ARE WAITING FOR YOU!

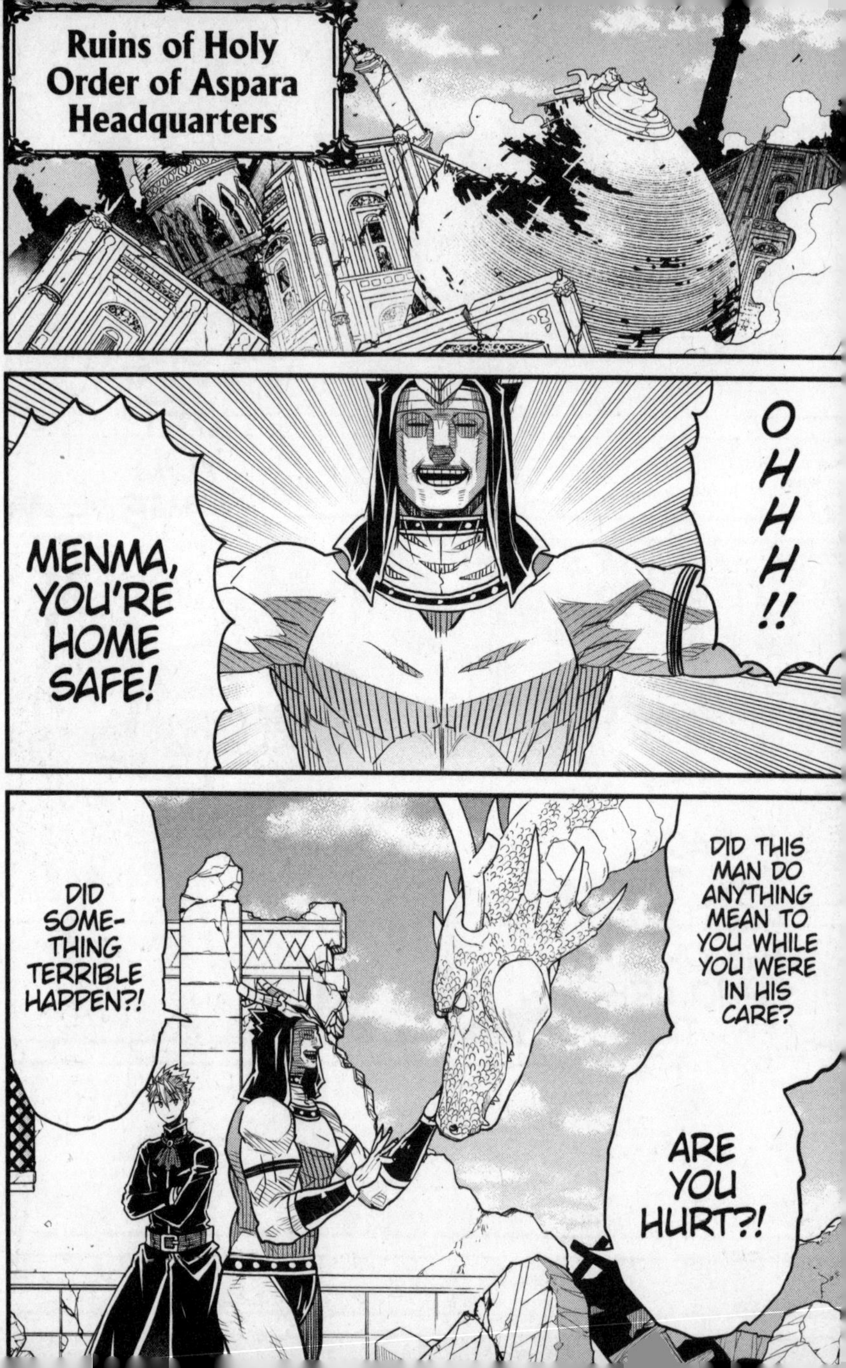
Ruins of Holy Order of Aspara Headquarters
OHHH!!
MENMA, YOU'RE HOME SAFE!
DID THIS MAN DO ANYTHING MEAN TO YOU WHILE YOU WERE IN HIS CARE?
ARE YOU HURT?!
DID SOME-THING TERRIBLE HAPPEN?!

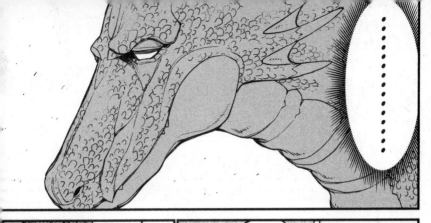

．．．．．．

RIGHT THEN.

I'VE FULFILLED MY PART OF THE BARGAIN.

O-OH...

MENMA?!

...

TRUDGE

．．．．．．

VERY WELL.

NOW IT'S YOUR TURN TO MAKE GOOD ON THE HOSTAGE.

RELEASE LUVELLIA-SENPAI AT ONCE!

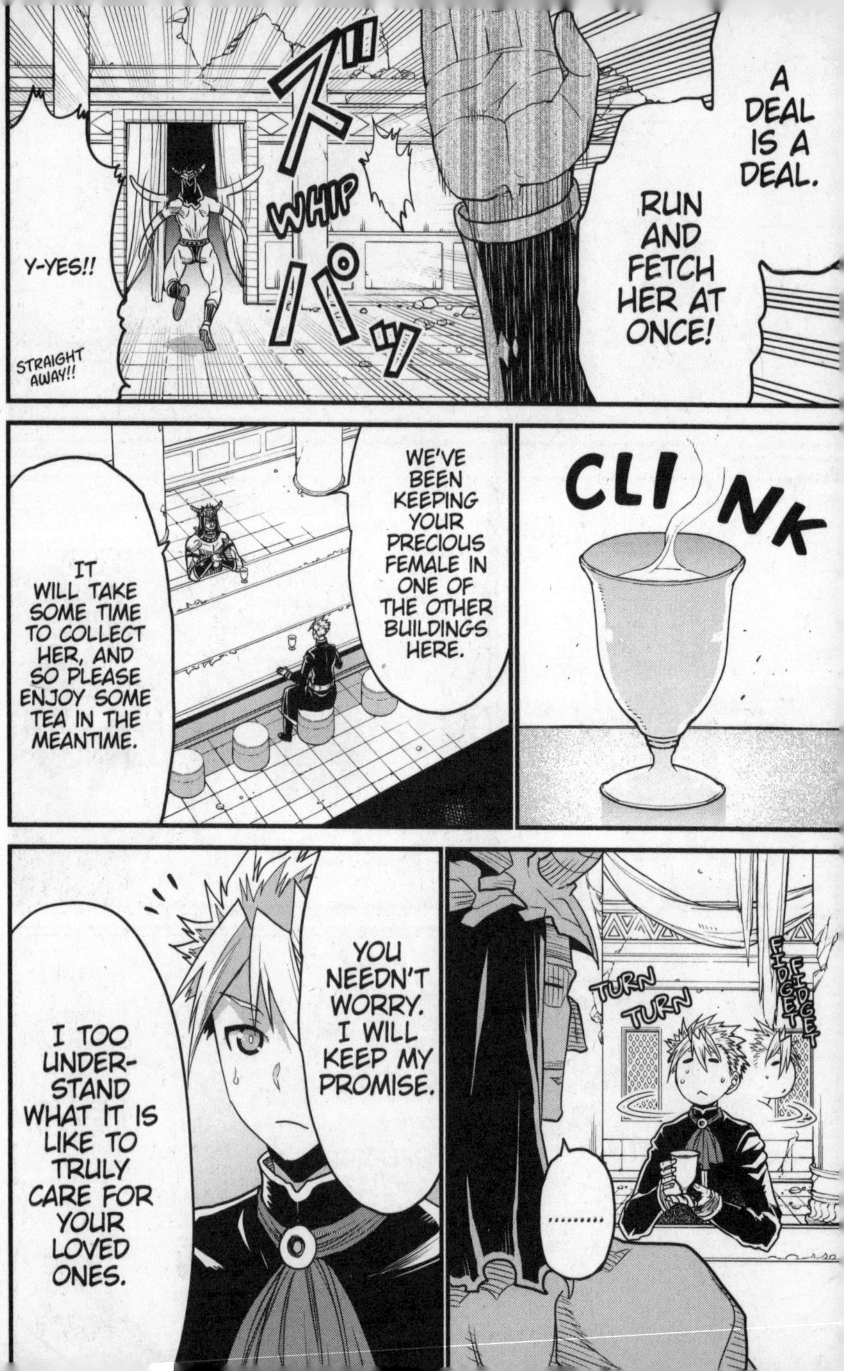
A DEAL IS A DEAL.
RUN AND FETCH HER AT ONCE!
WHIP
Y-YES!!
STRAIGHT AWAY!!
CLINK
WE'VE BEEN KEEPING YOUR PRECIOUS FEMALE IN ONE OF THE OTHER BUILDINGS HERE.
IT WILL TAKE SOME TIME TO COLLECT HER, AND SO PLEASE ENJOY SOME TEA IN THE MEANTIME.
TURN TURN
FIDGET FIDGET
....
YOU NEEDN'T WORRY. I WILL KEEP MY PROMISE.
I TOO UNDER-STAND WHAT IT IS LIKE TO TRULY CARE FOR YOUR LOVED ONES.

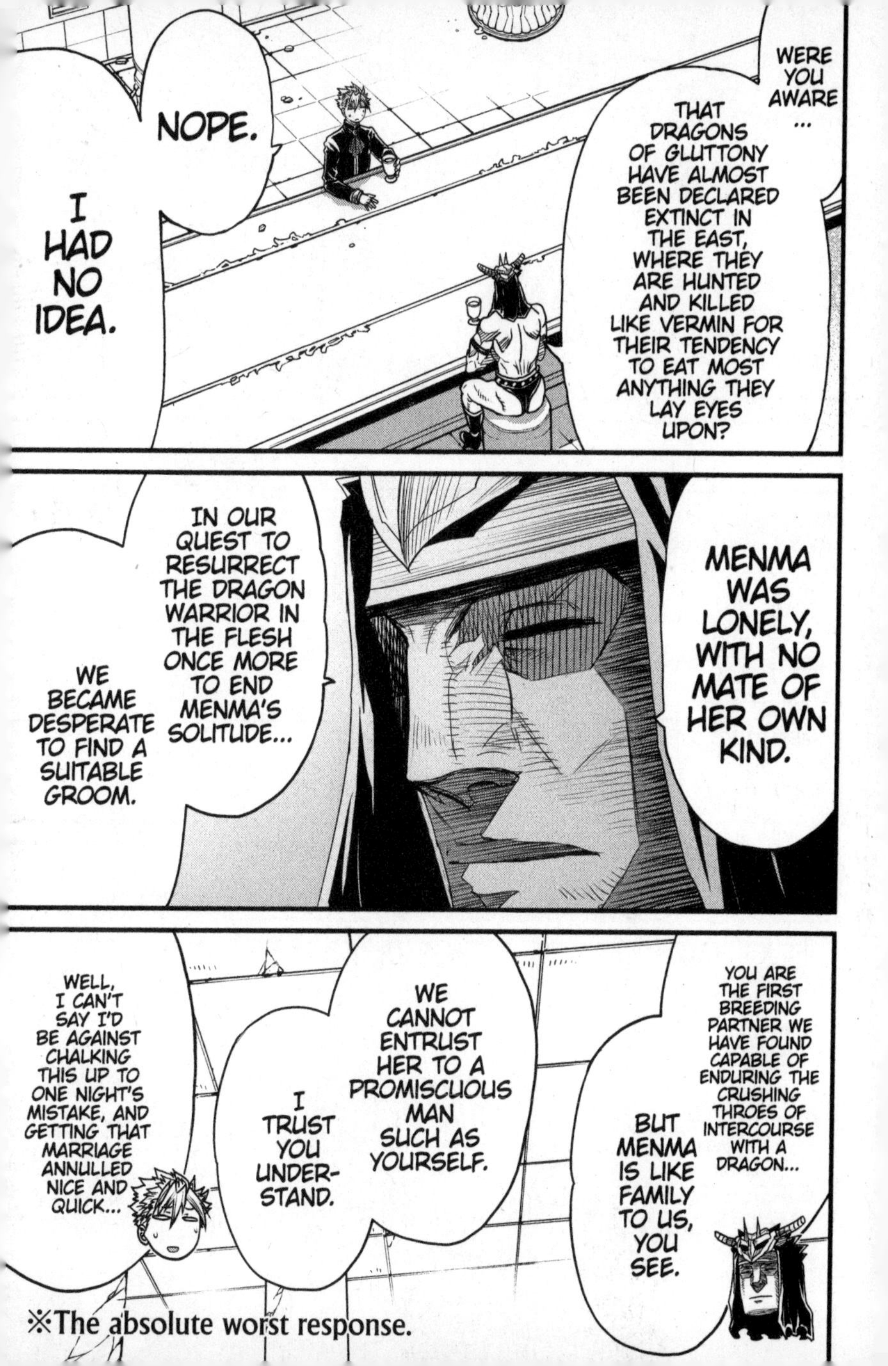
WERE YOU AWARE...
THAT DRAGONS OF GLUTTONY HAVE ALMOST BEEN DECLARED EXTINCT IN THE EAST, WHERE THEY ARE HUNTED AND KILLED LIKE VERMIN FOR THEIR TENDENCY TO EAT MOST ANYTHING THEY LAY EYES UPON?
NOPE.
I HAD NO IDEA.
MENMA WAS LONELY, WITH NO MATE OF HER OWN KIND.
IN OUR QUEST TO RESURRECT THE DRAGON WARRIOR IN THE FLESH ONCE MORE TO END MENMA'S SOLITUDE...
WE BECAME DESPERATE TO FIND A SUITABLE GROOM.
YOU ARE THE FIRST BREEDING PARTNER WE HAVE FOUND CAPABLE OF ENDURING THE CRUSHING THROES OF INTERCOURSE WITH A DRAGON...
BUT MENMA IS LIKE FAMILY TO US, YOU SEE.
WE CANNOT ENTRUST HER TO A PROMISCUOUS MAN SUCH AS YOURSELF.
I TRUST YOU UNDER-STAND.
WELL, I CAN'T SAY I'D BE AGAINST CHALKING THIS UP TO ONE NIGHT'S MISTAKE, AND GETTING THAT MARRIAGE ANNULLED NICE AND QUICK...
※The absolute worst response.

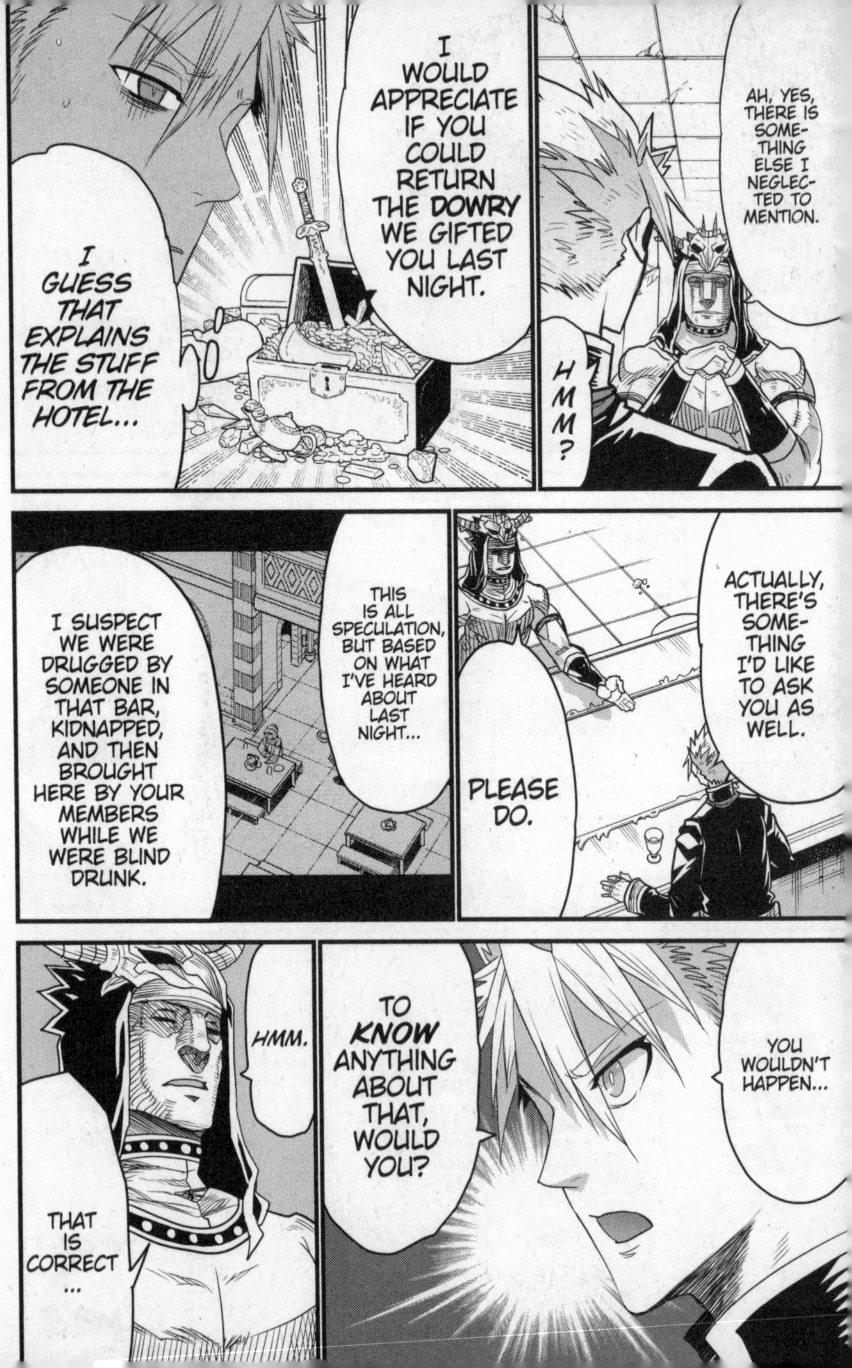
AH, YES, THERE IS SOMETHING ELSE I NEGLECTED TO MENTION.
HMM?
I WOULD APPRECIATE IF YOU COULD RETURN THE DOWRY WE GIFTED YOU LAST NIGHT.
I GUESS THAT EXPLAINS THE STUFF FROM THE HOTEL...
ACTUALLY, THERE'S SOMETHING I'D LIKE TO ASK YOU AS WELL.
PLEASE DO.
THIS IS ALL SPECULATION, BUT BASED ON WHAT I'VE HEARD ABOUT LAST NIGHT...
I SUSPECT WE WERE DRUGGED BY SOMEONE IN THAT BAR, KIDNAPPED, AND THEN BROUGHT HERE BY YOUR MEMBERS WHILE WE WERE BLIND DRUNK.
YOU WOULDN'T HAPPEN...
TO KNOW ANYTHING ABOUT THAT, WOULD YOU?
HMM.
THAT IS CORRECT...

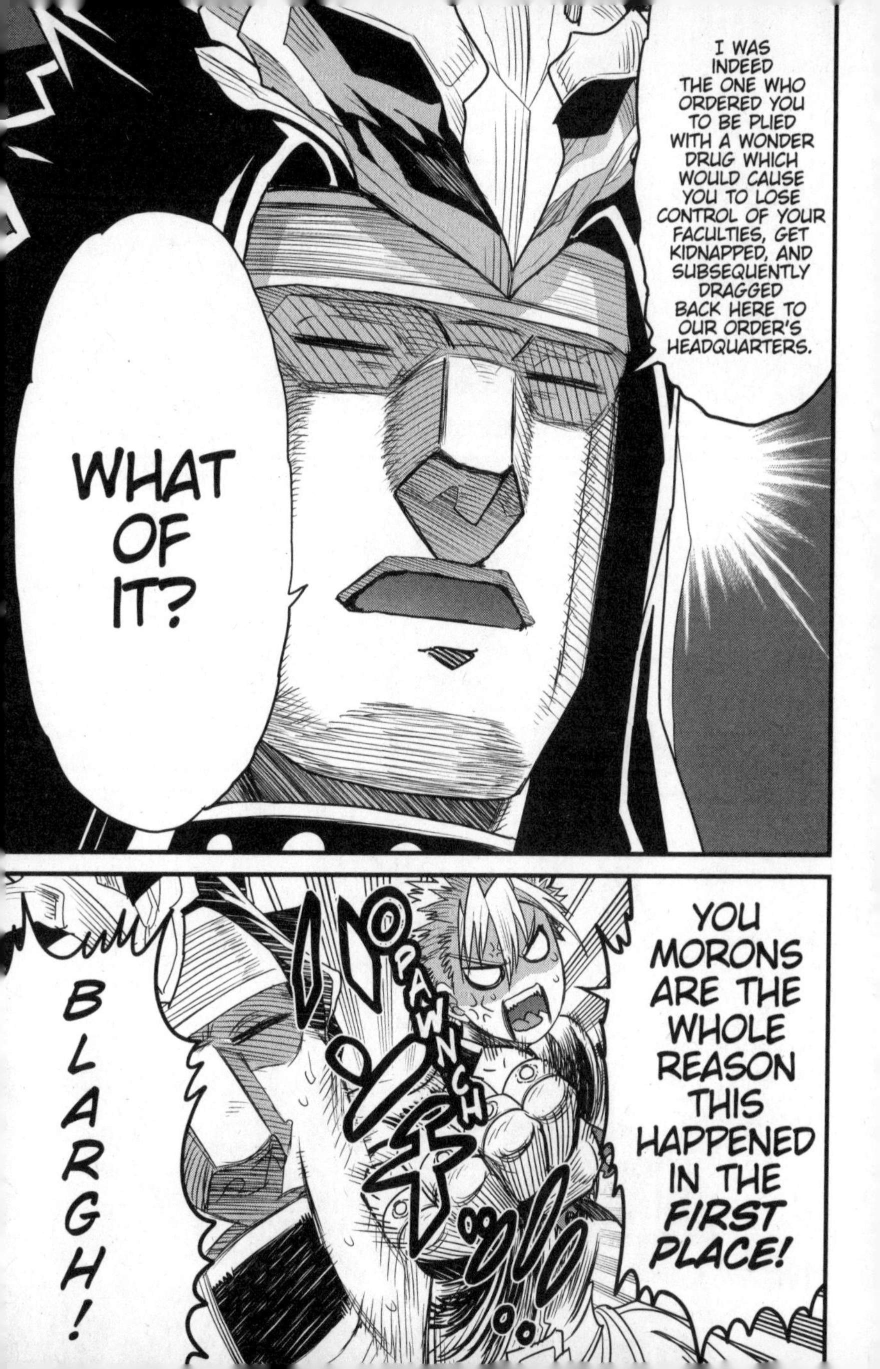
I WAS INDEED THE ONE WHO ORDERED YOU TO BE PLIED WITH A WONDER DRUG WHICH WOULD CAUSE YOU TO LOSE CONTROL OF YOUR FACULTIES, GET KIDNAPPED, AND SUBSEQUENTLY DRAGGED BACK HERE TO OUR ORDER'S HEADQUARTERS.
WHAT OF IT?
YOU MORONS ARE THE WHOLE REASON THIS HAPPENED IN THE *FIRST PLACE!*
PAWNCH
BLARGH!

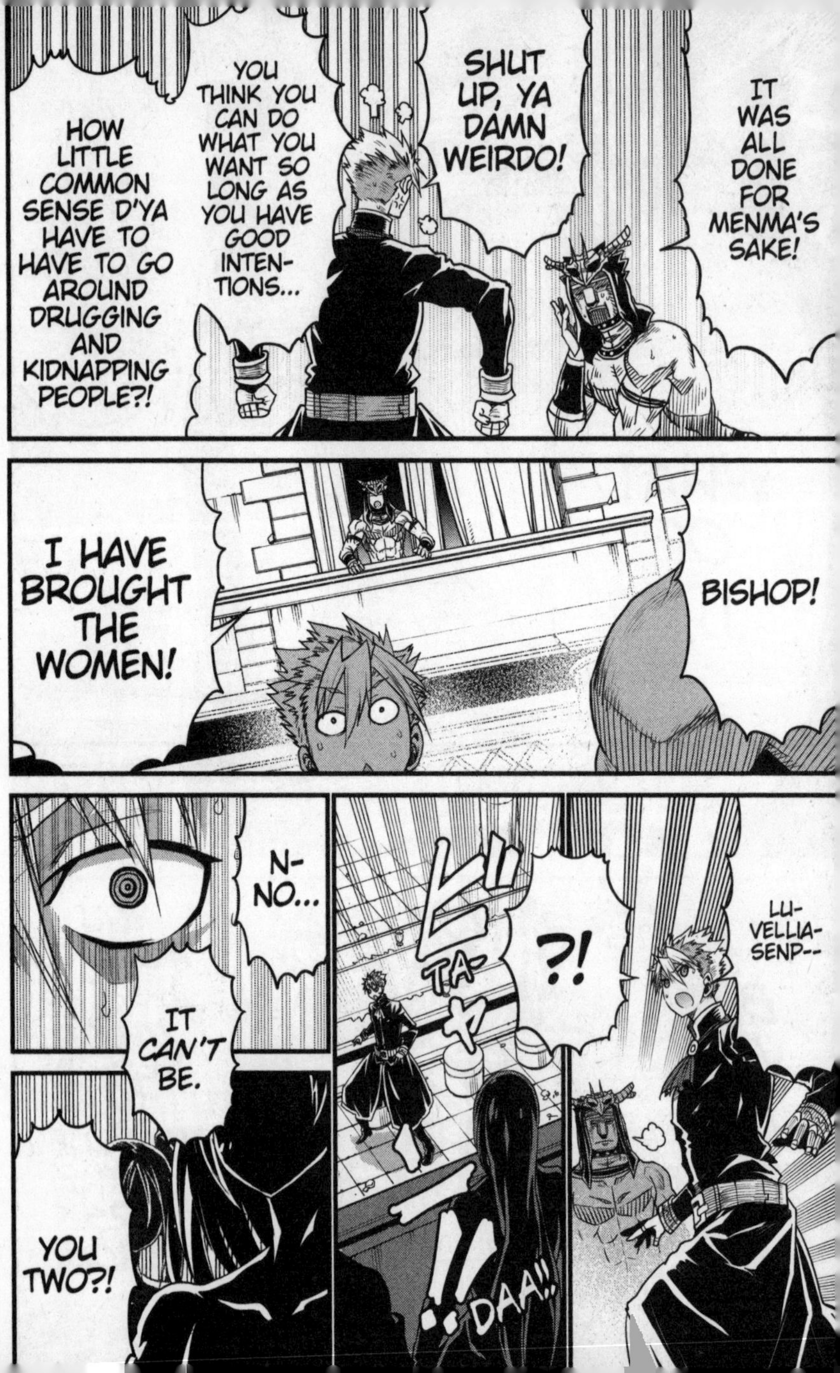
IT WAS ALL DONE FOR MENMA'S SAKE!
SHUT UP, YA DAMN WEIRDO!
YOU THINK YOU CAN DO WHAT YOU WANT SO LONG AS YOU HAVE GOOD INTEN-TIONS...
HOW LITTLE COMMON SENSE D'YA HAVE TO HAVE TO GO AROUND DRUGGING AND KIDNAPPING PEOPLE?!
BISHOP!
I HAVE BROUGHT THE WOMEN!
LU-VELLIA-SENP--
?!
TA
DAA!!
N-NO...
IT CAN'T BE.
YOU TWO?!

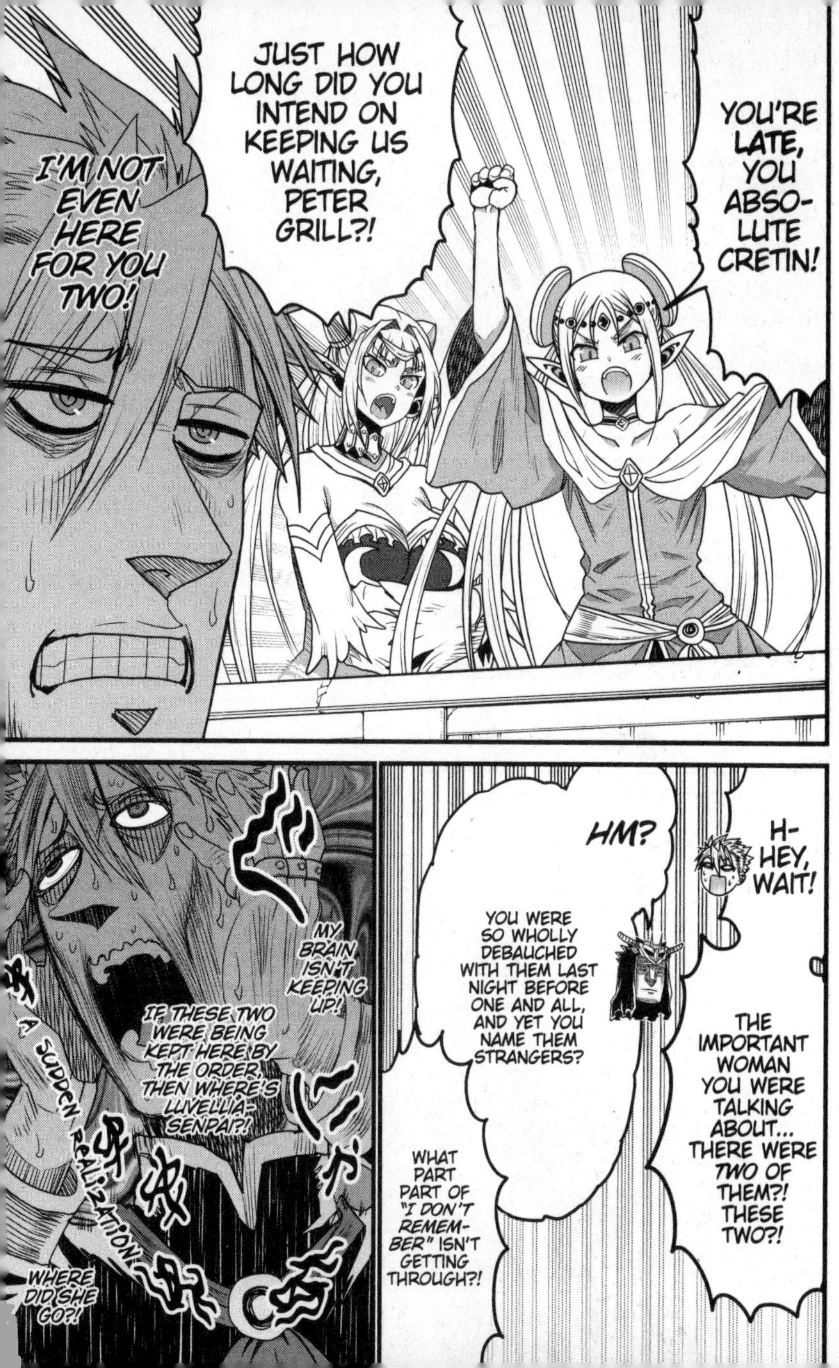
YOU'RE LATE, YOU ABSOLUTE CRETIN!
JUST HOW LONG DID YOU INTEND ON KEEPING US WAITING, PETER GRILL?!
I'M NOT EVEN HERE FOR YOU TWO!
H-HEY, WAIT!
HM?
THE IMPORTANT WOMAN YOU WERE TALKING ABOUT... THERE WERE TWO OF THEM?! THESE TWO?!
YOU WERE SO WHOLLY DEBAUCHED WITH THEM LAST NIGHT BEFORE ONE AND ALL, AND YET YOU NAME THEM STRANGERS?
WHAT PART PART OF "I DON'T REMEMBER" ISN'T GETTING THROUGH?!
MY BRAIN ISN'T KEEPING UP!
IF THESE TWO WERE BEING KEPT HERE BY THE ORDER, THEN WHERE'S LUVELLIA-SENPAI?!
A SUDDEN REALIZATION
WHERE DID SHE GO?!

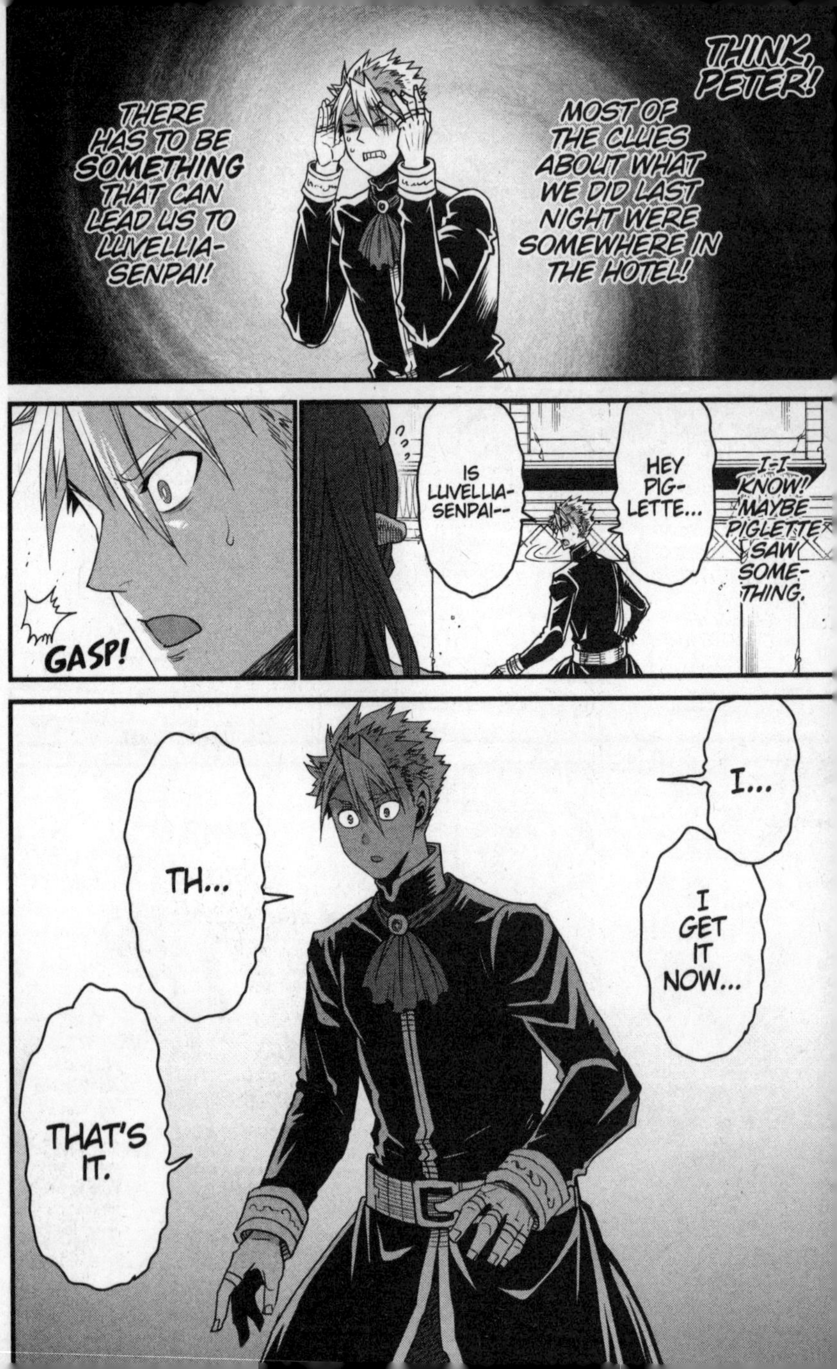
THINK, PETER!
MOST OF THE CLUES ABOUT WHAT WE DID LAST NIGHT WERE SOMEWHERE IN THE HOTEL!
THERE HAS TO BE SOMETHING THAT CAN LEAD US TO LUVELLIA-SENPAI!
I-I KNOW! MAYBE PIGLETTE SAW SOMETHING.
HEY PIGLETTE...
IS LUVELLIA-SENPAI--
GASP!
I...
I GET IT NOW...
TH...
THAT'S IT.

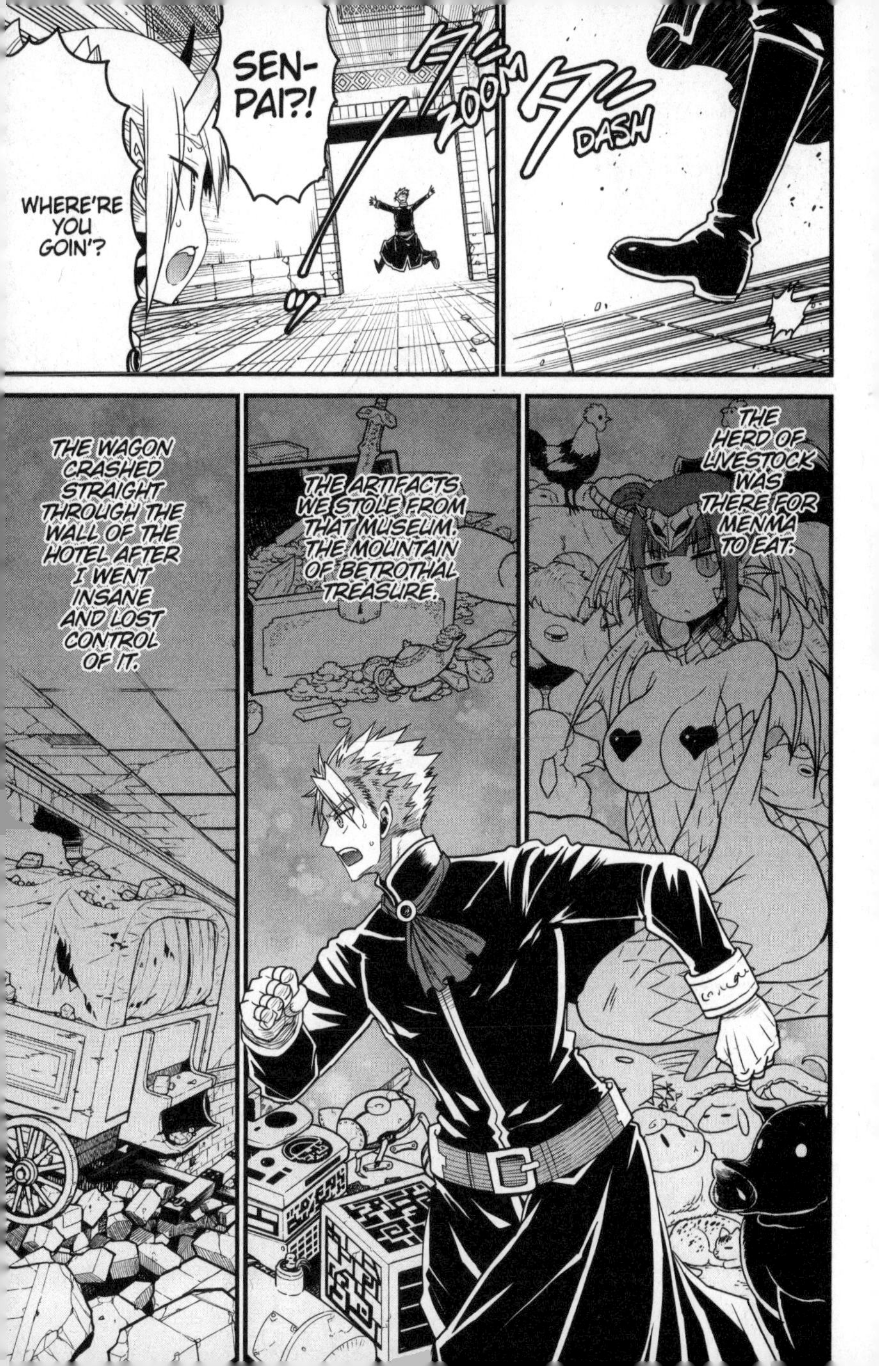
DASH
ZOOM
SEN-PAI?!
WHERE'RE YOU GOIN'?
THE HERD OF LIVESTOCK WAS THERE FOR MENMA TO EAT.
THE ARTIFACTS WE STOLE FROM THAT MUSEUM. THE MOUNTAIN OF BETROTHAL TREASURE.
THE WAGON CRASHED STRAIGHT THROUGH THE WALL OF THE HOTEL AFTER I WENT INSANE AND LOST CONTROL OF IT.

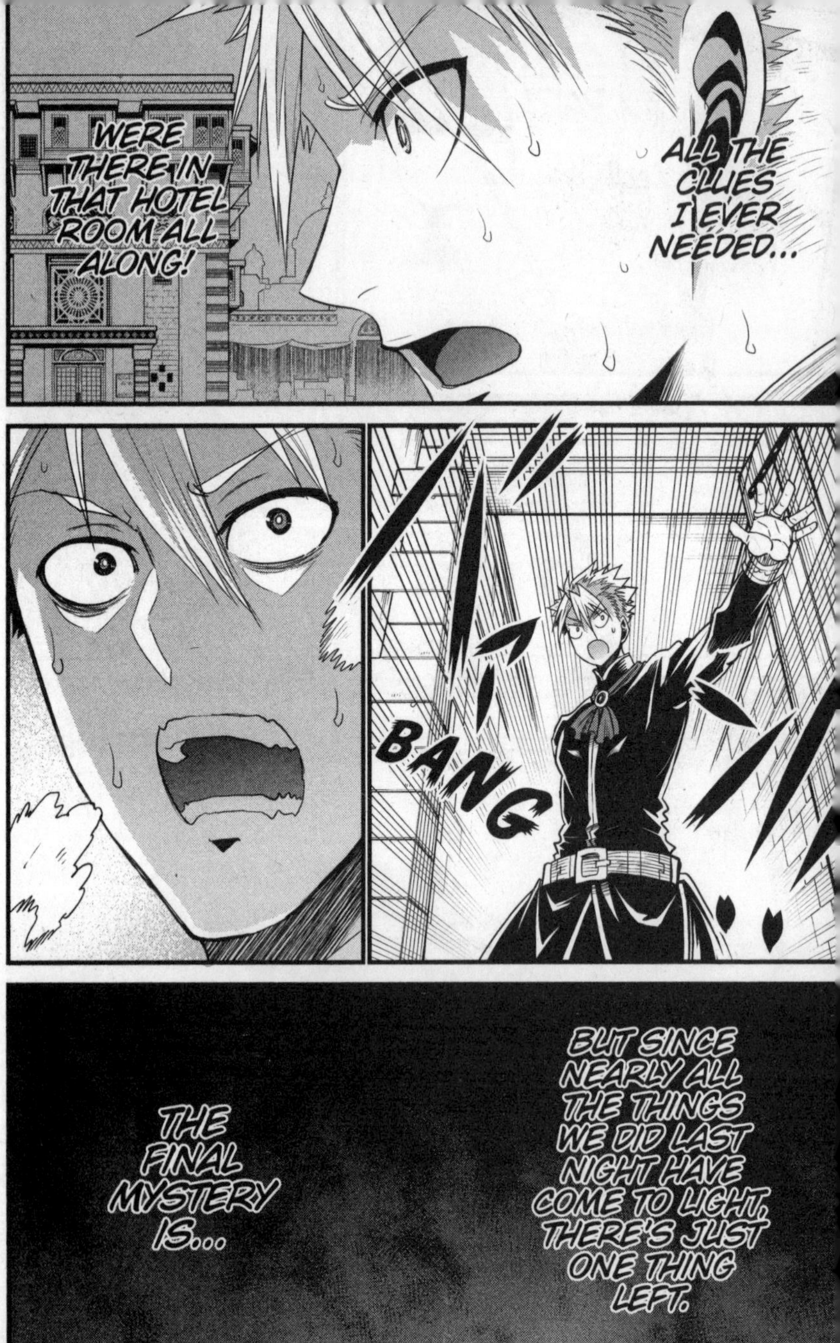
ALL THE CLUES I EVER NEEDED...
WERE THERE IN THAT HOTEL ROOM ALL ALONG!
BANG
BUT SINCE NEARLY ALL THE THINGS WE DID LAST NIGHT HAVE COME TO LIGHT, THERE'S JUST ONE THING LEFT.
THE FINAL MYSTERY IS...

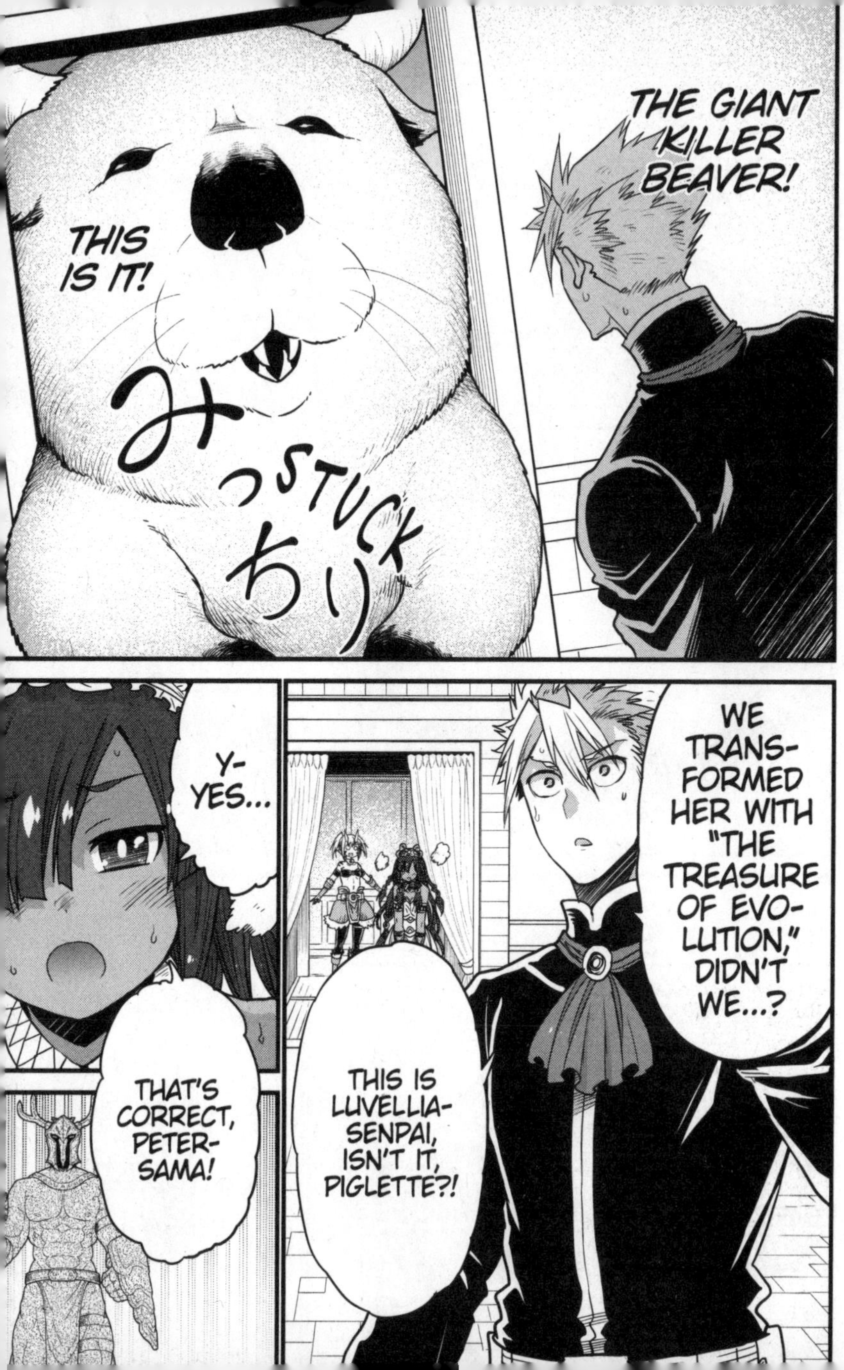
THE GIANT KILLER BEAVER!
THIS IS IT!
みっSTUCKちり
WE TRANS-FORMED HER WITH "THE TREASURE OF EVO-LUTION," DIDN'T WE...?
THIS IS LUVELLIA-SENPAI, ISN'T IT, PIGLETTE?!
Y-YES...
THAT'S CORRECT, PETER-SAMA!

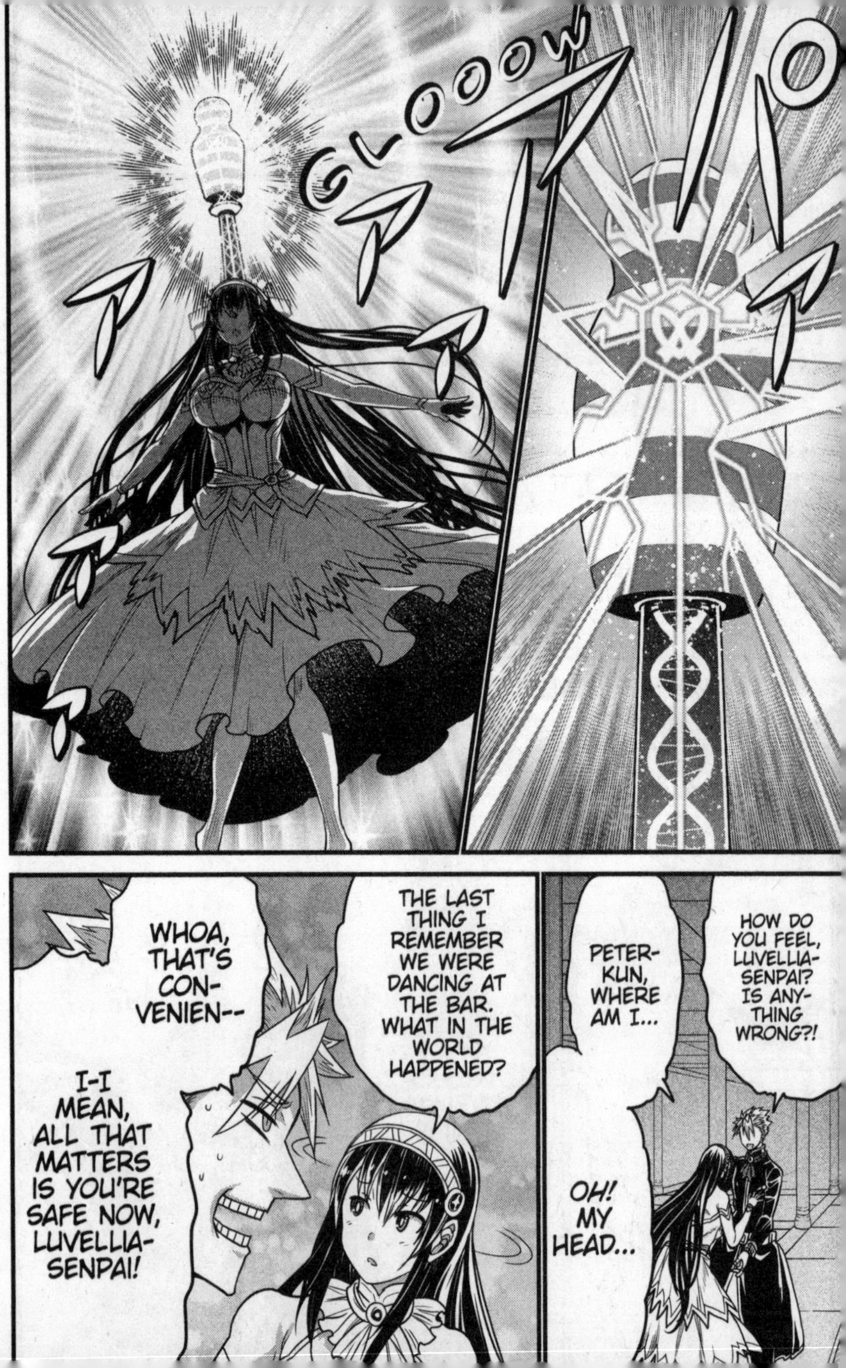
GLOOOW
HOW DO YOU FEEL, LUVELLIA-SENPAI? IS ANYTHING WRONG?!
PETER-KUN, WHERE AM I...
OH! MY HEAD...
THE LAST THING I REMEMBER WE WERE DANCING AT THE BAR. WHAT IN THE WORLD HAPPENED?
WHOA, THAT'S CON-VENIEN--
I-I MEAN, ALL THAT MATTERS IS YOU'RE SAFE NOW, LUVELLIA-SENPAI!

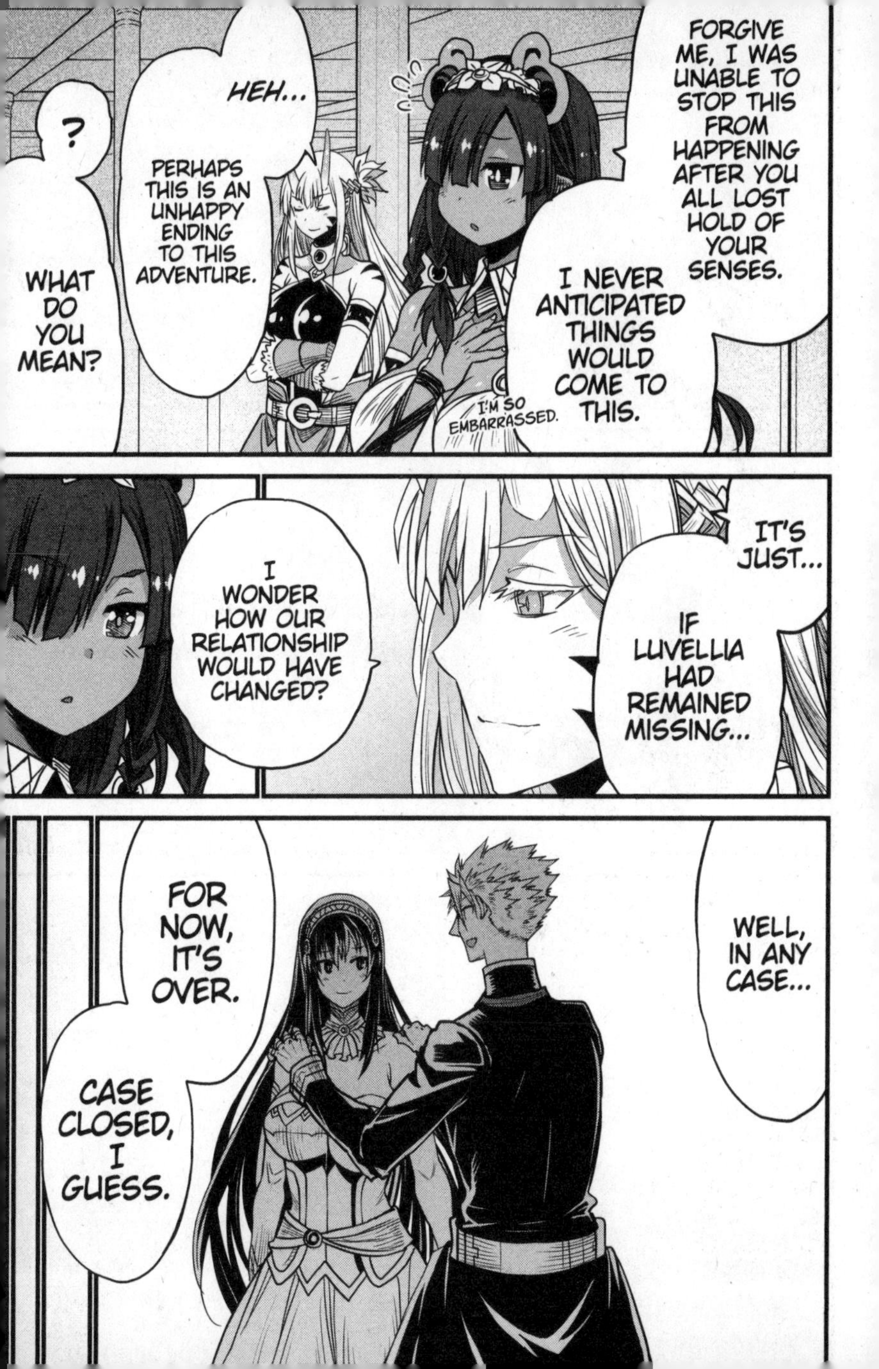
FORGIVE ME, I WAS UNABLE TO STOP THIS FROM HAPPENING AFTER YOU ALL LOST HOLD OF YOUR SENSES.
I NEVER ANTICIPATED THINGS WOULD COME TO THIS.
I'M SO EMBARRASSED.
HEH...
PERHAPS THIS IS AN UNHAPPY ENDING TO THIS ADVENTURE.
?
WHAT DO YOU MEAN?
IT'S JUST...
IF LUVELLIA HAD REMAINED MISSING...
I WONDER HOW OUR RELATIONSHIP WOULD HAVE CHANGED?
WELL, IN ANY CASE...
FOR NOW, IT'S OVER.
CASE CLOSED, I GUESS.

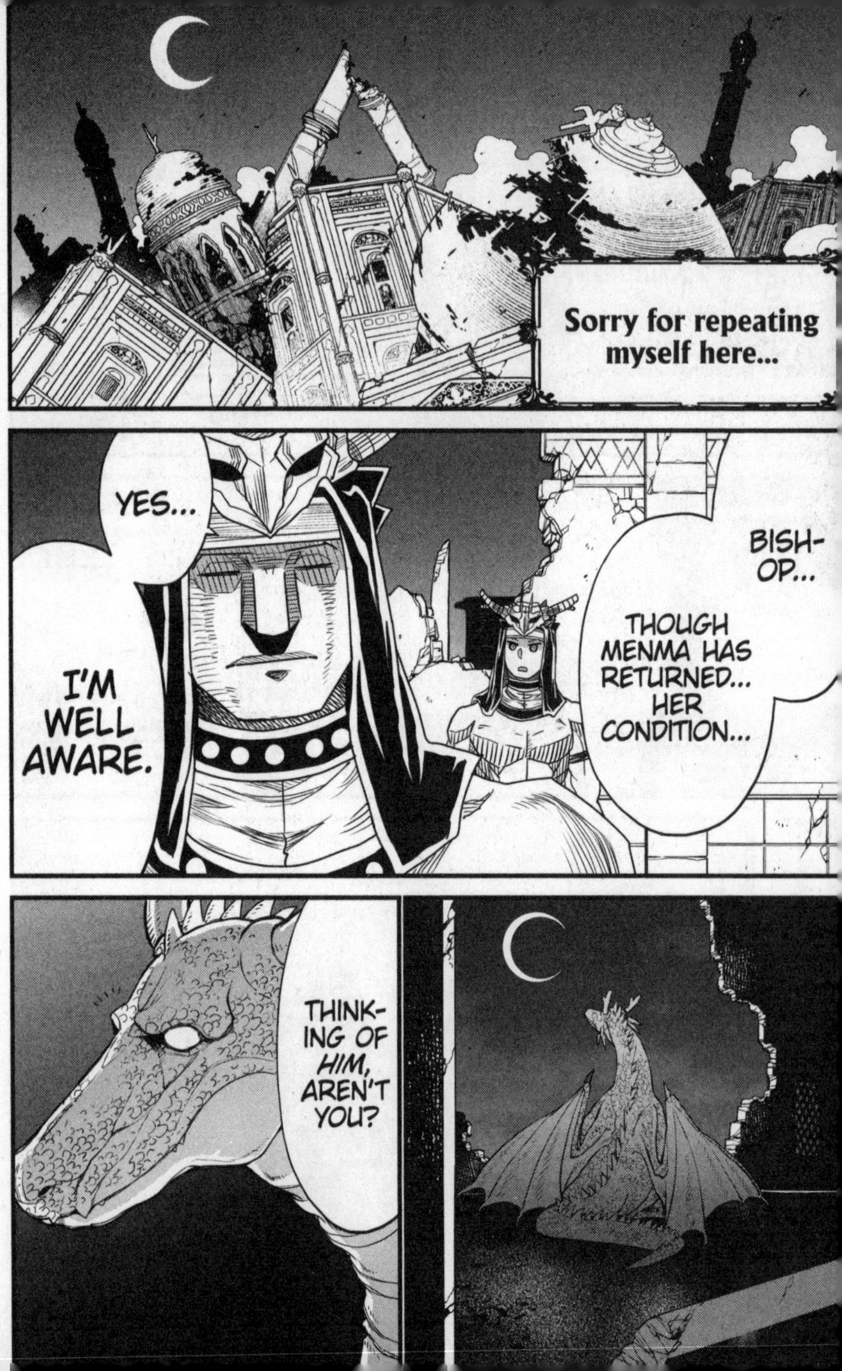
Sorry for repeating myself here...
BISH-OP...
THOUGH MENMA HAS RETURNED... HER CONDITION...
YES...
I'M WELL AWARE.
THINK-ING OF *HIM*, AREN'T YOU?

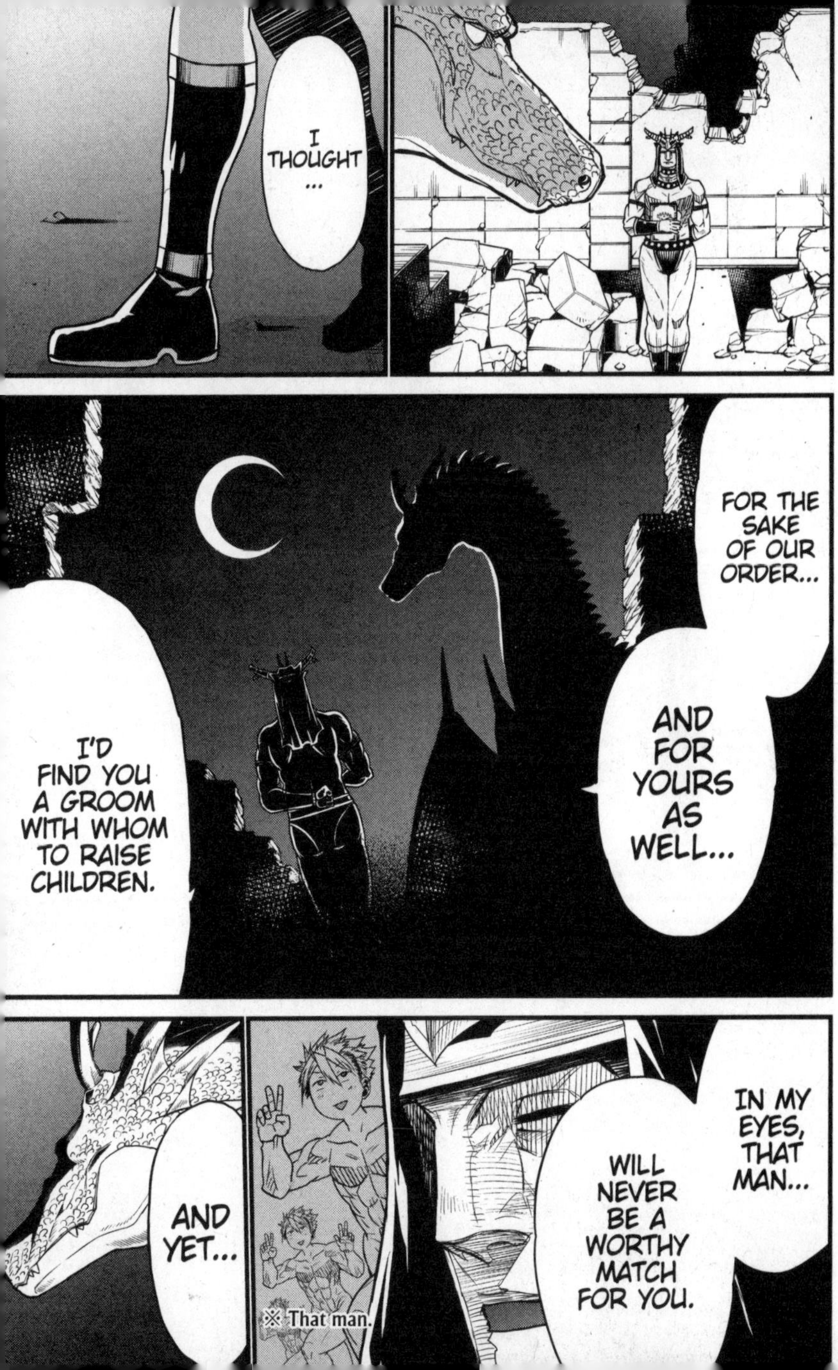
I THOUGHT...
FOR THE SAKE OF OUR ORDER...
AND FOR YOURS AS WELL...
I'D FIND YOU A GROOM WITH WHOM TO RAISE CHILDREN.
IN MY EYES, THAT MAN...
WILL NEVER BE A WORTHY MATCH FOR YOU.
※ That man.
AND YET...

MOST OF ALL...

I WISH TO RESPECT YOUR DECISION ON THE MATTER.

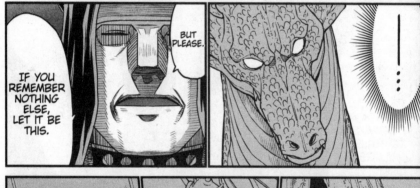

IF YOU REMEMBER NOTHING ELSE, LET IT BE THIS.

BUT PLEASE.

!
:

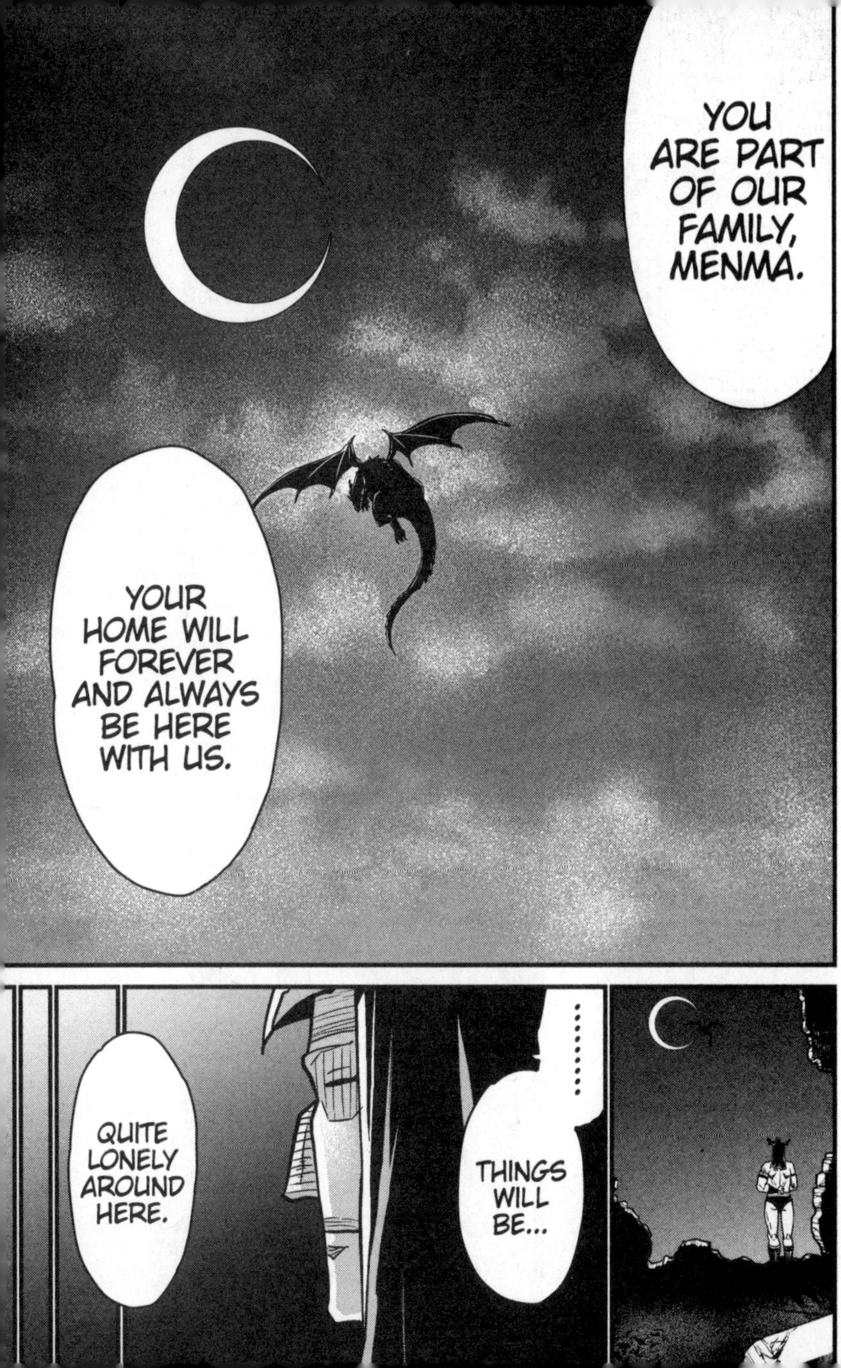
YOU ARE PART OF OUR FAMILY, MENMA.
YOUR HOME WILL FOREVER AND ALWAYS BE HERE WITH US.
......
THINGS WILL BE...
QUITE LONELY AROUND HERE.

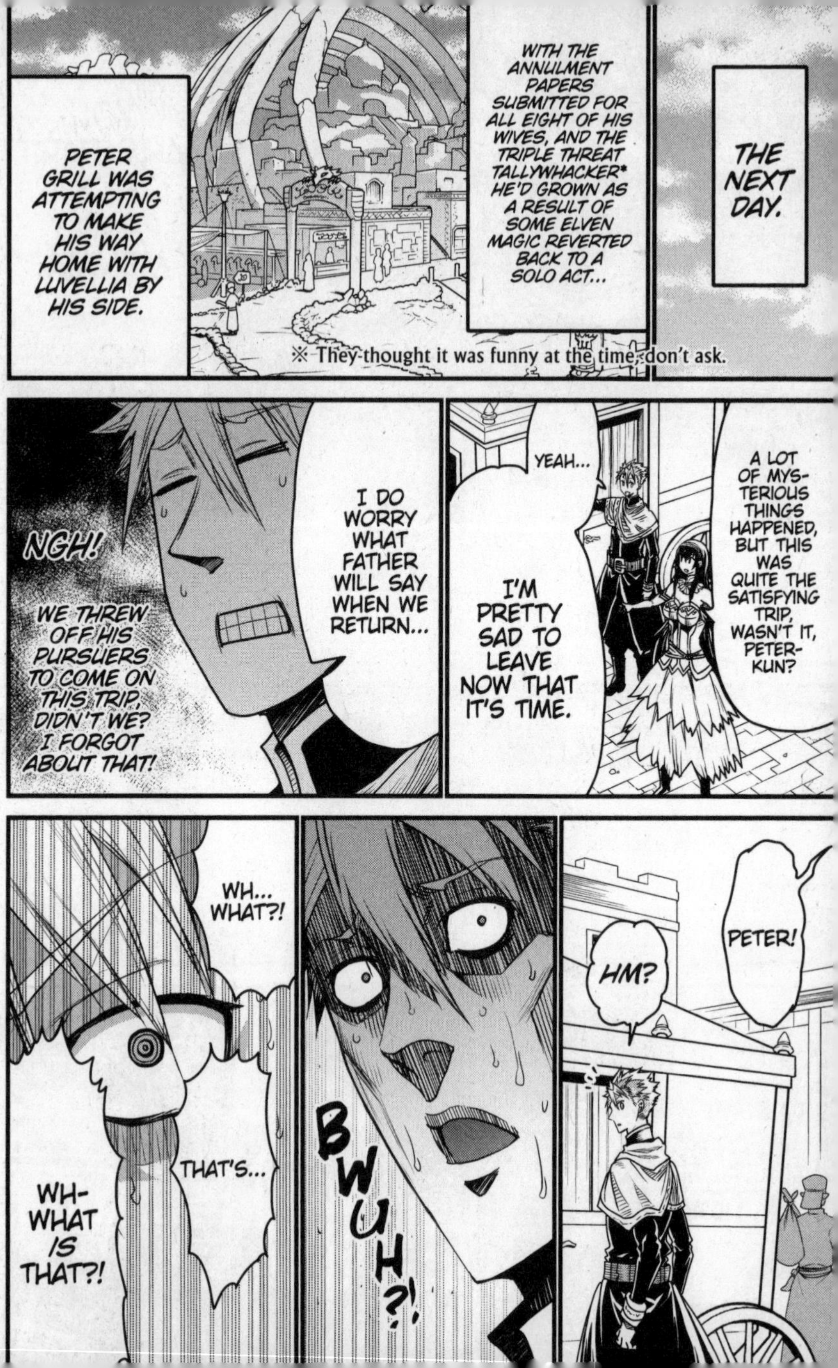
THE NEXT DAY.
WITH THE ANNULMENT PAPERS SUBMITTED FOR ALL EIGHT OF HIS WIVES, AND THE TRIPLE THREAT TALLYWHACKER* HE'D GROWN AS A RESULT OF SOME ELVEN MAGIC REVERTED BACK TO A SOLO ACT...
PETER GRILL WAS ATTEMPTING TO MAKE HIS WAY HOME WITH LUVELLIA BY HIS SIDE.
※ They thought it was funny at the time, don't ask.
A LOT OF MYSTERIOUS THINGS HAPPENED, BUT THIS WAS QUITE THE SATISFYING TRIP, WASN'T IT, PETER-KUN?
YEAH...
I'M PRETTY SAD TO LEAVE NOW THAT IT'S TIME.
I DO WORRY WHAT FATHER WILL SAY WHEN WE RETURN...
NGH!
WE THREW OFF HIS PURSUERS TO COME ON THIS TRIP, DIDN'T WE? I FORGOT ABOUT THAT!
PETER!
HM?
BWUH?!
WH... WHAT?!
THAT'S...
WH- WHAT IS THAT?!

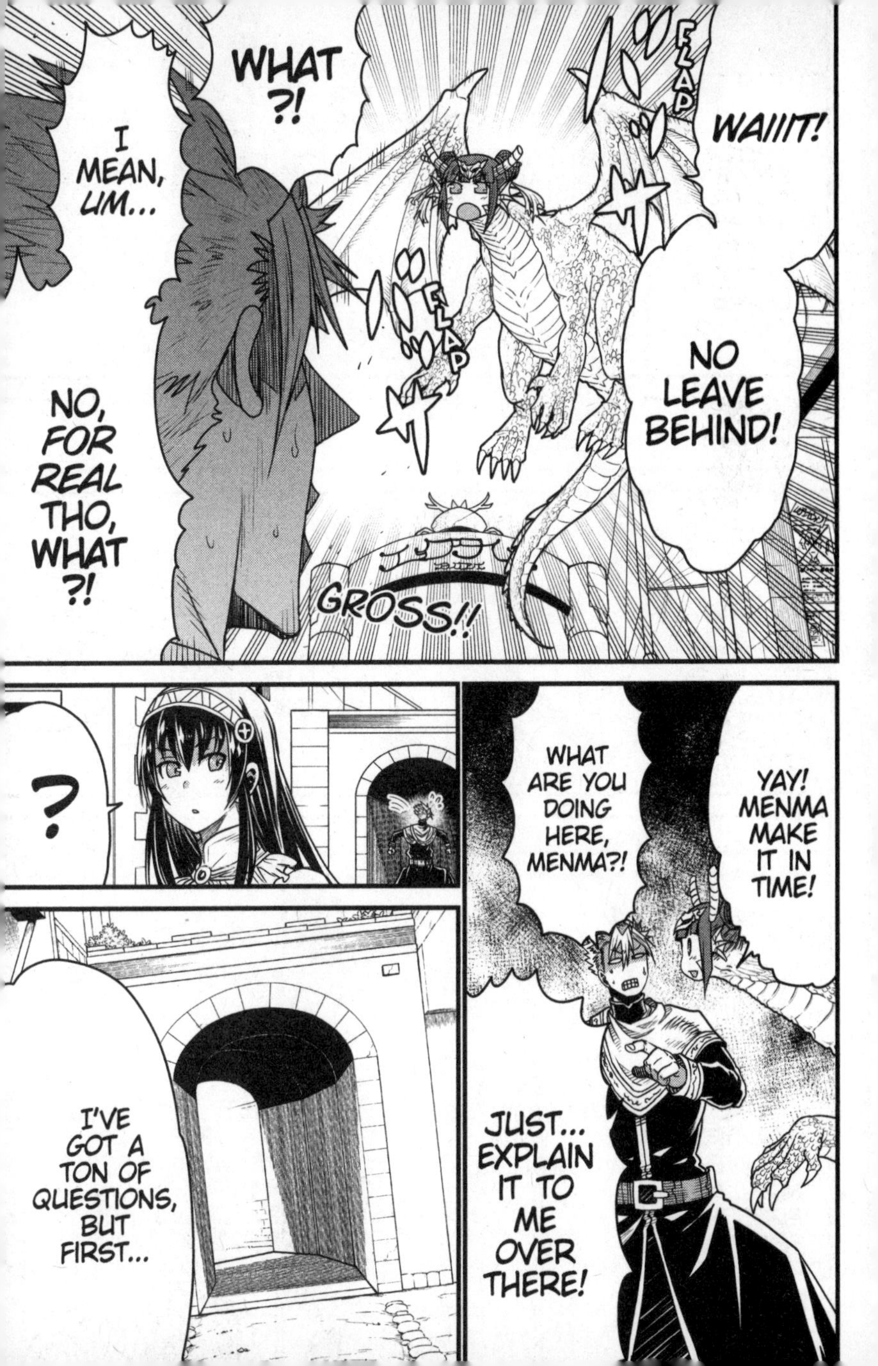
FLAP
FLAP
WAIIIT!
WHAT ?!
I MEAN, UM...
NO LEAVE BEHIND!
FLAP
NO, FOR REAL THO, WHAT ?!
GROSS!!
YAY! MENMA MAKE IT IN TIME!
WHAT ARE YOU DOING HERE, MENMA?!
JUST... EXPLAIN IT TO ME OVER THERE!
?
I'VE GOT A TON OF QUESTIONS, BUT FIRST...

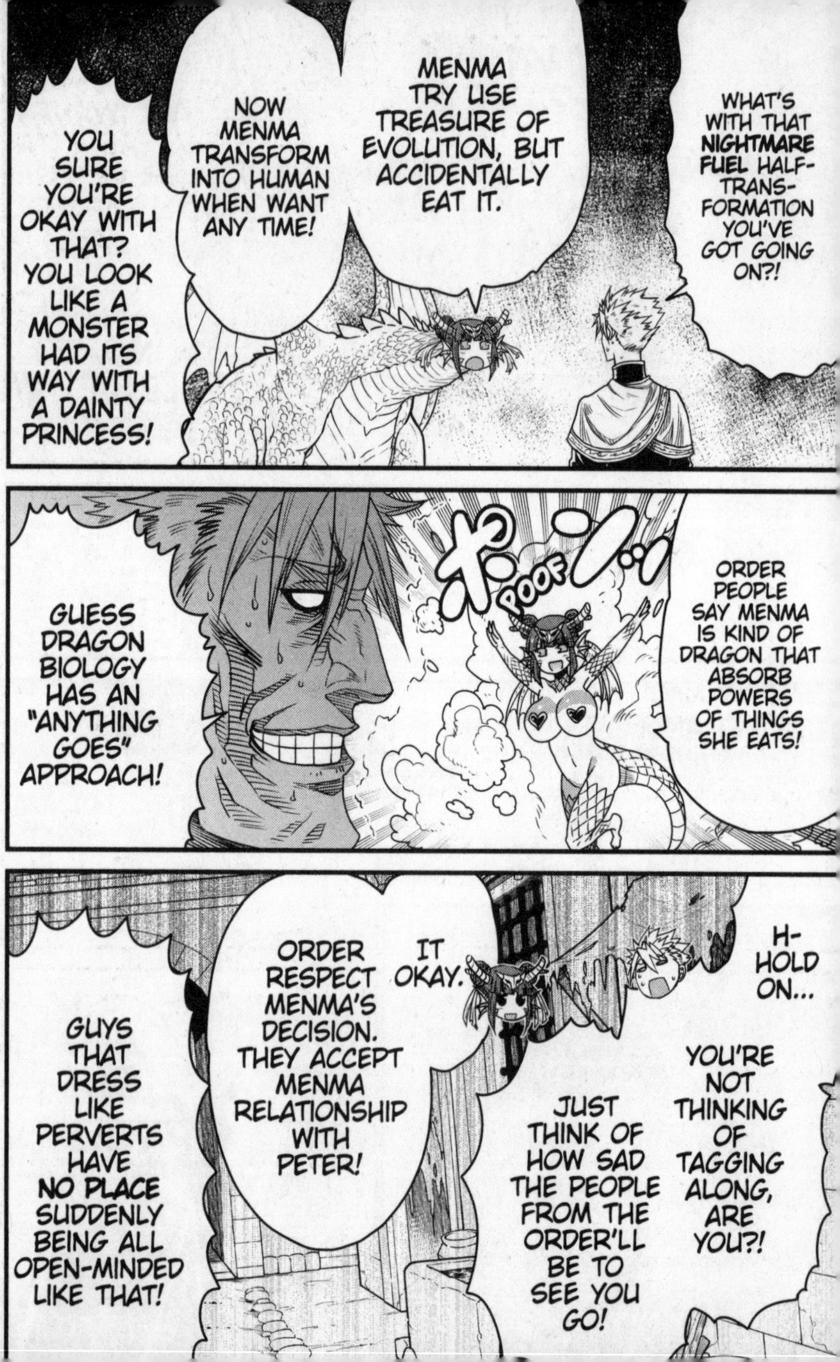
WHAT'S WITH THAT NIGHTMARE FUEL HALF-TRANSFORMATION YOU'VE GOT GOING ON?!
MENMA TRY USE TREASURE OF EVOLUTION, BUT ACCIDENTALLY EAT IT.
NOW MENMA TRANSFORM INTO HUMAN WHEN WANT ANY TIME!
YOU SURE YOU'RE OKAY WITH THAT? YOU LOOK LIKE A MONSTER HAD ITS WAY WITH A DAINTY PRINCESS!
ORDER PEOPLE SAY MENMA IS KIND OF DRAGON THAT ABSORB POWERS OF THINGS SHE EATS!
POOF
GUESS DRAGON BIOLOGY HAS AN "ANYTHING GOES" APPROACH!
H-HOLD ON...
YOU'RE NOT THINKING OF TAGGING ALONG, ARE YOU?!
JUST THINK OF HOW SAD THE PEOPLE FROM THE ORDER'LL BE TO SEE YOU GO!
IT OKAY.
ORDER RESPECT MENMA'S DECISION. THEY ACCEPT MENMA RELATIONSHIP WITH PETER!
GUYS THAT DRESS LIKE PERVERTS HAVE NO PLACE SUDDENLY BEING ALL OPEN-MINDED LIKE THAT!

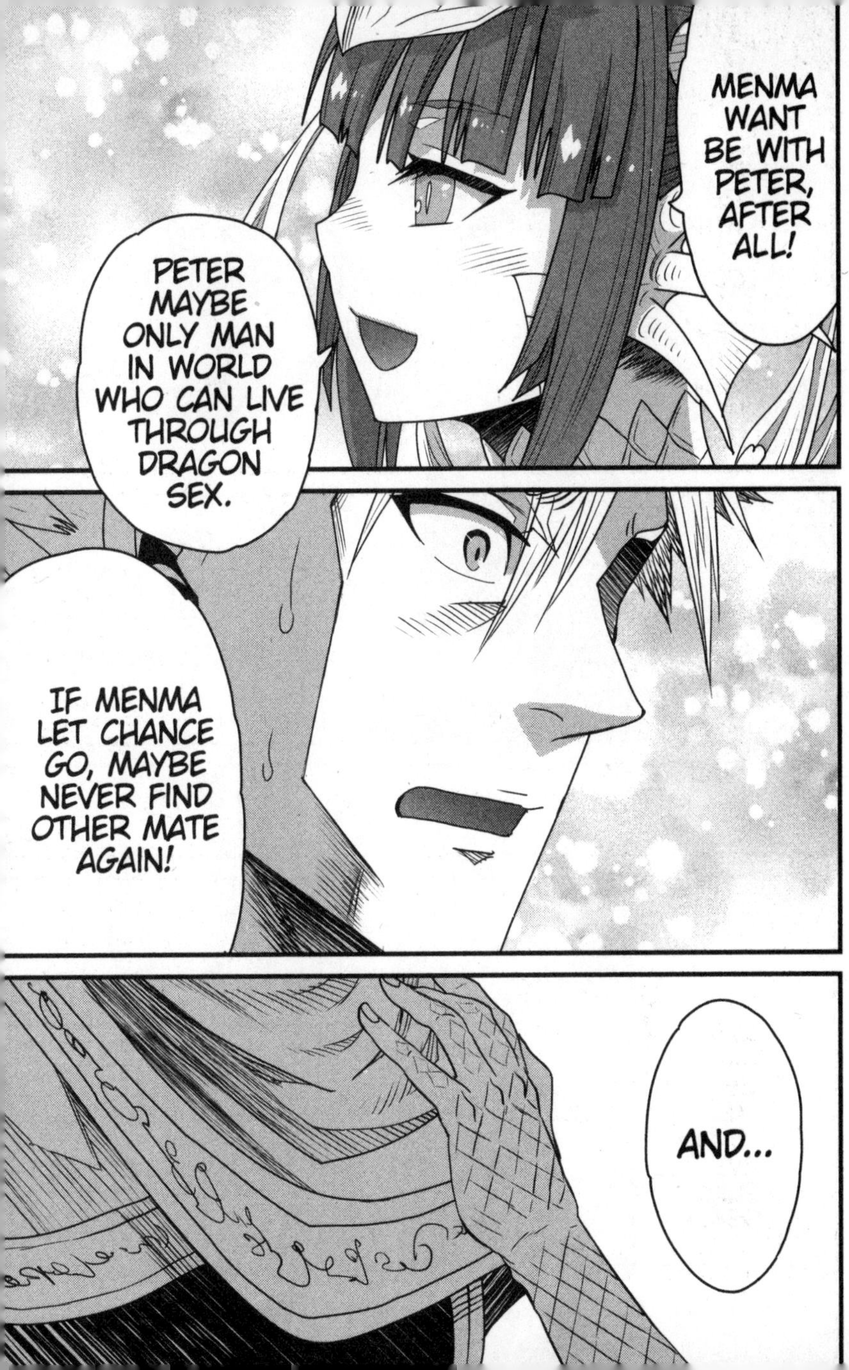
MENMA WANT BE WITH PETER, AFTER ALL!
PETER MAYBE ONLY MAN IN WORLD WHO CAN LIVE THROUGH DRAGON SEX.
IF MENMA LET CHANCE GO, MAYBE NEVER FIND OTHER MATE AGAIN!
AND...

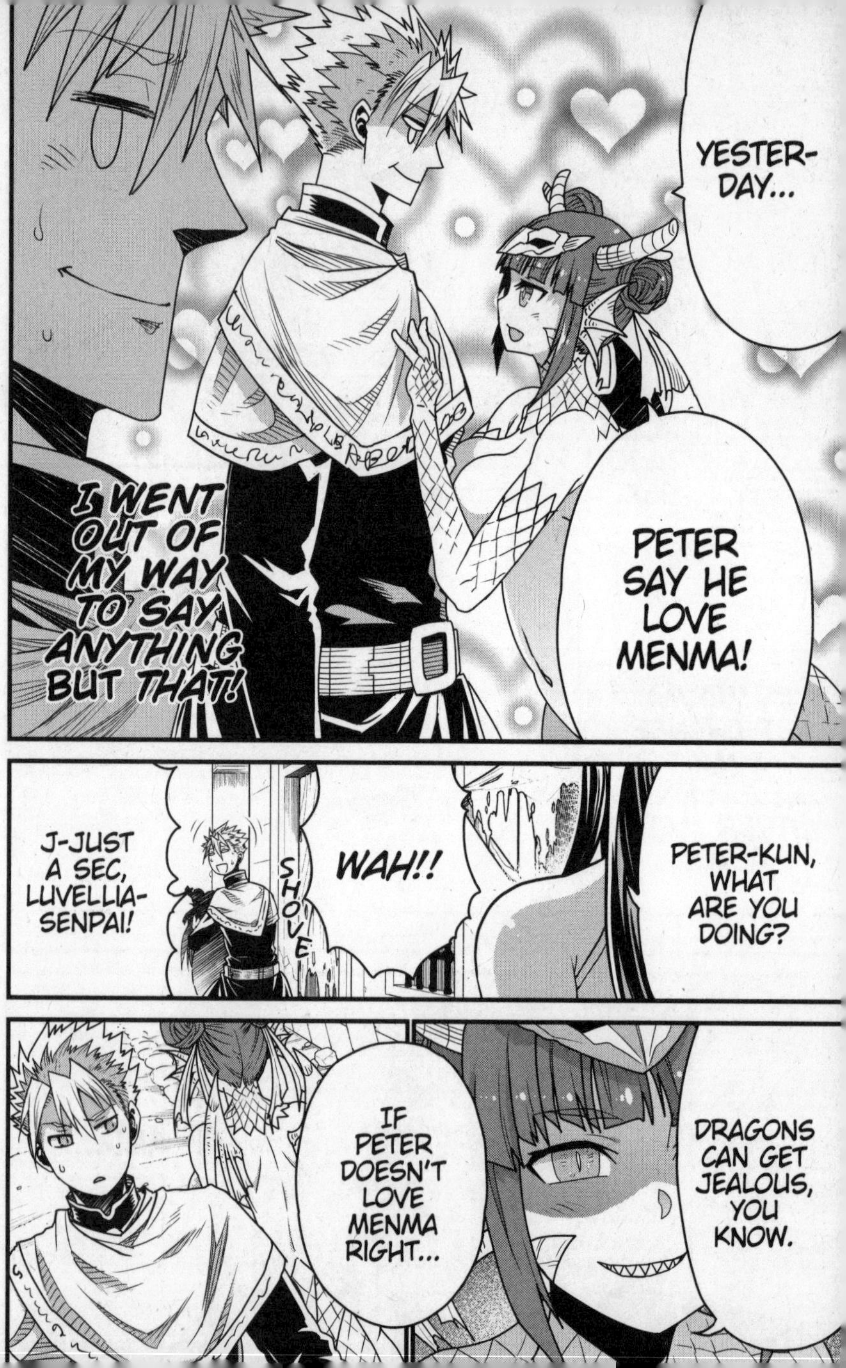
YESTER-DAY...
PETER SAY HE LOVE MENMA!
I WENT OUT OF MY WAY TO SAY ANYTHING BUT THAT!
PETER-KUN, WHAT ARE YOU DOING?
WAH!!
SHOVE
J-JUST A SEC, LUVELLIA-SENPAI!
DRAGONS CAN GET JEALOUS, YOU KNOW.
IF PETER DOESN'T LOVE MENMA RIGHT...

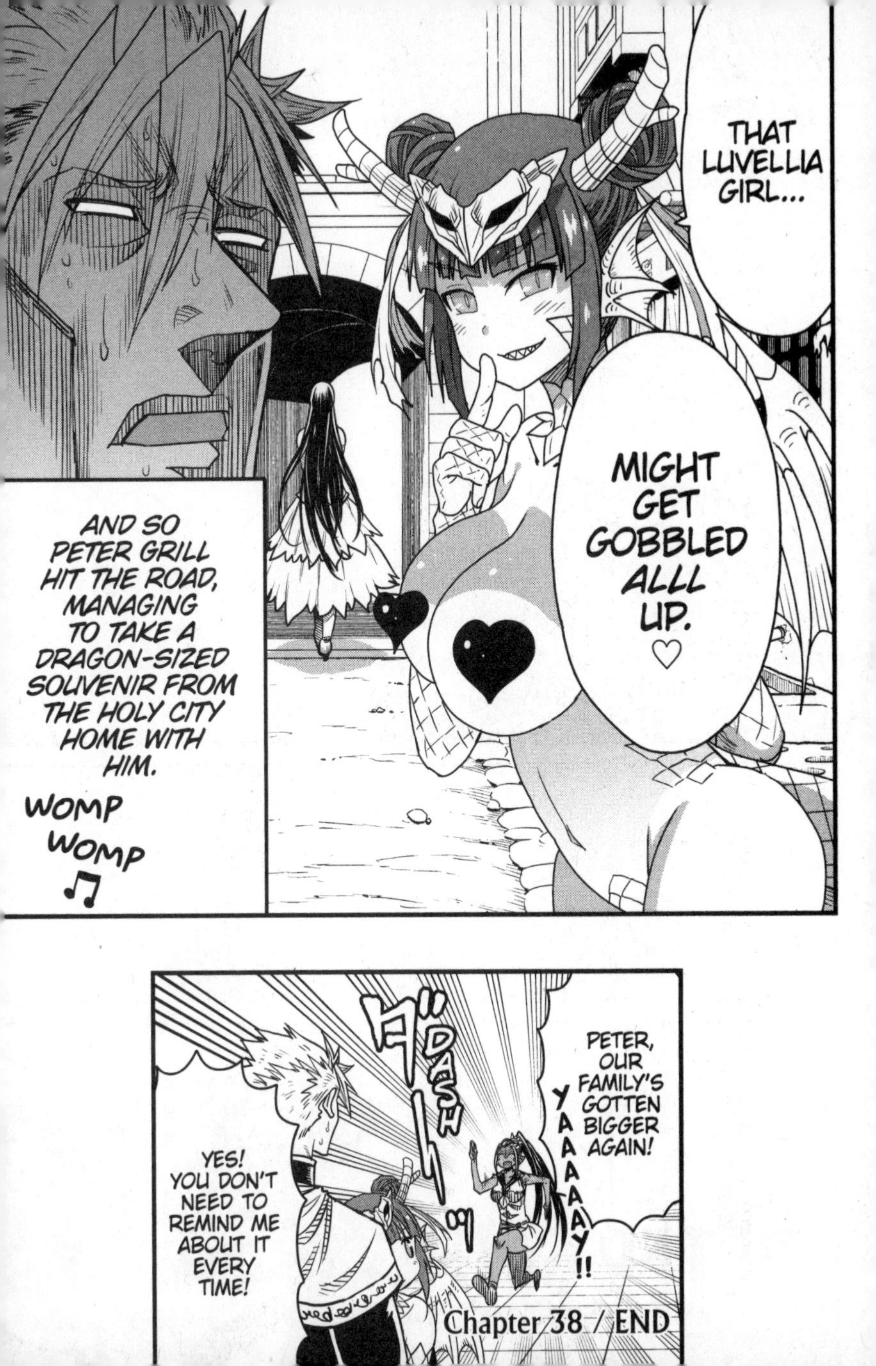
THAT LUVELLIA GIRL...
MIGHT GET GOBBLED ALLL UP. ♡
AND SO PETER GRILL HIT THE ROAD, MANAGING TO TAKE A DRAGON-SIZED SOUVENIR FROM THE HOLY CITY HOME WITH HIM.
WOMP WOMP ♫
PETER, OUR FAMILY'S GOTTEN BIGGER AGAIN!
YAAAAAAAY!!
DASH
YES! YOU DON'T NEED TO REMIND ME ABOUT IT EVERY TIME!
Chapter 38 / END

PETER GRILL
AND THE PHILOSOPHER'S TIME

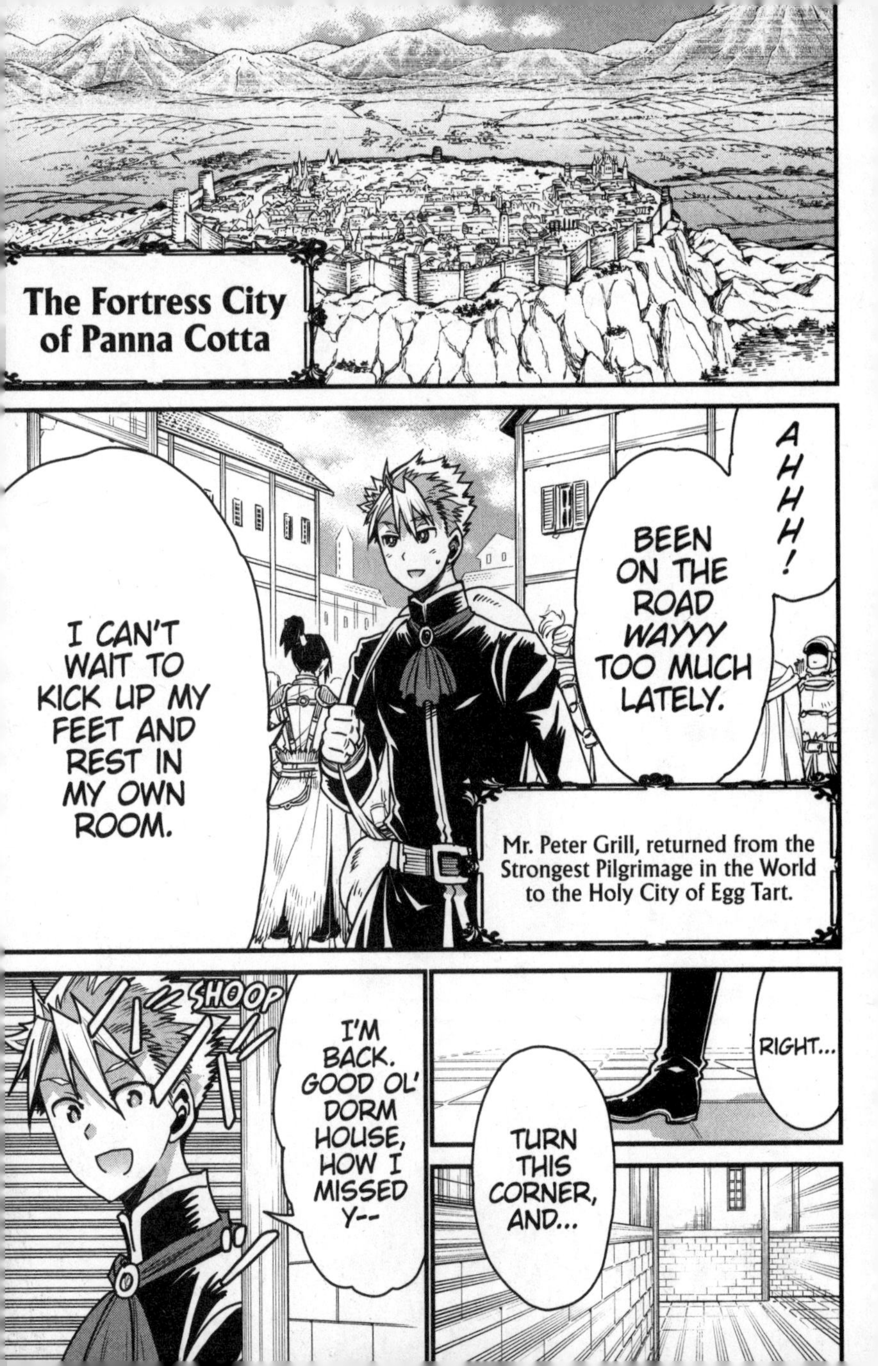
The Fortress City of Panna Cotta
AHHHH!
BEEN ON THE ROAD WAYYY TOO MUCH LATELY.
I CAN'T WAIT TO KICK UP MY FEET AND REST IN MY OWN ROOM.
Mr. Peter Grill, returned from the Strongest Pilgrimage in the World to the Holy City of Egg Tart.
RIGHT...
TURN THIS CORNER, AND...
SHOOP
I'M BACK. GOOD OL' DORM HOUSE, HOW I MISSED Y--

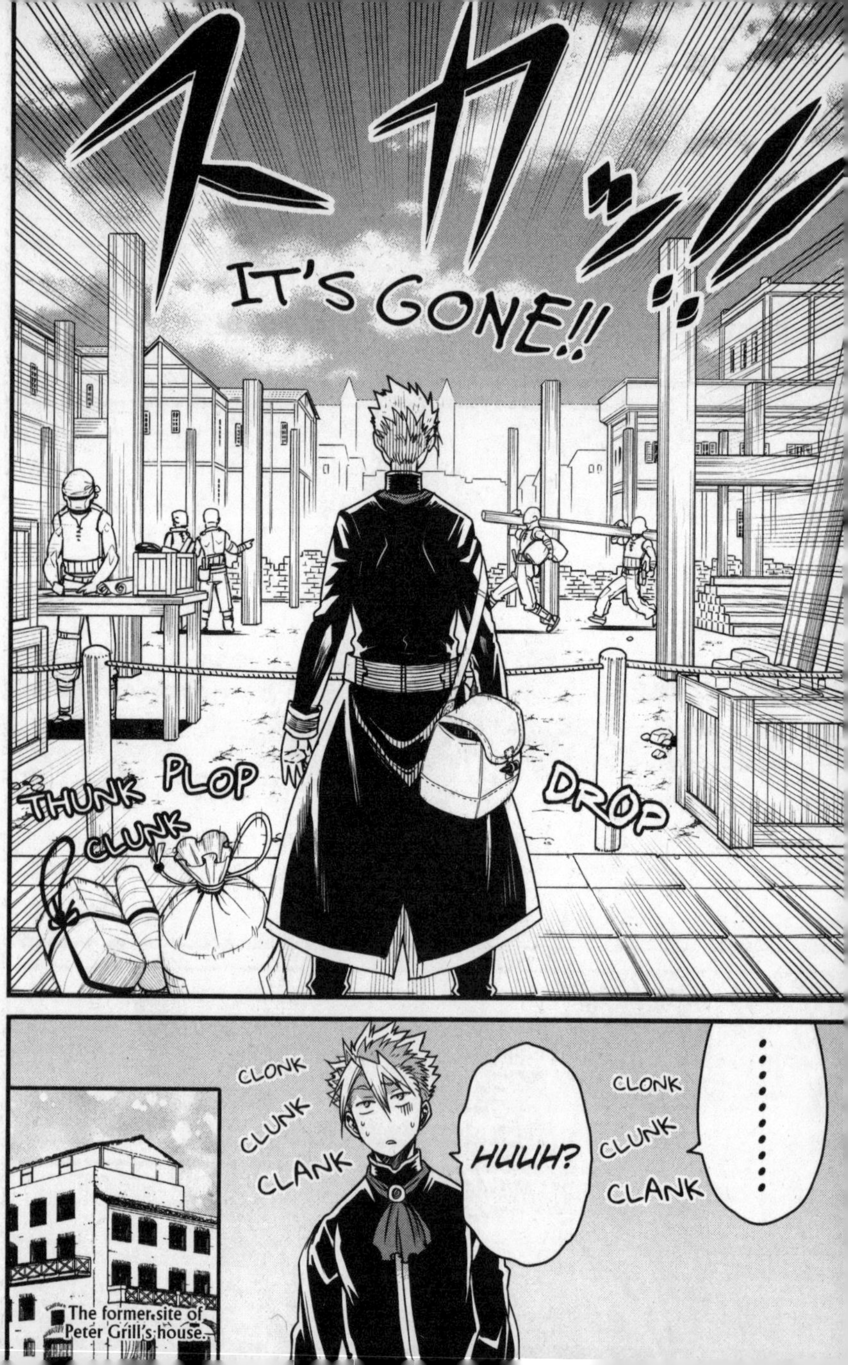
スカッ!!
IT'S GONE!!
DROP
PLOP
THUNK
CLUNK
......
CLONK
CLUNK
CLANK
HUUH?
CLONK
CLUNK
CLANK
The former site of Peter Grill's house.

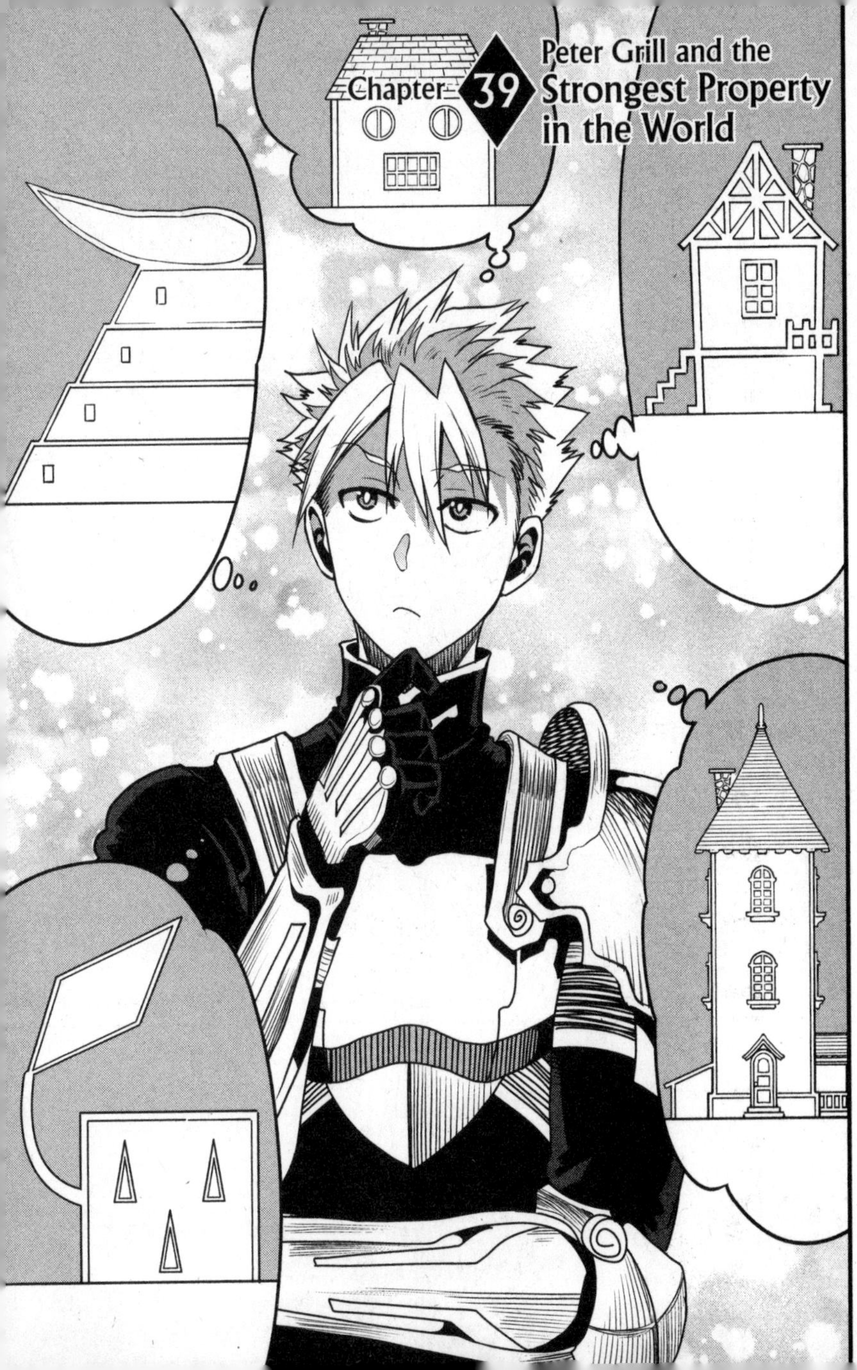
Chapter 39
Peter Grill and the Strongest Property in the World

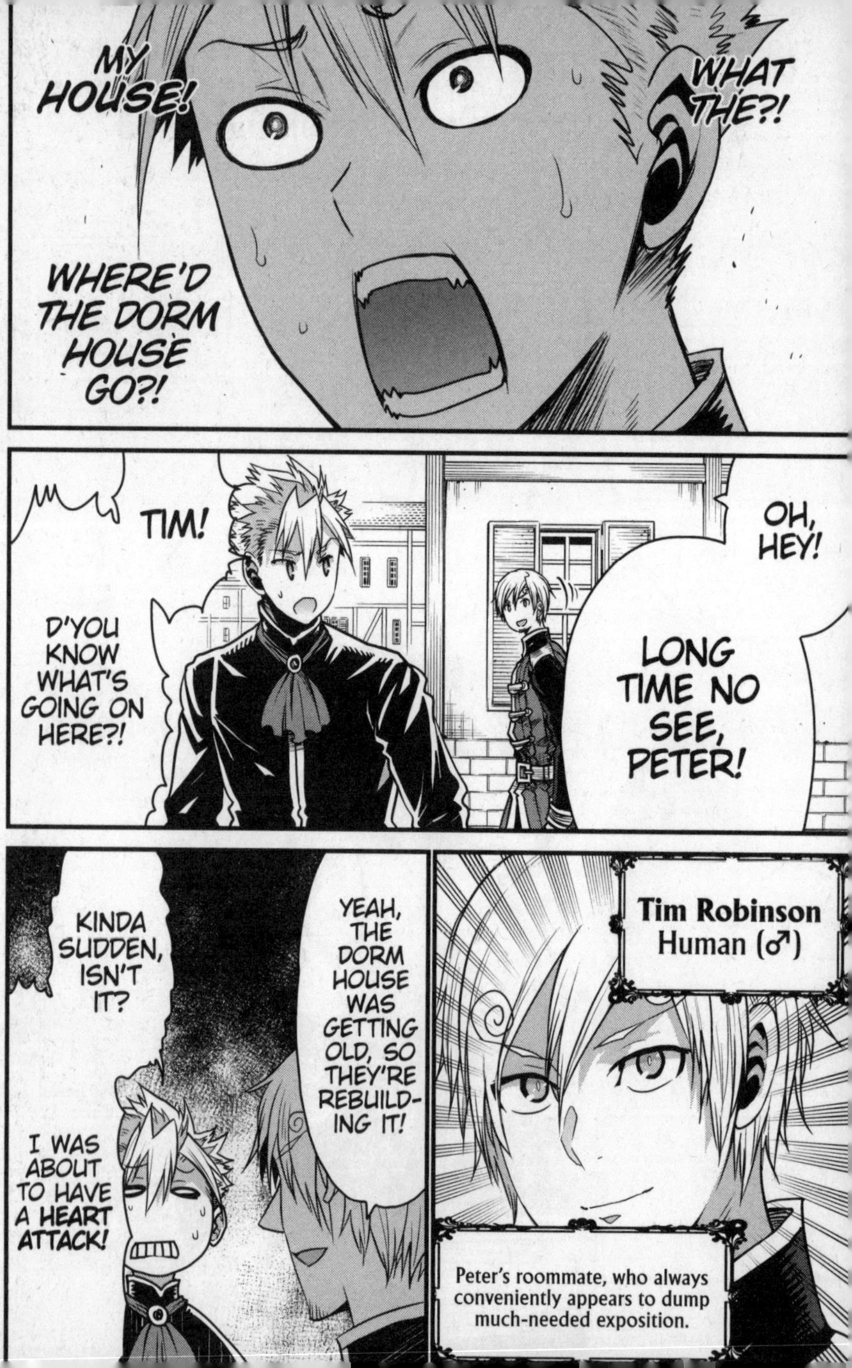
WHAT THE?!
MY HOUSE!
WHERE'D THE DORM HOUSE GO?!
OH, HEY!
LONG TIME NO SEE, PETER!
TIM!
D'YOU KNOW WHAT'S GOING ON HERE?!
Tim Robinson
Human (♂)
Peter's roommate, who always conveniently appears to dump much-needed exposition.
YEAH, THE DORM HOUSE WAS GETTING OLD, SO THEY'RE REBUILD-ING IT!
KINDA SUDDEN, ISN'T IT?
I WAS ABOUT TO HAVE A HEART ATTACK!

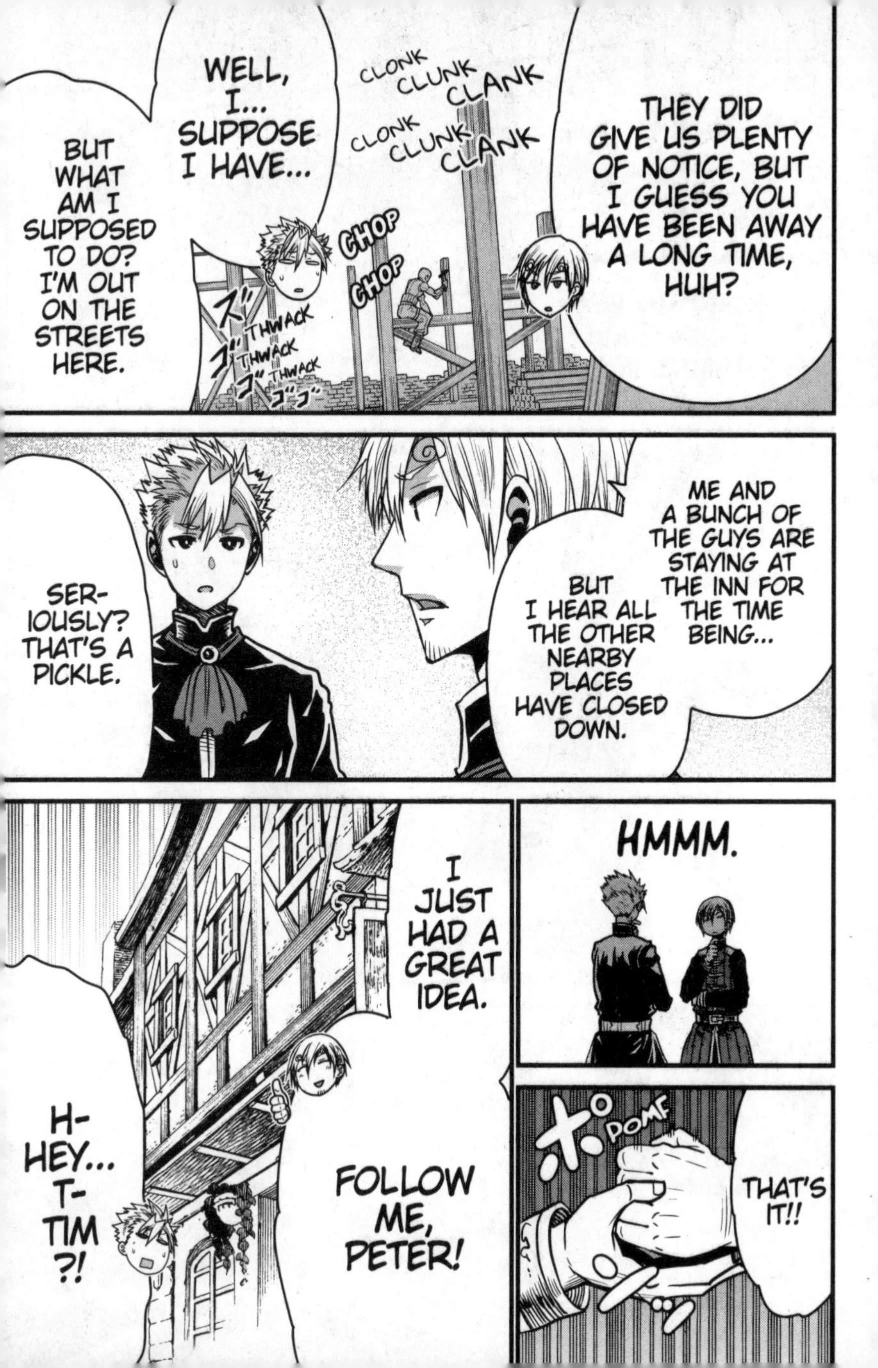
THEY DID GIVE US PLENTY OF NOTICE, BUT I GUESS YOU HAVE BEEN AWAY A LONG TIME, HUH?
CLONK CLUNK CLANK
CLONK CLUNK CLANK
CHOP
CHOP
WELL, I... SUPPOSE I HAVE...
THWACK
THWACK
THWACK
BUT WHAT AM I SUPPOSED TO DO? I'M OUT ON THE STREETS HERE.
ME AND A BUNCH OF THE GUYS ARE STAYING AT THE INN FOR THE TIME BEING...
BUT I HEAR ALL THE OTHER NEARBY PLACES HAVE CLOSED DOWN.
SER-IOUSLY? THAT'S A PICKLE.
HMMM.
POMF
THAT'S IT!!
I JUST HAD A GREAT IDEA.
FOLLOW ME, PETER!
H-HEY... T-TIM?!

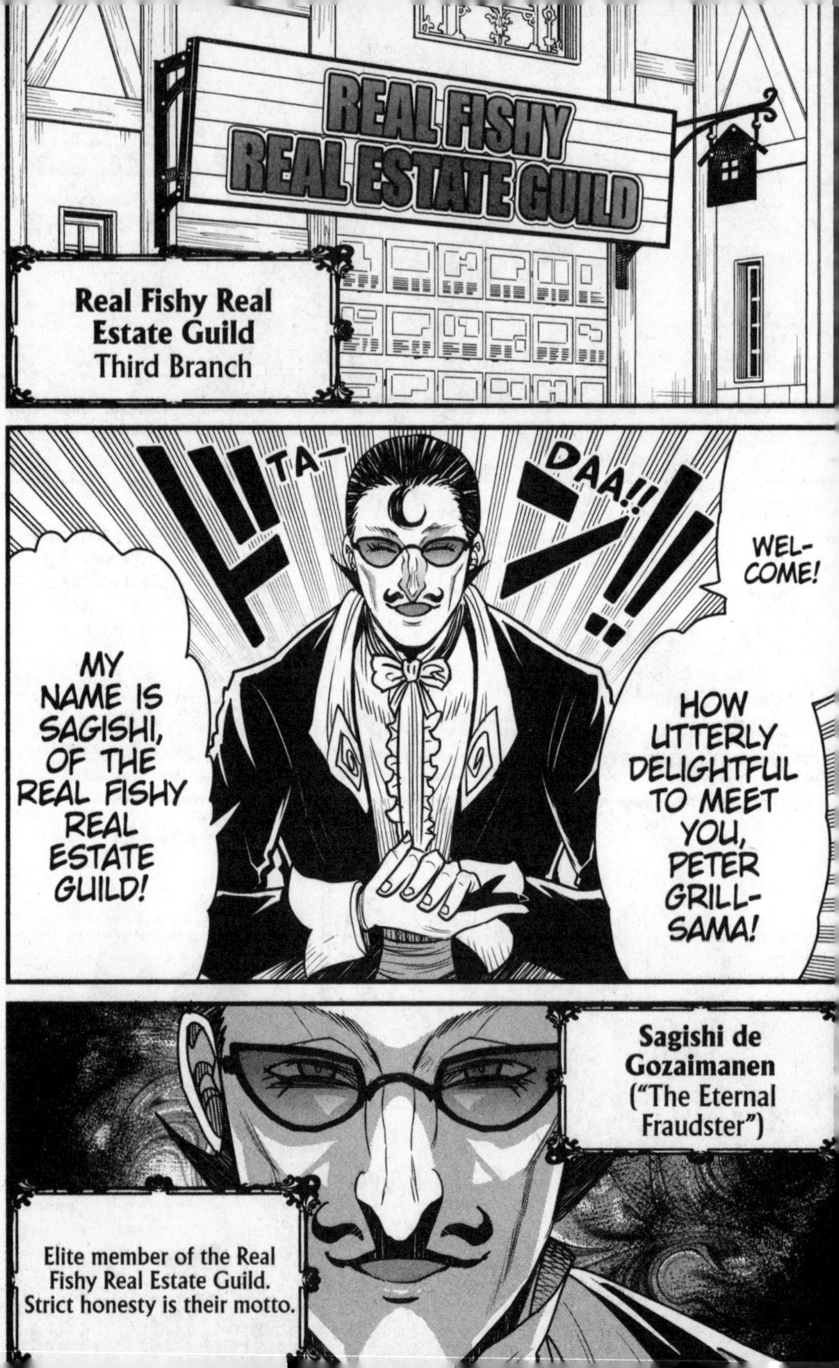
REAL FISHY REAL ESTATE GUILD
Real Fishy Real Estate Guild Third Branch
WEL-COME!
TA-DAA!!
HOW UTTERLY DELIGHTFUL TO MEET YOU, PETER GRILL-SAMA!
MY NAME IS SAGISHI, OF THE REAL FISHY REAL ESTATE GUILD!
Sagishi de Gozaimanen ("The Eternal Fraudster")
Elite member of the Real Fishy Real Estate Guild. Strict honesty is their motto.

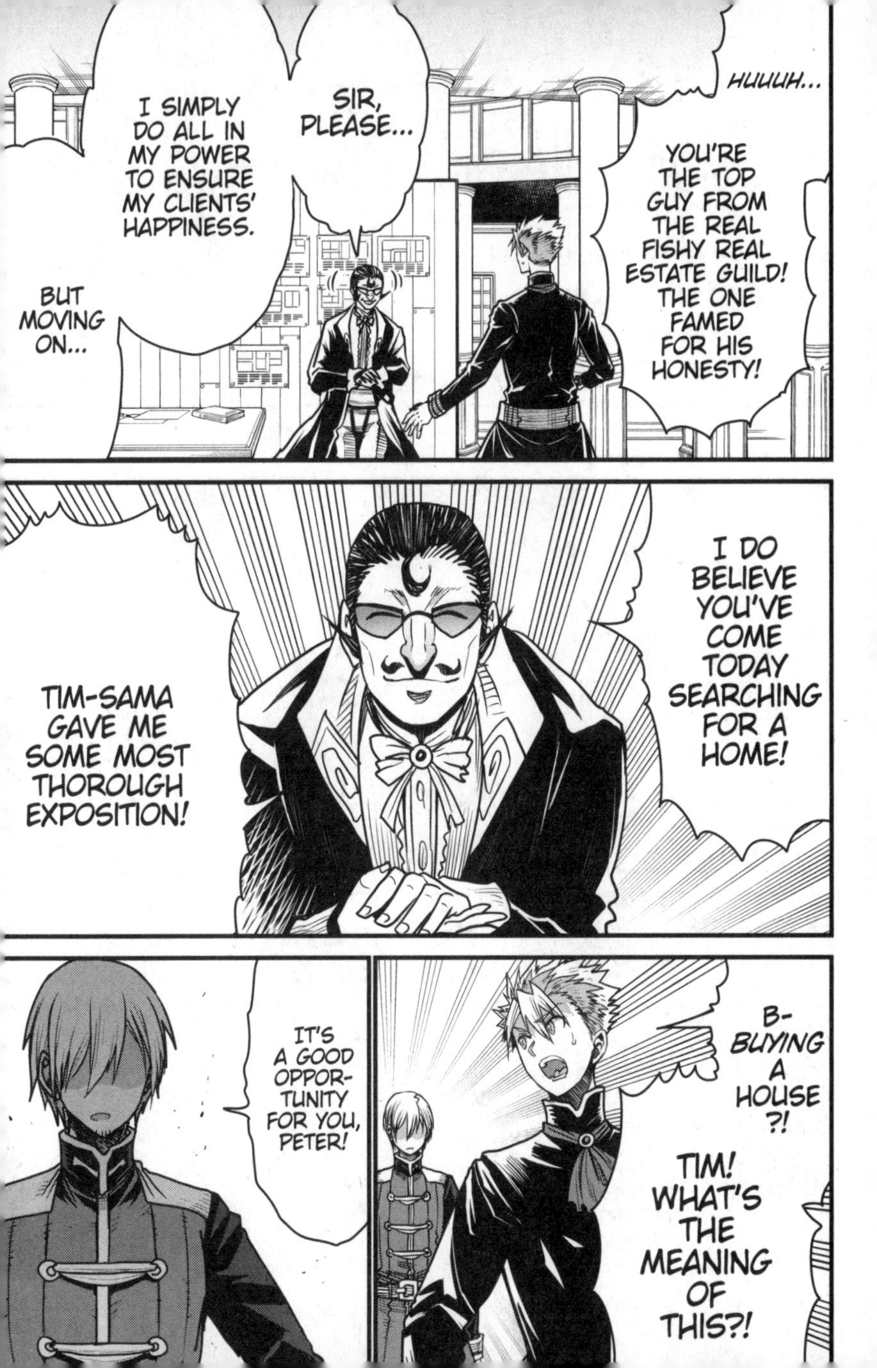
HUUUH...
YOU'RE THE TOP GUY FROM THE REAL FISHY REAL ESTATE GUILD! THE ONE FAMED FOR HIS HONESTY!
SIR, PLEASE...
I SIMPLY DO ALL IN MY POWER TO ENSURE MY CLIENTS' HAPPINESS.
BUT MOVING ON...
I DO BELIEVE YOU'VE COME TODAY SEARCHING FOR A HOME!
TIM-SAMA GAVE ME SOME MOST THOROUGH EXPOSITION!
B-BUYING A HOUSE?!
TIM! WHAT'S THE MEANING OF THIS?!
IT'S A GOOD OPPORTUNITY FOR YOU, PETER!

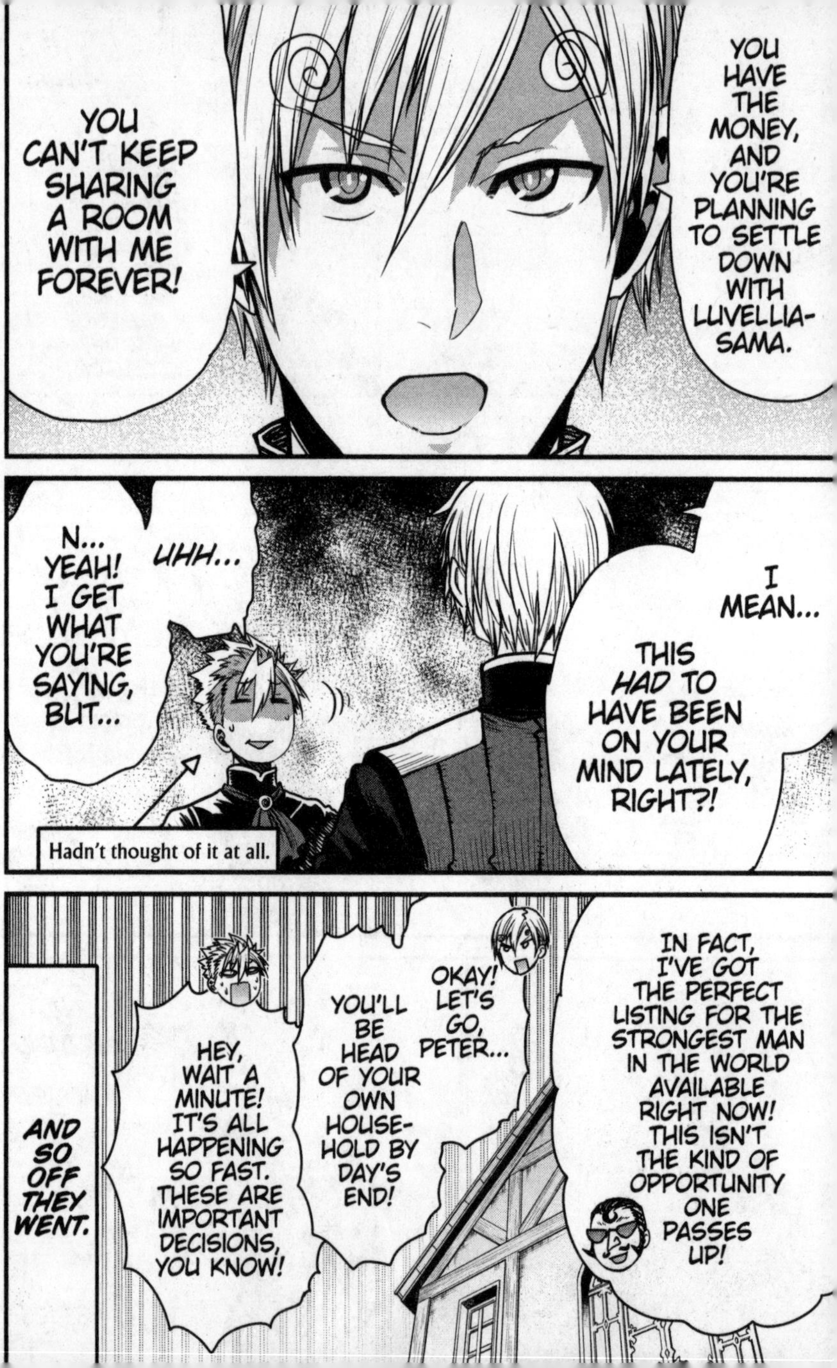
YOU HAVE THE MONEY, AND YOU'RE PLANNING TO SETTLE DOWN WITH LUVELLIA-SAMA.
YOU CAN'T KEEP SHARING A ROOM WITH ME FOREVER!
I MEAN...
THIS *HAD* TO HAVE BEEN ON YOUR MIND LATELY, RIGHT?!
UHH...
N... YEAH! I GET WHAT YOU'RE SAYING, BUT...
Hadn't thought of it at all.
IN FACT, I'VE GOT THE PERFECT LISTING FOR THE STRONGEST MAN IN THE WORLD AVAILABLE RIGHT NOW! THIS ISN'T THE KIND OF OPPORTUNITY ONE PASSES UP!
OKAY! LET'S GO, PETER...
YOU'LL BE HEAD OF YOUR OWN HOUSE-HOLD BY DAY'S END!
HEY, WAIT A MINUTE! IT'S ALL HAPPENING SO FAST. THESE ARE IMPORTANT DECISIONS, YOU KNOW!
AND SO OFF THEY WENT.

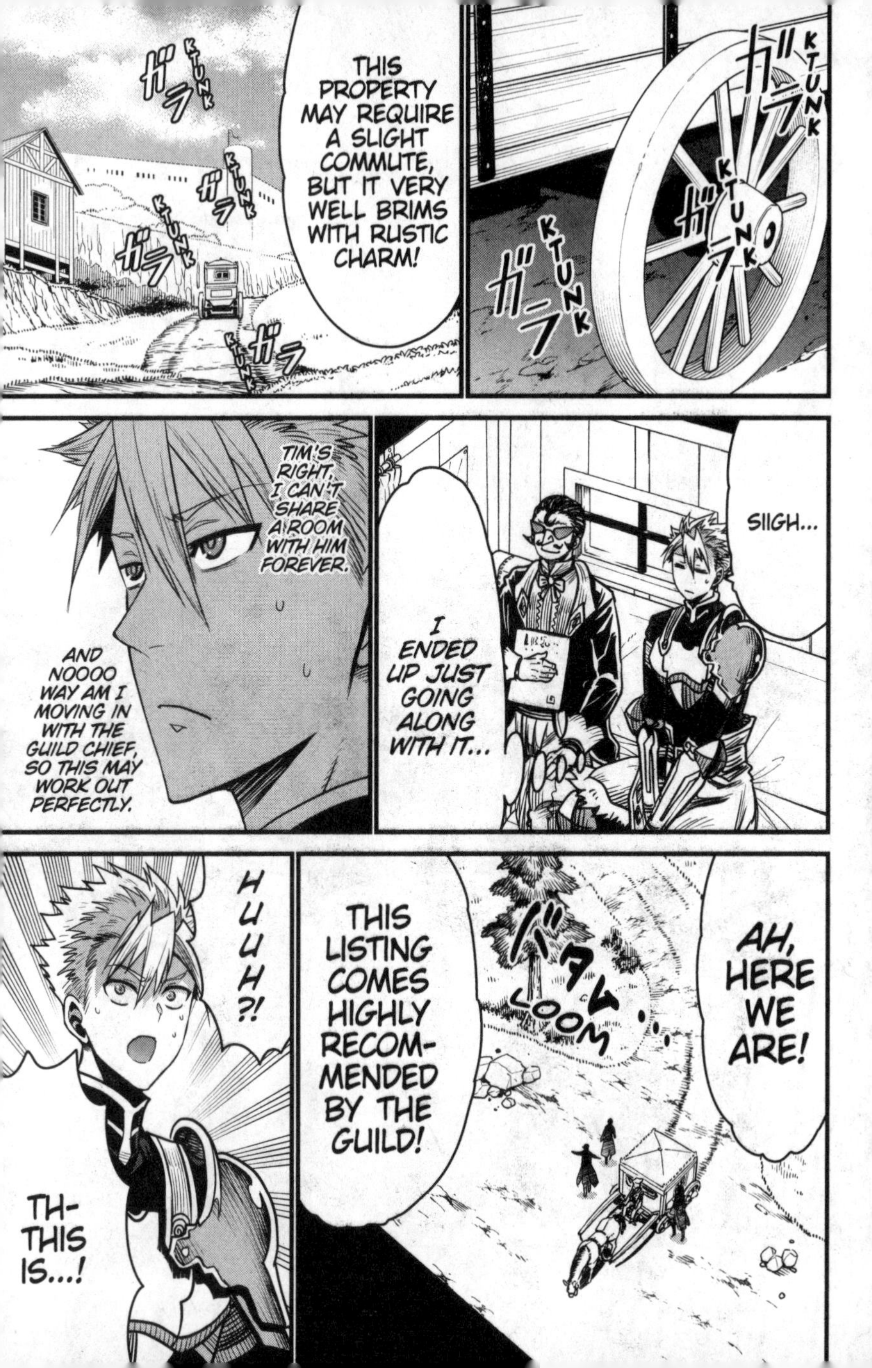
ガラ KTUNK
ガラ KTUNK
ガーラ KTUNK
THIS PROPERTY MAY REQUIRE A SLIGHT COMMUTE, BUT IT VERY WELL BRIMS WITH RUSTIC CHARM!
ガラ KTUNK
ガラ KTUNK
ガラ KTUNK
ガラ KTUNK
SIIGH...
I ENDED UP JUST GOING ALONG WITH IT...
TIM'S RIGHT. I CAN'T SHARE A ROOM WITH HIM FOREVER.
AND NOOOO WAY AM I MOVING IN WITH THE GUILD CHIEF, SO THIS MAY WORK OUT PERFECTLY.
AH, HERE WE ARE!
THIS LISTING COMES HIGHLY RECOM-MENDED BY THE GUILD!
バタム LOOM
HUUUH?!
TH-THIS IS...!

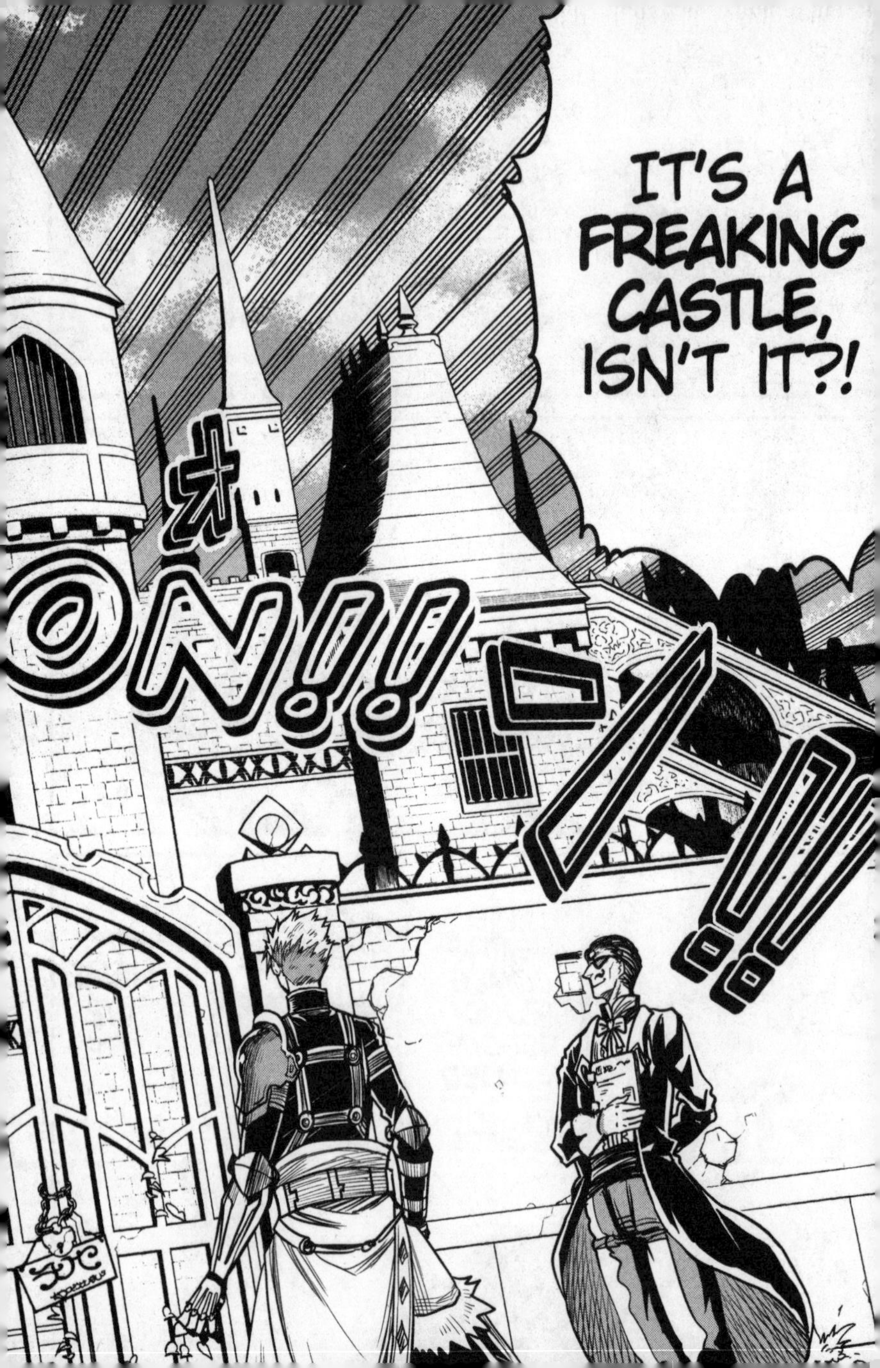
IT'S A FREAKING CASTLE, ISN'T IT?!
ON!!

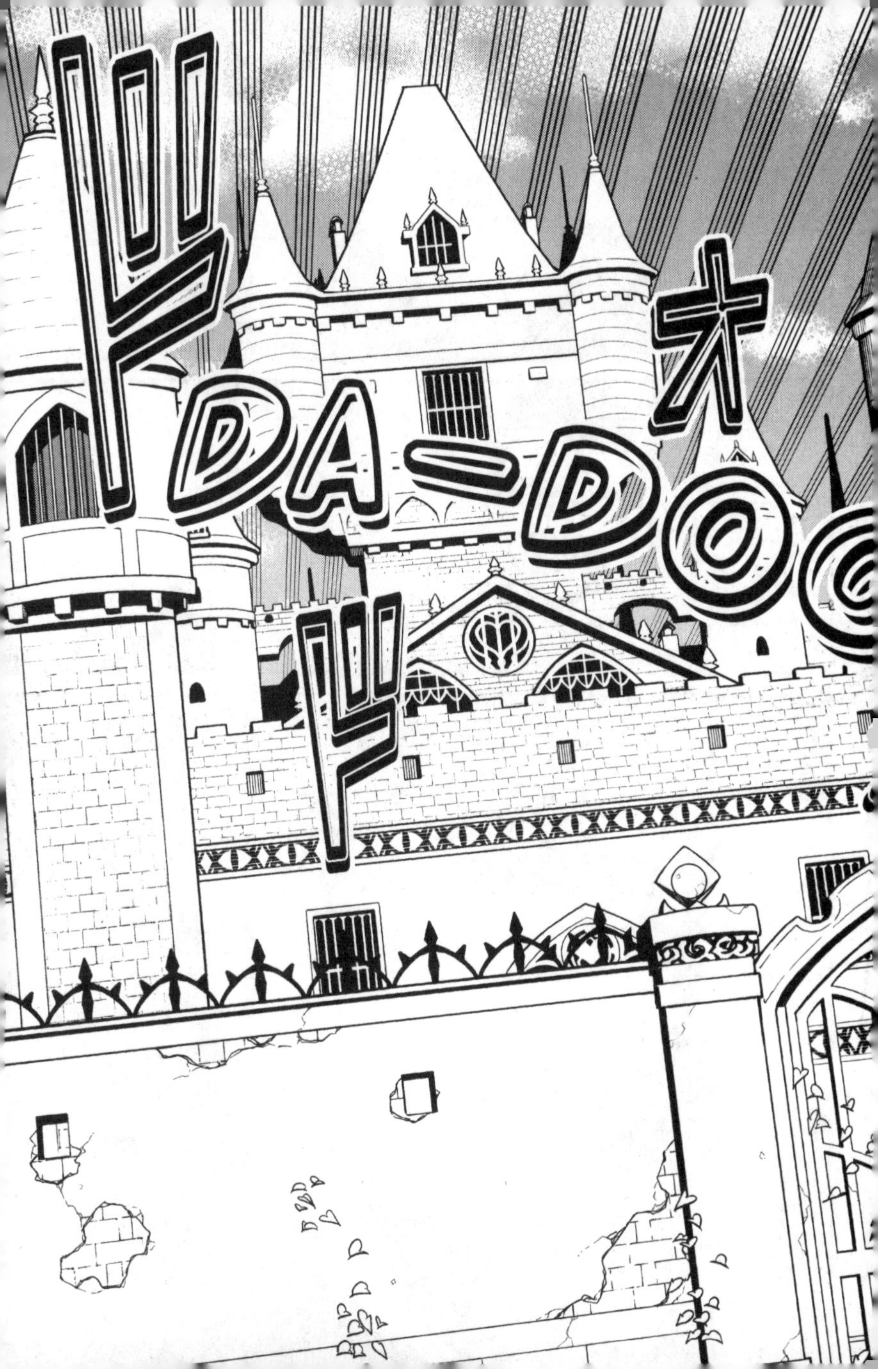
ドオッ
DA-DOOM
ドッ

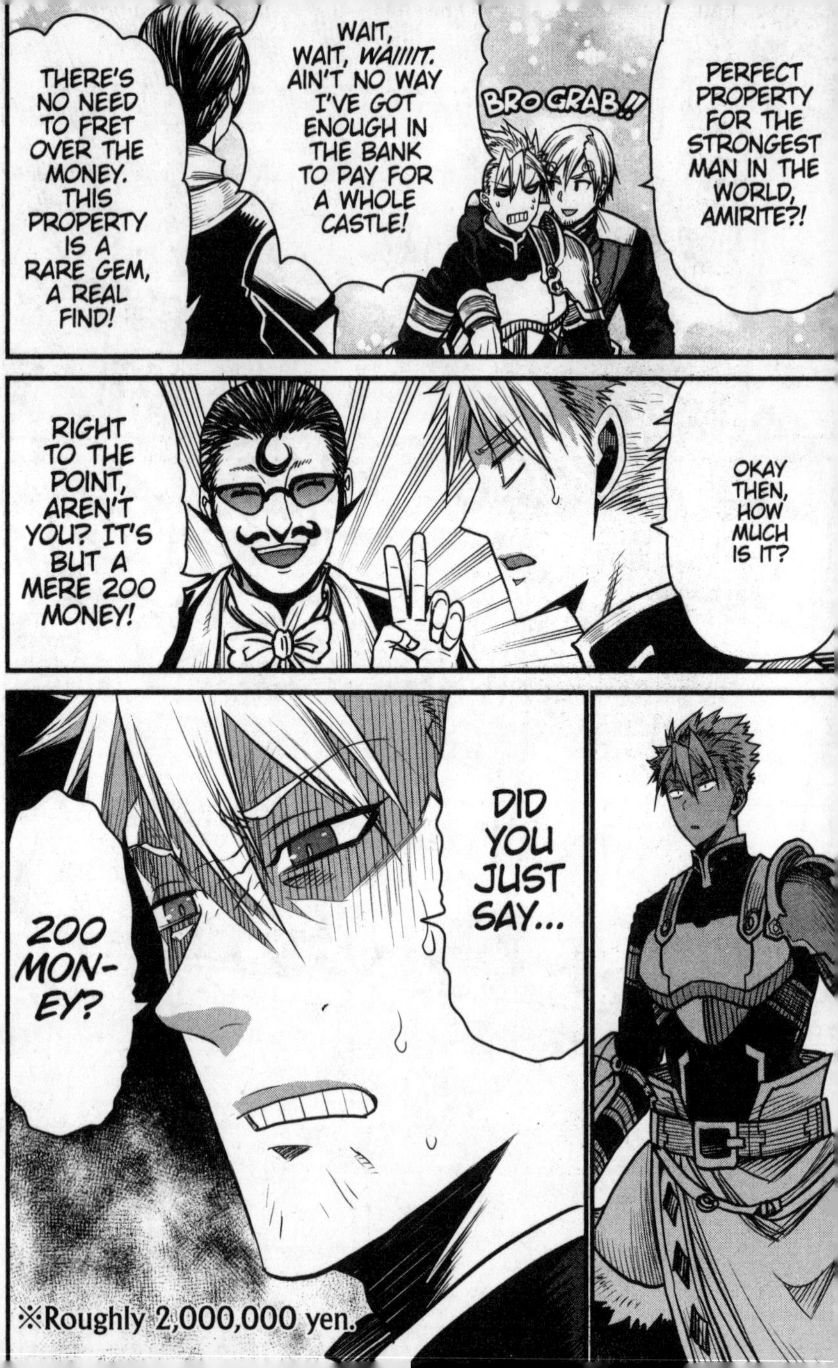
PERFECT PROPERTY FOR THE STRONGEST MAN IN THE WORLD, AMIRITE?!
BRO GRAB!!
WAIT, WAIT, WAIIIIT. AIN'T NO WAY I'VE GOT ENOUGH IN THE BANK TO PAY FOR A WHOLE CASTLE!
THERE'S NO NEED TO FRET OVER THE MONEY. THIS PROPERTY IS A RARE GEM, A REAL FIND!
OKAY THEN, HOW MUCH IS IT?
RIGHT TO THE POINT, AREN'T YOU? IT'S BUT A MERE 200 MONEY!
DID YOU JUST SAY...
200 MON-EY?
※Roughly 2,000,000 yen.

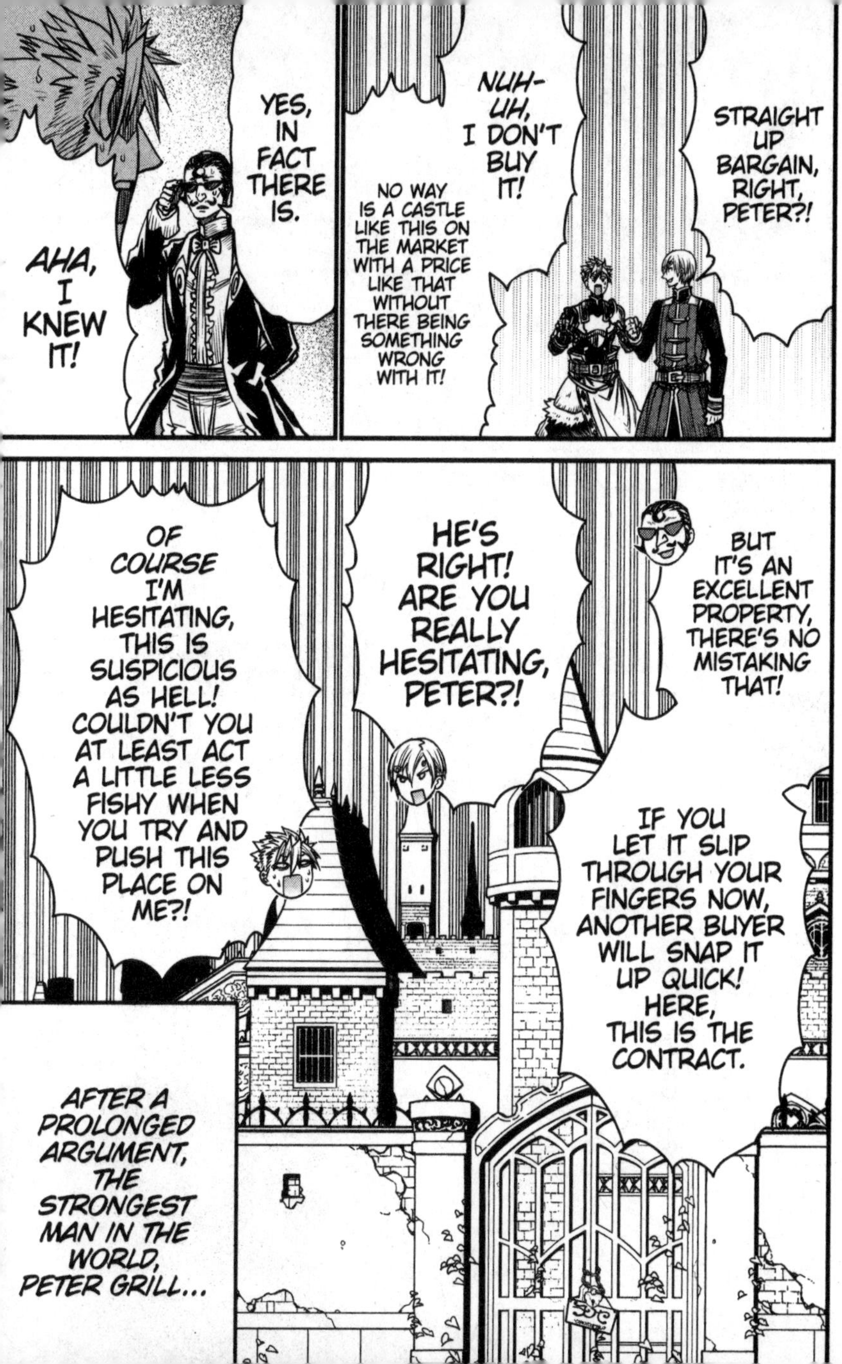
STRAIGHT UP BARGAIN, RIGHT, PETER?!
NUH-UH, I DON'T BUY IT!
NO WAY IS A CASTLE LIKE THIS ON THE MARKET WITH A PRICE LIKE THAT WITHOUT THERE BEING SOMETHING WRONG WITH IT!
YES, IN FACT THERE IS.
AHA, I KNEW IT!
BUT IT'S AN EXCELLENT PROPERTY, THERE'S NO MISTAKING THAT!
IF YOU LET IT SLIP THROUGH YOUR FINGERS NOW, ANOTHER BUYER WILL SNAP IT UP QUICK! HERE, THIS IS THE CONTRACT.
HE'S RIGHT! ARE YOU REALLY HESITATING, PETER?!
OF COURSE I'M HESITATING, THIS IS SUSPICIOUS AS HELL! COULDN'T YOU AT LEAST ACT A LITTLE LESS FISHY WHEN YOU TRY AND PUSH THIS PLACE ON ME?!
AFTER A PROLONGED ARGUMENT, THE STRONGEST MAN IN THE WORLD, PETER GRILL...

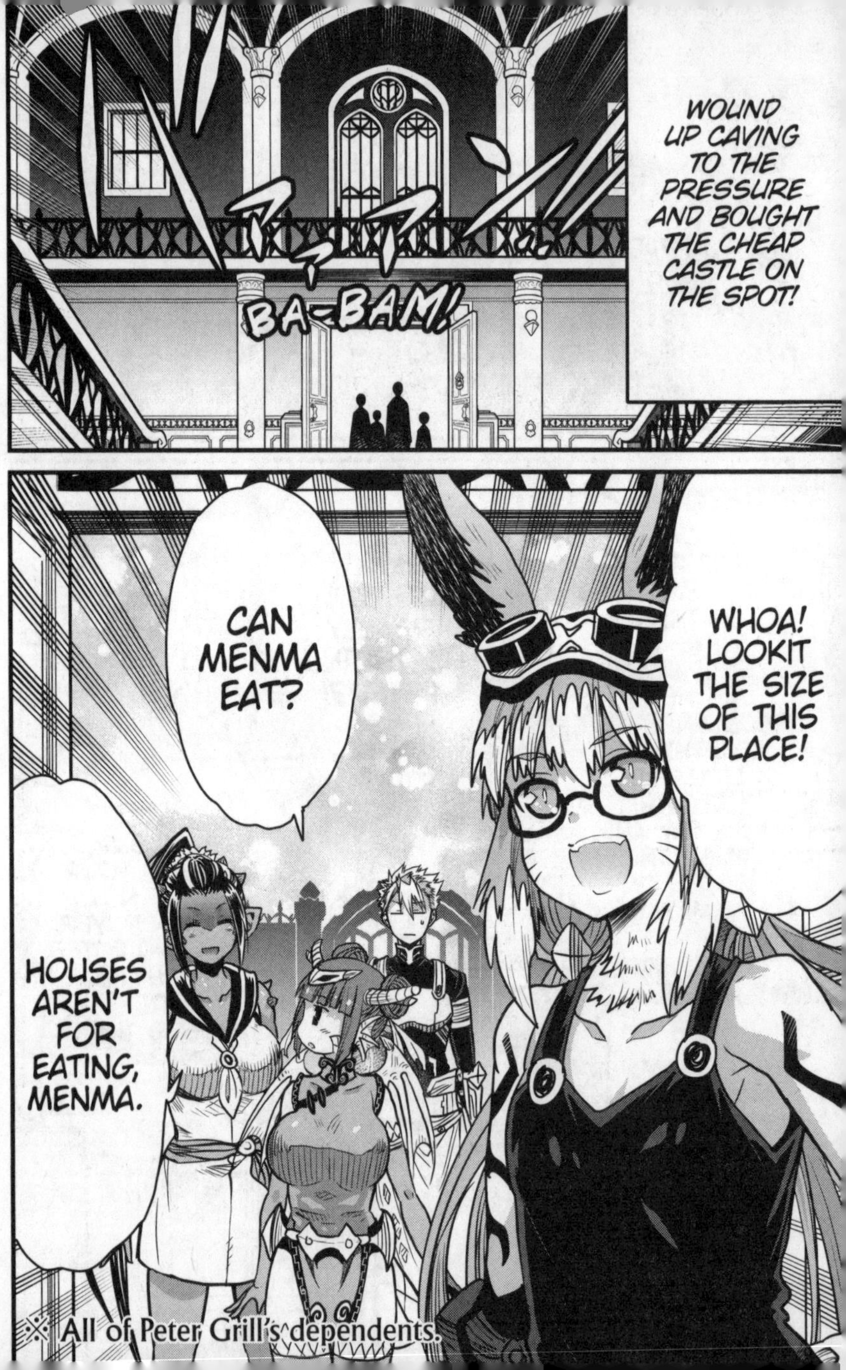
WOUND UP CAVING TO THE PRESSURE AND BOUGHT THE CHEAP CASTLE ON THE SPOT!
BA-BAM!
WHOA! LOOKIT THE SIZE OF THIS PLACE!
CAN MENMA EAT?
HOUSES AREN'T FOR EATING, MENMA.

※ All of Peter Grill's dependents.

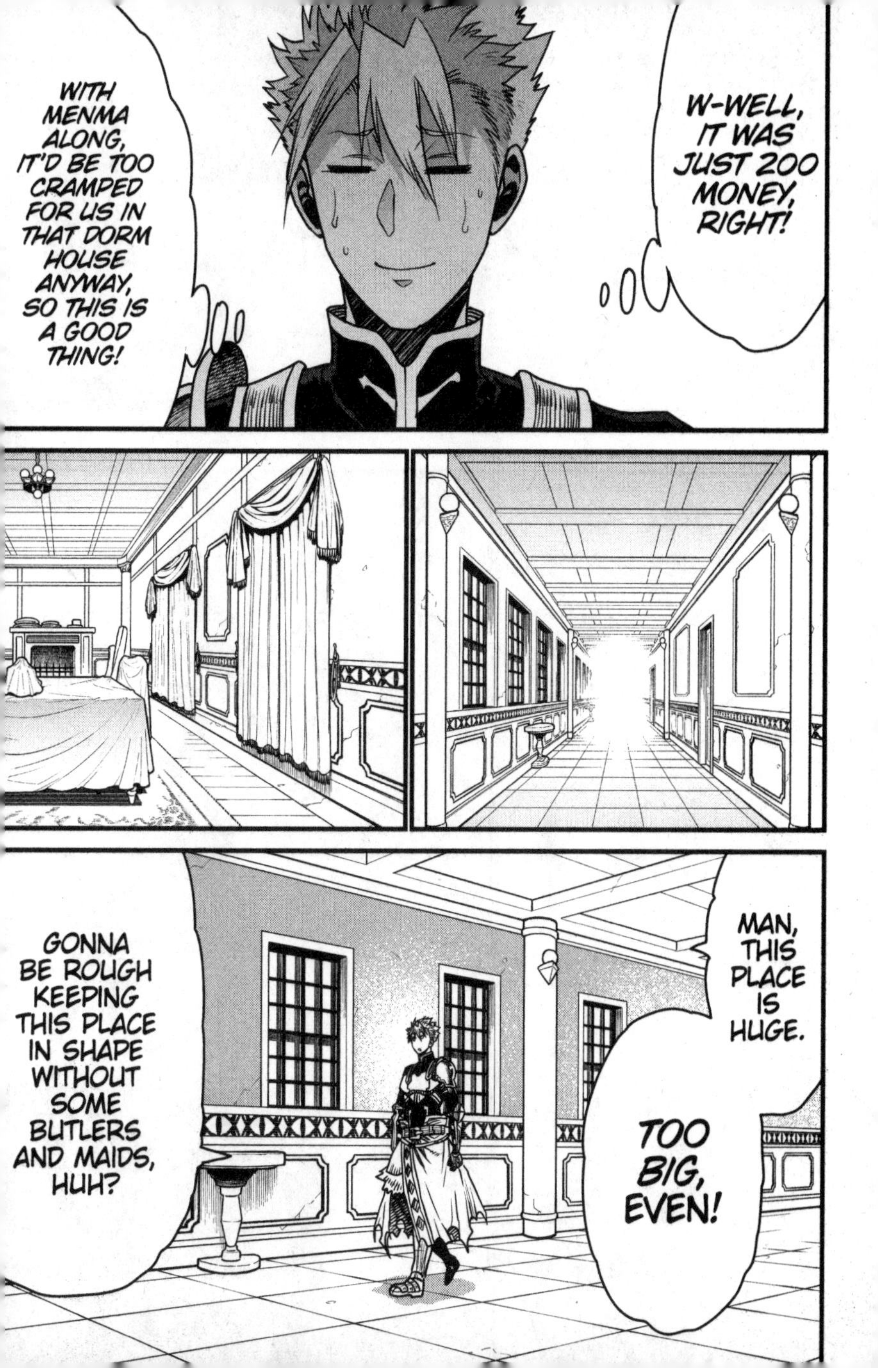
W-WELL, IT WAS JUST 200 MONEY, RIGHT!
WITH MENMA ALONG, IT'D BE TOO CRAMPED FOR US IN THAT DORM HOUSE ANYWAY, SO THIS IS A GOOD THING!
MAN, THIS PLACE IS HUGE.
TOO BIG, EVEN!
GONNA BE ROUGH KEEPING THIS PLACE IN SHAPE WITHOUT SOME BUTLERS AND MAIDS, HUH?

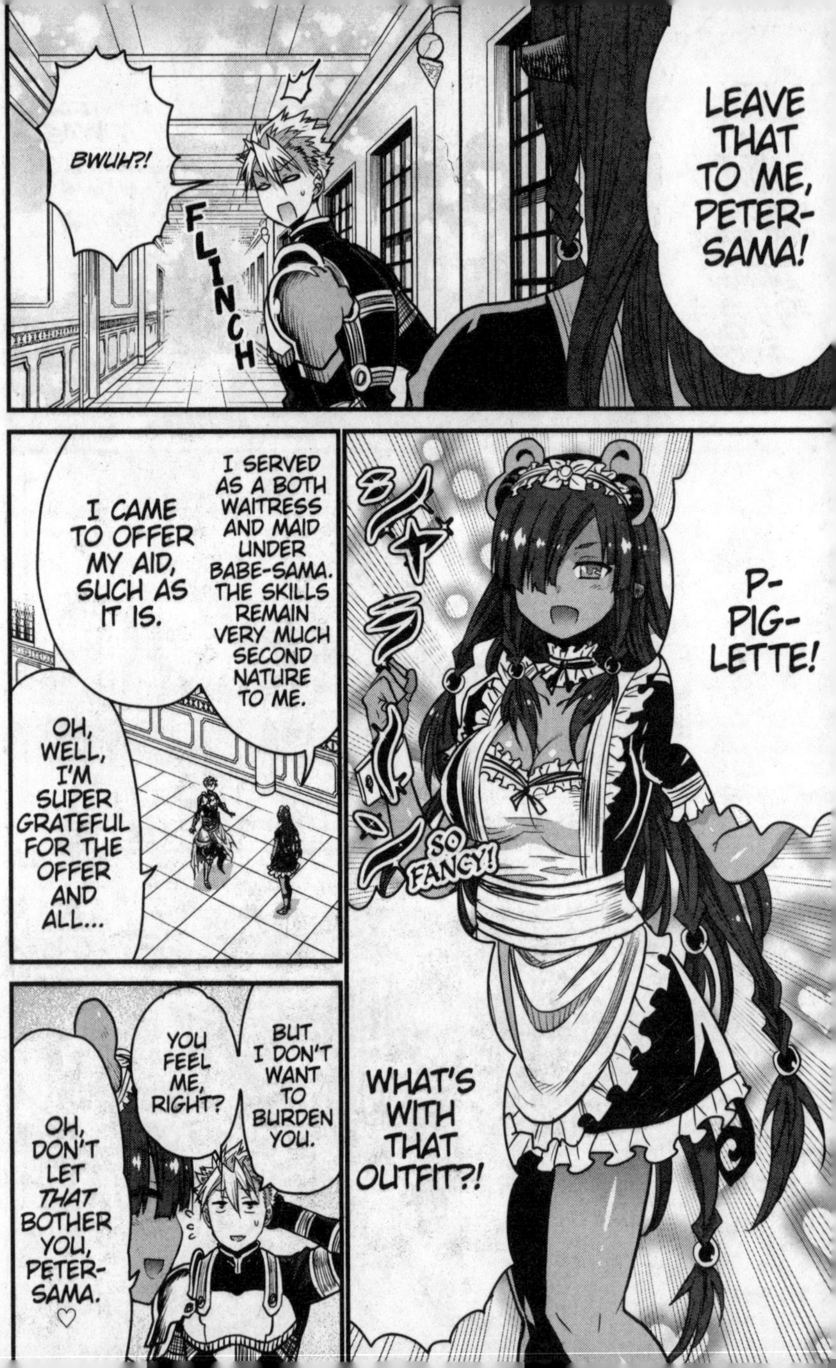
LEAVE THAT TO ME, PETER-SAMA!
BWUH?!
FLINCH
P-PIGLETTE!
SO FANCY!
WHAT'S WITH THAT OUTFIT?!
I SERVED AS A BOTH WAITRESS AND MAID UNDER BABE-SAMA. THE SKILLS REMAIN VERY MUCH SECOND NATURE TO ME.
I CAME TO OFFER MY AID, SUCH AS IT IS.
OH, WELL, I'M SUPER GRATEFUL FOR THE OFFER AND ALL...
BUT I DON'T WANT TO BURDEN YOU.
YOU FEEL ME, RIGHT?
OH, DON'T LET *THAT* BOTHER YOU, PETER-SAMA. ♡

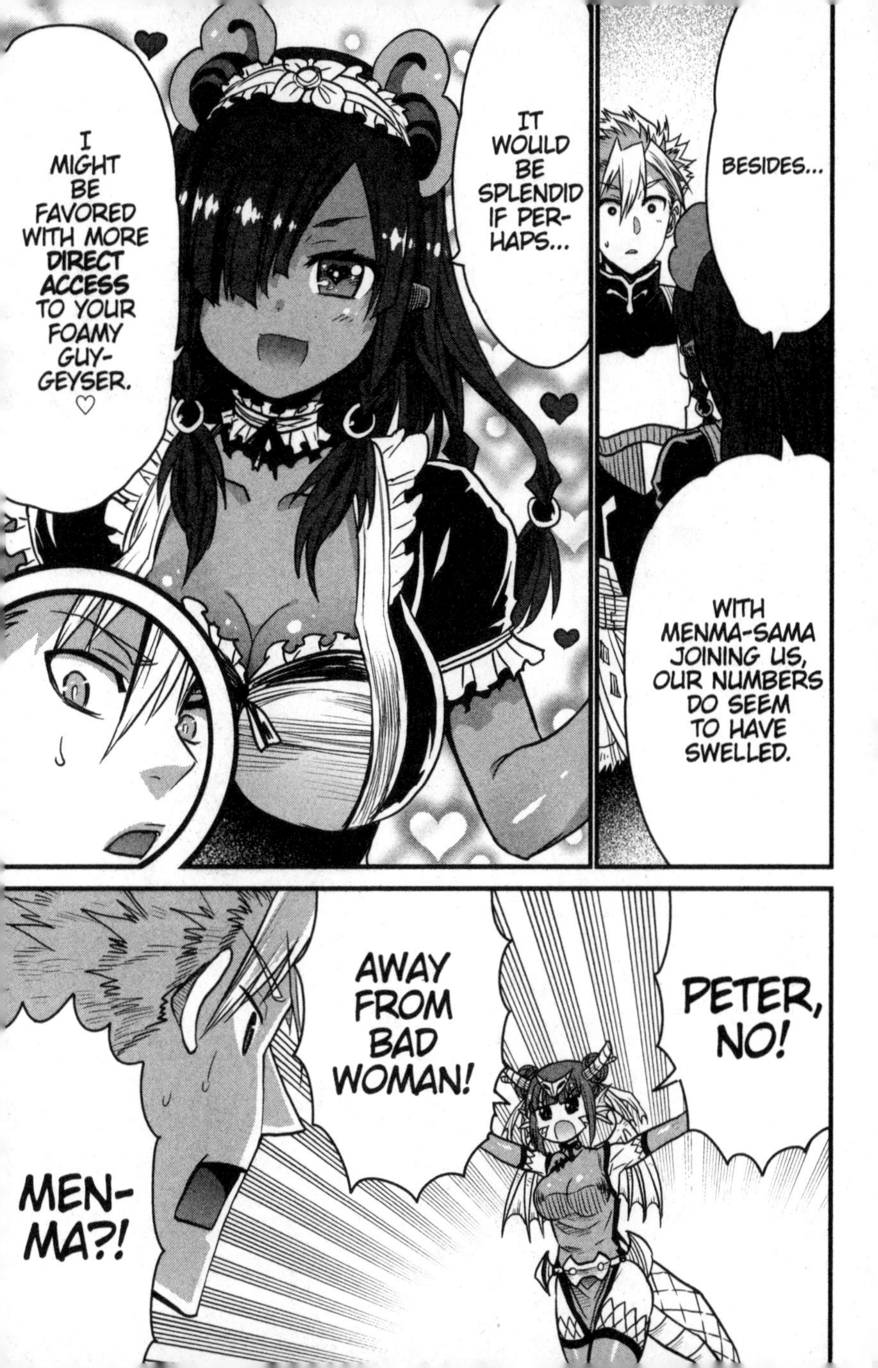
BESIDES...
WITH MENMA-SAMA JOINING US, OUR NUMBERS DO SEEM TO HAVE SWELLED.
IT WOULD BE SPLENDID IF PER-HAPS...
I MIGHT BE FAVORED WITH MORE DIRECT ACCESS TO YOUR FOAMY GUY-GEYSER. ♡
PETER, NO!
AWAY FROM BAD WOMAN!
MEN-MA?!

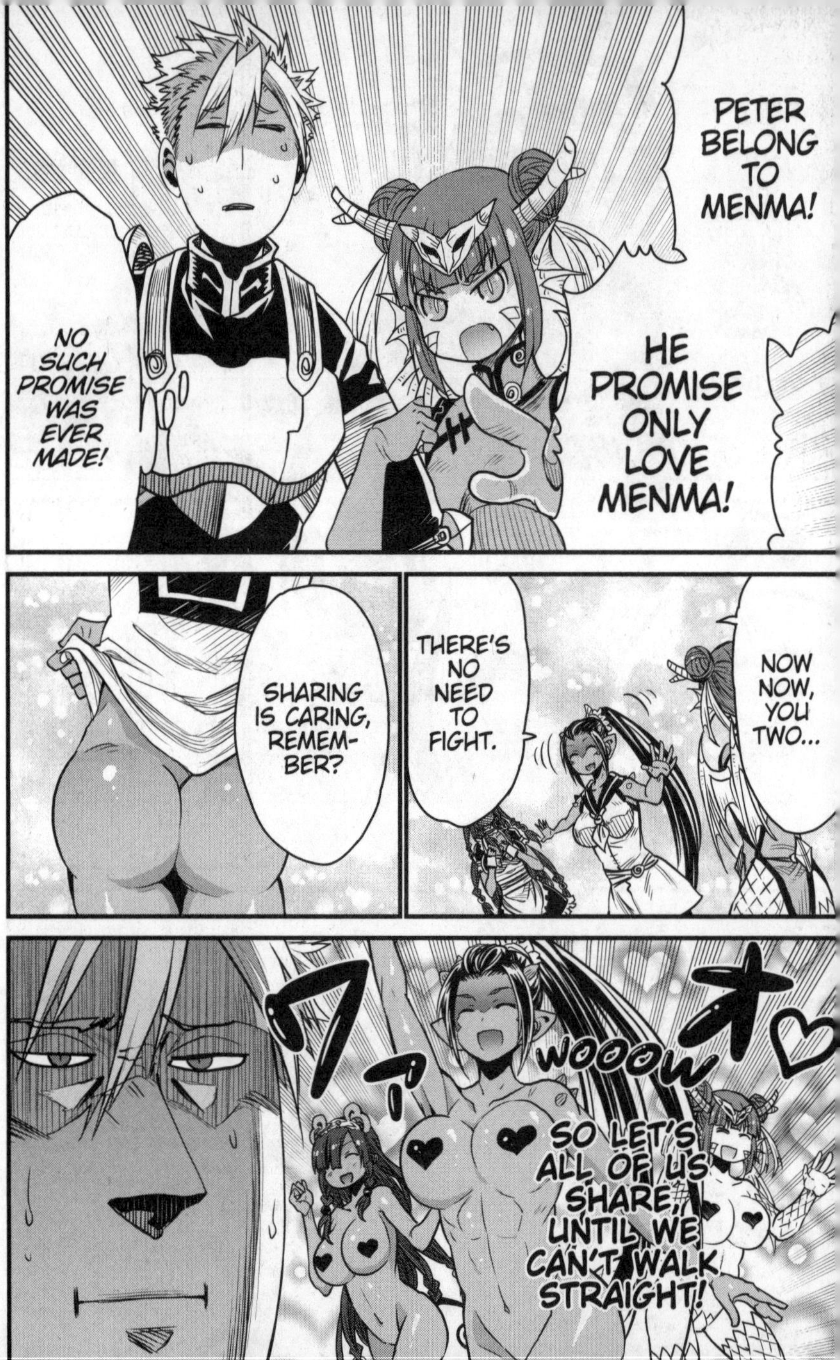
PETER BELONG TO MENMA!
HE PROMISE ONLY LOVE MENMA!
NO SUCH PROMISE WAS EVER MADE!
NOW NOW, YOU TWO...
THERE'S NO NEED TO FIGHT.
SHARING IS CARING, REMEMBER?
ワァオ♡
WOOOW
SO LET'S ALL OF US SHARE, UNTIL WE CAN'T WALK STRAIGHT!

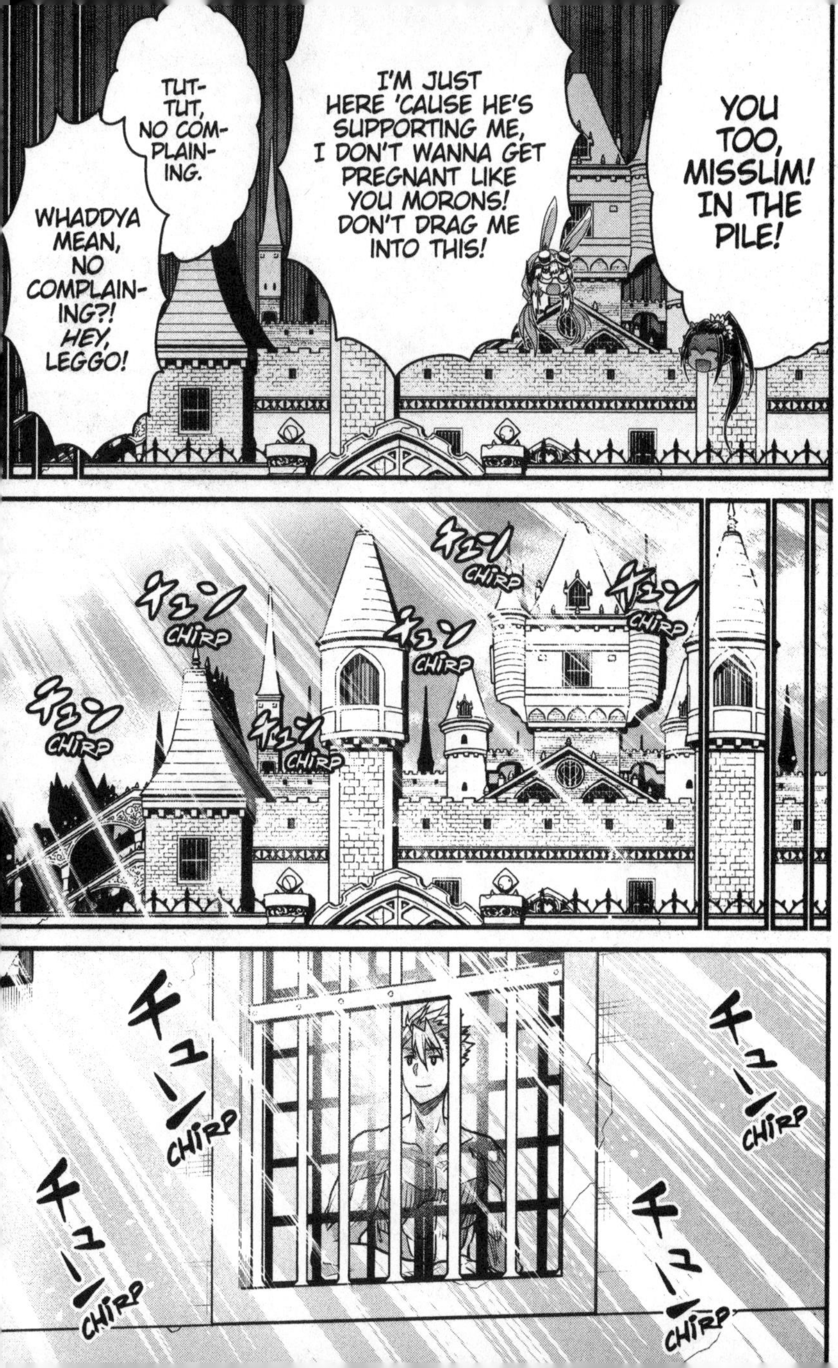
YOU TOO, MISSLIM! IN THE PILE!
I'M JUST HERE 'CAUSE HE'S SUPPORTING ME, I DON'T WANNA GET PREGNANT LIKE YOU MORONS! DON'T DRAG ME INTO THIS!
TUT-TUT, NO COMPLAINING.
WHADDYA MEAN, NO COMPLAINING?! HEY, LEGGO!
CHIRP
CHIRP
CHIRP
CHIRP
CHIRP
CHIRP
CHIRP
CHIRP
CHIRP
CHIRP

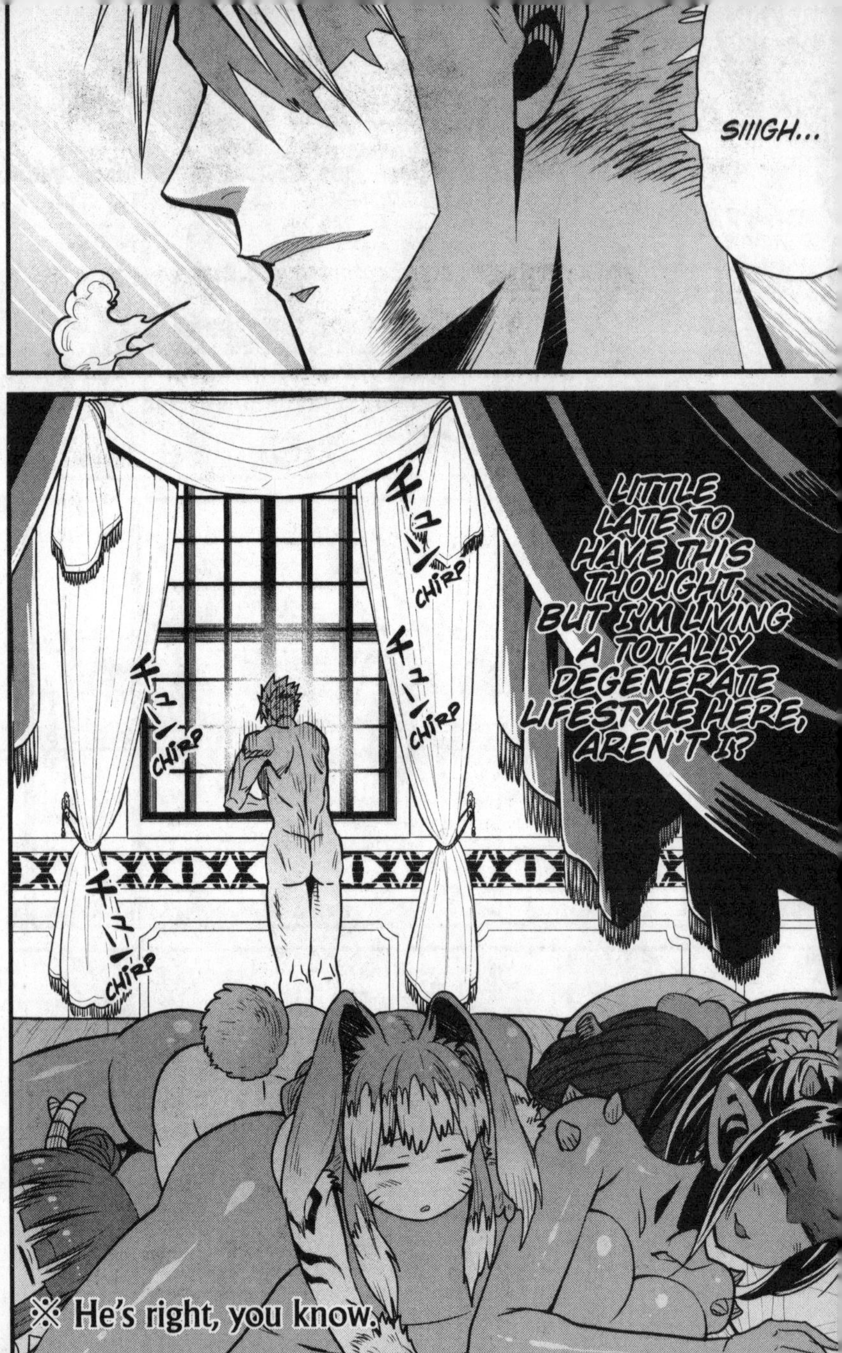
SIIIGH...
LITTLE LATE TO HAVE THIS THOUGHT, BUT I'M LIVING A TOTALLY DEGENERATE LIFESTYLE HERE, AREN'T I?
チュン CHIRP
チュン CHIRP
チュン CHIRP
チュン CHIRP
※ He's right, you know.

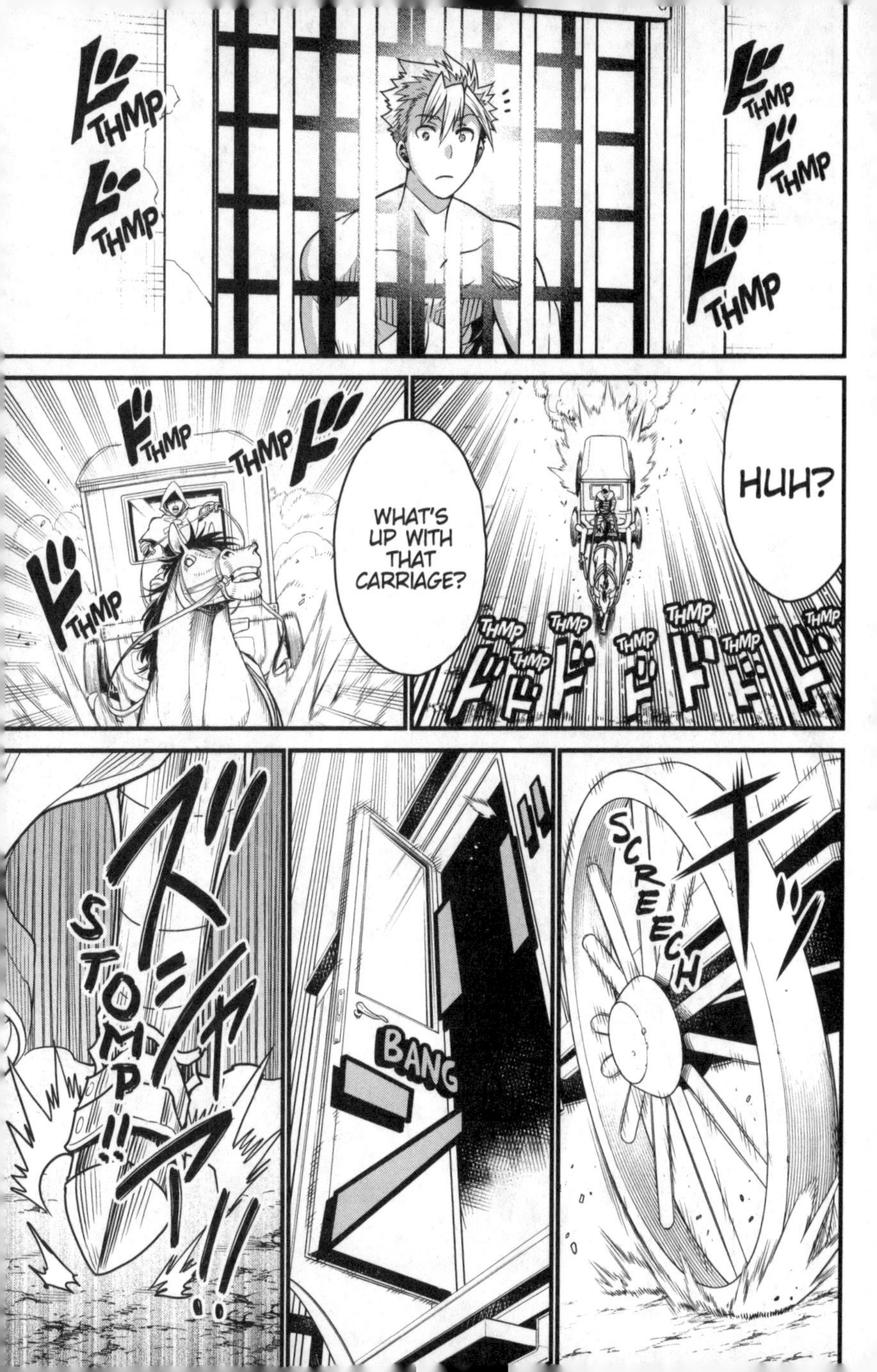
THMP
THMP
THMP
THMP
THMP
HUH?
THMP
THMP
THMP
THMP
THMP
THMP
THMP
WHAT'S UP WITH THAT CARRIAGE?
THMP
THMP
THMP
SCREECH
BANG
STOMP!!

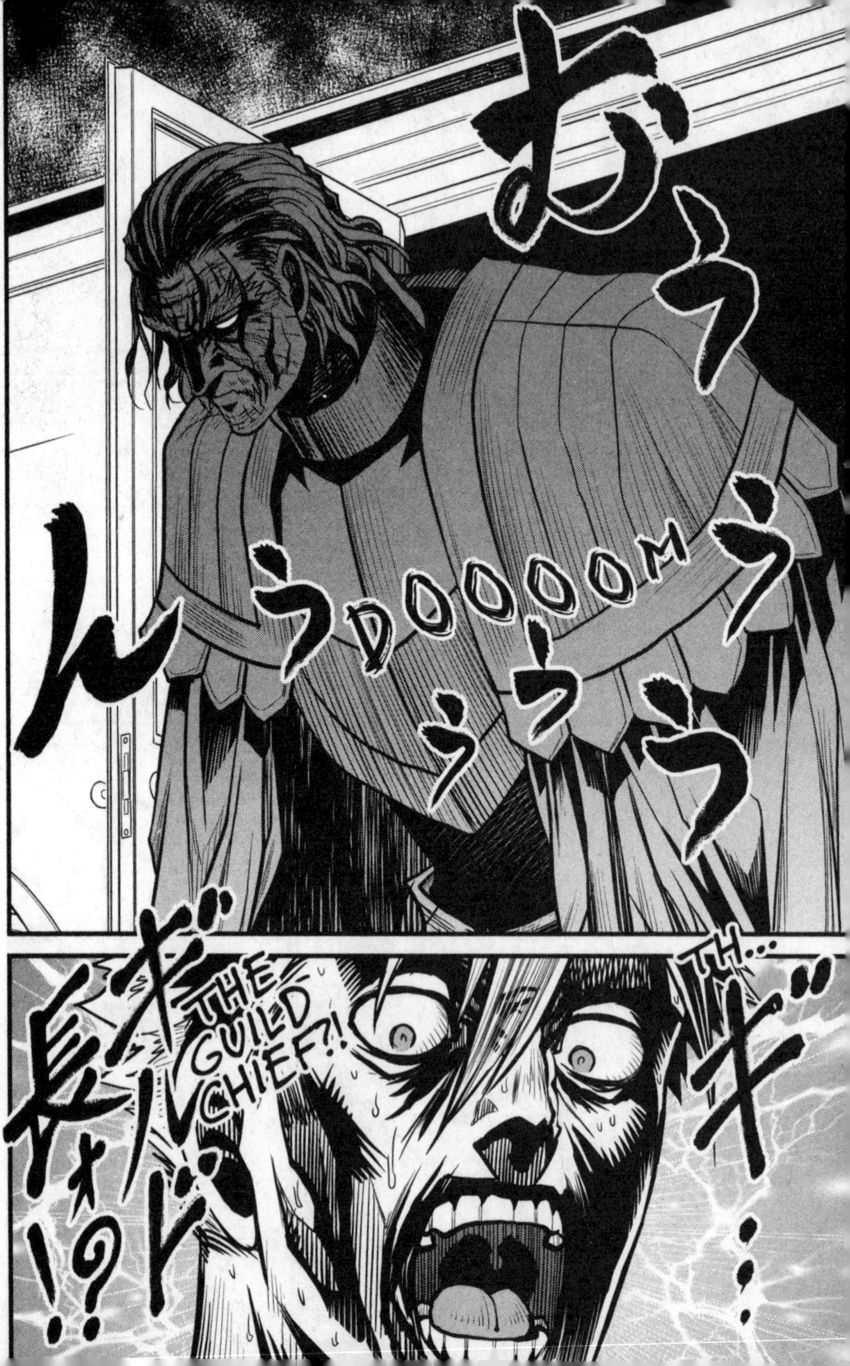
DOOOOM
TH...
THE GUILD CHIEF?!

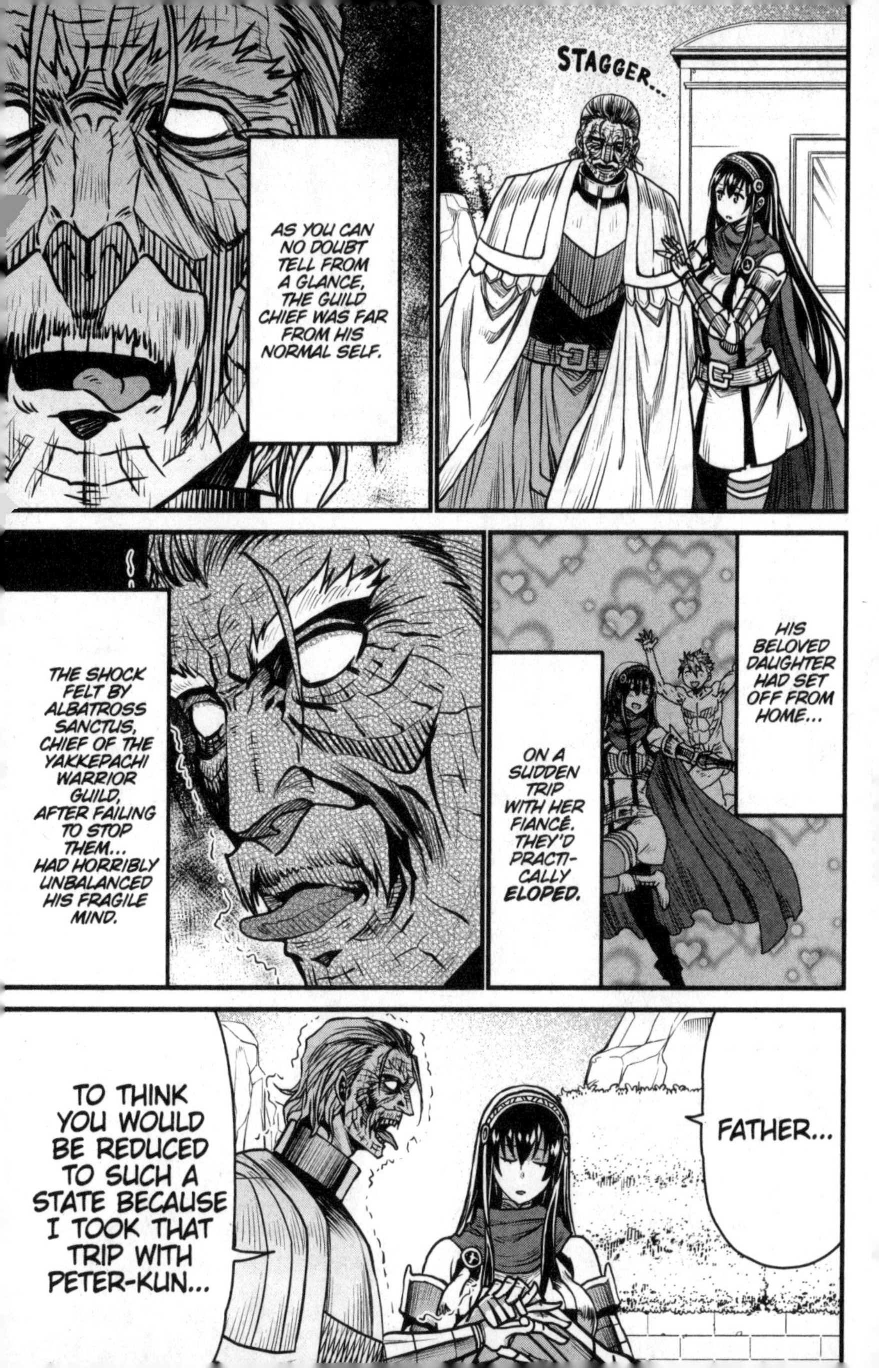
STAGGER...
AS YOU CAN NO DOUBT TELL FROM A GLANCE, THE GUILD CHIEF WAS FAR FROM HIS NORMAL SELF.
HIS BELOVED DAUGHTER HAD SET OFF FROM HOME...
ON A SUDDEN TRIP WITH HER FIANCÉ. THEY'D PRACTI-CALLY ELOPED.
THE SHOCK FELT BY ALBATROSS SANCTUS, CHIEF OF THE YAKKEPACHI WARRIOR GUILD, AFTER FAILING TO STOP THEM... HAD HORRIBLY UNBALANCED HIS FRAGILE MIND.
FATHER...
TO THINK YOU WOULD BE REDUCED TO SUCH A STATE BECAUSE I TOOK THAT TRIP WITH PETER-KUN...

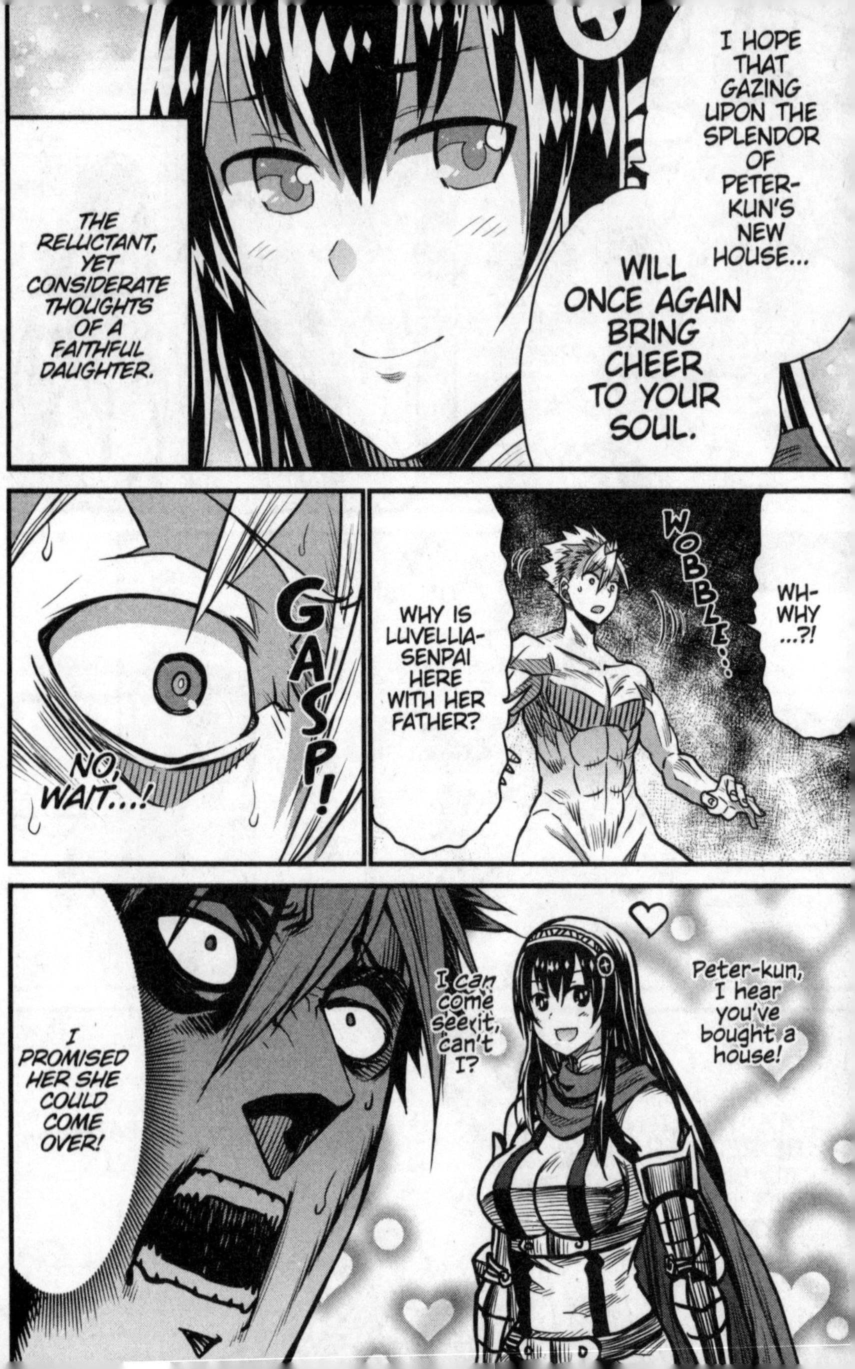
I HOPE THAT GAZING UPON THE SPLENDOR OF PETER-KUN'S NEW HOUSE...
WILL ONCE AGAIN BRING CHEER TO YOUR SOUL.
THE RELUCTANT, YET CONSIDERATE THOUGHTS OF A FAITHFUL DAUGHTER.
WOBBLE...
WH-WHY...?!
WHY IS LUVELLIA-SENPAI HERE WITH HER FATHER?
GASP!
NO, WAIT...!
Peter-kun, I hear you've bought a house!
I can come see it, can't I?
I PROMISED HER SHE COULD COME OVER!

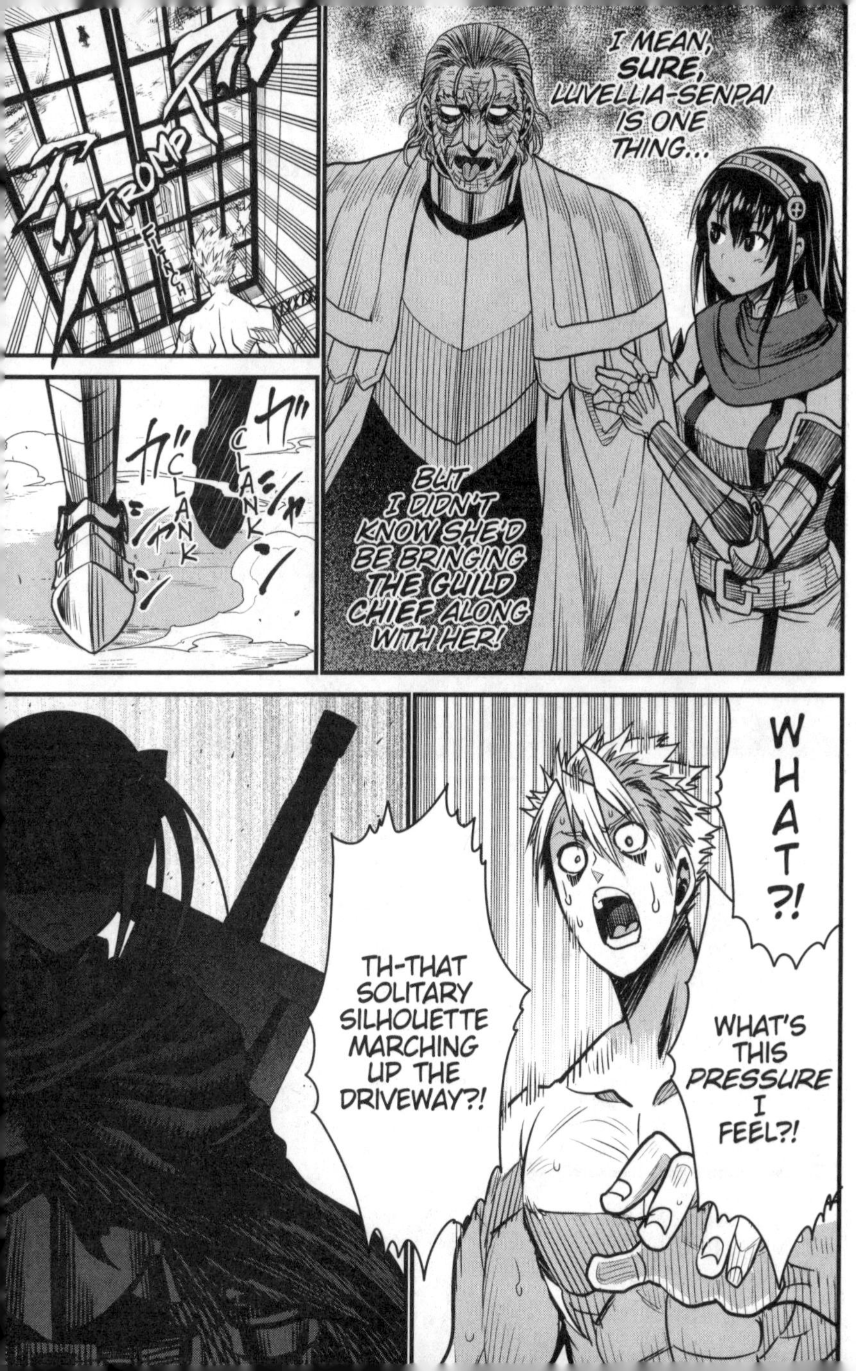
I MEAN, SURE, LUVELLIA-SENPAI IS ONE THING...
BUT I DIDN'T KNOW SHE'D BE BRINGING THE GUILD CHIEF ALONG WITH HER!
TROMP
FLINCH
CLANK
CLANK
WHAT?!
WHAT'S THIS PRESSURE I FEEL?!
TH-THAT SOLITARY SILHOUETTE MARCHING UP THE DRIVEWAY?!

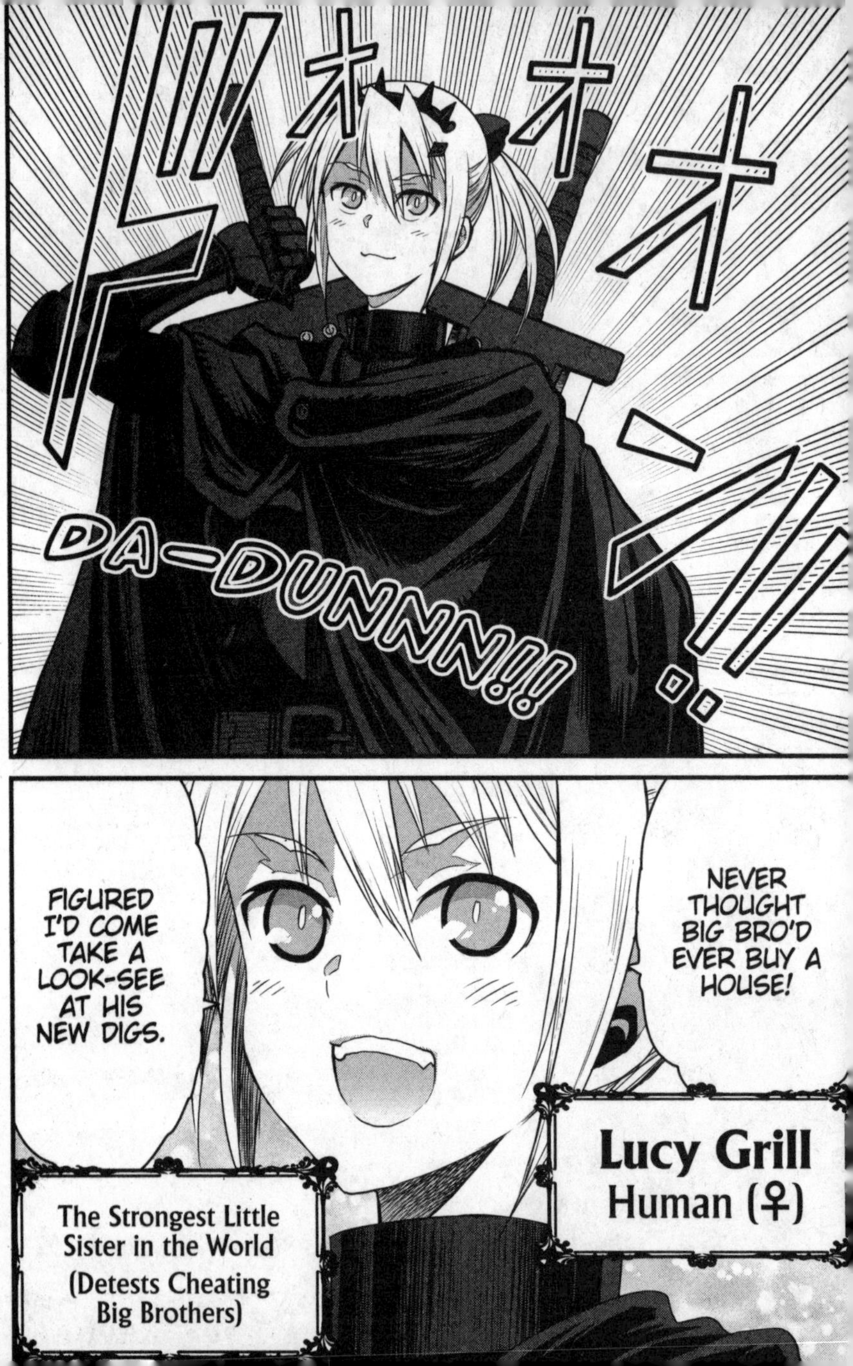
DA-DUNNNN!!
NEVER THOUGHT BIG BRO'D EVER BUY A HOUSE!
FIGURED I'D COME TAKE A LOOK-SEE AT HIS NEW DIGS.
Lucy Grill
Human (♀)
The Strongest Little Sister in the World
(Detests Cheating Big Brothers)

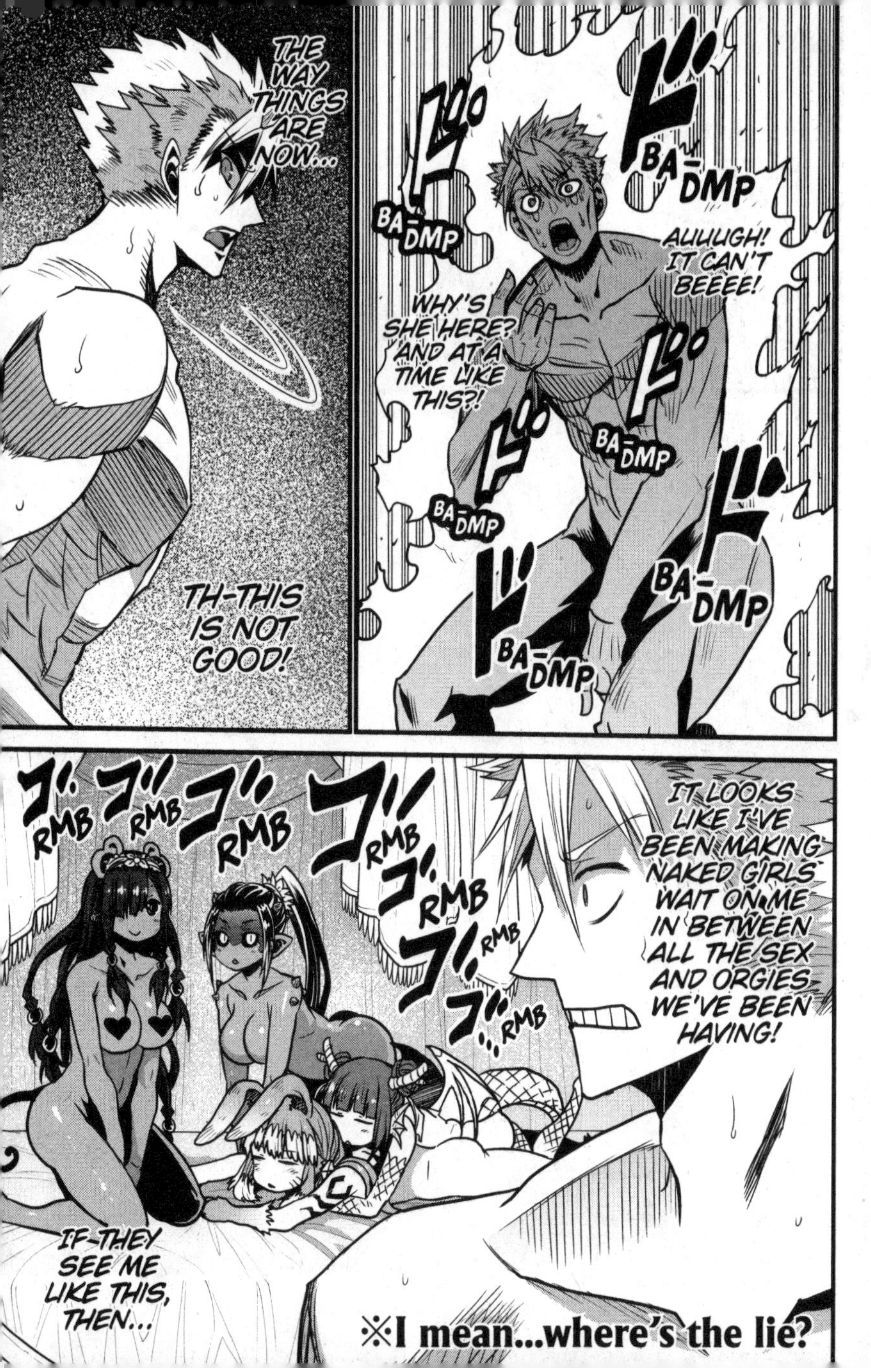
ド BA-DMP
AUUUGH! IT CAN'T BEEEE!
WHY'S SHE HERE? AND AT A TIME LIKE THIS?!
ド BA-DMP
ド BA-DMP
ド BA-DMP
ド BA-DMP
ド BA-DMP
ド BA-DMP
THE WAY THINGS ARE NOW...
TH-THIS IS NOT GOOD!
ゴ RMB
ゴ RMB
ゴ RMB
ゴ RMB
ゴ RMB
ゴ RMB
ゴ RMB
IT LOOKS LIKE I'VE BEEN MAKING NAKED GIRLS WAIT ON ME IN BETWEEN ALL THE SEX AND ORGIES WE'VE BEEN HAVING!
IF THEY SEE ME LIKE THIS, THEN...
※I mean...where's the lie?

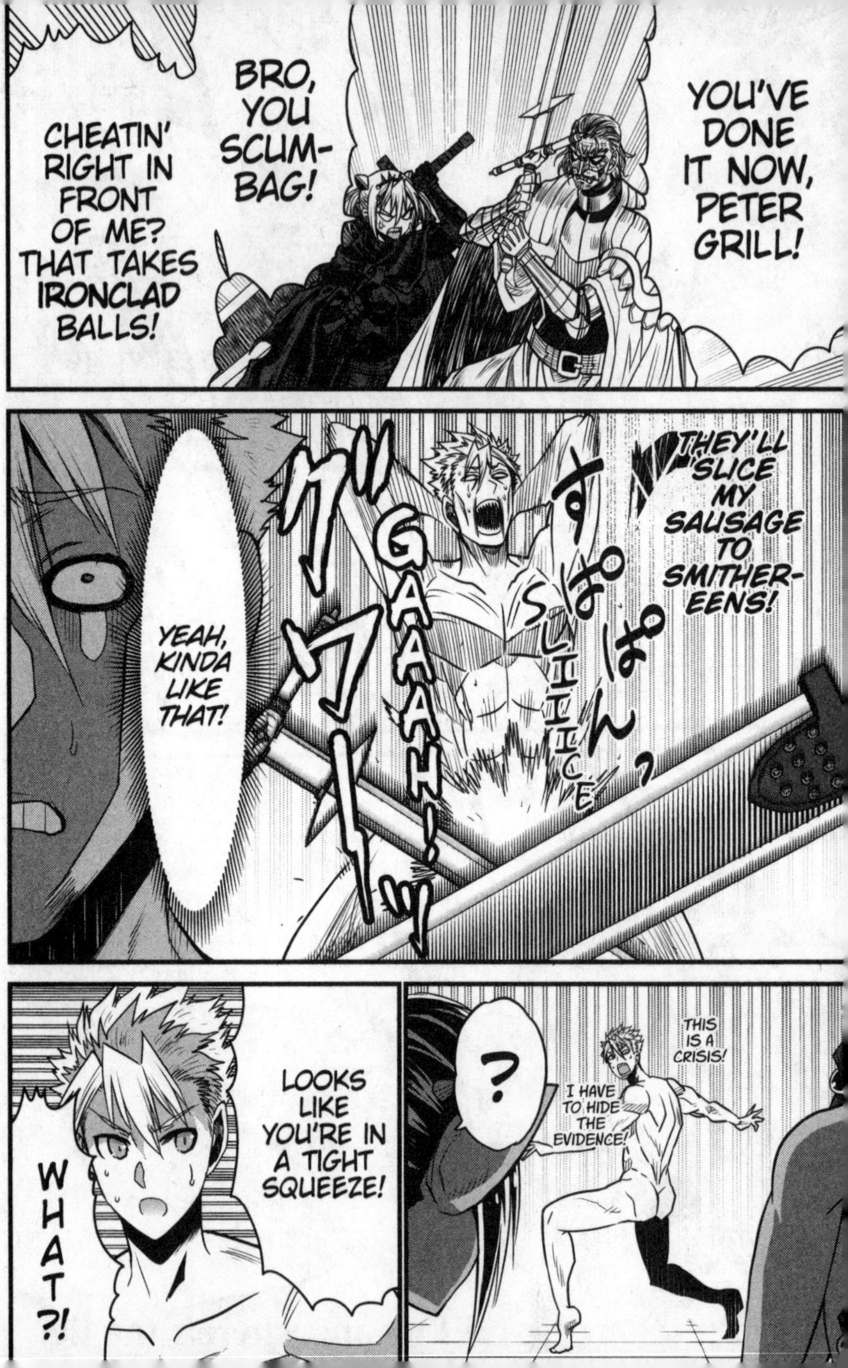
YOU'VE DONE IT NOW, PETER GRILL!
BRO, YOU SCUMBAG!
CHEATIN' RIGHT IN FRONT OF ME? THAT TAKES IRONCLAD BALLS!
THEY'LL SLICE MY SAUSAGE TO SMITHEREENS!
すぱぱん
SLIIIICE
GAAAH!!
YEAH, KINDA LIKE THAT!
THIS IS A CRISIS!
I HAVE TO HIDE THE EVIDENCE!
?
LOOKS LIKE YOU'RE IN A TIGHT SQUEEZE!
WHAT?!

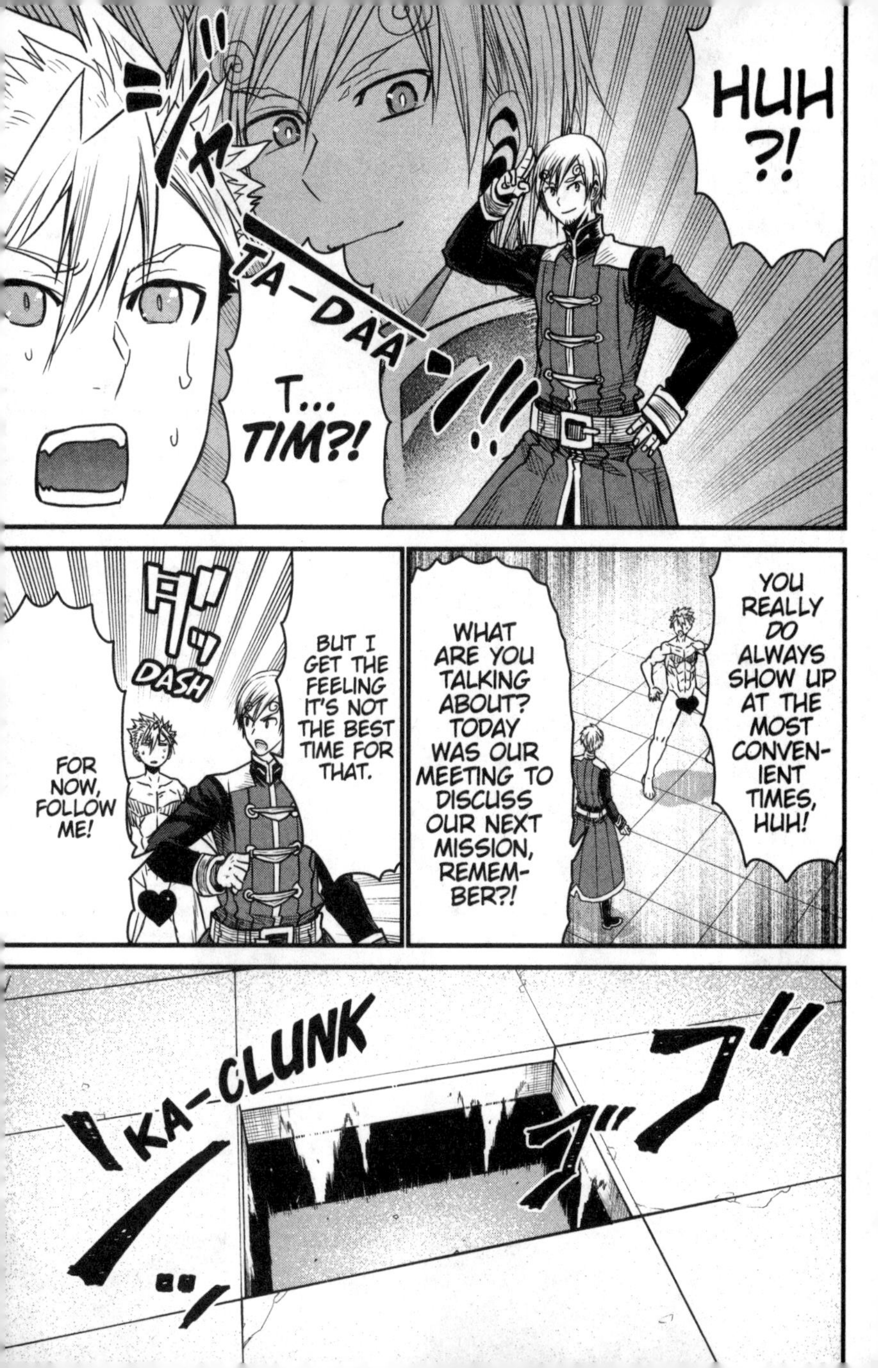
HUH?!
TA-DAA
T... TIM?!
YOU REALLY DO ALWAYS SHOW UP AT THE MOST CONVEN-IENT TIMES, HUH!
WHAT ARE YOU TALKING ABOUT? TODAY WAS OUR MEETING TO DISCUSS OUR NEXT MISSION, REMEM-BER?!
BUT I GET THE FEELING IT'S NOT THE BEST TIME FOR THAT.
DASH
FOR NOW, FOLLOW ME!
KA-CLUNK

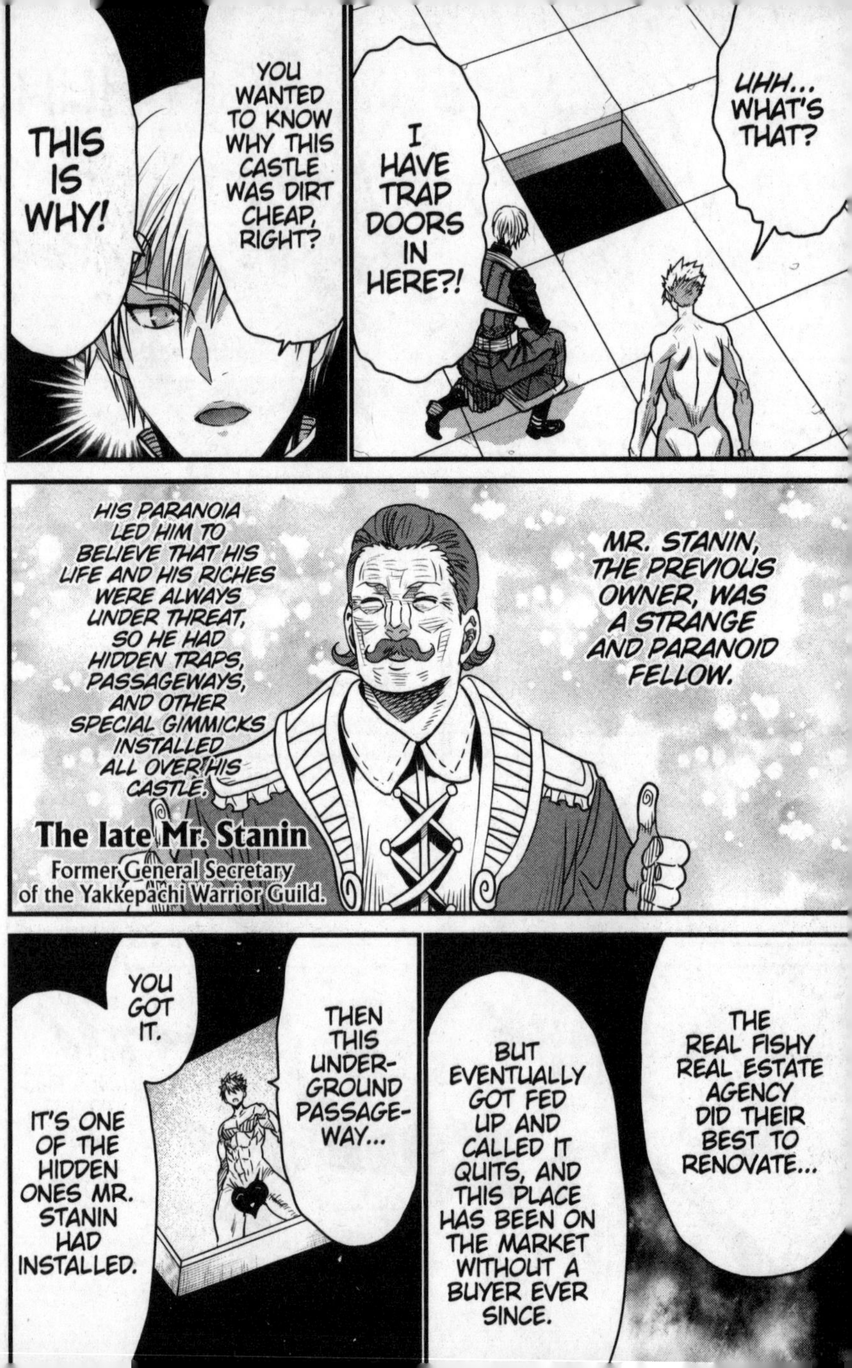
UHH... WHAT'S THAT?
I HAVE TRAP DOORS IN HERE?!
YOU WANTED TO KNOW WHY THIS CASTLE WAS DIRT CHEAP, RIGHT?
THIS IS WHY!
MR. STANIN, THE PREVIOUS OWNER, WAS A STRANGE AND PARANOID FELLOW.
HIS PARANOIA LED HIM TO BELIEVE THAT HIS LIFE AND HIS RICHES WERE ALWAYS UNDER THREAT, SO HE HAD HIDDEN TRAPS, PASSAGEWAYS, AND OTHER SPECIAL GIMMICKS INSTALLED ALL OVER HIS CASTLE.
The late Mr. Stanin
Former General Secretary of the Yakkepachi Warrior Guild.
THE REAL FISHY REAL ESTATE AGENCY DID THEIR BEST TO RENOVATE...
BUT EVENTUALLY GOT FED UP AND CALLED IT QUITS, AND THIS PLACE HAS BEEN ON THE MARKET WITHOUT A BUYER EVER SINCE.
THEN THIS UNDER-GROUND PASSAGE-WAY...
YOU GOT IT.
IT'S ONE OF THE HIDDEN ONES MR. STANIN HAD INSTALLED.

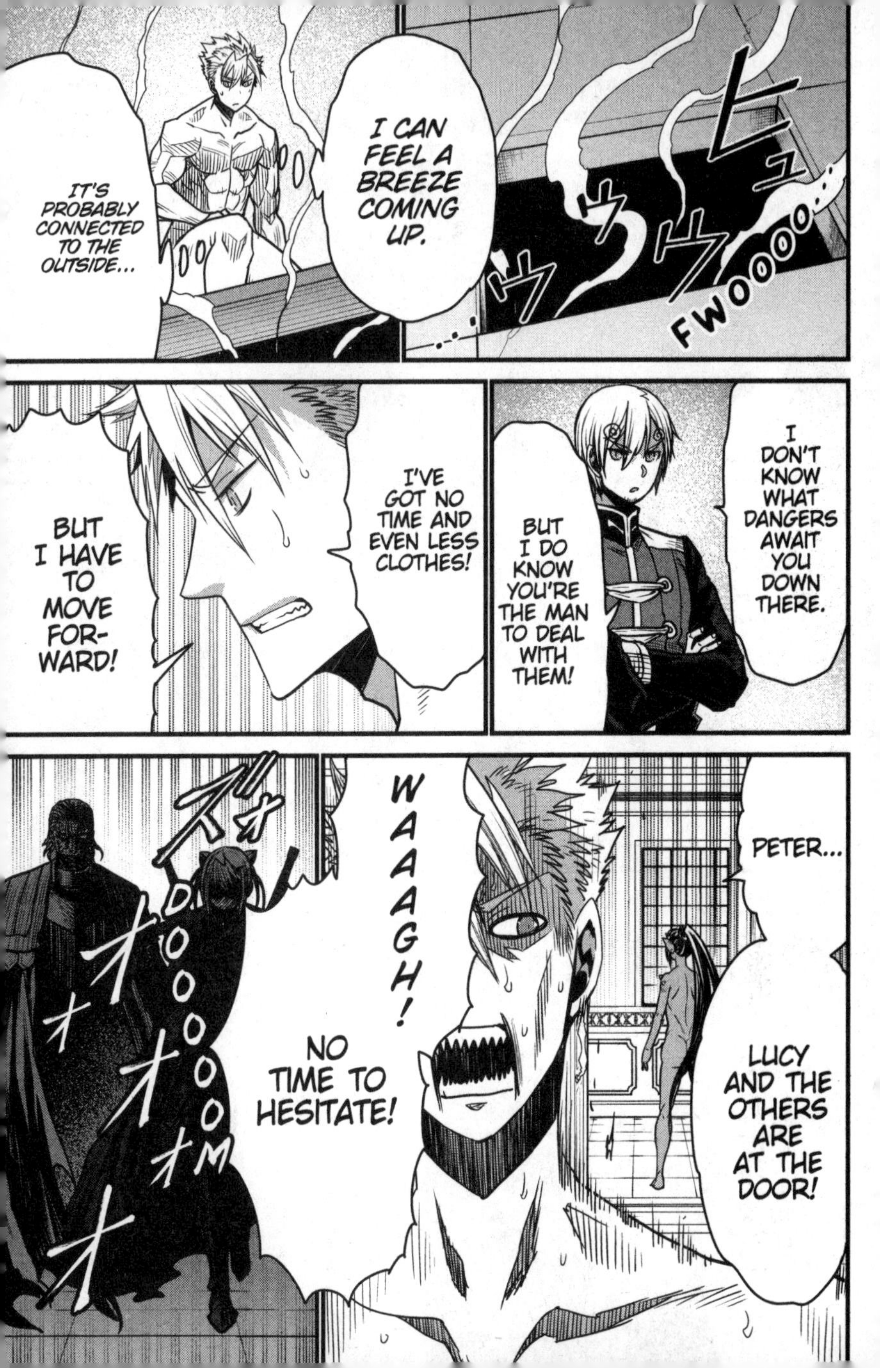
FWOOOO...
I CAN FEEL A BREEZE COMING UP.
IT'S PROBABLY CONNECTED TO THE OUTSIDE...
I DON'T KNOW WHAT DANGERS AWAIT YOU DOWN THERE.
BUT I DO KNOW YOU'RE THE MAN TO DEAL WITH THEM!
I'VE GOT NO TIME AND EVEN LESS CLOTHES!
BUT I HAVE TO MOVE FOR-WARD!
PETER...
LUCY AND THE OTHERS ARE AT THE DOOR!
WAAAAGH!
NO TIME TO HESITATE!
DOOOOOOM

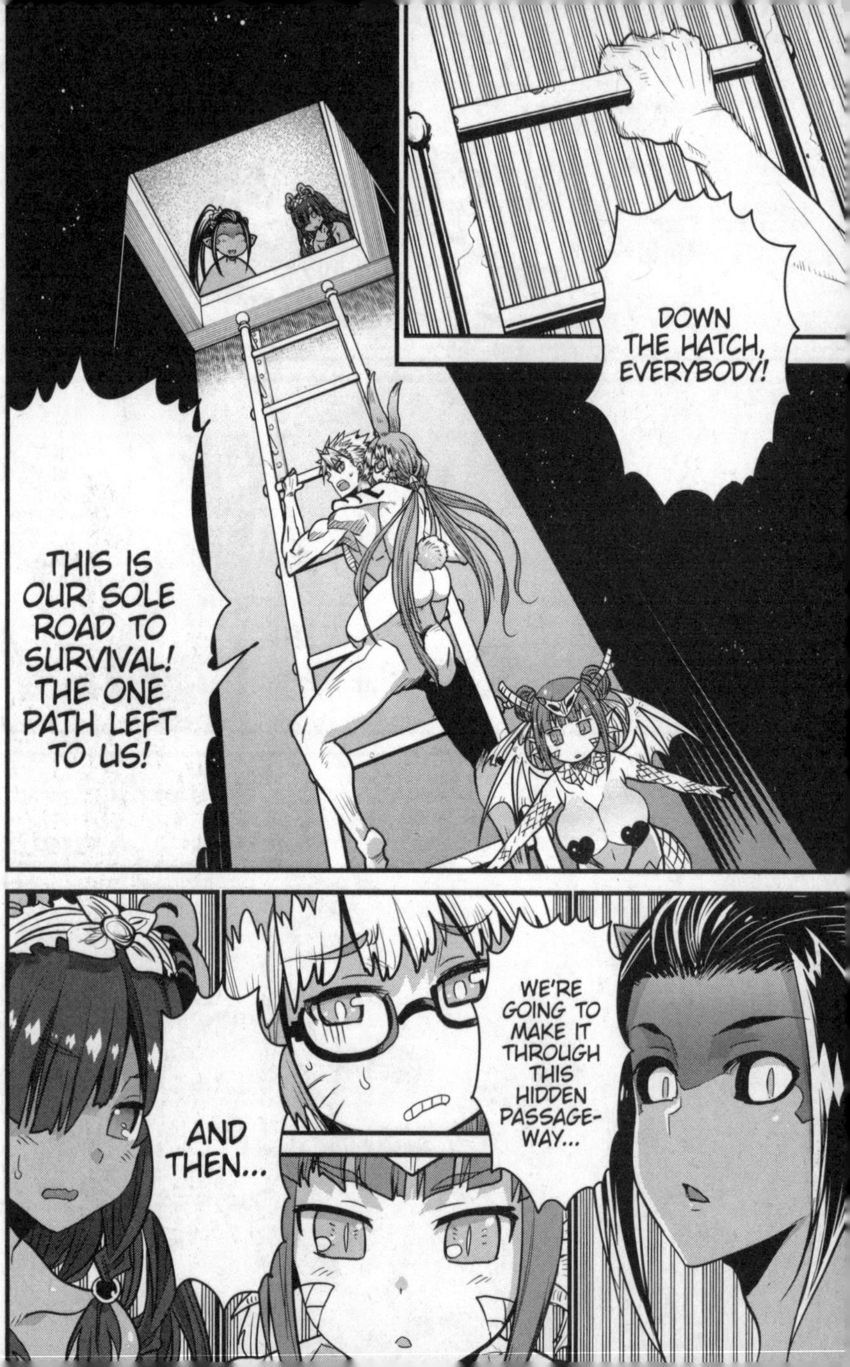
DOWN THE HATCH, EVERYBODY!
THIS IS OUR SOLE ROAD TO SURVIVAL! THE ONE PATH LEFT TO US!
WE'RE GOING TO MAKE IT THROUGH THIS HIDDEN PASSAGE-WAY...
AND THEN...

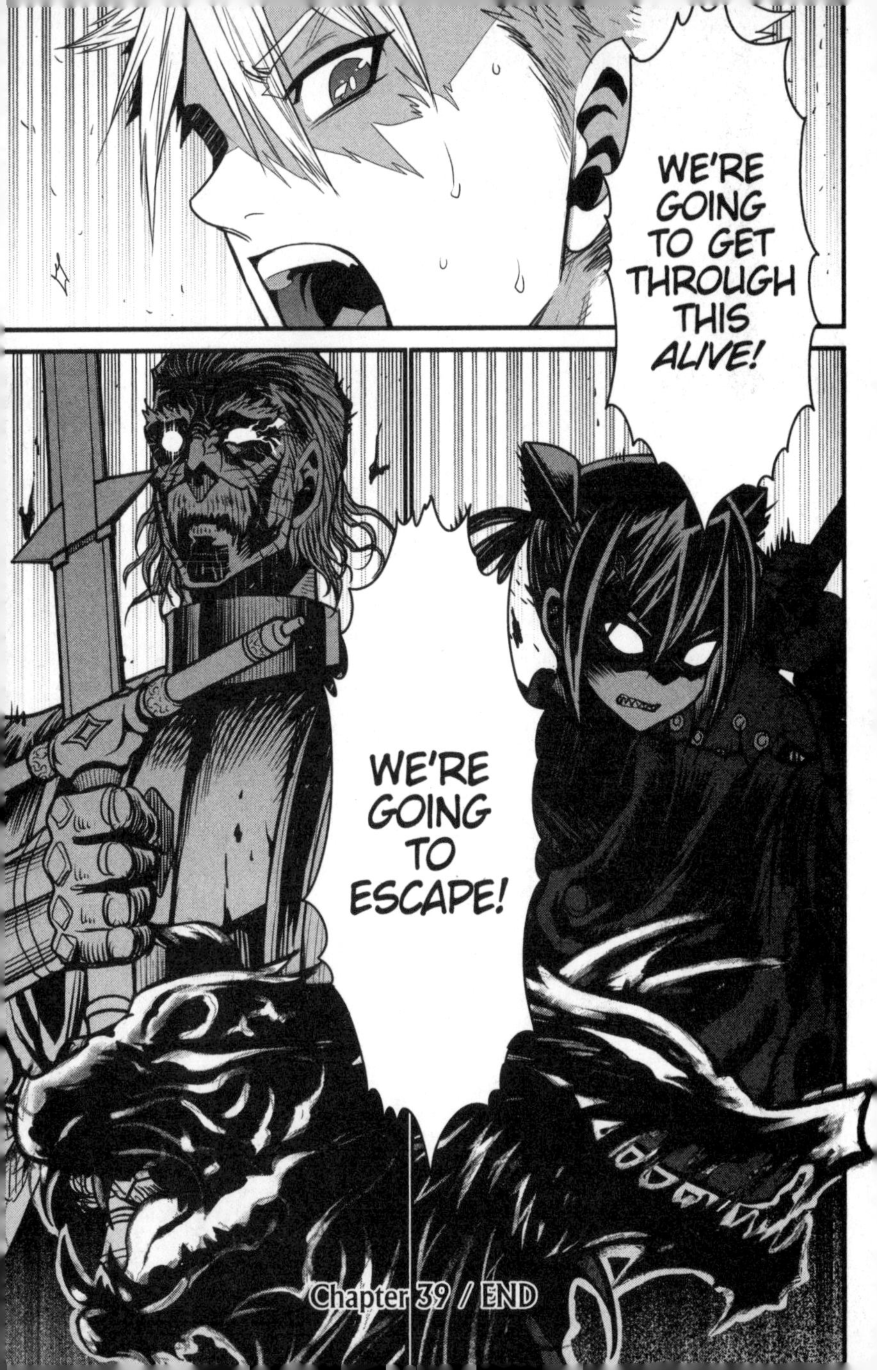
WE'RE GOING TO GET THROUGH THIS ALIVE!
WE'RE GOING TO ESCAPE!
Chapter 39 / END

PETER GRILL
AND THE PHILOSOPHER'S TIME

Previously, on *Peter Grill...*

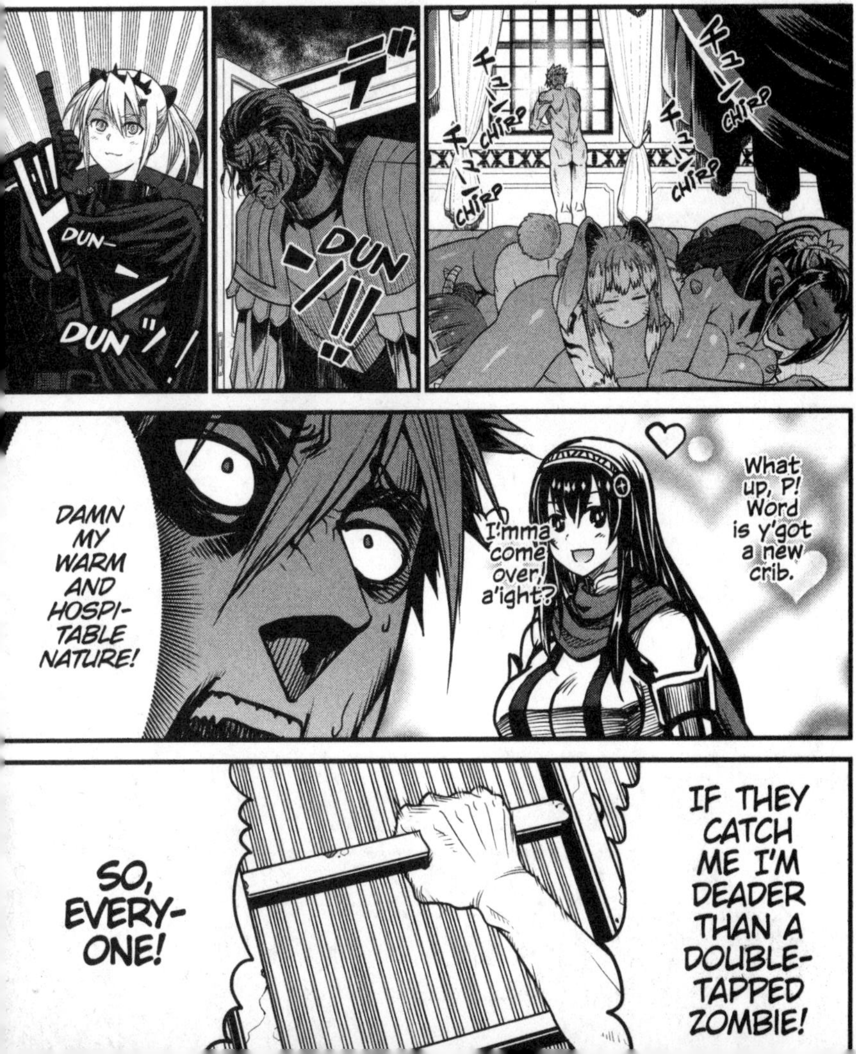
CHIRP
CHIRP
CHIRP
CHIRP
DUN
!!
DUN-
DUN
What up, P! Word is y'got a new crib.
I'mma come over, a'ight?
DAMN MY WARM AND HOSPI-TABLE NATURE!
IF THEY CATCH ME I'M DEADER THAN A DOUBLE-TAPPED ZOMBIE!
SO, EVERY-ONE!

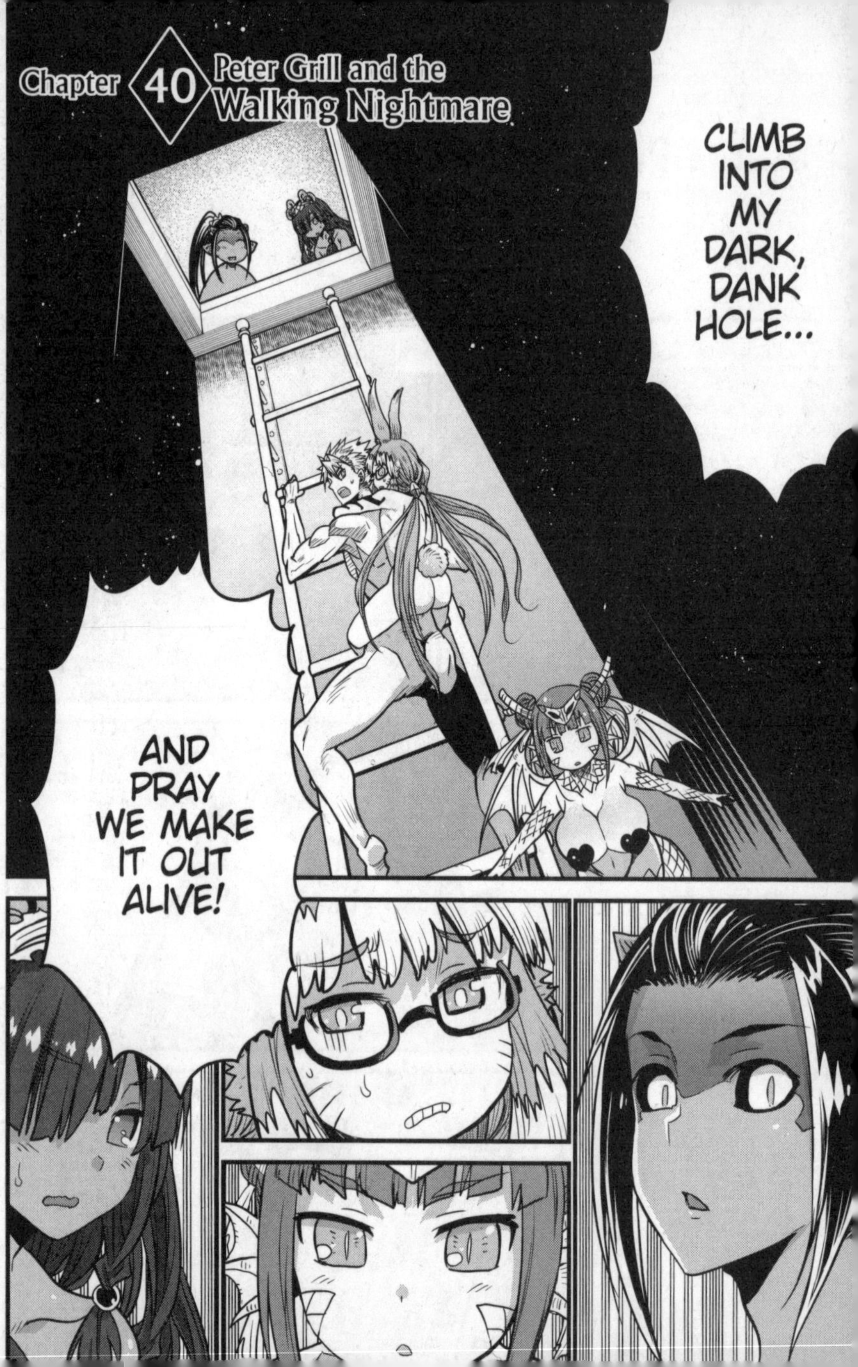
Chapter 40 Peter Grill and the Walking Nightmare
CLIMB INTO MY DARK, DANK HOLE...
AND PRAY WE MAKE IT OUT ALIVE!

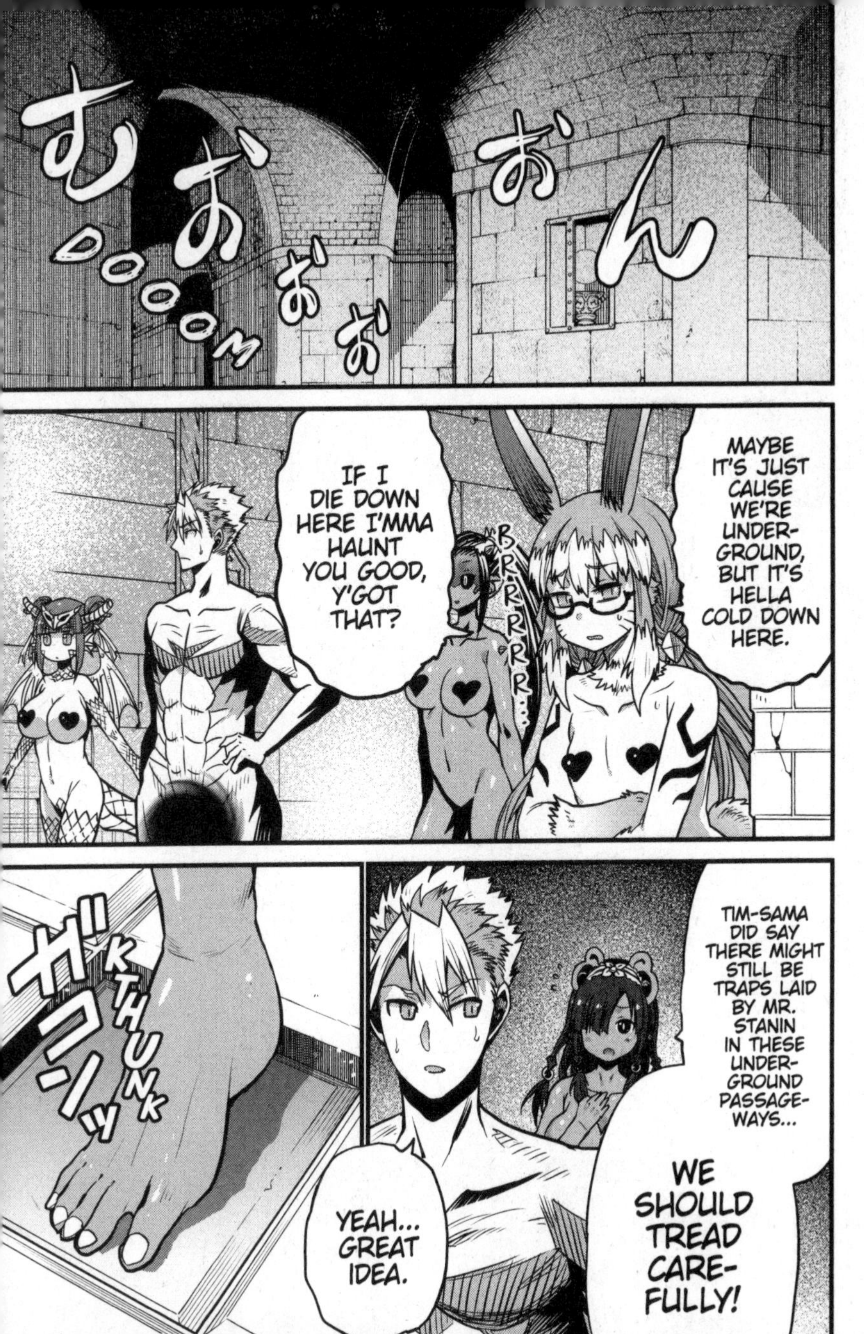
むおぉぉおん
DOOOOOM
MAYBE IT'S JUST CAUSE WE'RE UNDERGROUND, BUT IT'S HELLA COLD DOWN HERE.
BRRRRRR...
IF I DIE DOWN HERE I'MMA HAUNT YOU GOOD, Y'GOT THAT?
TIM-SAMA DID SAY THERE MIGHT STILL BE TRAPS LAID BY MR. STANIN IN THESE UNDERGROUND PASSAGEWAYS...
WE SHOULD TREAD CAREFULLY!
YEAH... GREAT IDEA.
ガコーッ
KTHUNK

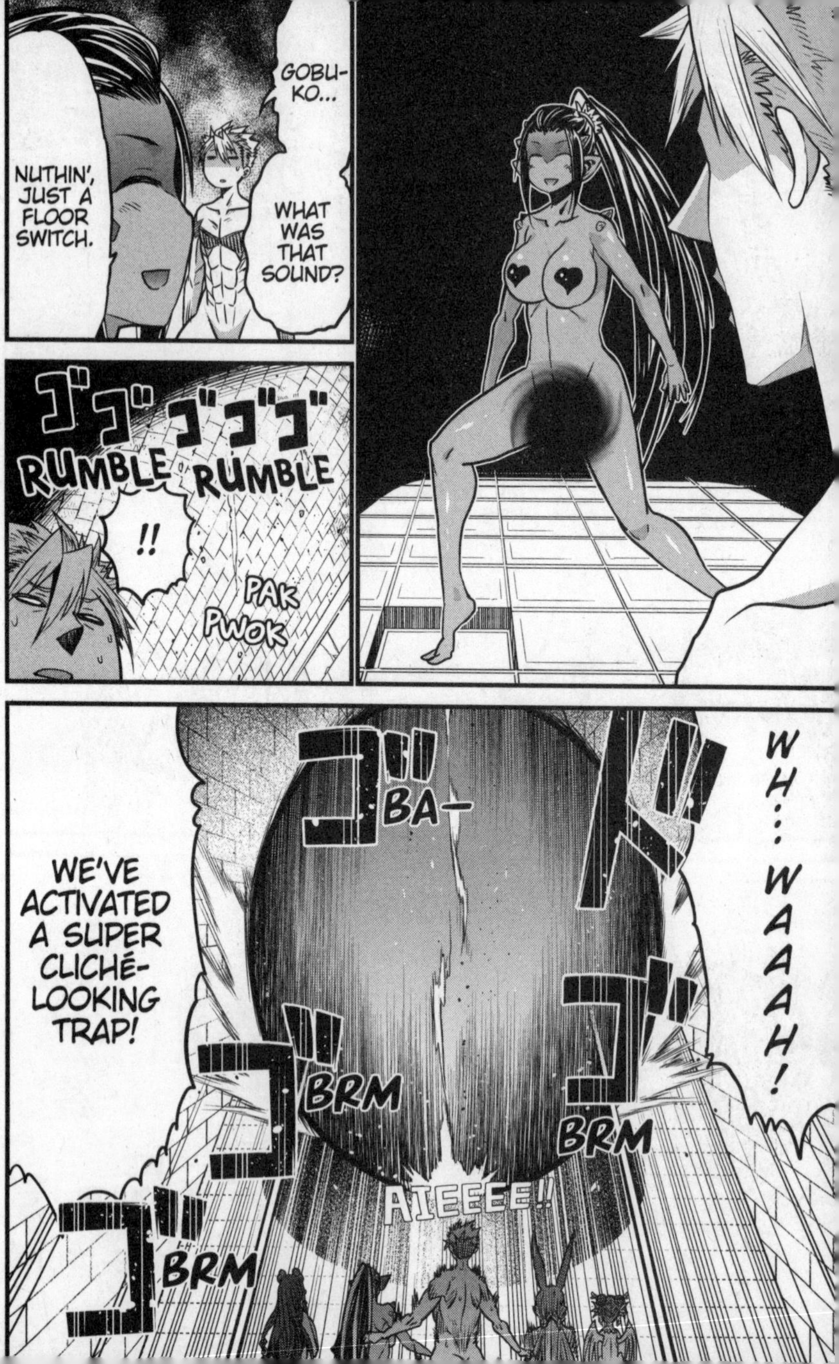
GOBU-KO...
WHAT WAS THAT SOUND?
NUTHIN', JUST A FLOOR SWITCH.
ゴゴ
ゴゴゴ
RUMBLE RUMBLE
!!
PAK PWOK
WH... WAAAAH!
BA—
WE'VE ACTIVATED A SUPER CLICHÉ-LOOKING TRAP!
BRM
BRM
AIEEEE!!
BRM

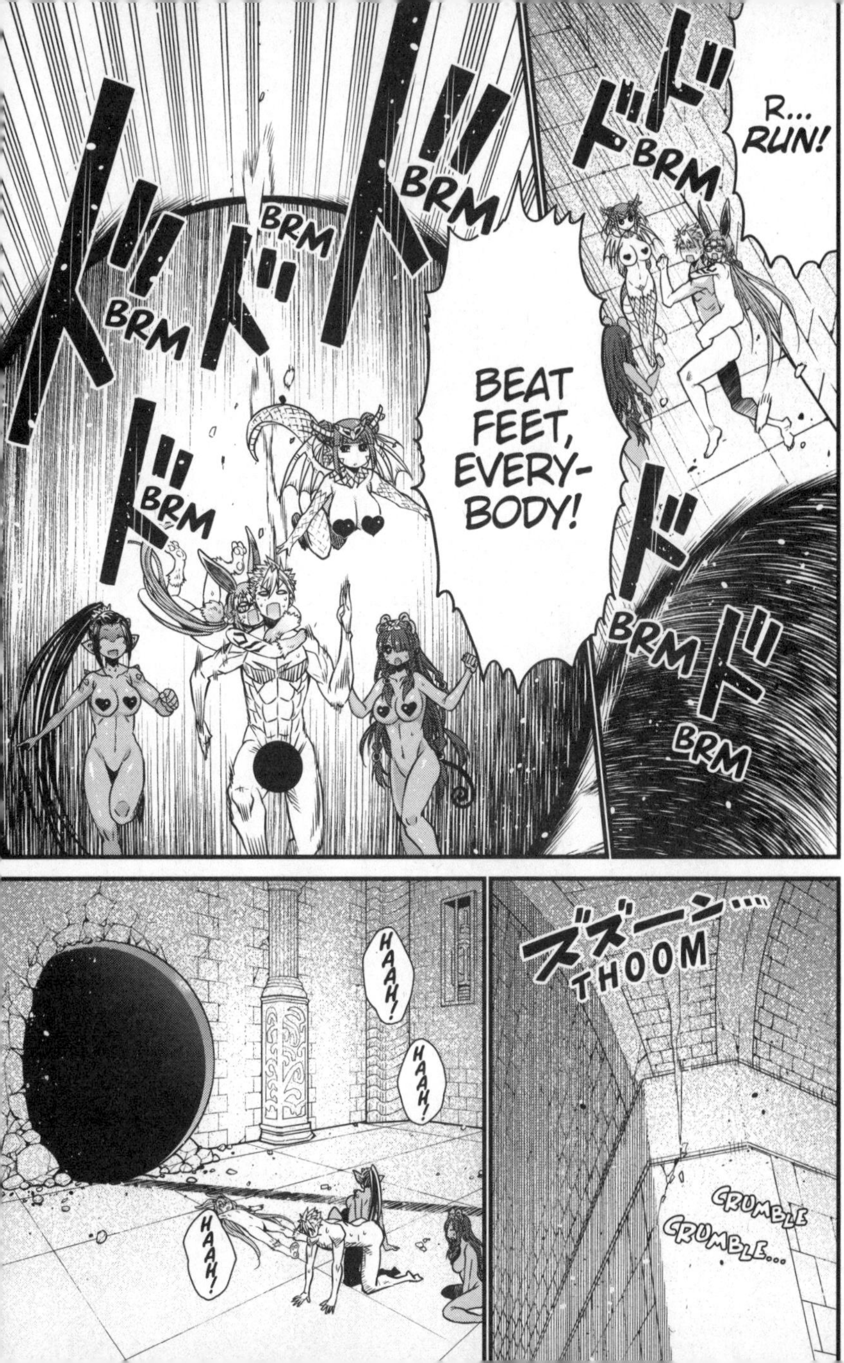
ドドド
BRM
R... RUN!
ドドド
BRM
BRM
ドドドドド
BRM
BRM
BRM
BRM
BRM
BEAT FEET, EVERY-BODY!
ズズーン…
THOOM
CRUMBLE
CRUMBLE...
HAAH!
HAAH!
HAAH!

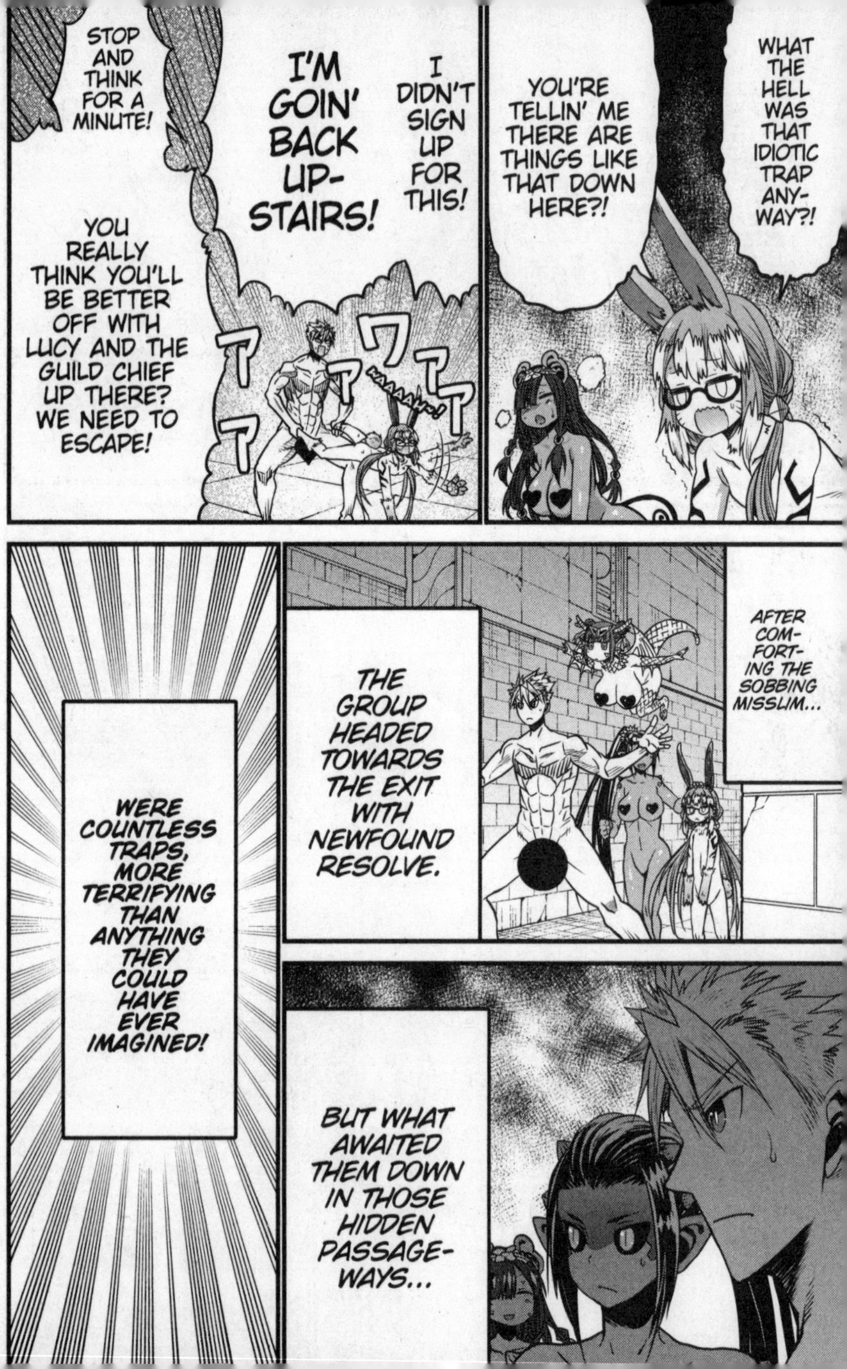
WHAT THE HELL WAS THAT IDIOTIC TRAP ANY-WAY?!
YOU'RE TELLIN' ME THERE ARE THINGS LIKE THAT DOWN HERE?!
I DIDN'T SIGN UP FOR THIS!
I'M GOIN' BACK UP-STAIRS!
STOP AND THINK FOR A MINUTE!
YOU REALLY THINK YOU'LL BE BETTER OFF WITH LUCY AND THE GUILD CHIEF UP THERE? WE NEED TO ESCAPE!
AFTER COM-FORT-ING THE SOBBING MISSLIM...
THE GROUP HEADED TOWARDS THE EXIT WITH NEWFOUND RESOLVE.
BUT WHAT AWAITED THEM DOWN IN THOSE HIDDEN PASSAGE-WAYS...
WERE COUNTLESS TRAPS, MORE TERRIFYING THAN ANYTHING THEY COULD HAVE EVER IMAGINED!

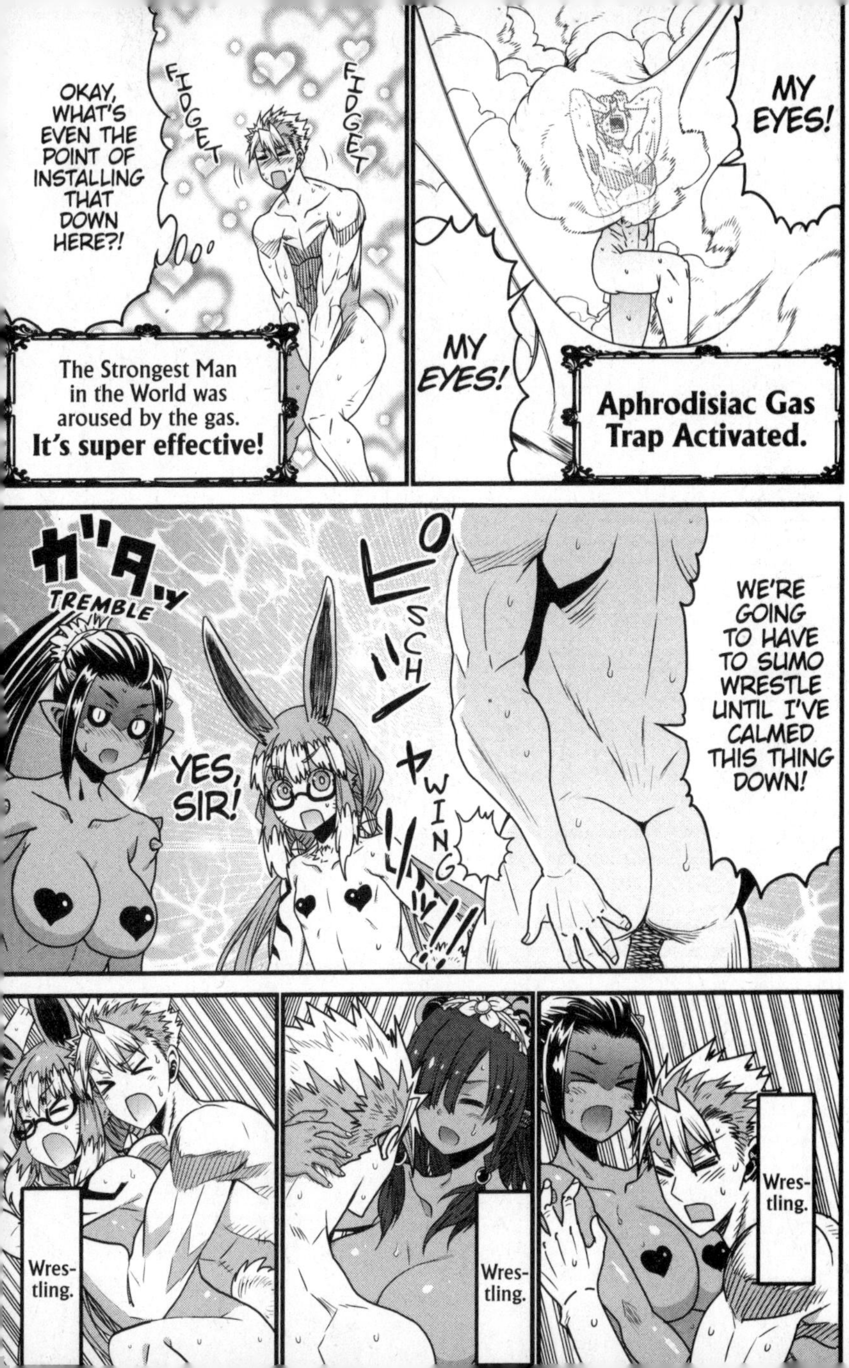
MY EYES!
MY EYES!
Aphrodisiac Gas Trap Activated.
FIDGET
FIDGET
OKAY, WHAT'S EVEN THE POINT OF INSTALLING THAT DOWN HERE?!
The Strongest Man in the World was aroused by the gas. It's super effective!
WE'RE GOING TO HAVE TO SUMO WRESTLE UNTIL I'VE CALMED THIS THING DOWN!
SCH
WING
YES, SIR!
TREMBLE
Wres-tling.
Wres-tling.
Wres-tling.

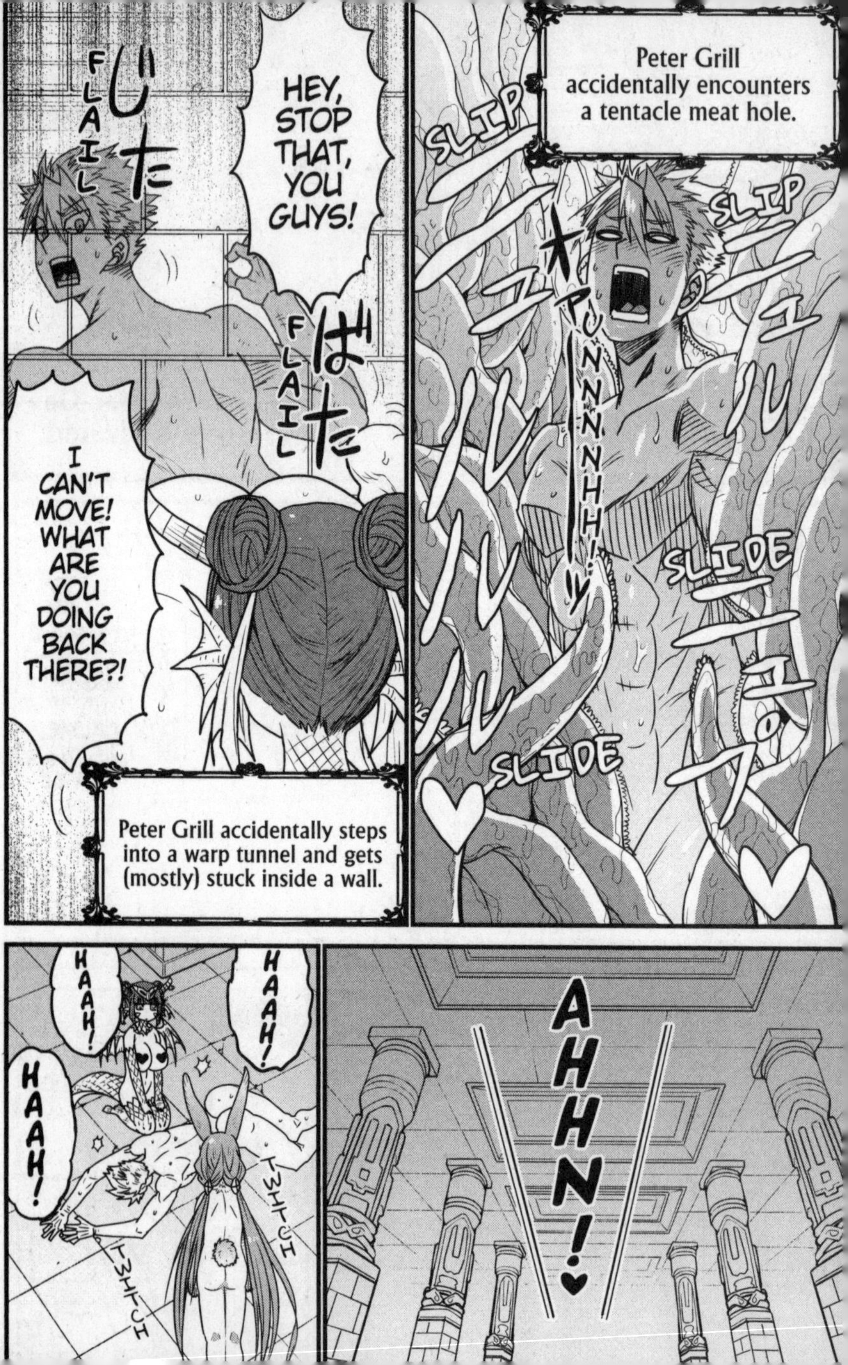
Peter Grill accidentally encounters a tentacle meat hole.
SLIP
SLIP
PUNNNNNHH!!
SLIDE
SLIDE
HEY, STOP THAT, YOU GUYS!
FLAIL
じた
FLAIL
ばた
I CAN'T MOVE! WHAT ARE YOU DOING BACK THERE?!
Peter Grill accidentally steps into a warp tunnel and gets (mostly) stuck inside a wall.
AHHN!♥
HAAAH!
HAAAH!
HAAAH!
TWITCH
TWITCH

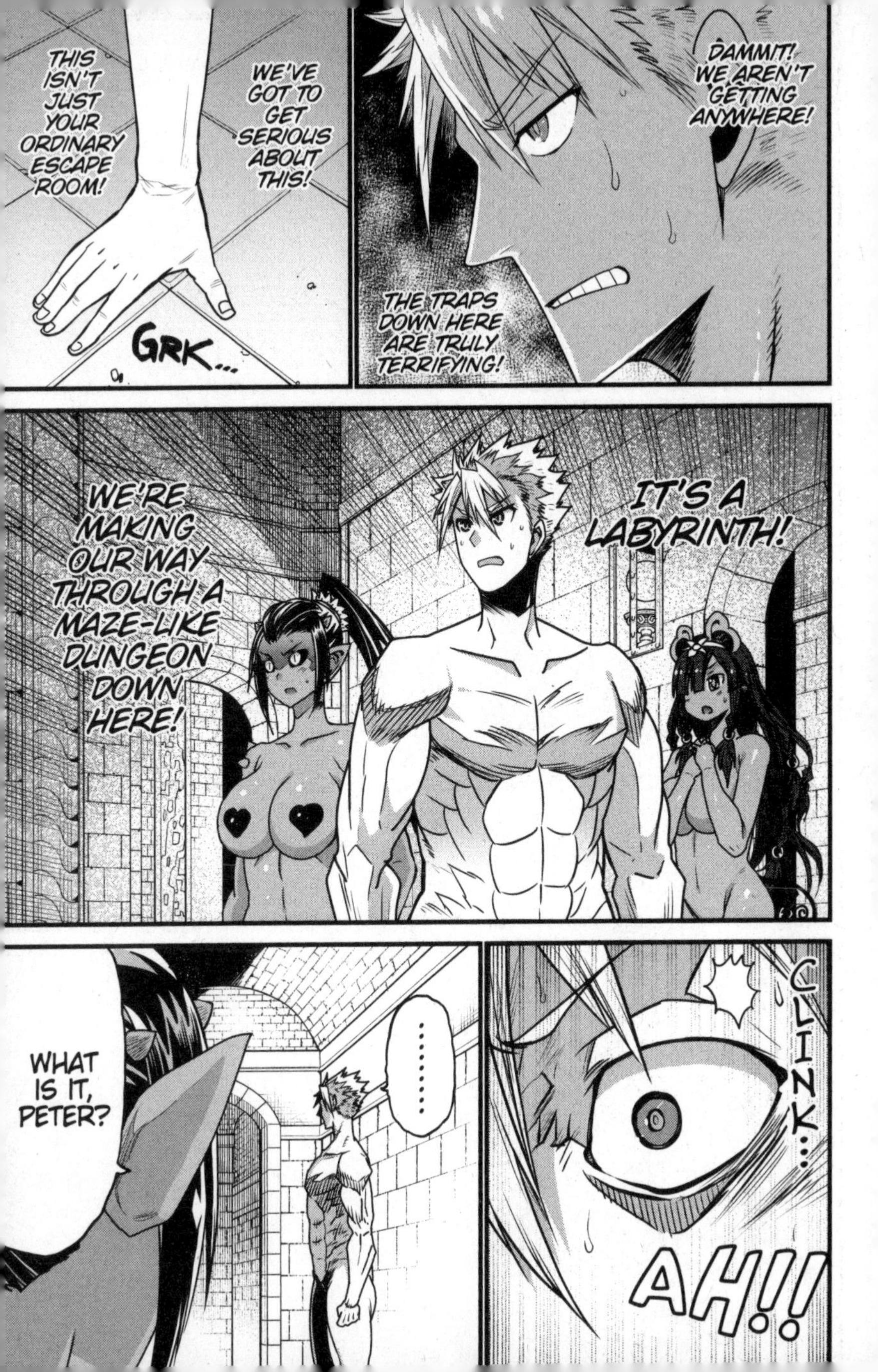

DAMMIT! WE AREN'T GETTING ANYWHERE!
THE TRAPS DOWN HERE ARE TRULY TERRIFYING!
WE'VE GOT TO GET SERIOUS ABOUT THIS!
THIS ISN'T JUST YOUR ORDINARY ESCAPE ROOM!
GRK...
IT'S A LABYRINTH!
WE'RE MAKING OUR WAY THROUGH A MAZE-LIKE DUNGEON DOWN HERE!
CLINK...
AH!!
......
WHAT IS IT, PETER?

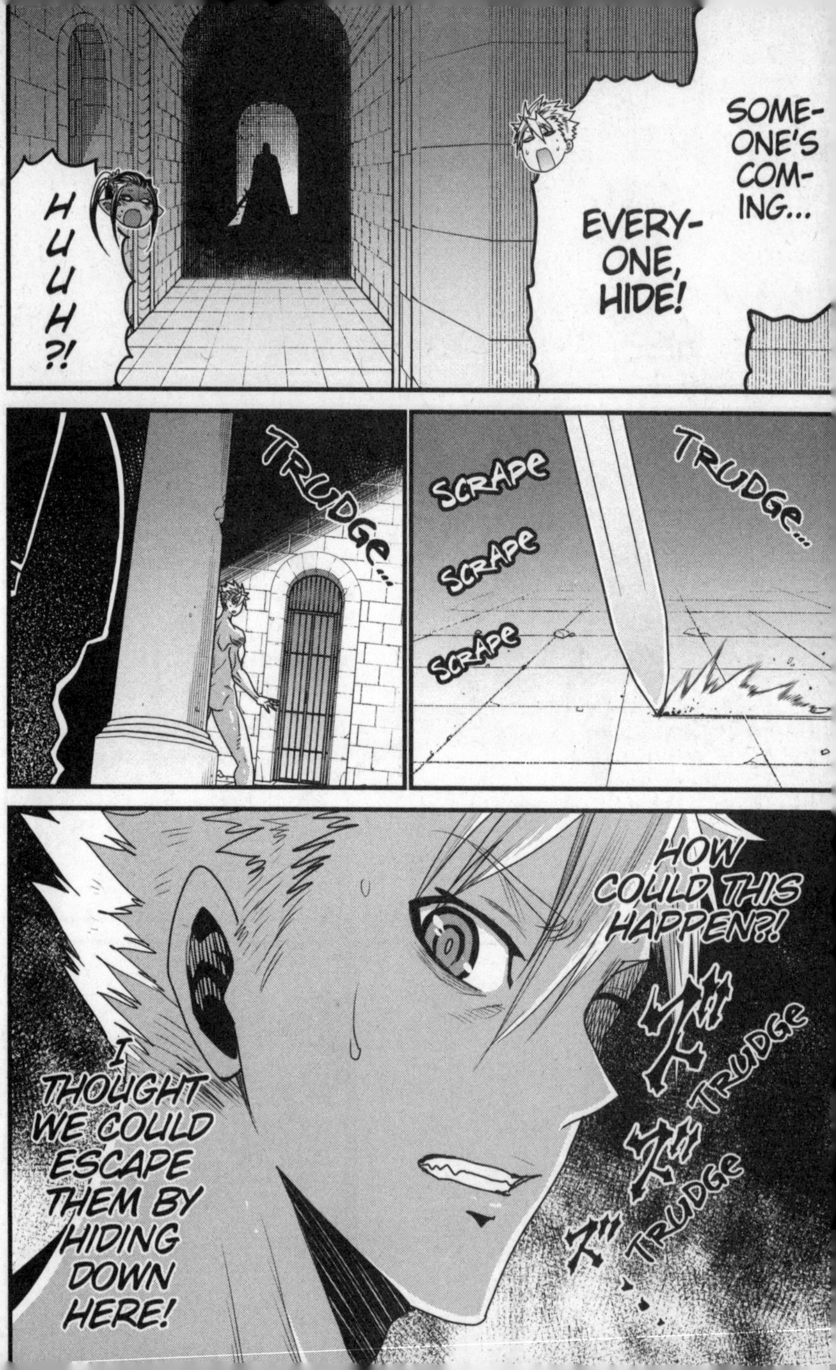
SOME-ONE'S COM-ING...
EVERY-ONE, HIDE!
HUUH?!
TRUDGE...
SCRAPE
SCRAPE
SCRAPE
TRUDGE...
HOW COULD THIS HAPPEN?!
ズ
TRUDGE
ズ
TRUDGE
ズ
I THOUGHT WE COULD ESCAPE THEM BY HIDING DOWN HERE!

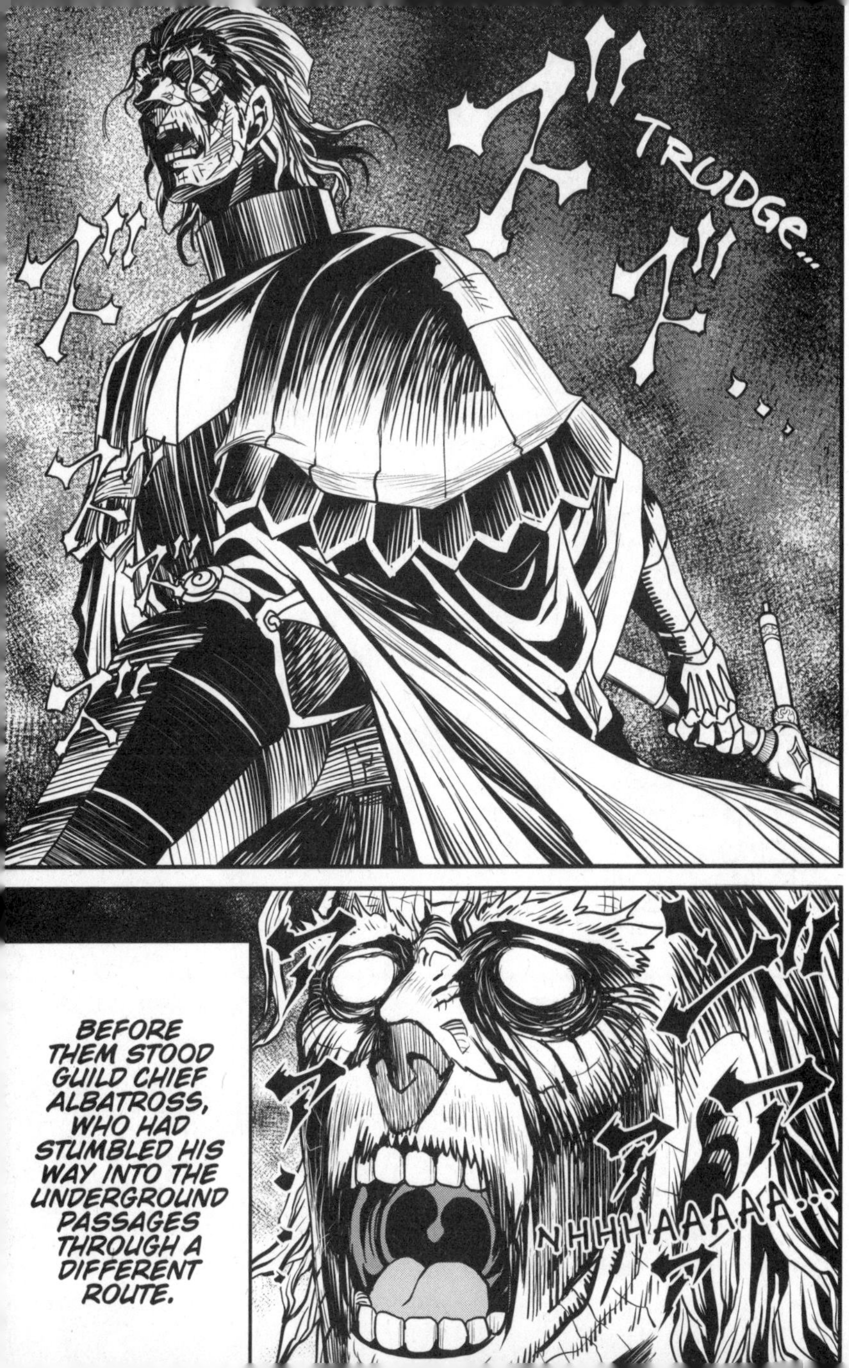
TRUDGE...
BEFORE THEM STOOD GUILD CHIEF ALBATROSS, WHO HAD STUMBLED HIS WAY INTO THE UNDERGROUND PASSAGES THROUGH A DIFFERENT ROUTE.
NHHHAAAAA...

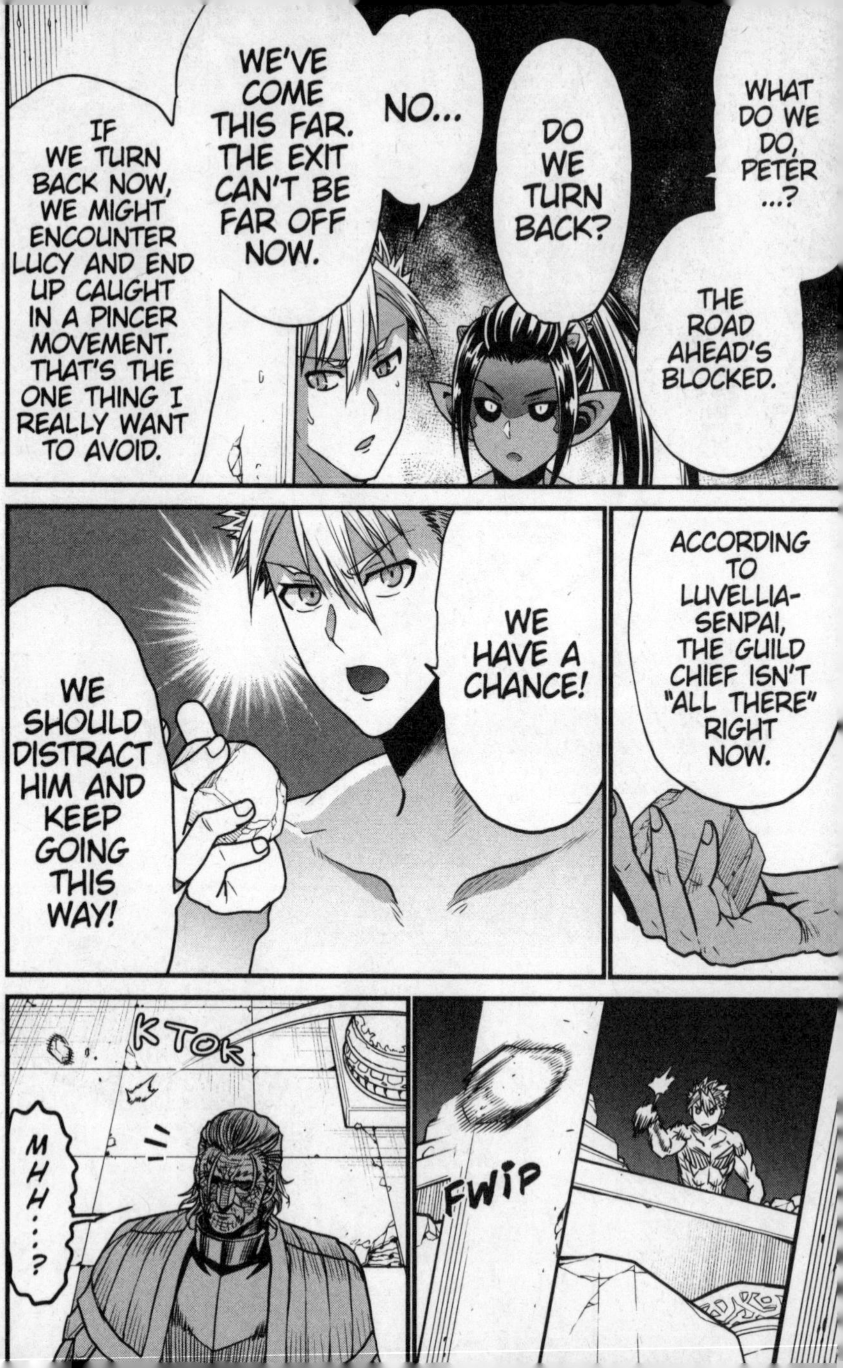
WHAT DO WE DO, PETER ...?
THE ROAD AHEAD'S BLOCKED.
DO WE TURN BACK?
NO...
WE'VE COME THIS FAR. THE EXIT CAN'T BE FAR OFF NOW.
IF WE TURN BACK NOW, WE MIGHT ENCOUNTER LUCY AND END UP CAUGHT IN A PINCER MOVEMENT. THAT'S THE ONE THING I REALLY WANT TO AVOID.
ACCORDING TO LUVELLIA-SENPAI, THE GUILD CHIEF ISN'T "ALL THERE" RIGHT NOW.
WE HAVE A CHANCE!
WE SHOULD DISTRACT HIM AND KEEP GOING THIS WAY!
FWIP
KTOK
MHH...?

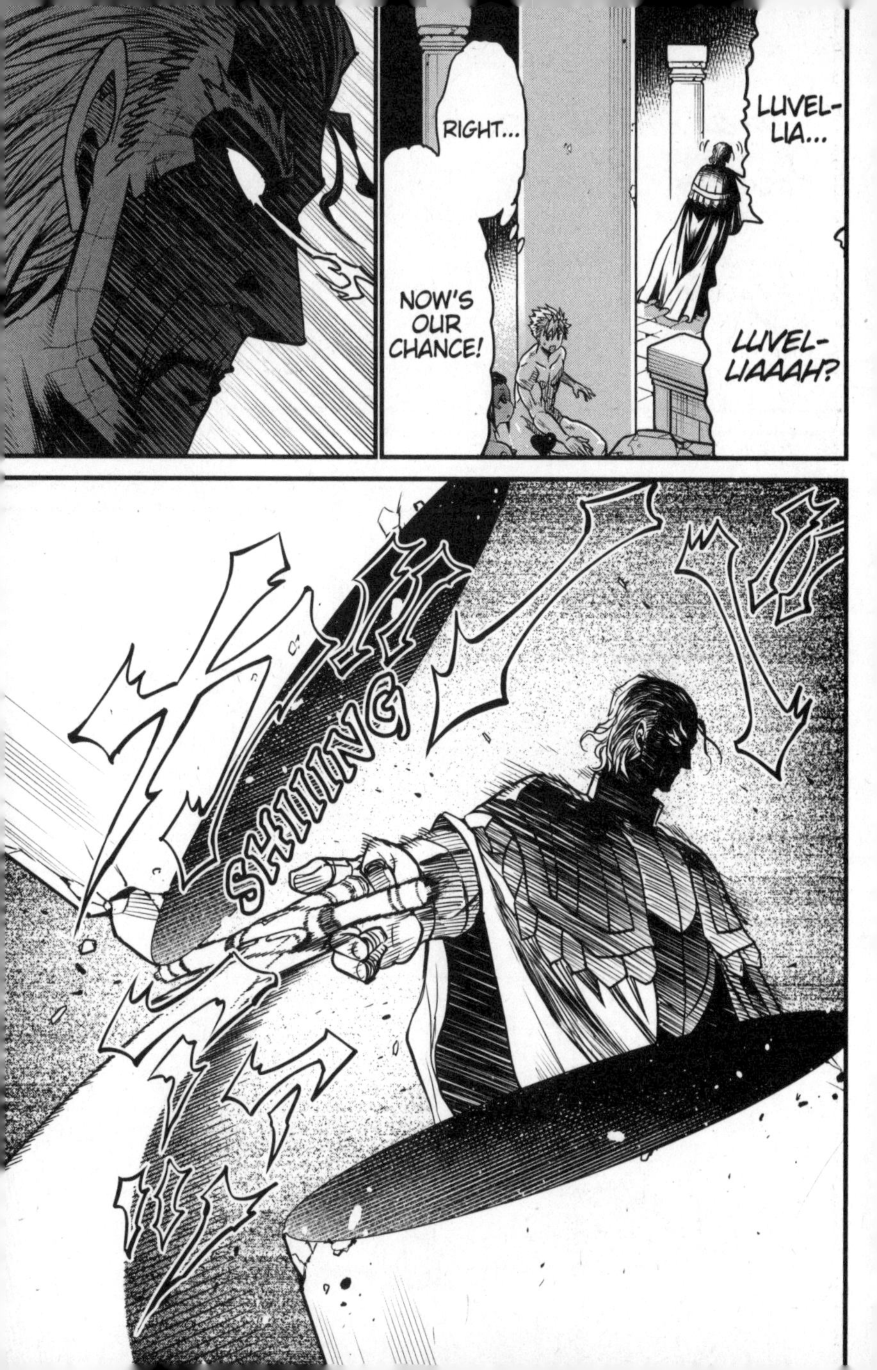
LUVEL-LIA...
LUVEL-LIAAAH?
RIGHT...
NOW'S OUR CHANCE!
SHIIIING

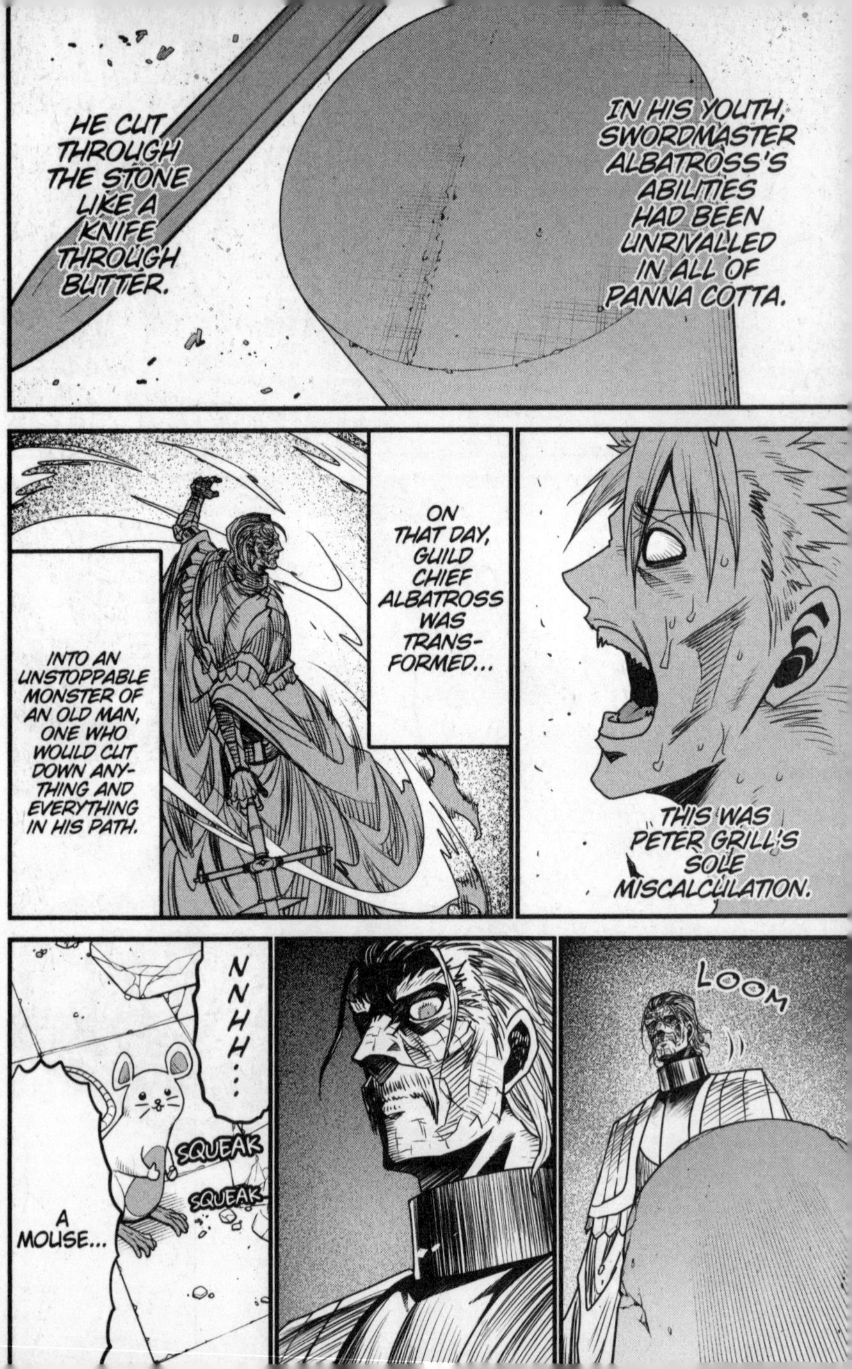
IN HIS YOUTH, SWORDMASTER ALBATROSS'S ABILITIES HAD BEEN UNRIVALLED IN ALL OF PANNA COTTA.
HE CUT THROUGH THE STONE LIKE A KNIFE THROUGH BUTTER.
THIS WAS PETER GRILL'S SOLE MISCALCULATION.
ON THAT DAY, GUILD CHIEF ALBATROSS WAS TRANS-FORMED...
INTO AN UNSTOPPABLE MONSTER OF AN OLD MAN, ONE WHO WOULD CUT DOWN ANY-THING AND EVERYTHING IN HIS PATH.
LOOM
NNHH...
SQUEAK
SQUEAK
A MOUSE...

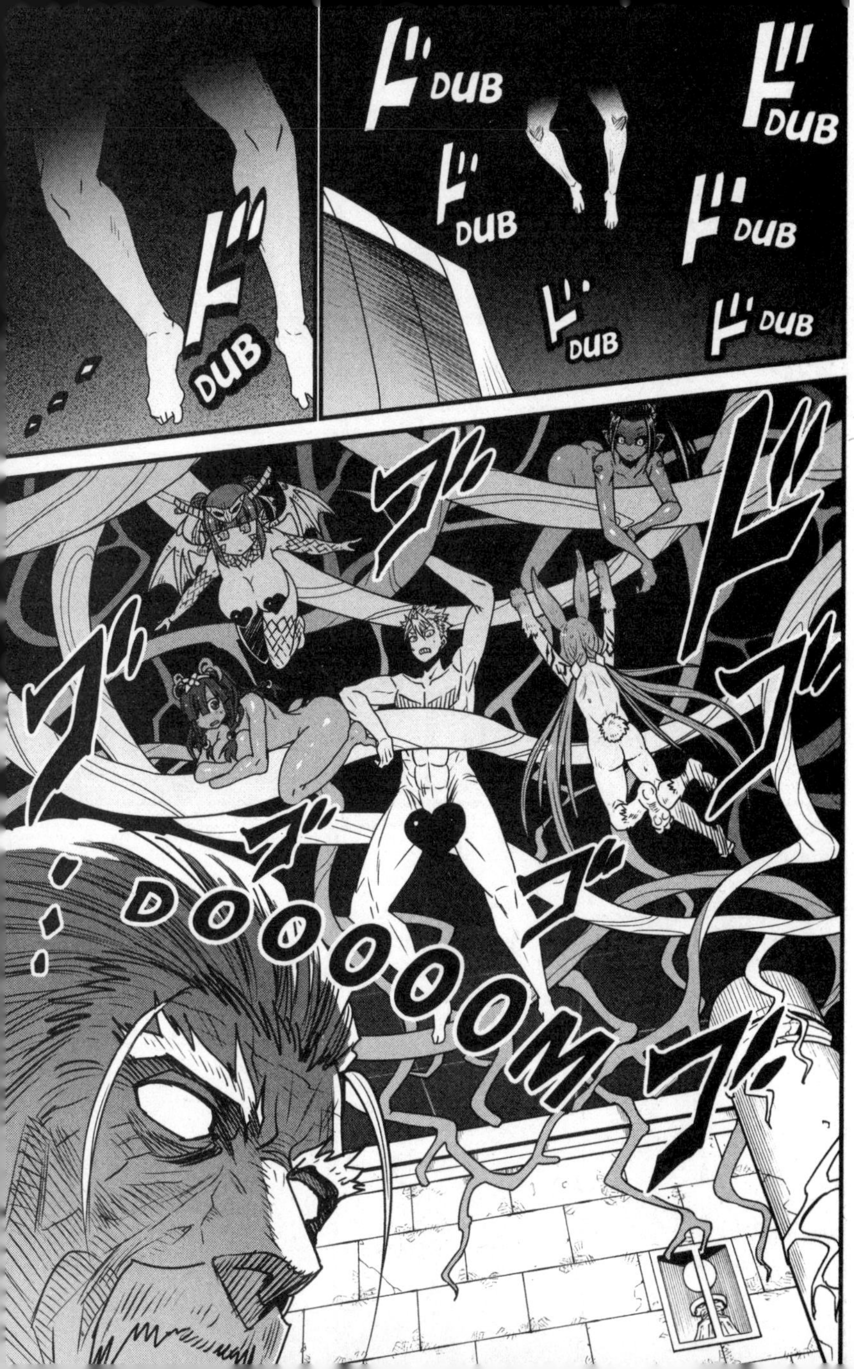
DUB
DUB
DUB
DUB
DUB
DUB
DUB
DOOOOOOM

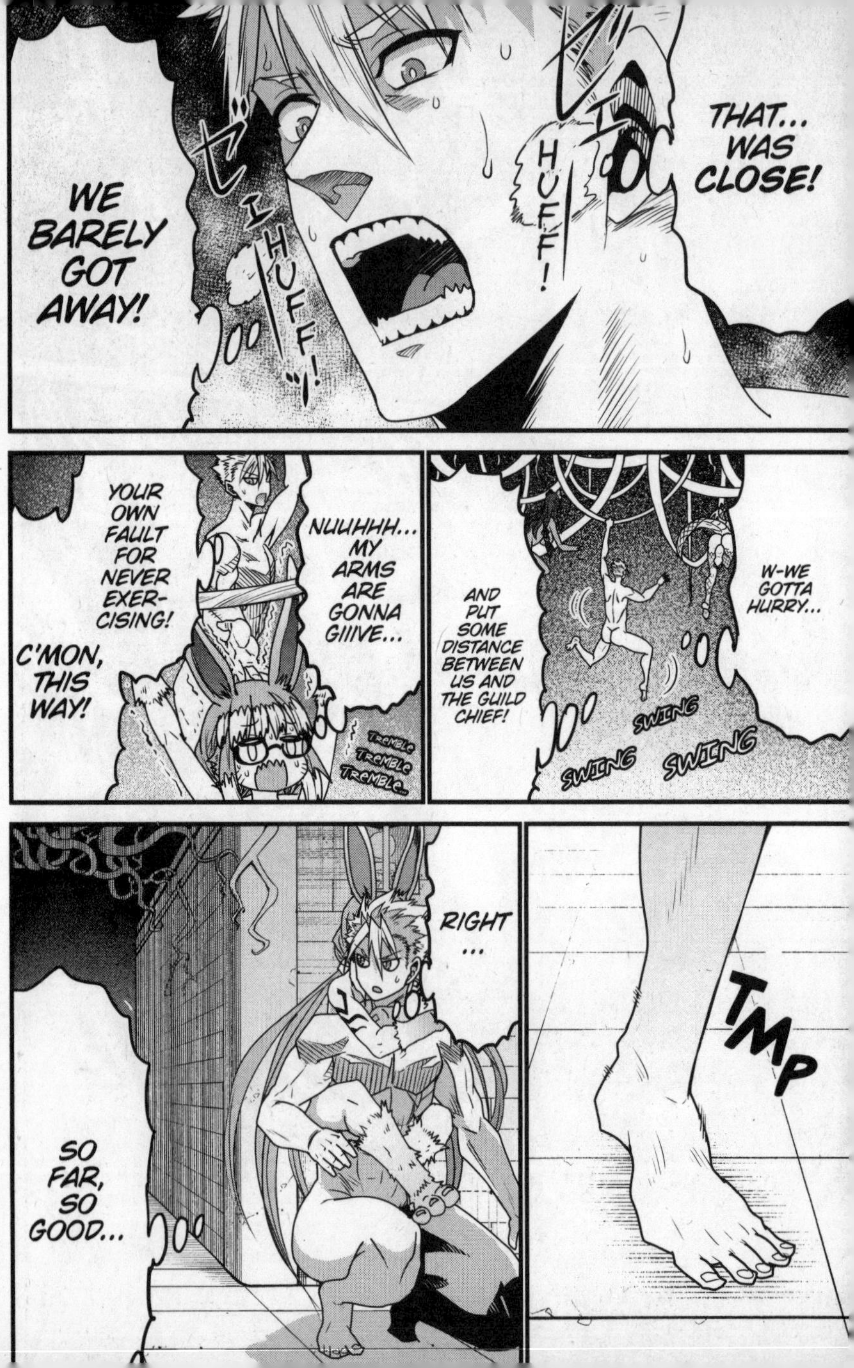
THAT... WAS CLOSE!
HUFF! HUFF!
WE BARELY GOT AWAY!
W-WE GOTTA HURRY...
AND PUT SOME DISTANCE BETWEEN US AND THE GUILD CHIEF!
SWING SWING SWING
NUUHHH... MY ARMS ARE GONNA GIIIVE...
TREMBLE TREMBLE TREMBLE...
YOUR OWN FAULT FOR NEVER EXER-CISING!
C'MON, THIS WAY!
TMP
RIGHT...
SO FAR, SO GOOD...

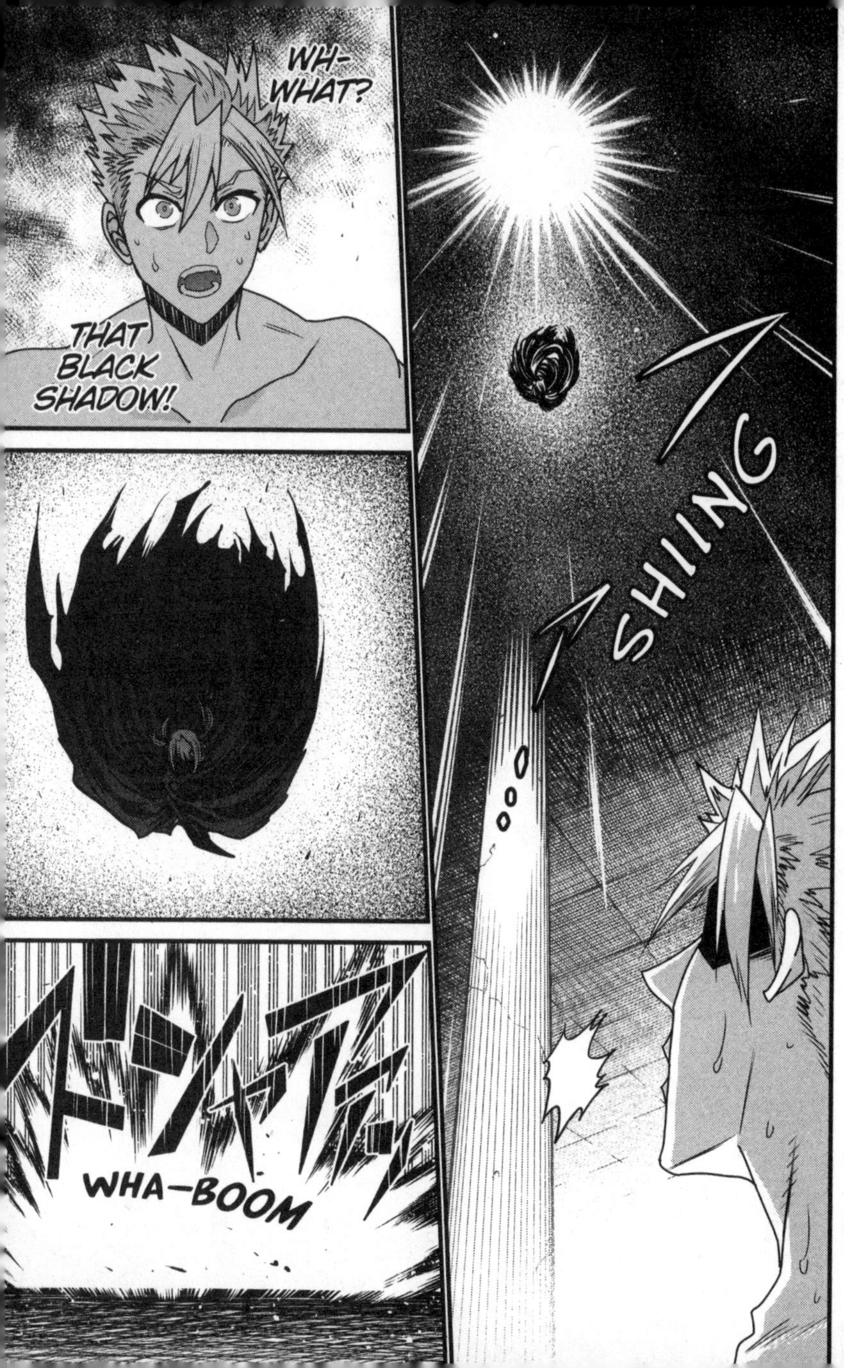
SHING
...
WH- WHAT?
THAT BLACK SHADOW!
WHA-BOOM

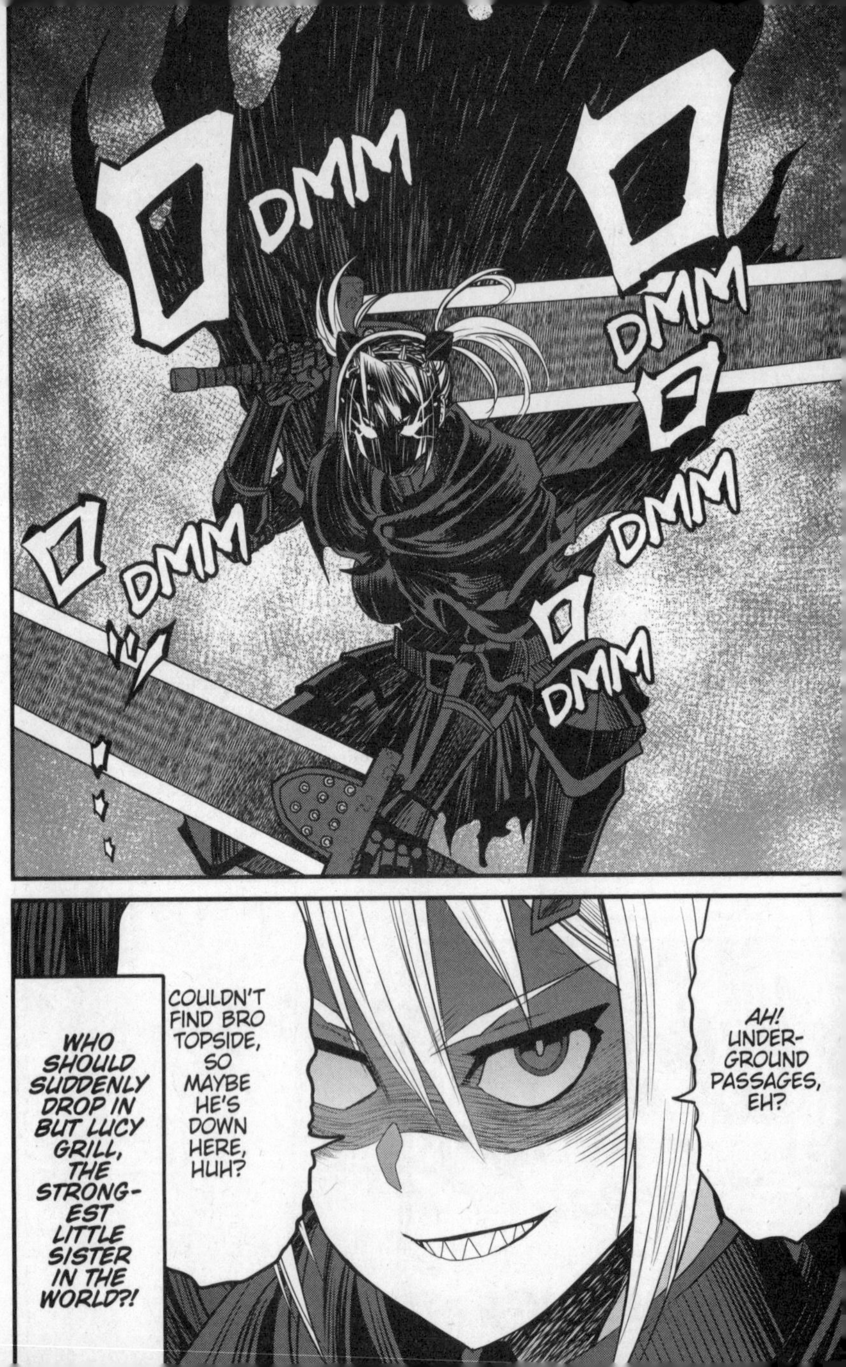
DMM
DMM
DMM
DMM
DMM
AH! UNDER-GROUND PASSAGES, EH?
COULDN'T FIND BRO TOPSIDE, SO MAYBE HE'S DOWN HERE, HUH?
WHO SHOULD SUDDENLY DROP IN BUT LUCY GRILL, THE STRONG-EST LITTLE SISTER IN THE WORLD?!

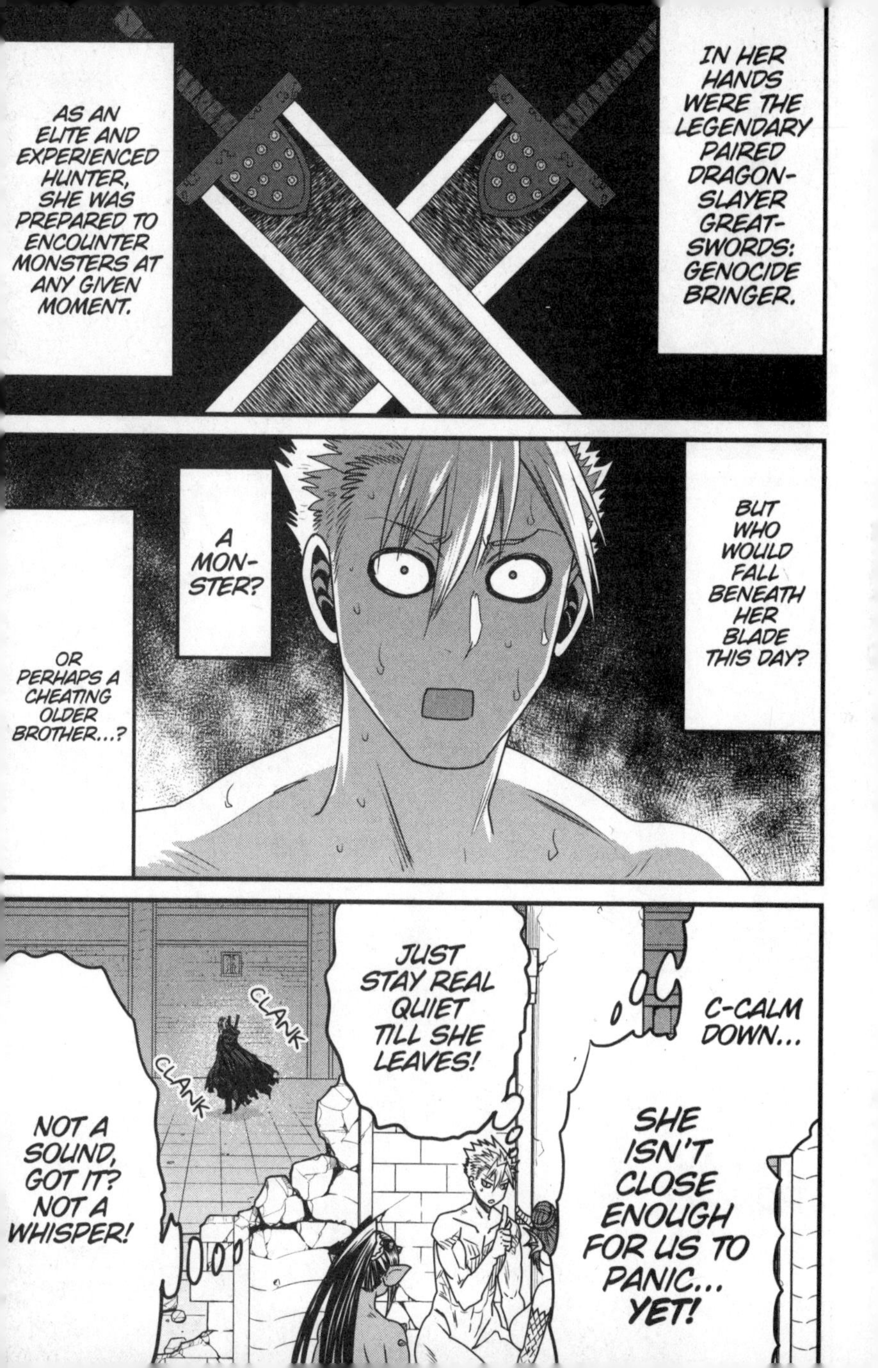
IN HER HANDS WERE THE LEGENDARY PAIRED DRAGON-SLAYER GREAT-SWORDS: GENOCIDE BRINGER.
AS AN ELITE AND EXPERIENCED HUNTER, SHE WAS PREPARED TO ENCOUNTER MONSTERS AT ANY GIVEN MOMENT.
BUT WHO WOULD FALL BENEATH HER BLADE THIS DAY?
A MON-STER?
OR PERHAPS A CHEATING OLDER BROTHER...?
C-CALM DOWN...
JUST STAY REAL QUIET TILL SHE LEAVES!
CLANK
CLANK
SHE ISN'T CLOSE ENOUGH FOR US TO PANIC... YET!
NOT A SOUND, GOT IT? NOT A WHISPER!

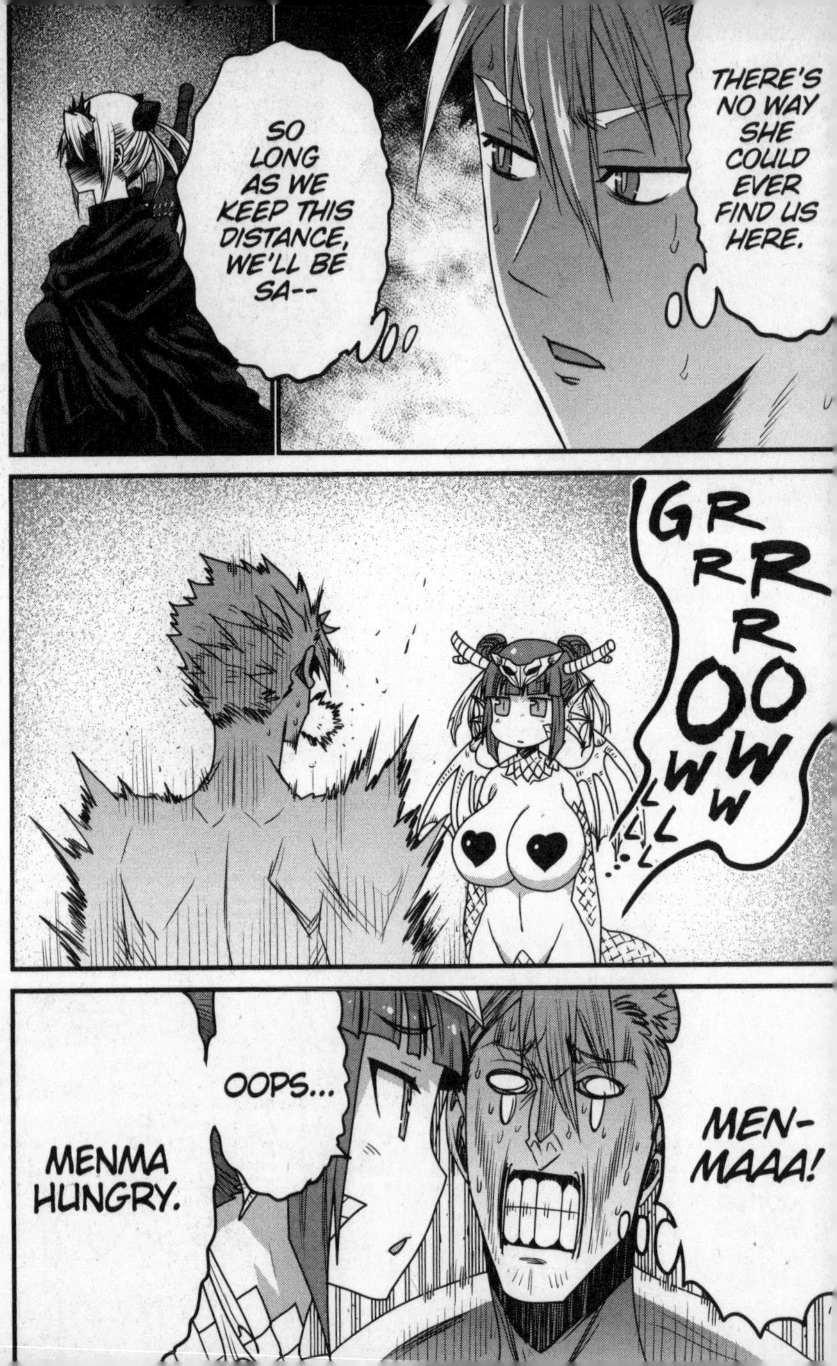
THERE'S NO WAY SHE COULD EVER FIND US HERE.
SO LONG AS WE KEEP THIS DISTANCE, WE'LL BE SA--
GRRRROOWWWW
OOPS... MENMA HUNGRY.
MEN-MAAA!

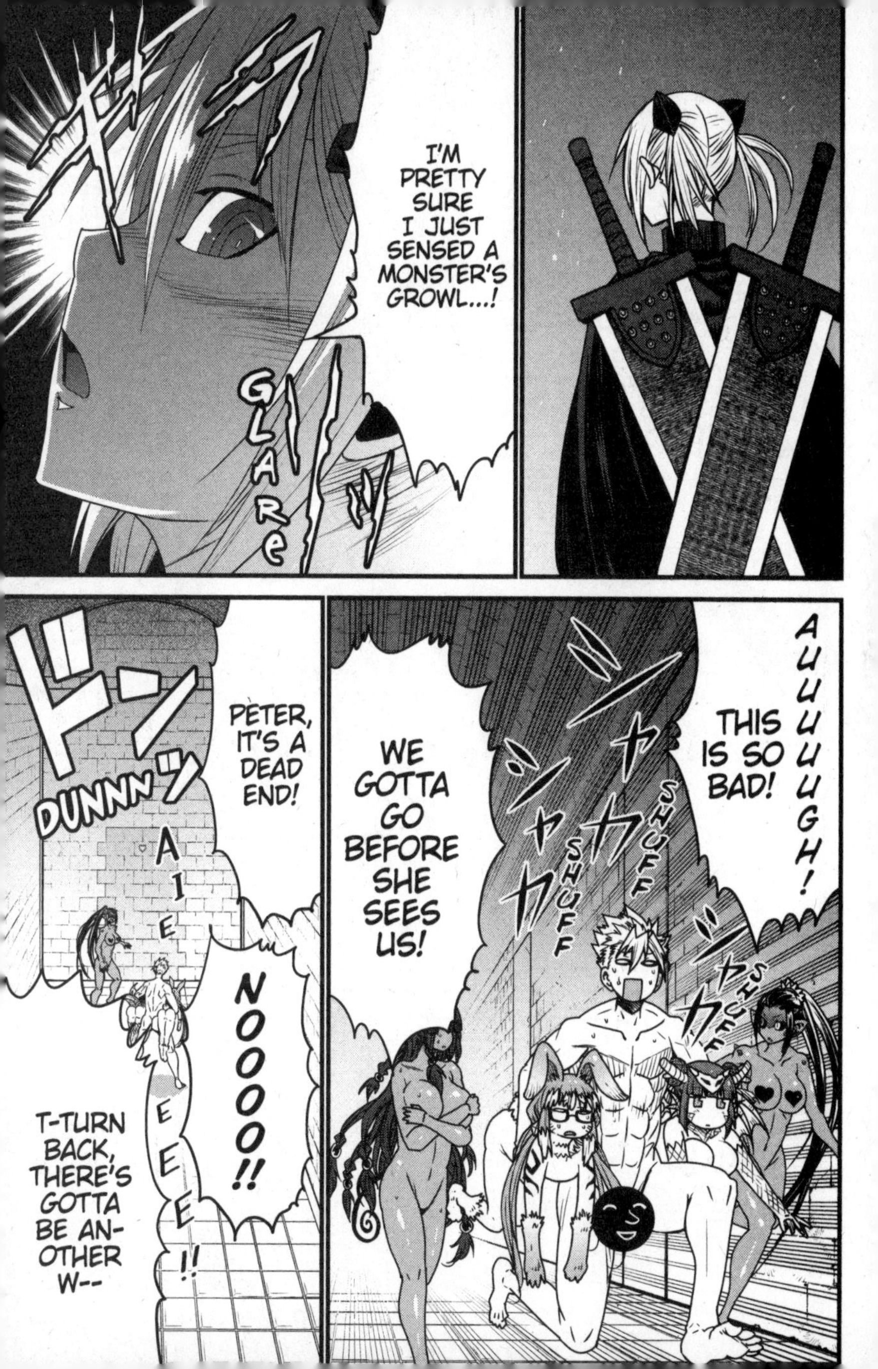
I'M PRETTY SURE I JUST SENSED A MONSTER'S GROWL...!
GLARE
AUUUUUUGH!
THIS IS SO BAD!
SHUFF
SHUFF
SHUFF
WE GOTTA GO BEFORE SHE SEES US!
PETER, IT'S A DEAD END!
DUNNN
NOOOOOO!!
AIEEEEE!!
T-TURN BACK, THERE'S GOTTA BE AN-OTHER W--

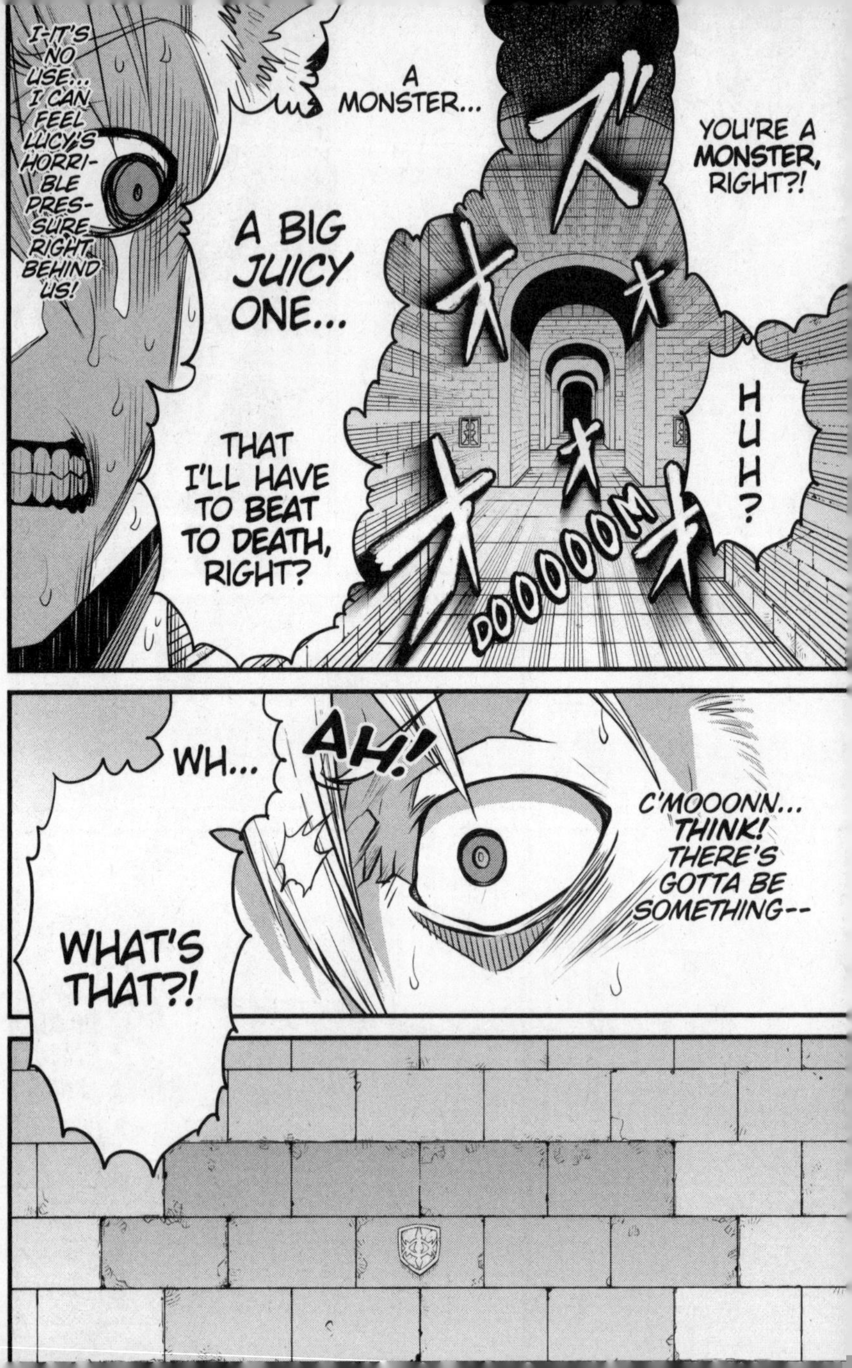
YOU'RE A MONSTER, RIGHT?!
HUH?
ズ
DOOOOOOM
A MONSTER...
A BIG JUICY ONE...
THAT I'LL HAVE TO BEAT TO DEATH, RIGHT?
I-IT'S NO USE... I CAN FEEL LUCY'S HORRIBLE PRESSURE RIGHT BEHIND US!
C'MOOONN... THINK! THERE'S GOTTA BE SOMETHING--
AH!
WH...
WHAT'S THAT?!

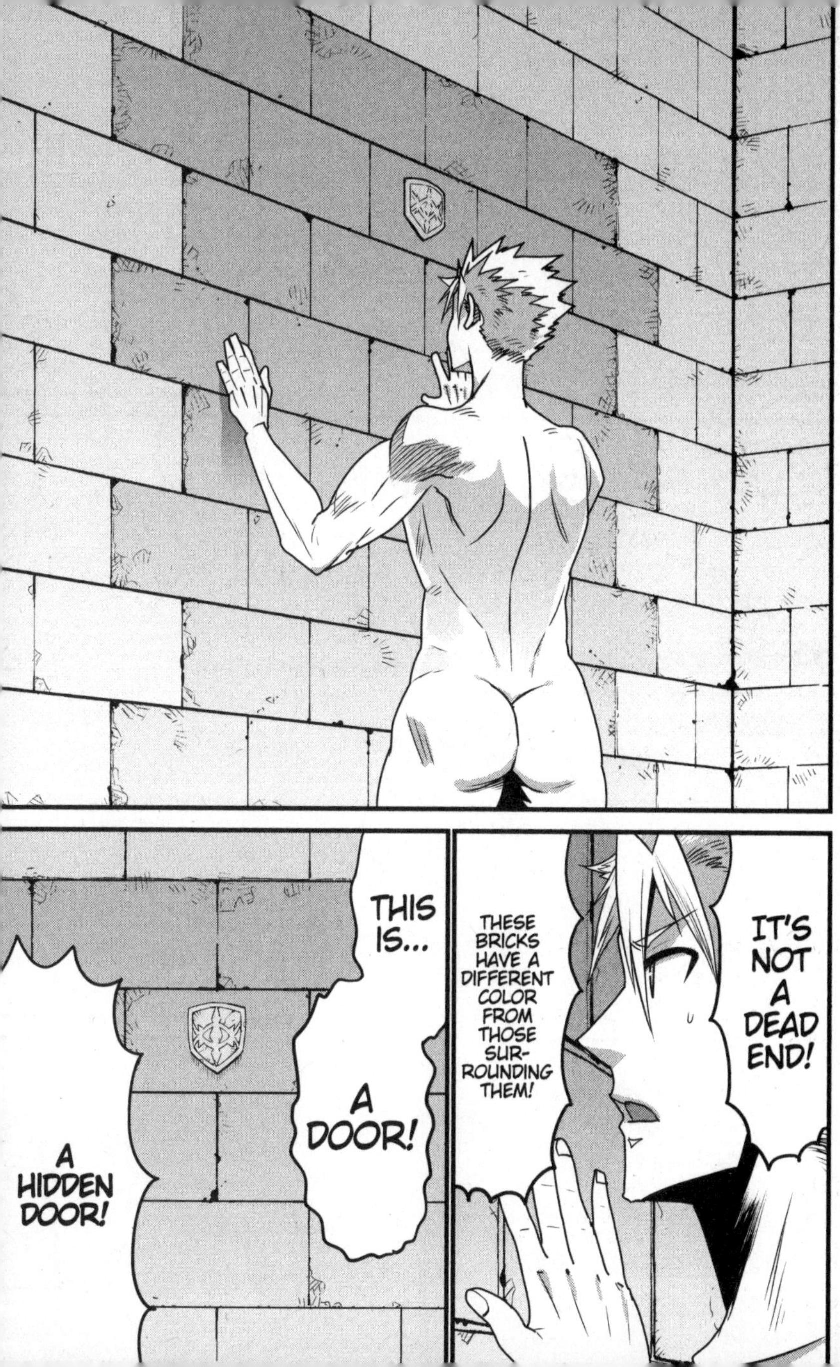
IT'S NOT A DEAD END!
THESE BRICKS HAVE A DIFFERENT COLOR FROM THOSE SUR-ROUNDING THEM!
THIS IS... A DOOR!
A HIDDEN DOOR!

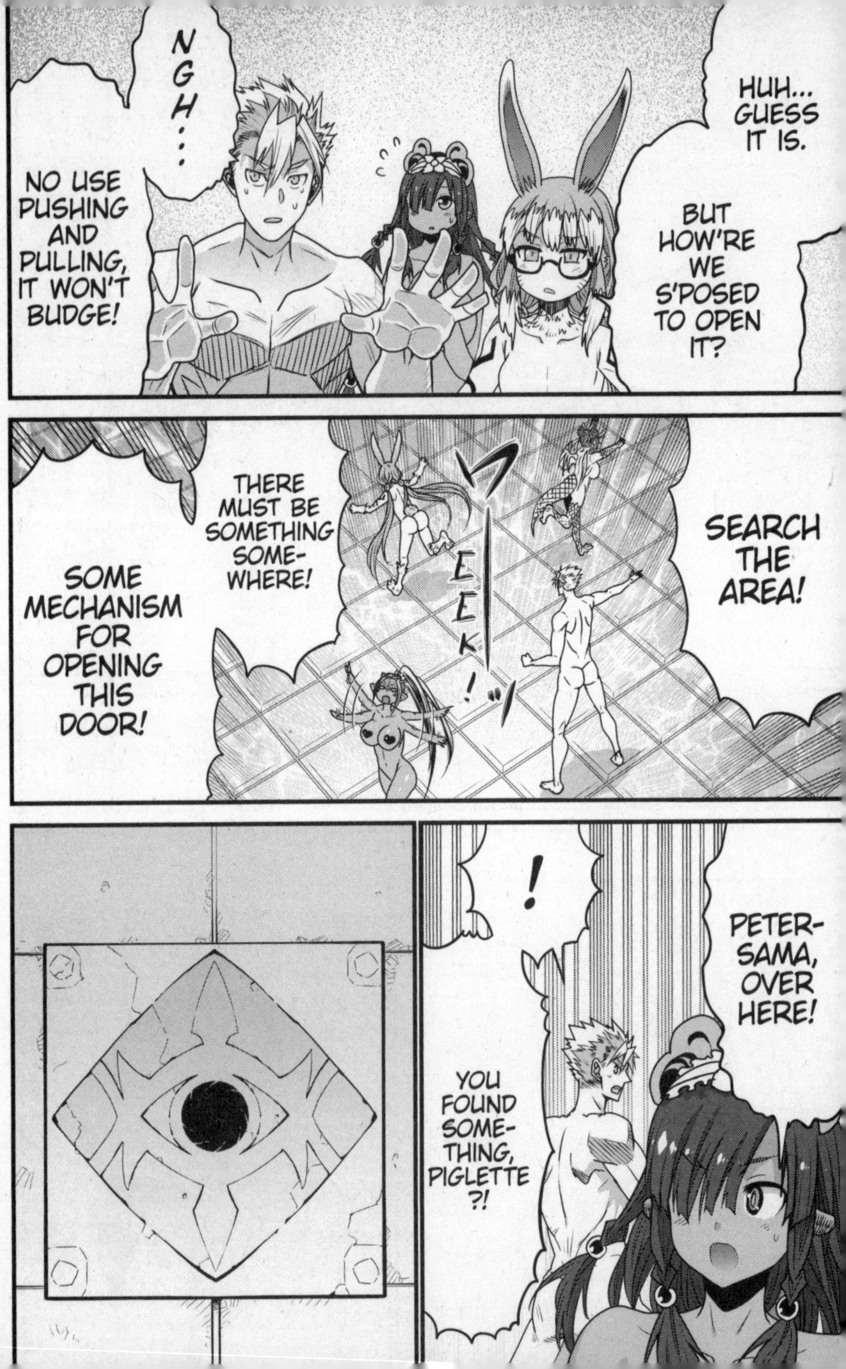
HUH... GUESS IT IS.
BUT HOW'RE WE S'POSED TO OPEN IT?
NGH...
NO USE PUSHING AND PULLING, IT WON'T BUDGE!
SEARCH THE AREA!
EEEK!!
THERE MUST BE SOMETHING SOME-WHERE!
SOME MECHANISM FOR OPENING THIS DOOR!
PETER-SAMA, OVER HERE!
!
YOU FOUND SOME-THING, PIGLETTE?!

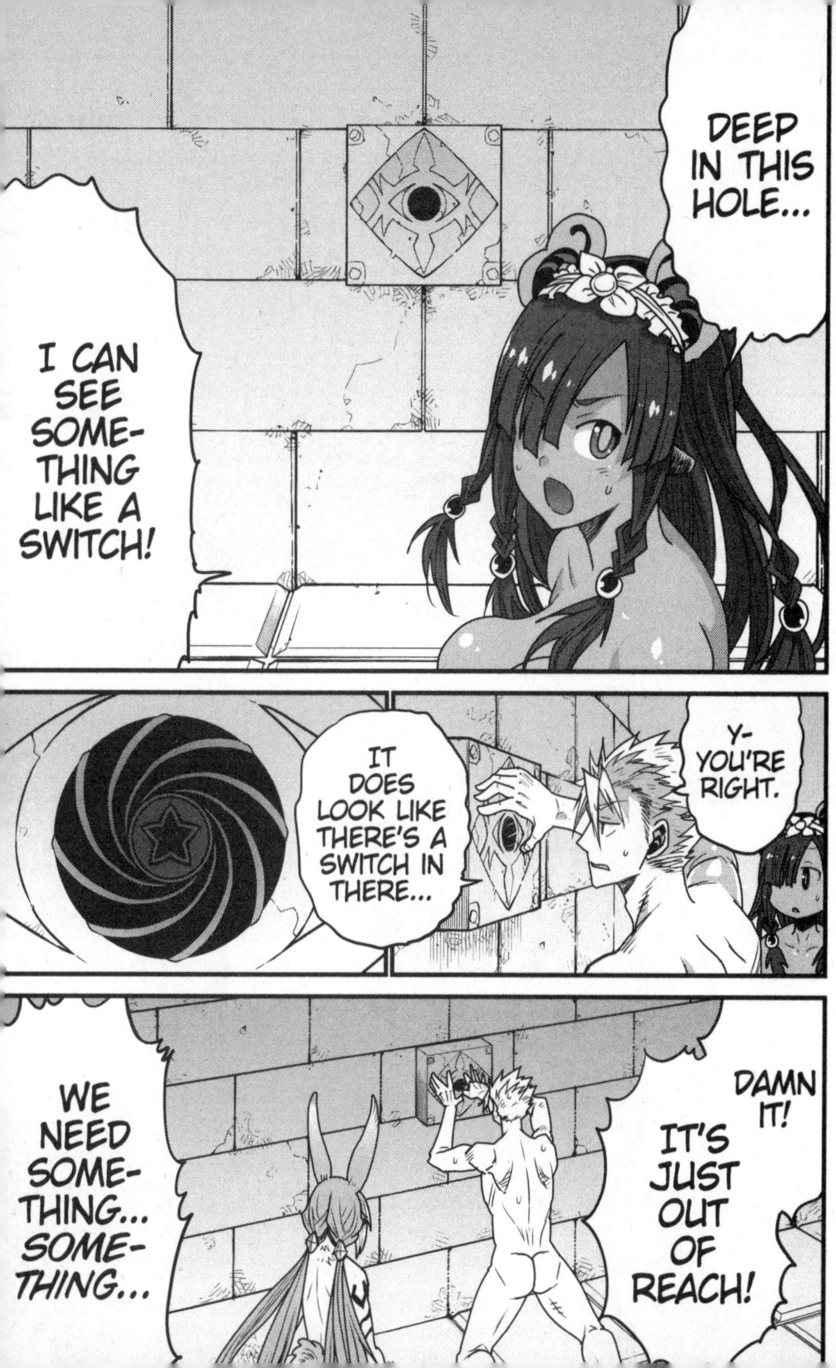
DEEP IN THIS HOLE...
I CAN SEE SOME-THING LIKE A SWITCH!
IT DOES LOOK LIKE THERE'S A SWITCH IN THERE...
Y-YOU'RE RIGHT.
DAMN IT!
IT'S JUST OUT OF REACH!
WE NEED SOME-THING... SOME-THING...

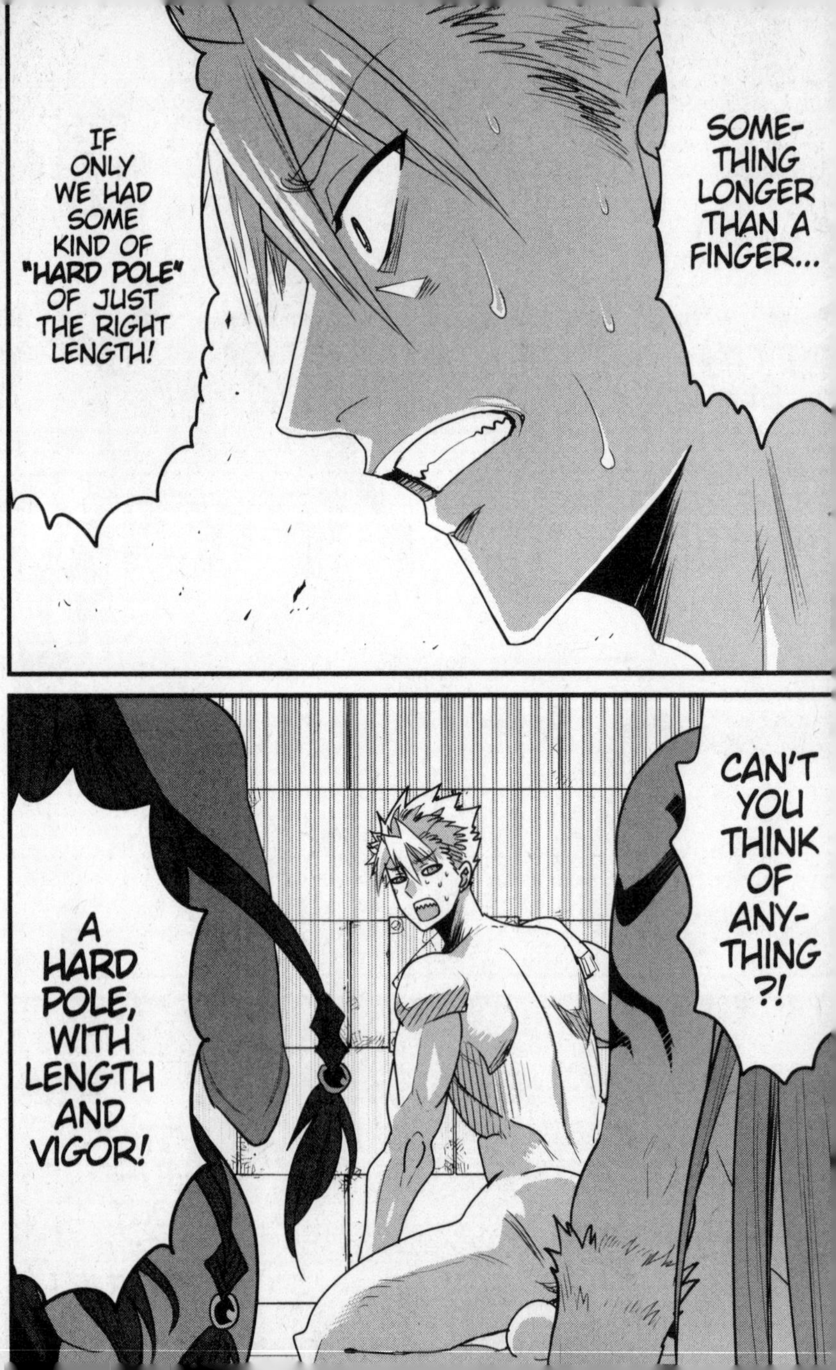
SOMETHING LONGER THAN A FINGER...
IF ONLY WE HAD SOME KIND OF "HARD POLE" OF JUST THE RIGHT LENGTH!
CAN'T YOU THINK OF ANYTHING?!
A HARD POLE, WITH LENGTH AND VIGOR!

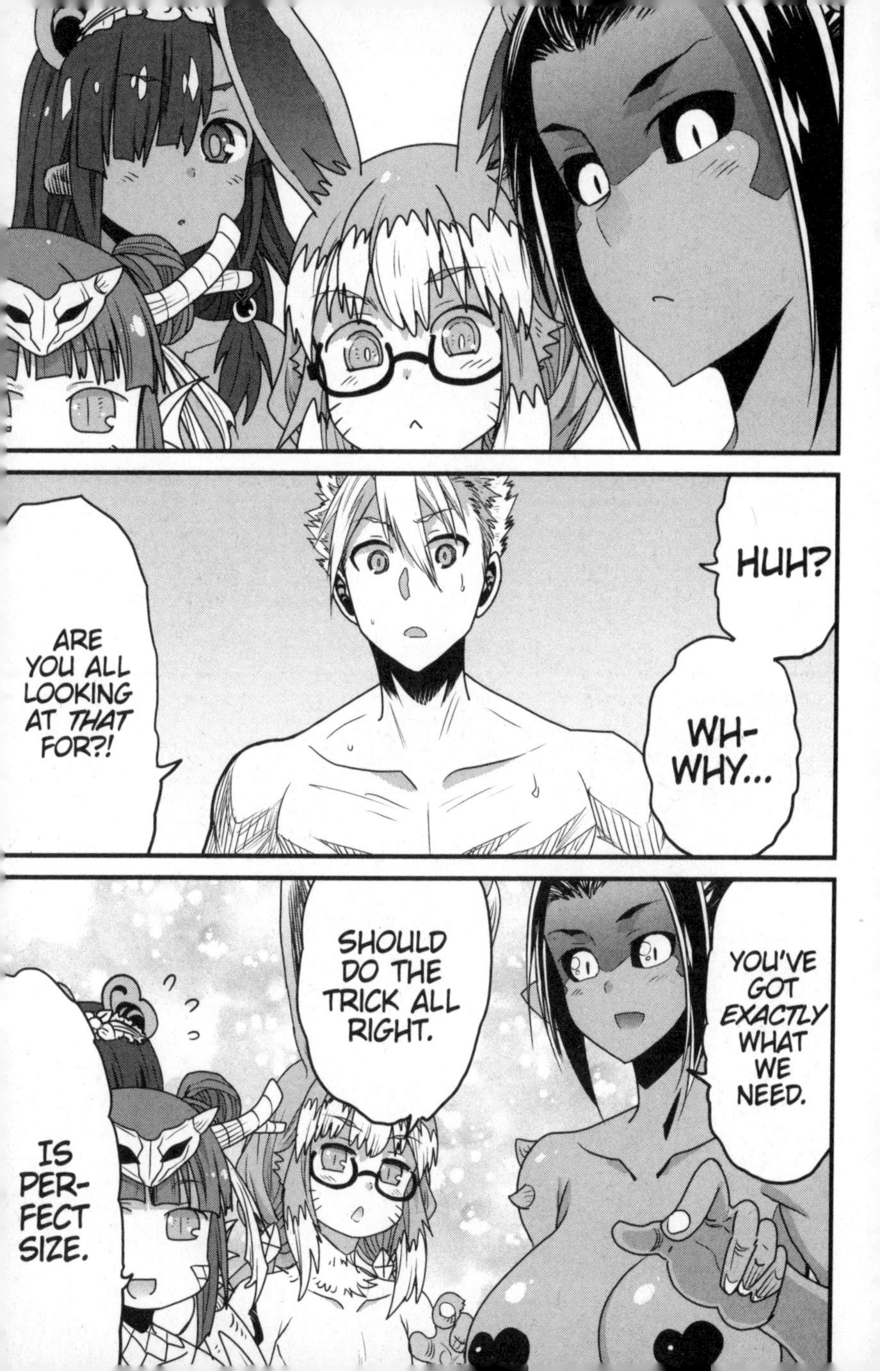
HUH?
WH-WHY...
ARE YOU ALL LOOKING AT *THAT* FOR?!
YOU'VE GOT *EXACTLY* WHAT WE NEED.
SHOULD DO THE TRICK ALL RIGHT.
IS PER-FECT SIZE.

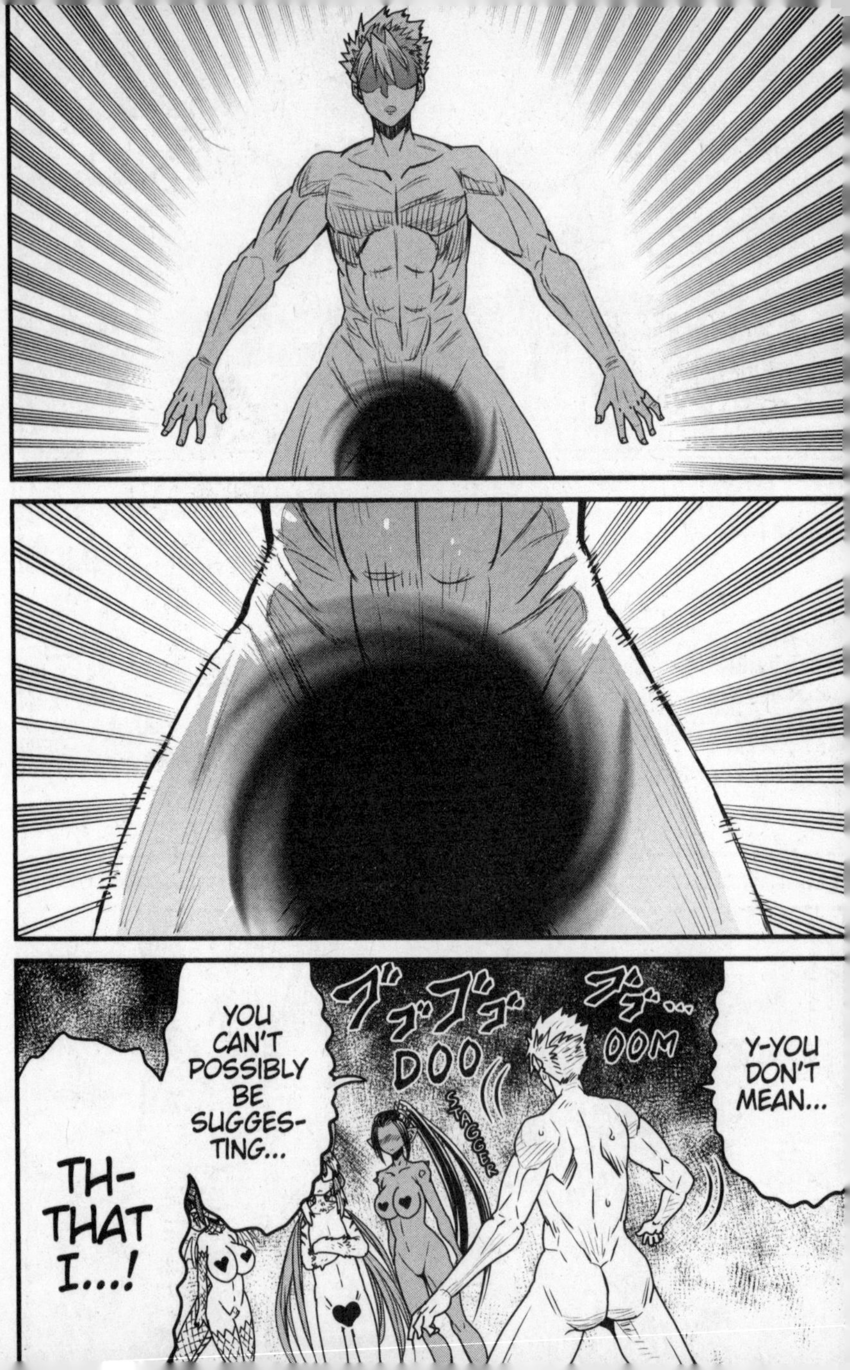

Y-YOU DON'T MEAN...
DOO
OOM
STAGGER
YOU CAN'T POSSIBLY BE SUGGES-TING...
TH-THAT I...!

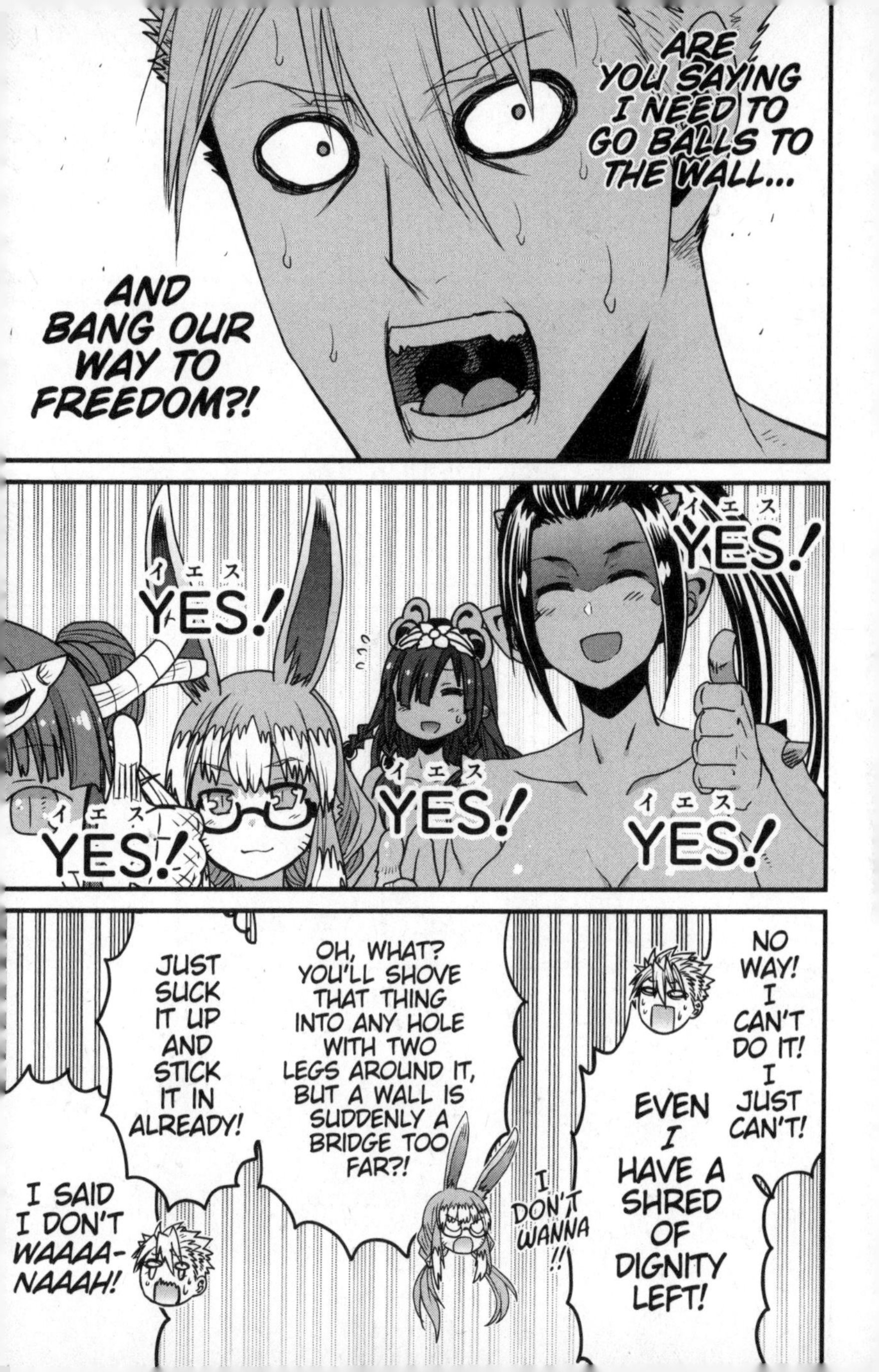
ARE YOU SAYING I NEED TO GO BALLS TO THE WALL...
AND BANG OUR WAY TO FREEDOM?!
YES!
YES!
YES!
YES!
YES!
NO WAY! I CAN'T DO IT! I JUST CAN'T!
EVEN I HAVE A SHRED OF DIGNITY LEFT!
I DON'T WANNA!!
OH, WHAT? YOU'LL SHOVE THAT THING INTO ANY HOLE WITH TWO LEGS AROUND IT, BUT A WALL IS SUDDENLY A BRIDGE TOO FAR?!
JUST SUCK IT UP AND STICK IT IN ALREADY!
I SAID I DON'T WAAAA-NAAAH!

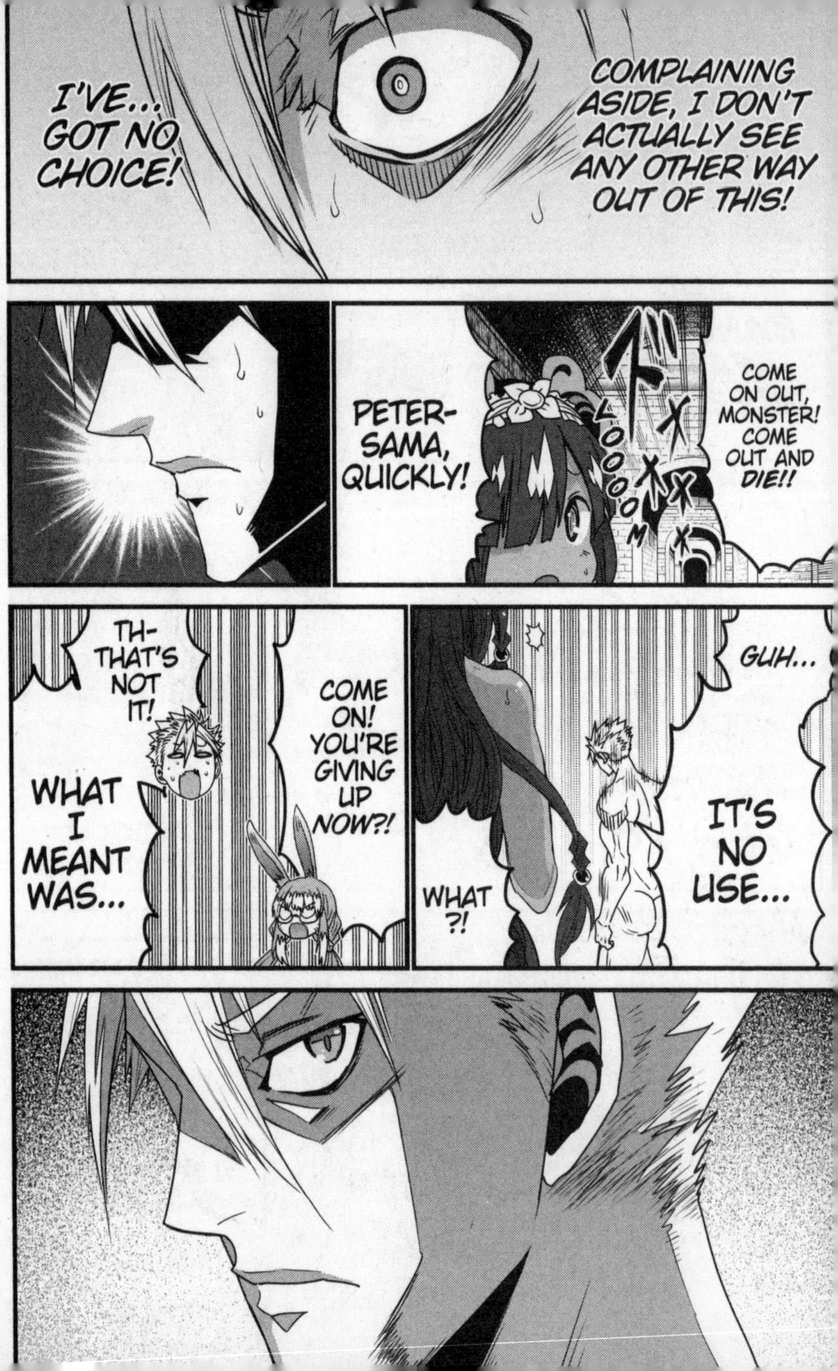
COMPLAINING ASIDE, I DON'T ACTUALLY SEE ANY OTHER WAY OUT OF THIS!
I'VE... GOT NO CHOICE!
COME ON OUT, MONSTER! COME OUT AND DIE!!
VOOOOM
PETER-SAMA, QUICKLY!
GUH...
IT'S NO USE...
WHAT?!
COME ON! YOU'RE GIVING UP NOW?!
TH-THAT'S NOT IT!
WHAT I MEANT WAS...

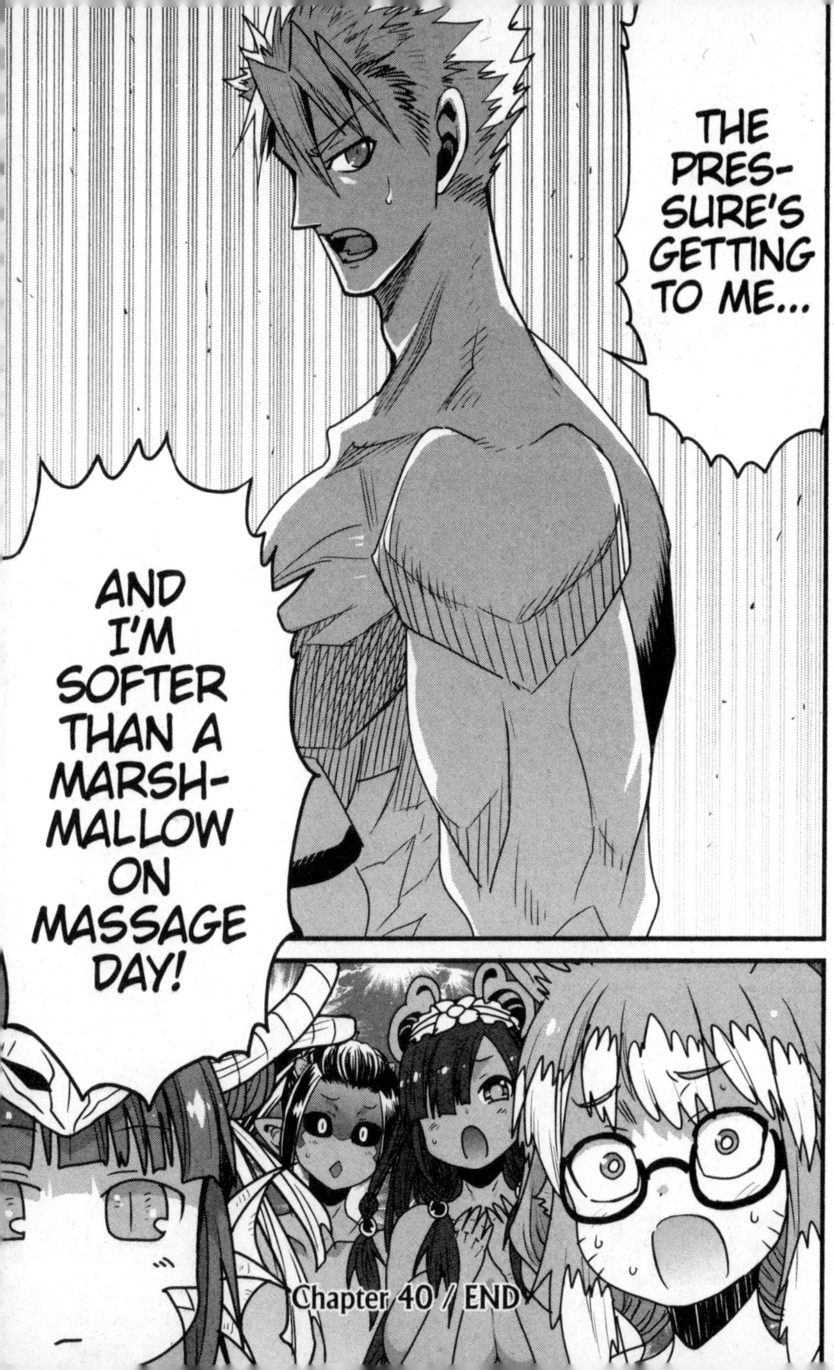
THE PRES-SURE'S GETTING TO ME...
AND I'M SOFTER THAN A MARSH-MALLOW ON MASSAGE DAY!
Chapter 40 / END

PETER GRILL
AND THE PHILOSOPHER'S TIME

Previously, on *Peter Grill*...

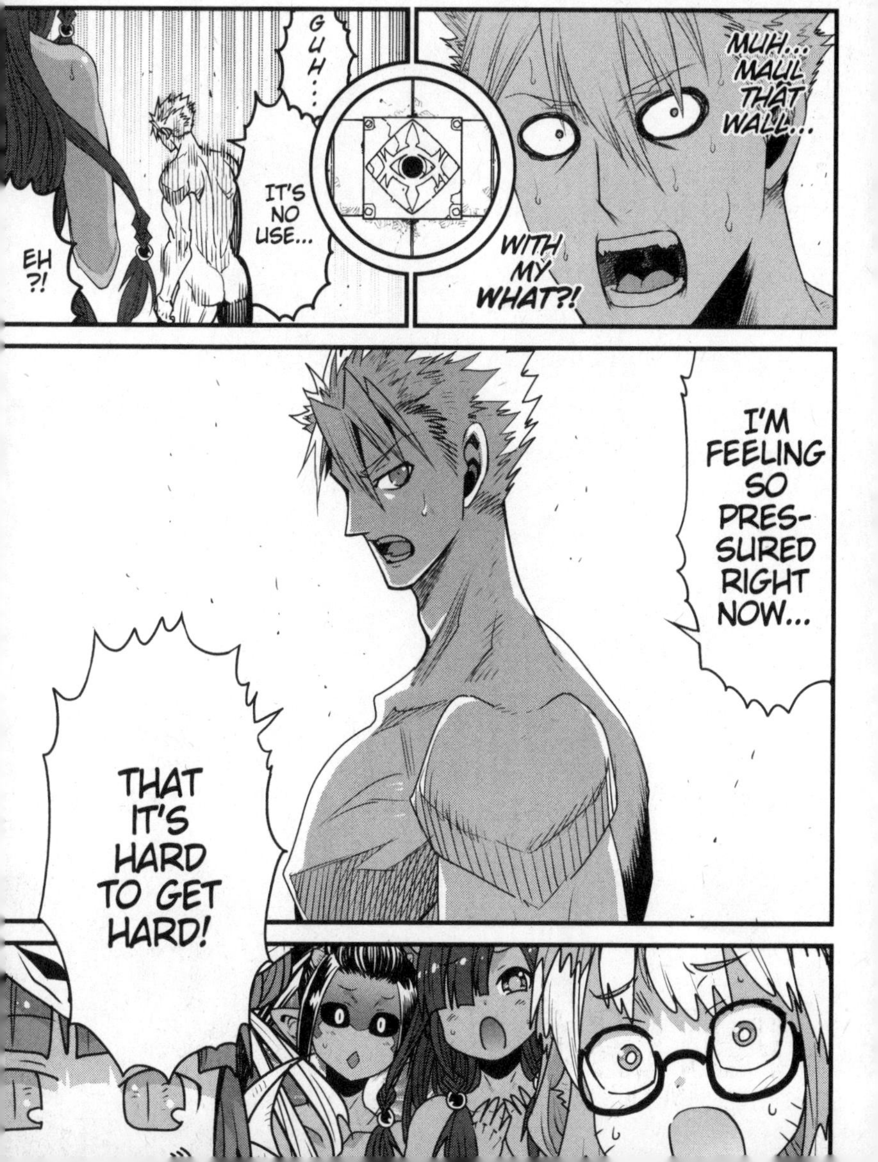
MUH... MAUL THAT WALL...
WITH MY WHAT?!
GUH...
IT'S NO USE...
EH?!
I'M FEELING SO PRES-SURED RIGHT NOW...
THAT IT'S HARD TO GET HARD!

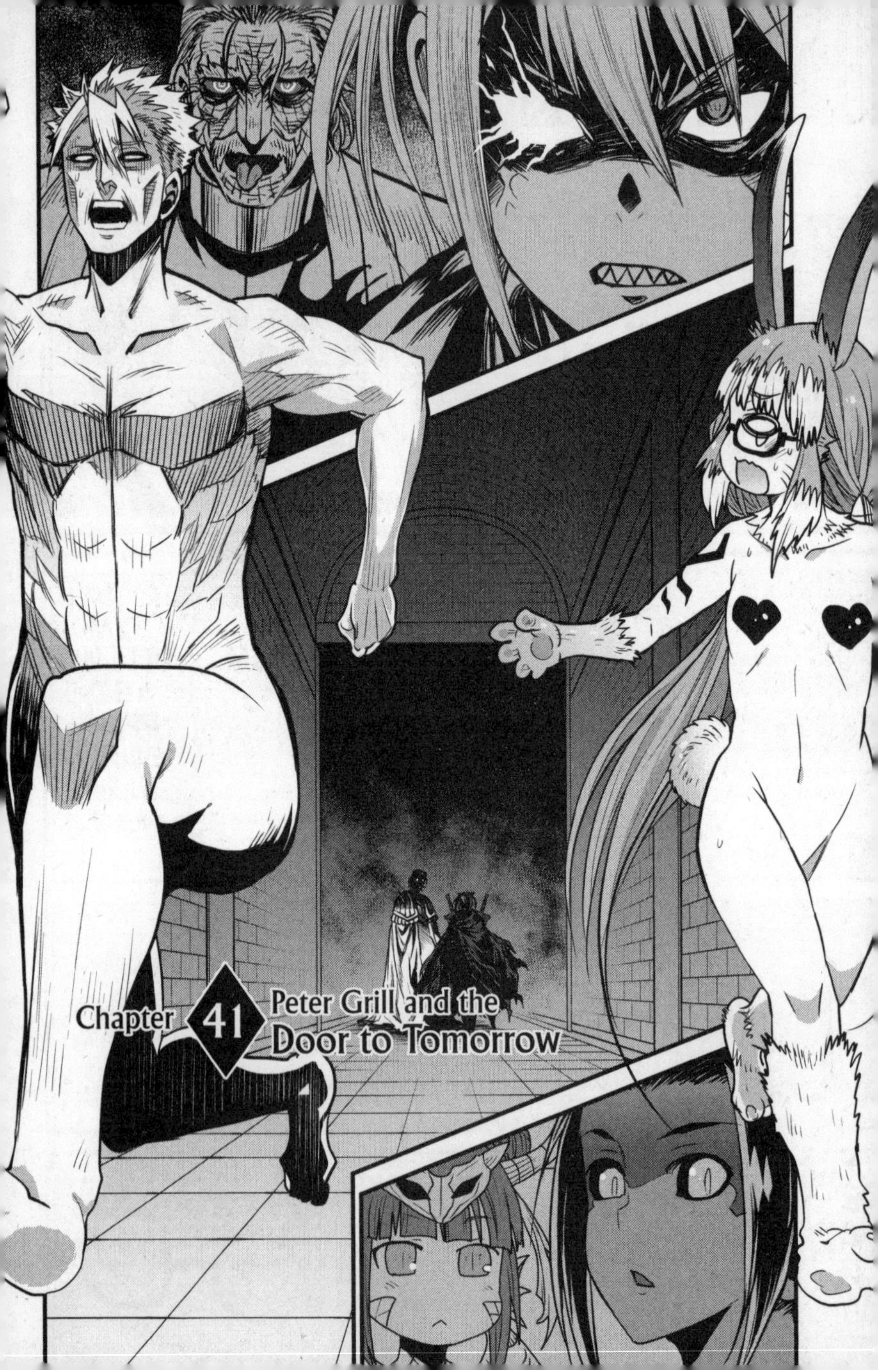
Chapter 41 Peter Grill and the Door to Tomorrow

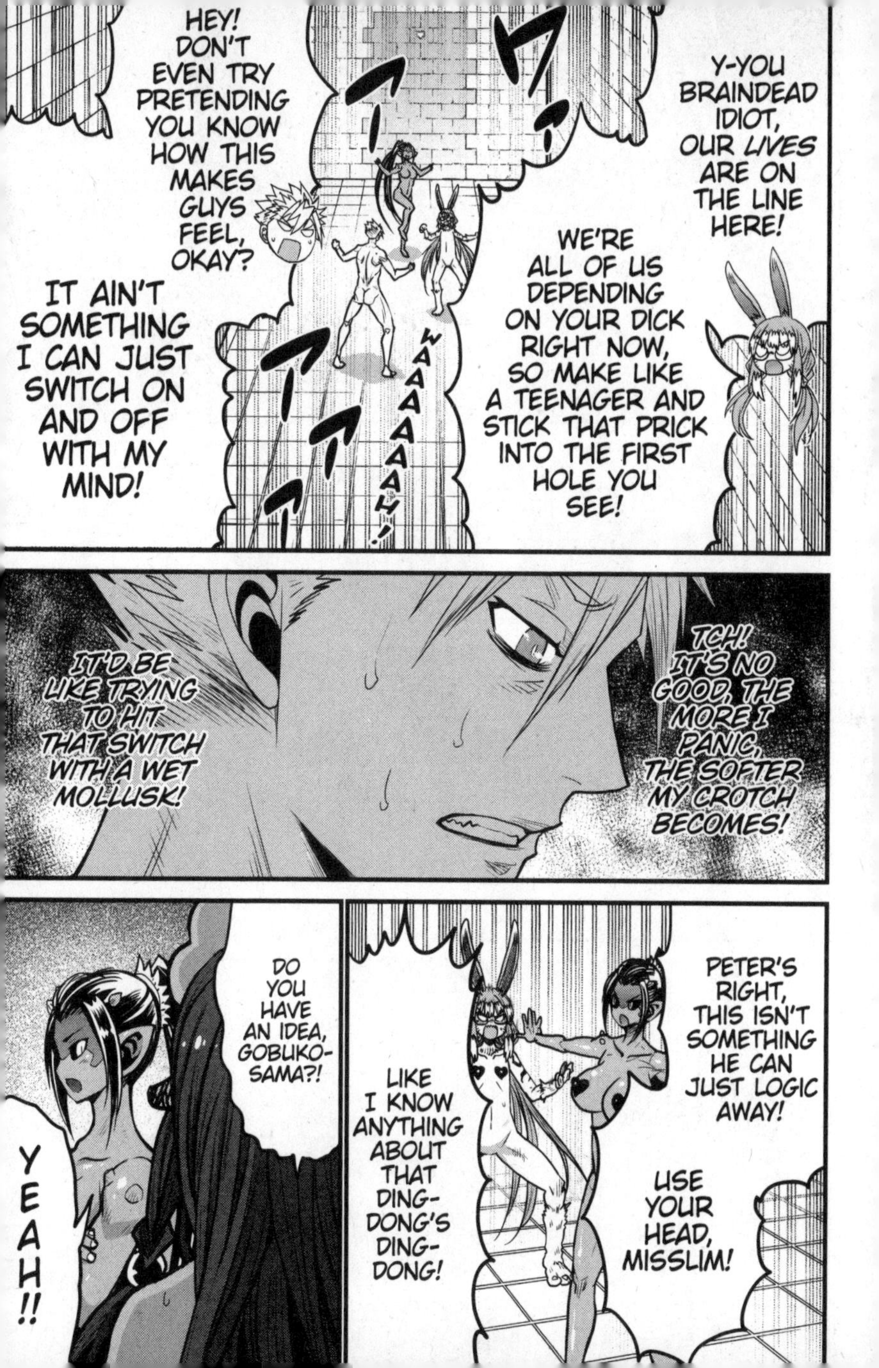
Y-YOU BRAINDEAD IDIOT, OUR LIVES ARE ON THE LINE HERE!
WE'RE ALL OF US DEPENDING ON YOUR DICK RIGHT NOW, SO MAKE LIKE A TEENAGER AND STICK THAT PRICK INTO THE FIRST HOLE YOU SEE!
WAAAAAAAH!
HEY! DON'T EVEN TRY PRETENDING YOU KNOW HOW THIS MAKES GUYS FEEL, OKAY?
IT AIN'T SOMETHING I CAN JUST SWITCH ON AND OFF WITH MY MIND!
TCH! IT'S NO GOOD, THE MORE I PANIC, THE SOFTER MY CROTCH BECOMES!
IT'D BE LIKE TRYING TO HIT THAT SWITCH WITH A WET MOLLUSK!
PETER'S RIGHT, THIS ISN'T SOMETHING HE CAN JUST LOGIC AWAY!
USE YOUR HEAD, MISSLIM!
LIKE I KNOW ANYTHING ABOUT THAT DING-DONG'S DING-DONG!
DO YOU HAVE AN IDEA, GOBUKO-SAMA?!
YEAH!!

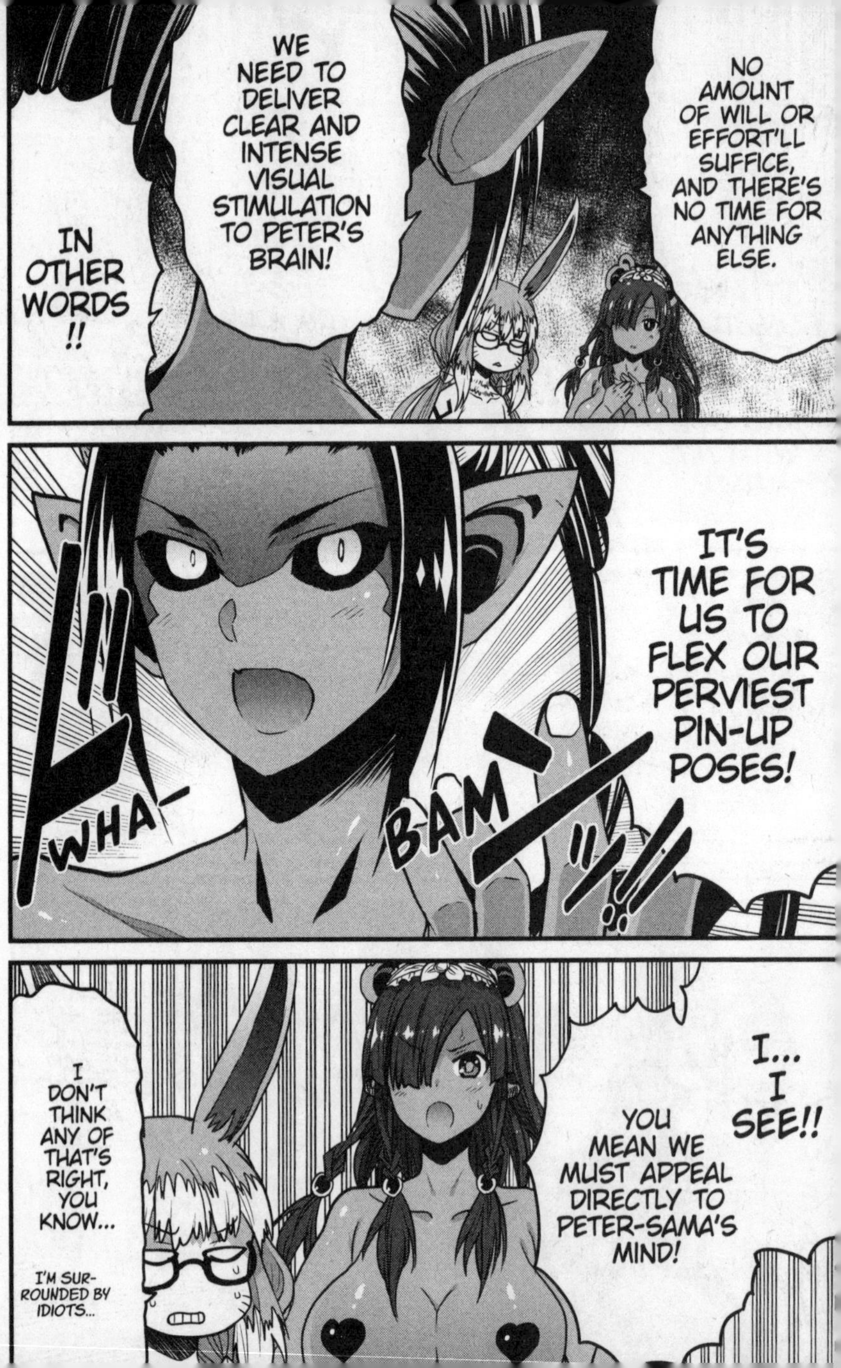
NO AMOUNT OF WILL OR EFFORT'LL SUFFICE, AND THERE'S NO TIME FOR ANYTHING ELSE.
WE NEED TO DELIVER CLEAR AND INTENSE VISUAL STIMULATION TO PETER'S BRAIN!
IN OTHER WORDS!!
IT'S TIME FOR US TO FLEX OUR PERVIEST PIN-UP POSES!
WHA-BAM!!
I... I SEE!!
YOU MEAN WE MUST APPEAL DIRECTLY TO PETER-SAMA'S MIND!
I DON'T THINK ANY OF THAT'S RIGHT, YOU KNOW...
I'M SURROUNDED BY IDIOTS...

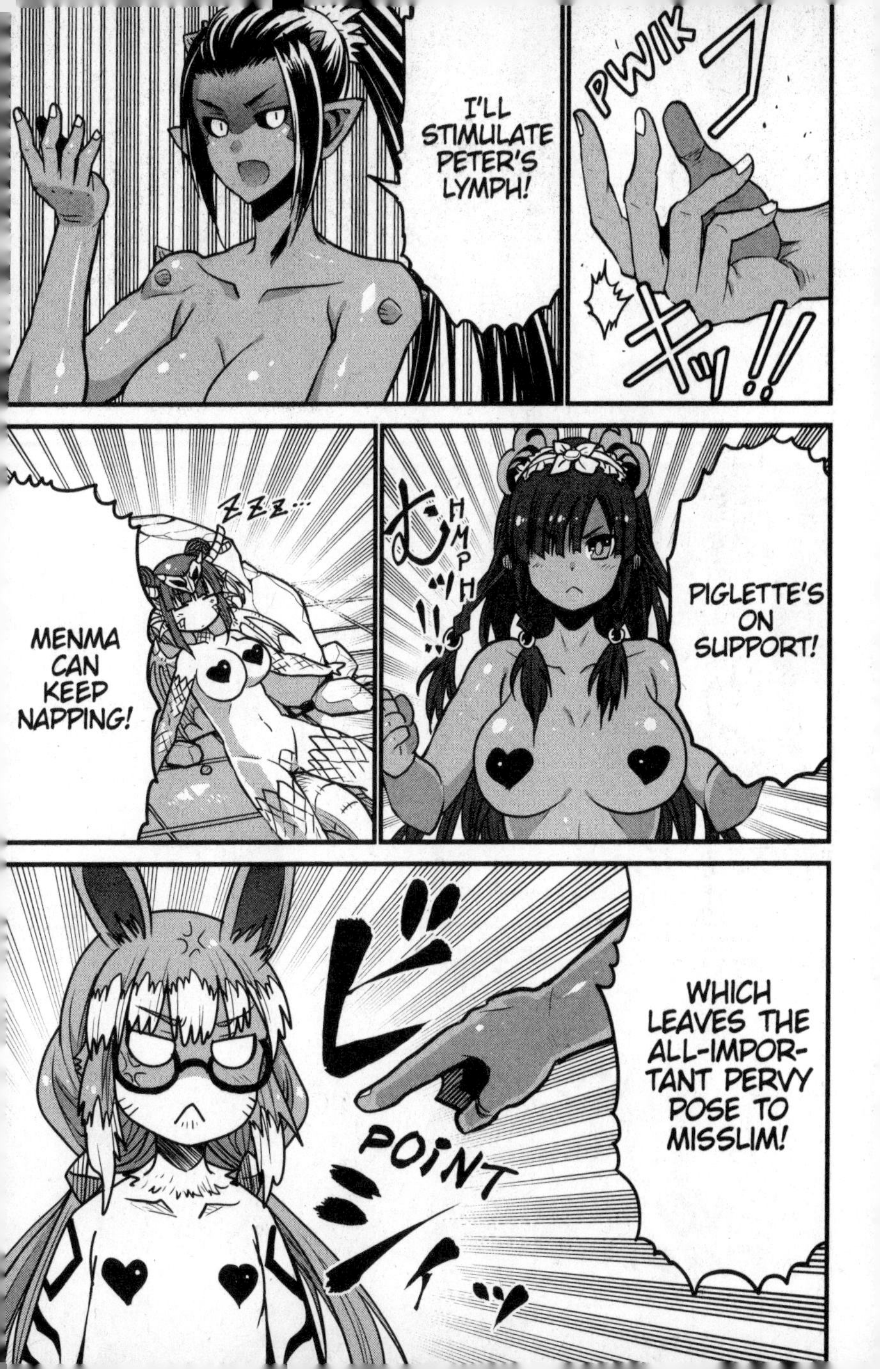
PWIK
I'LL STIMULATE PETER'S LYMPH!
むッ!!
HMPH
PIGLETTE'S ON SUPPORT!
ZZZ...
MENMA CAN KEEP NAPPING!
WHICH LEAVES THE ALL-IMPORTANT PERVY POSE TO MISSLIM!
POINT

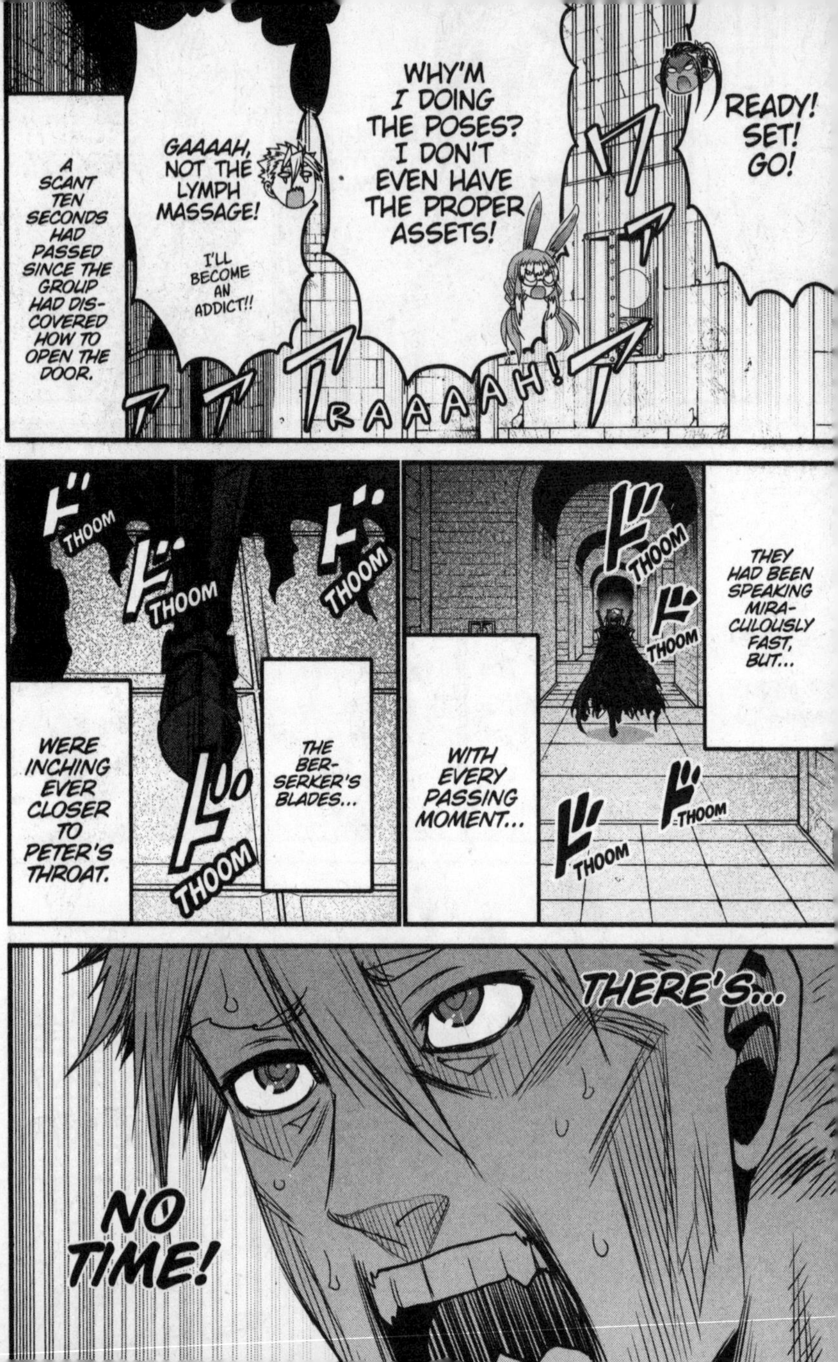
READY! SET! GO!
WHY'M I DOING THE POSES? I DON'T EVEN HAVE THE PROPER ASSETS!
GAAAAH, NOT THE LYMPH MASSAGE!
I'LL BECOME AN ADDICT!!
RAAAAAH!
A SCANT TEN SECONDS HAD PASSED SINCE THE GROUP HAD DIS-COVERED HOW TO OPEN THE DOOR.
THEY HAD BEEN SPEAKING MIRA-CULOUSLY FAST, BUT...
THOOM
THOOM
THOOM
THOOM
WITH EVERY PASSING MOMENT...
THOOM
THOOM
THOOM
THOOM
THE BER-SERKER'S BLADES...
WERE INCHING EVER CLOSER TO PETER'S THROAT.
THERE'S...
NO TIME!

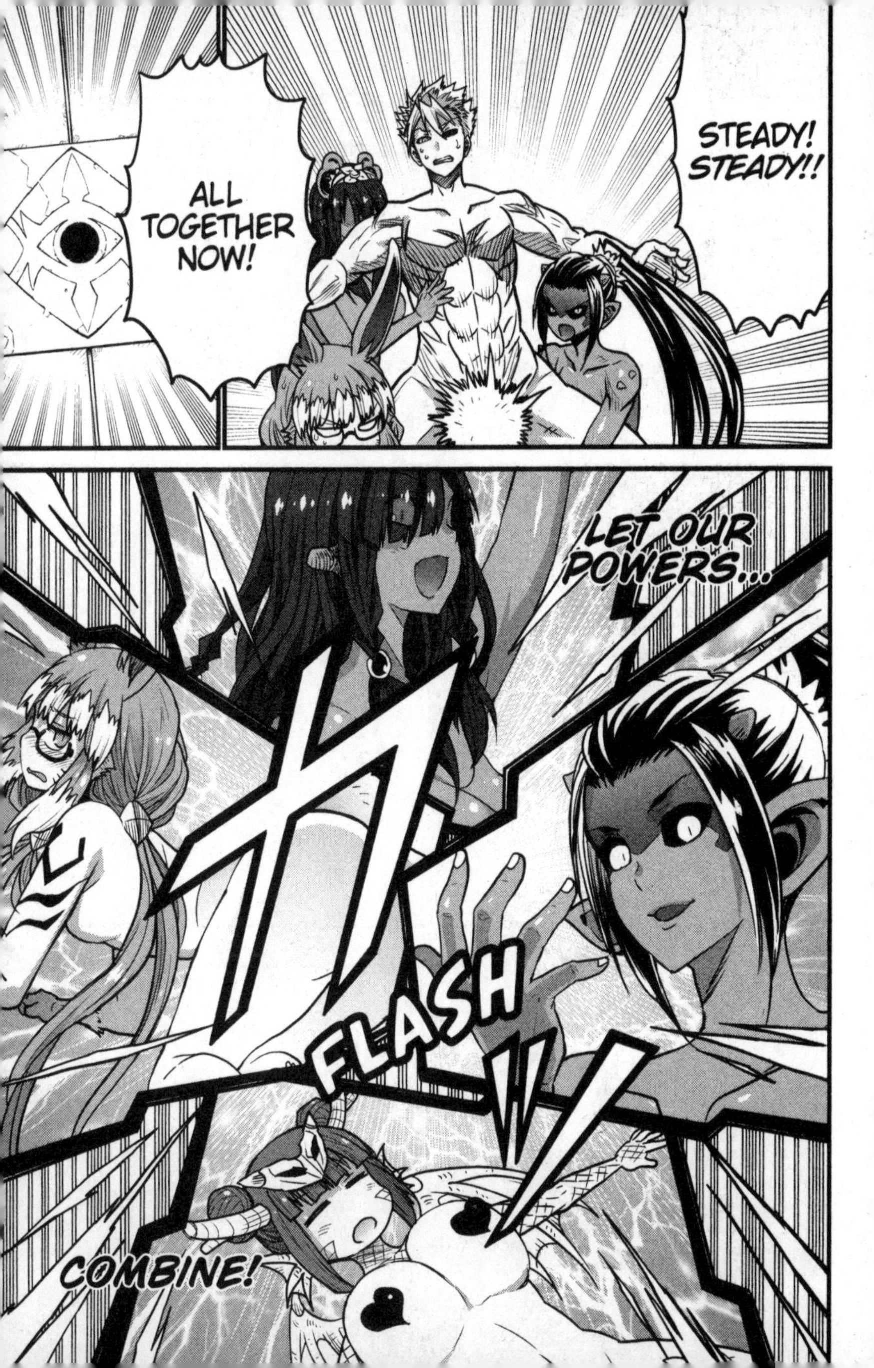
STEADY! STEADY!!
ALL TOGETHER NOW!
LET OUR POWERS...
FLASH
COMBINE!

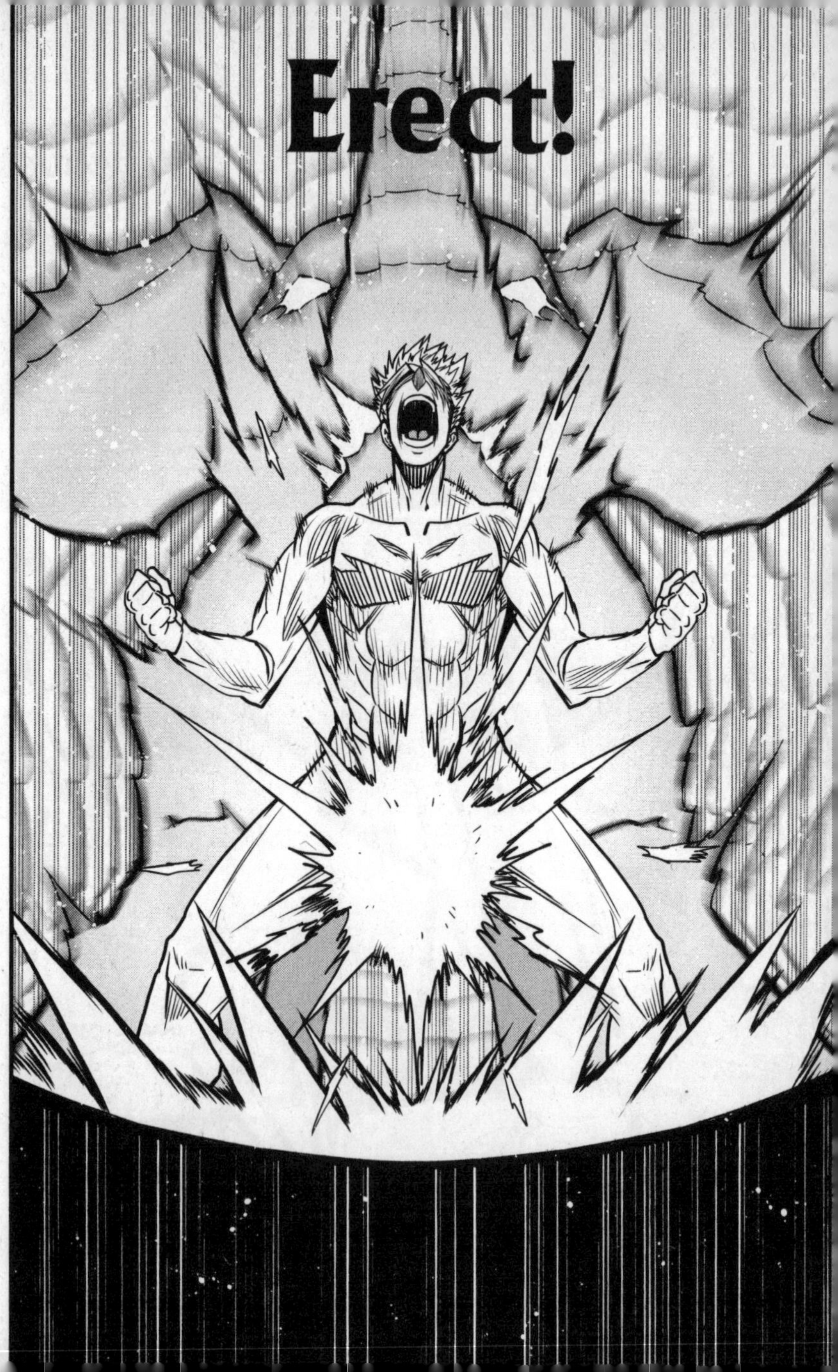
Erect!

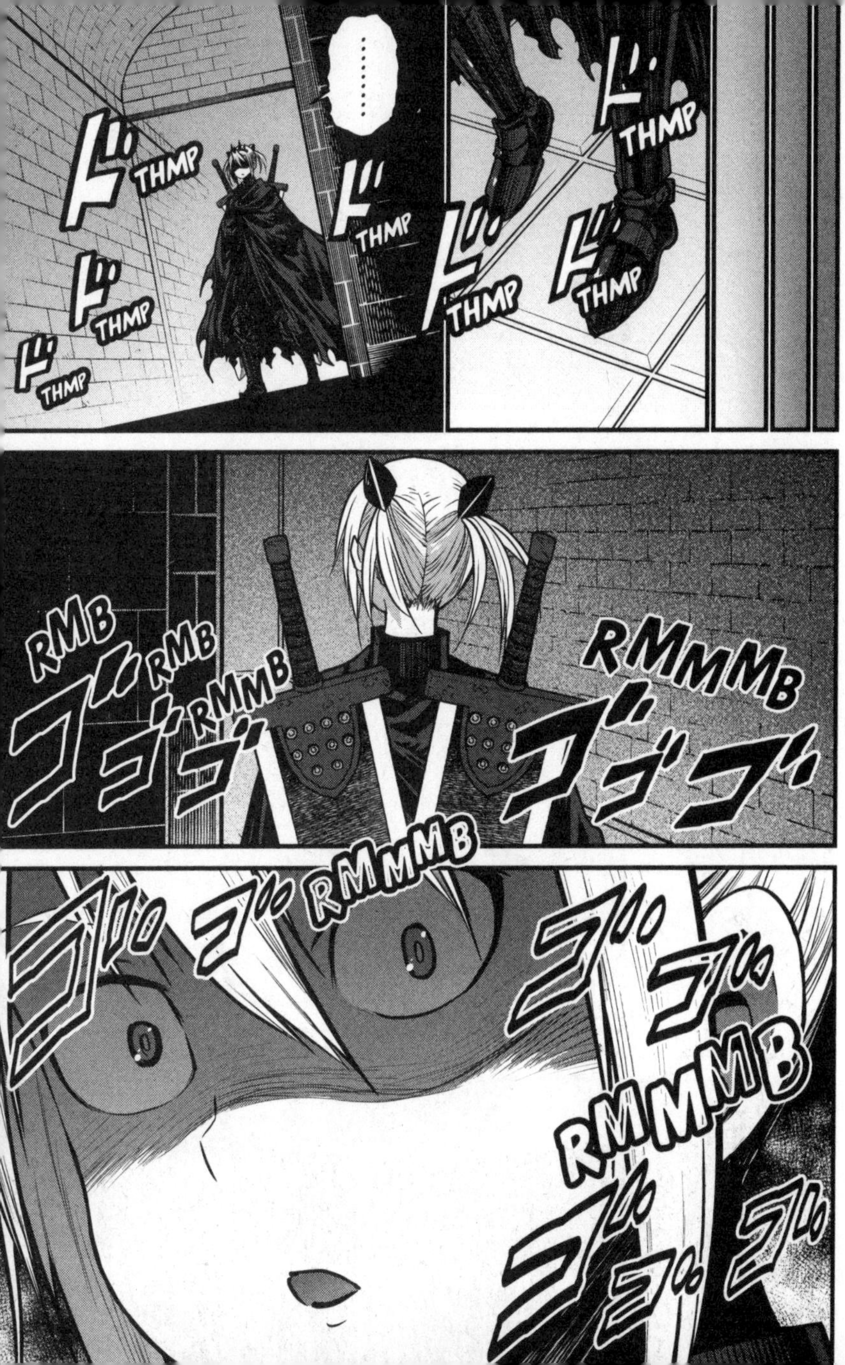
THMP
THMP
THMP
……
THMP
THMP
THMP
THMP
RMMMB
RMB
RMB
RMMMB
RMMMB
RMMMB

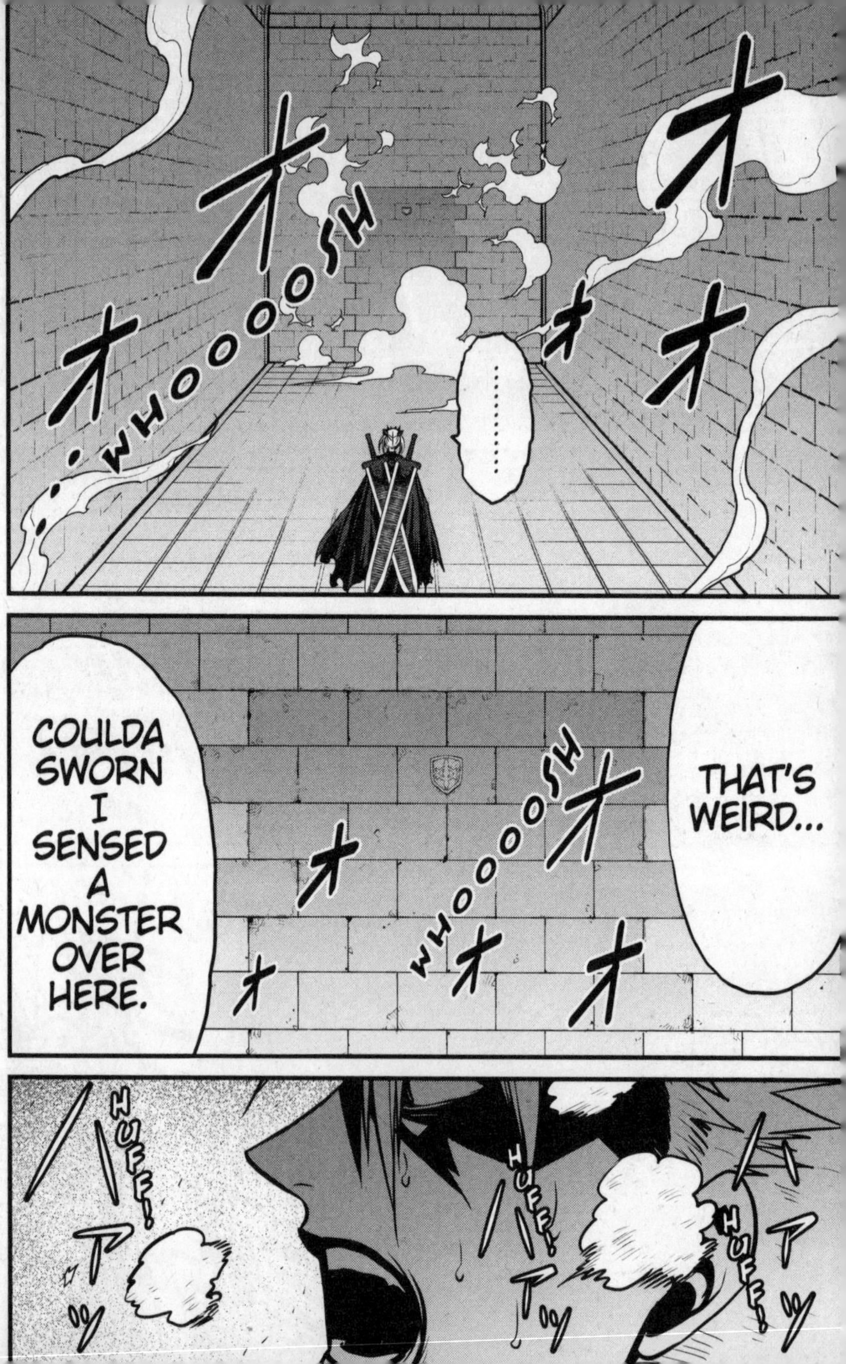
WHOOOOOSH
......
THAT'S WEIRD...
WHOOOOOSH
COULDA SWORN I SENSED A MONSTER OVER HERE.
HUFF!
HUFF!
HUFF!

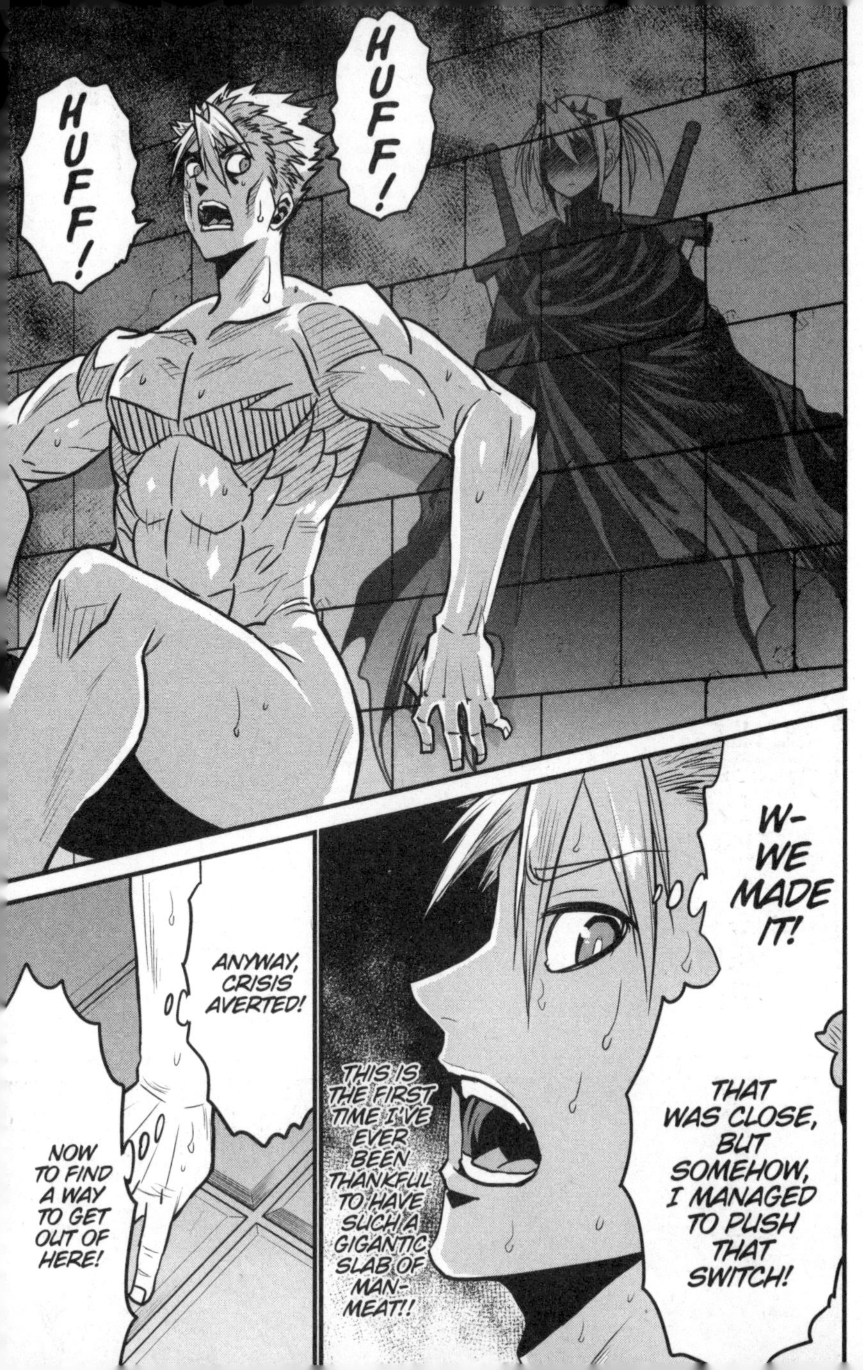
HUFF!
HUFF!
W-WE MADE IT!
THAT WAS CLOSE, BUT SOMEHOW, I MANAGED TO PUSH THAT SWITCH!
THIS IS THE FIRST TIME I'VE EVER BEEN THANKFUL TO HAVE SUCH A GIGANTIC SLAB OF MAN-MEAT!!
ANYWAY, CRISIS AVERTED!
NOW TO FIND A WAY TO GET OUT OF HERE!

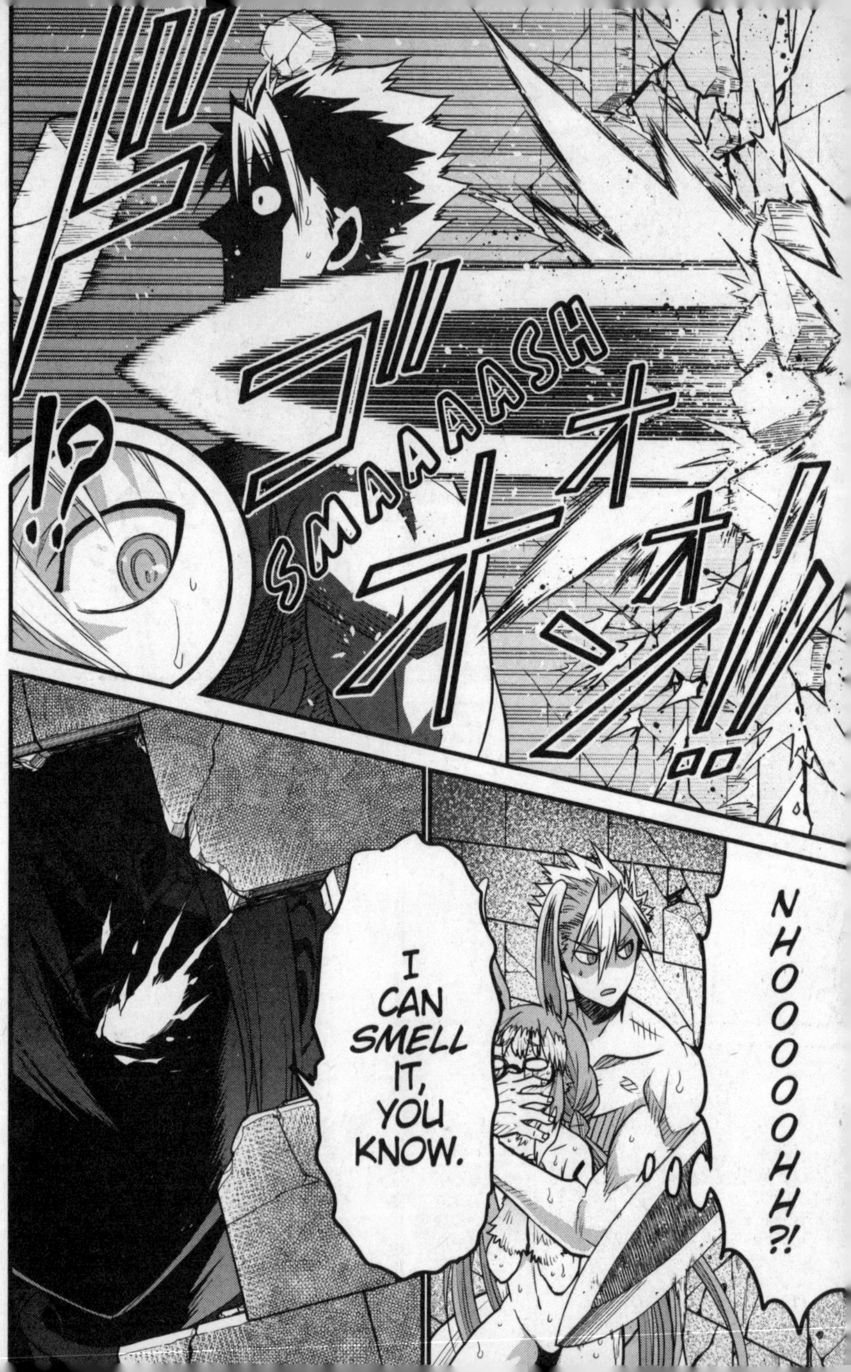
ドゴオーオッ!!
SMAAAASH
!?
NHOOOOOOHH?!
I CAN SMELL IT, YOU KNOW.

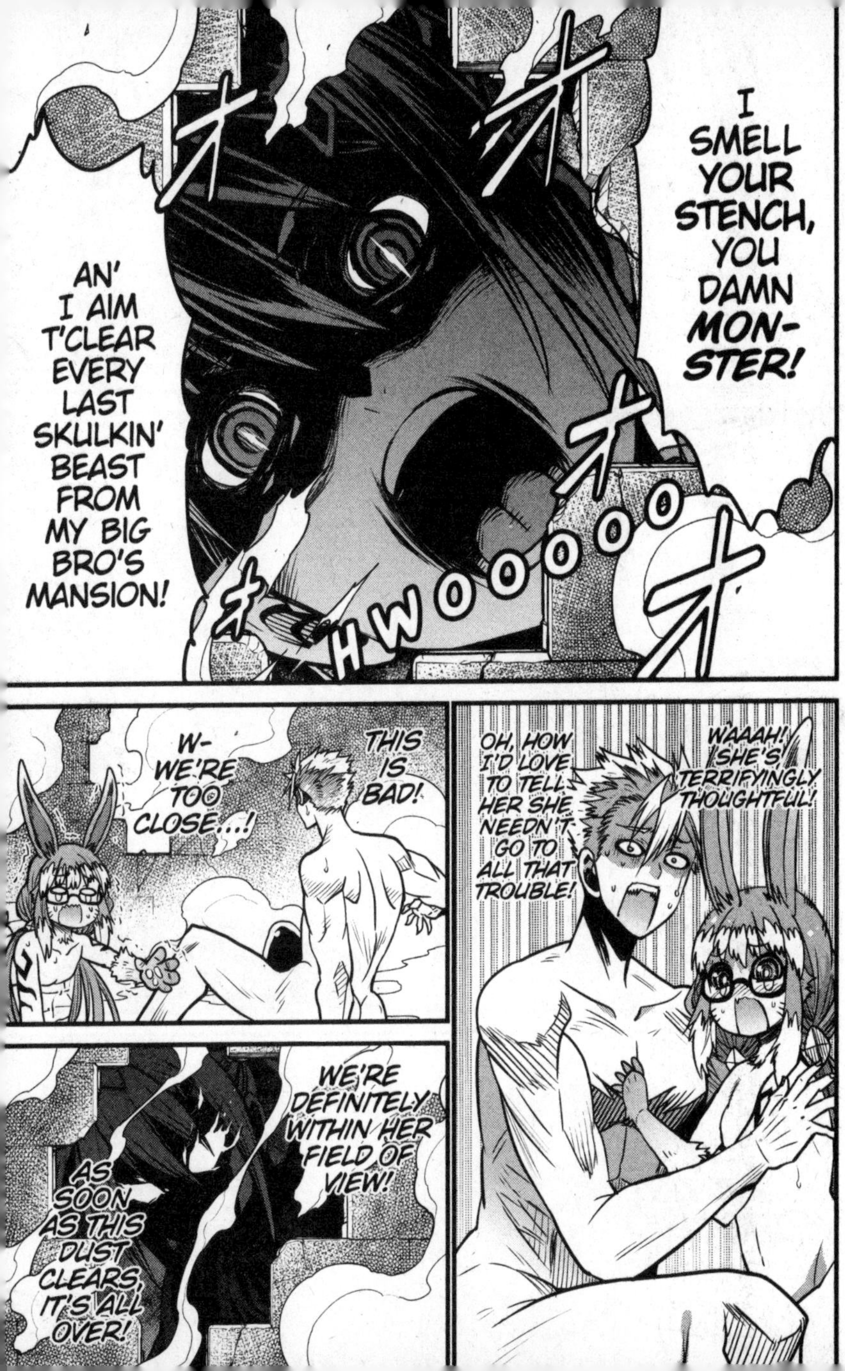
I SMELL YOUR STENCH, YOU DAMN MONSTER!
AN' I AIM T'CLEAR EVERY LAST SKULKIN' BEAST FROM MY BIG BRO'S MANSION!
HWOOOOOO
WAAAH! SHE'S TERRIFYINGLY THOUGHTFUL!
OH, HOW I'D LOVE TO TELL HER SHE NEEDN'T GO TO ALL THAT TROUBLE!
THIS IS BAD!
W-WE'RE TOO CLOSE...!
WE'RE DEFINITELY WITHIN HER FIELD OF VIEW!
AS SOON AS THIS DUST CLEARS, IT'S ALL OVER!

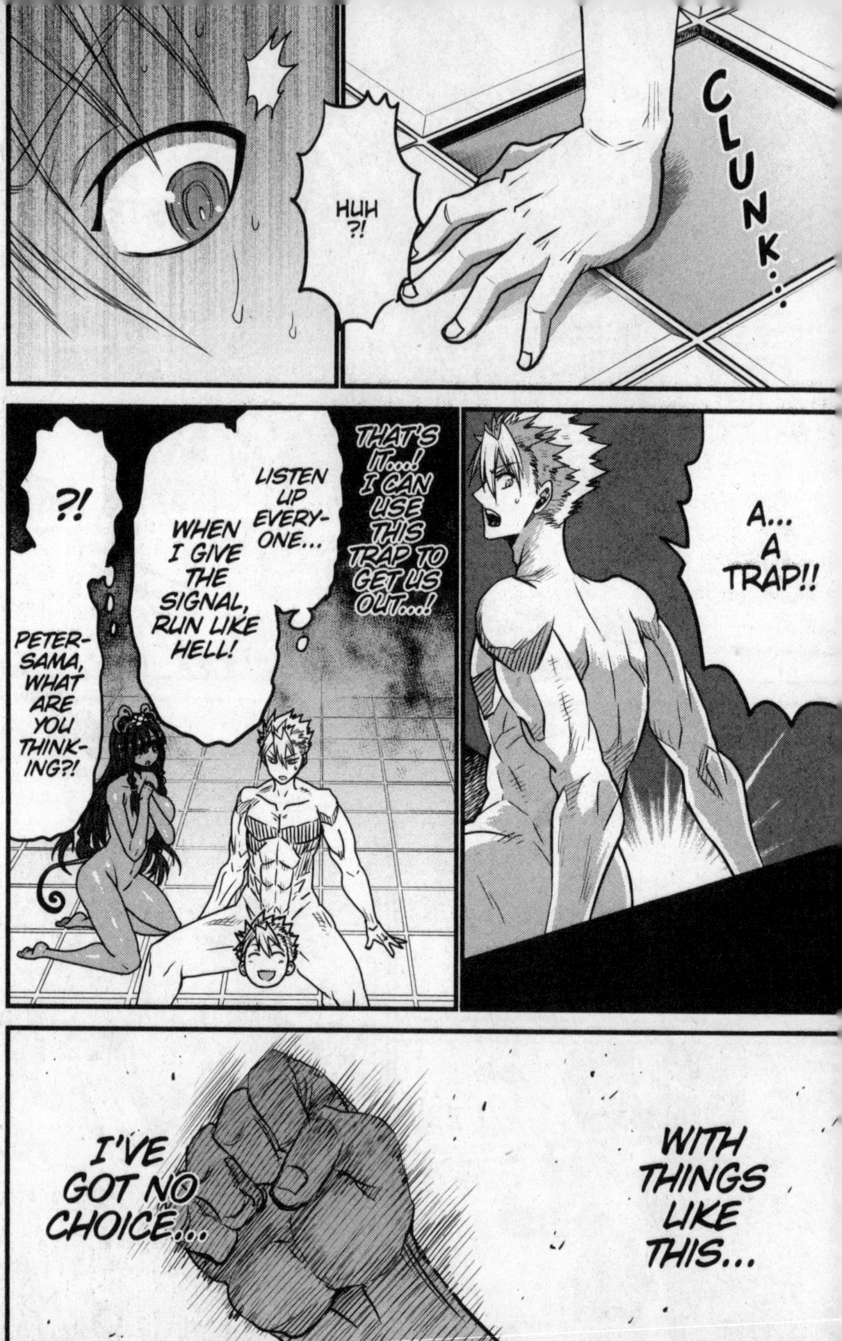
CLUNK...
HUH ?!
A... A TRAP!!
THAT'S IT...! I CAN USE THIS TRAP TO GET US OUT...!
LISTEN UP EVERYONE... WHEN I GIVE THE SIGNAL, RUN LIKE HELL!
?!
PETER-SAMA, WHAT ARE YOU THINKING?!
WITH THINGS LIKE THIS...
I'VE GOT NO CHOICE...

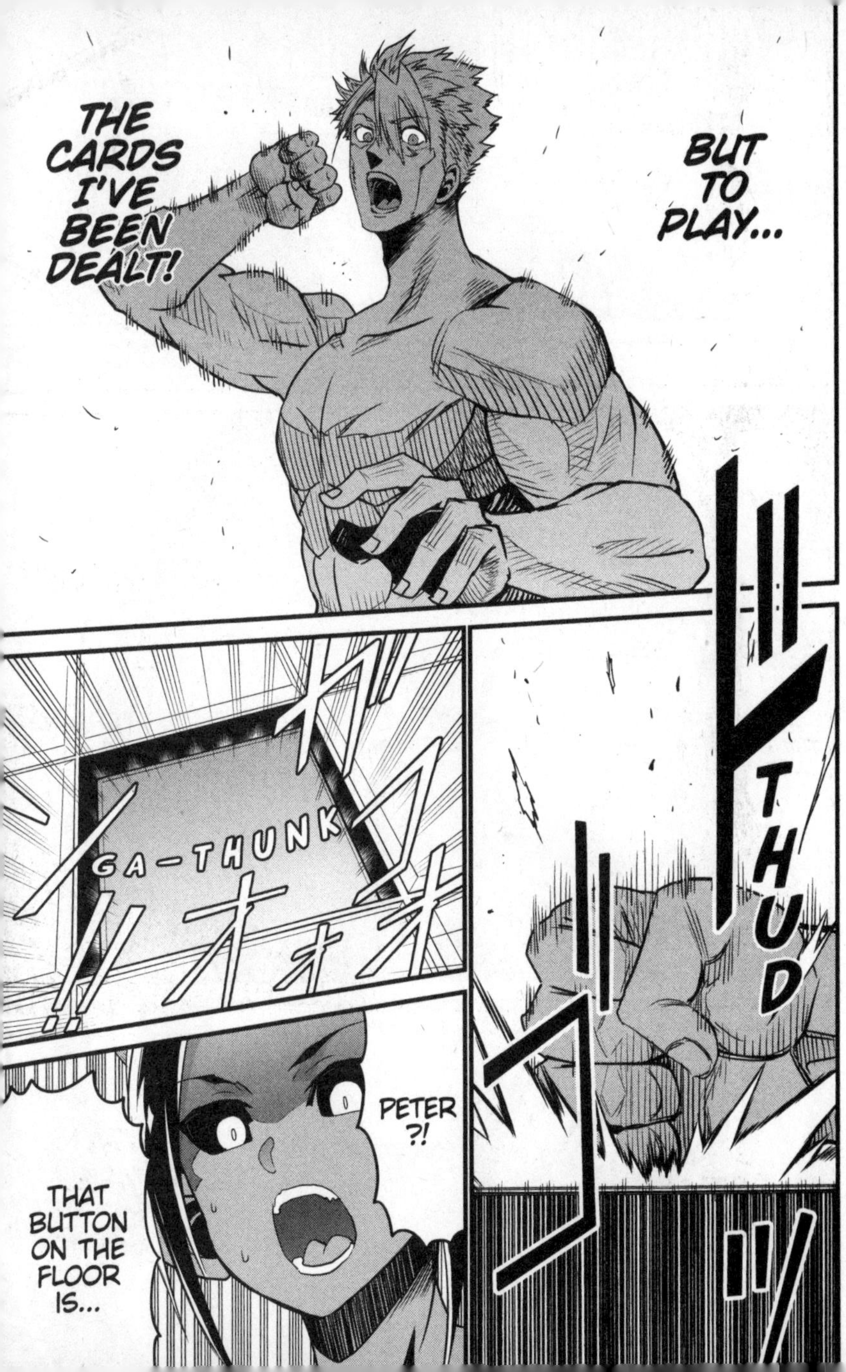
BUT TO PLAY...
THE CARDS I'VE BEEN DEALT!
THUD
GA-THUNK
PETER ?!
THAT BUTTON ON THE FLOOR IS...

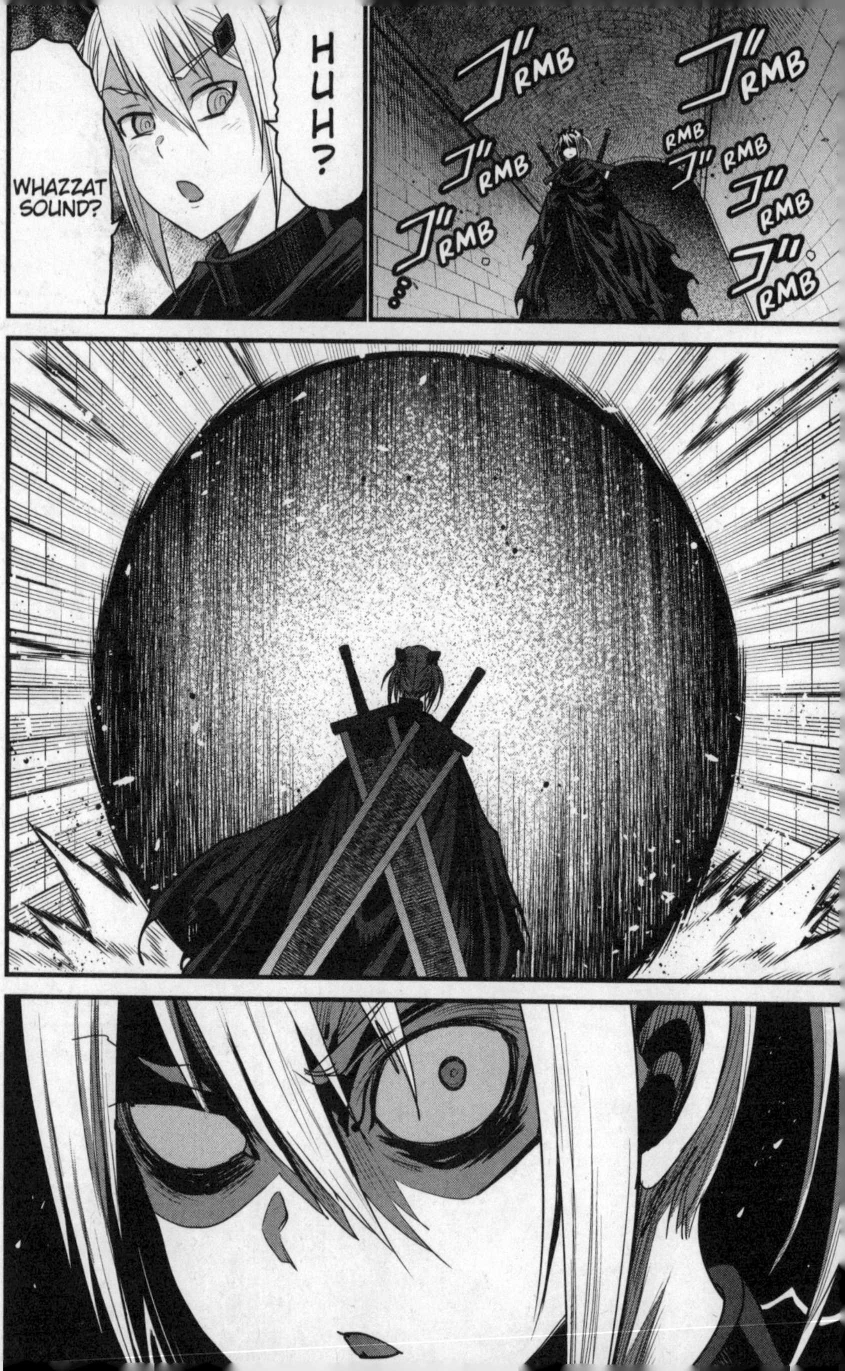
ゴ RMB
ゴ RMB
ゴ RMB
RMB ゴ RMB
ゴ RMB
ゴ RMB
ゴ RMB
ゴ RMB
...
HUH?
WHAZZAT SOUND?

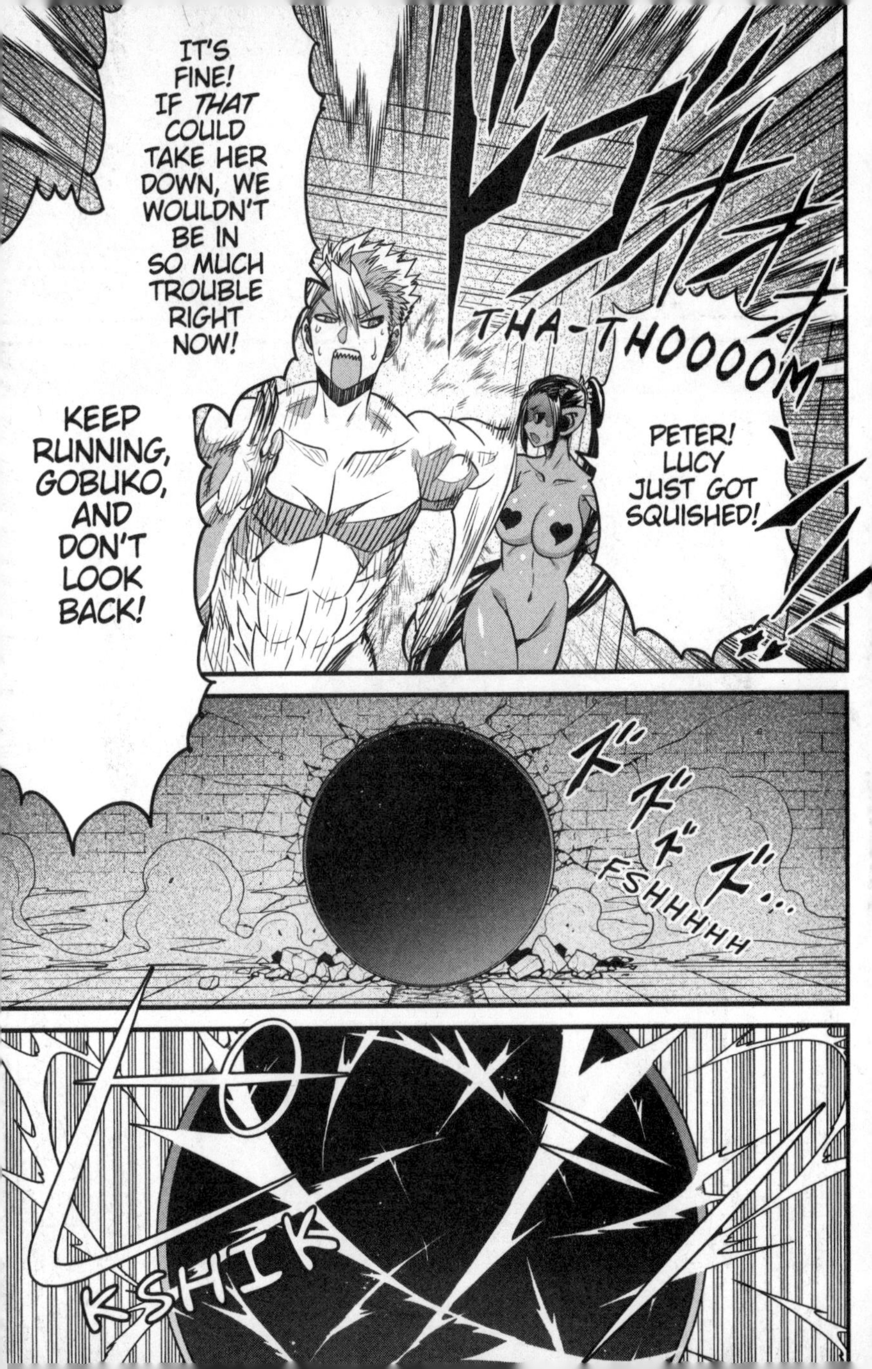
THA-THOOOOOM
PETER! LUCY JUST GOT SQUISHED!
IT'S FINE! IF *THAT* COULD TAKE HER DOWN, WE WOULDN'T BE IN SO MUCH TROUBLE RIGHT NOW!
KEEP RUNNING, GOBUKO, AND DON'T LOOK BACK!
FSHHHHHH
KSHIK

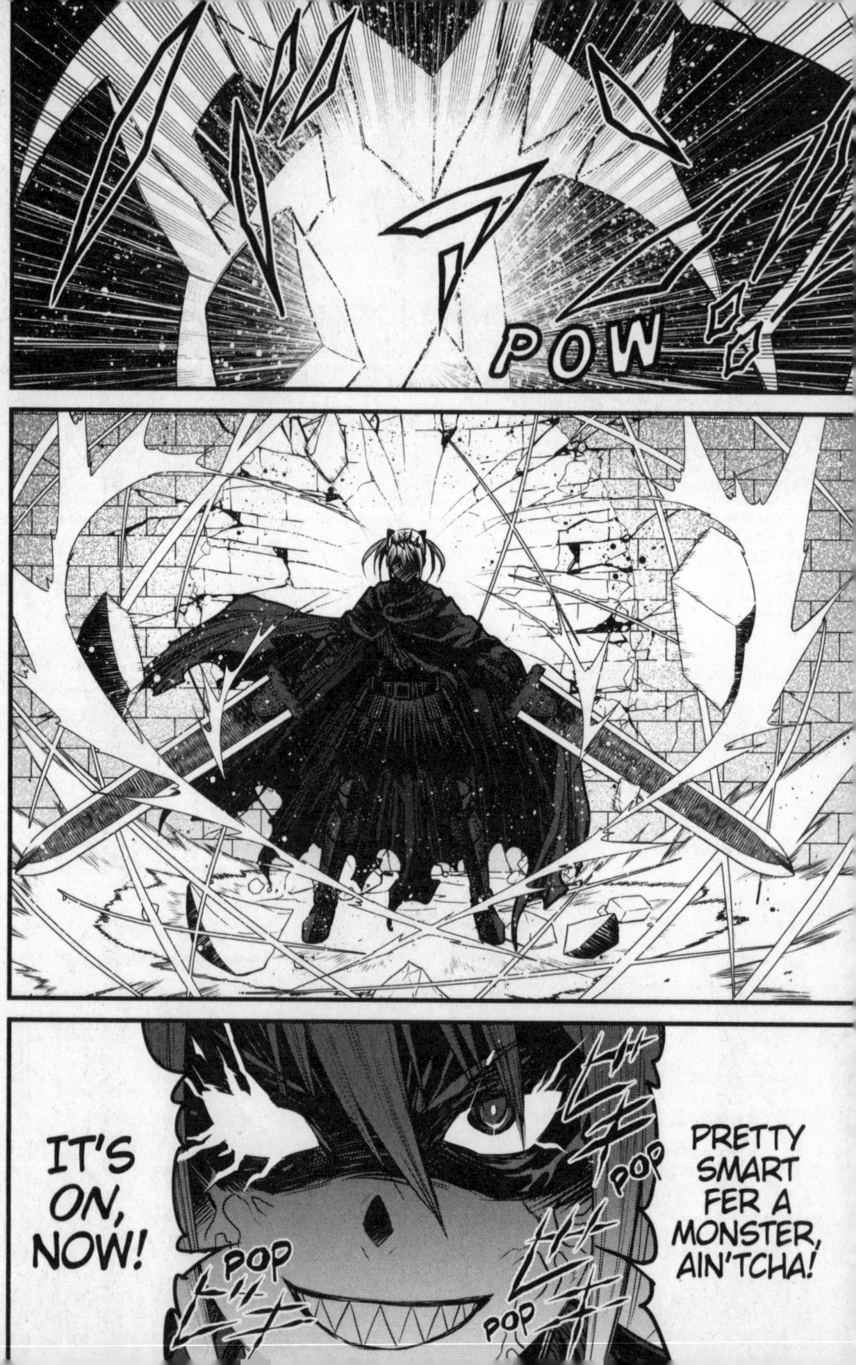
POW
PRETTY SMART FER A MONSTER, AIN'TCHA!
POP
IT'S ON, NOW!
POP
POP

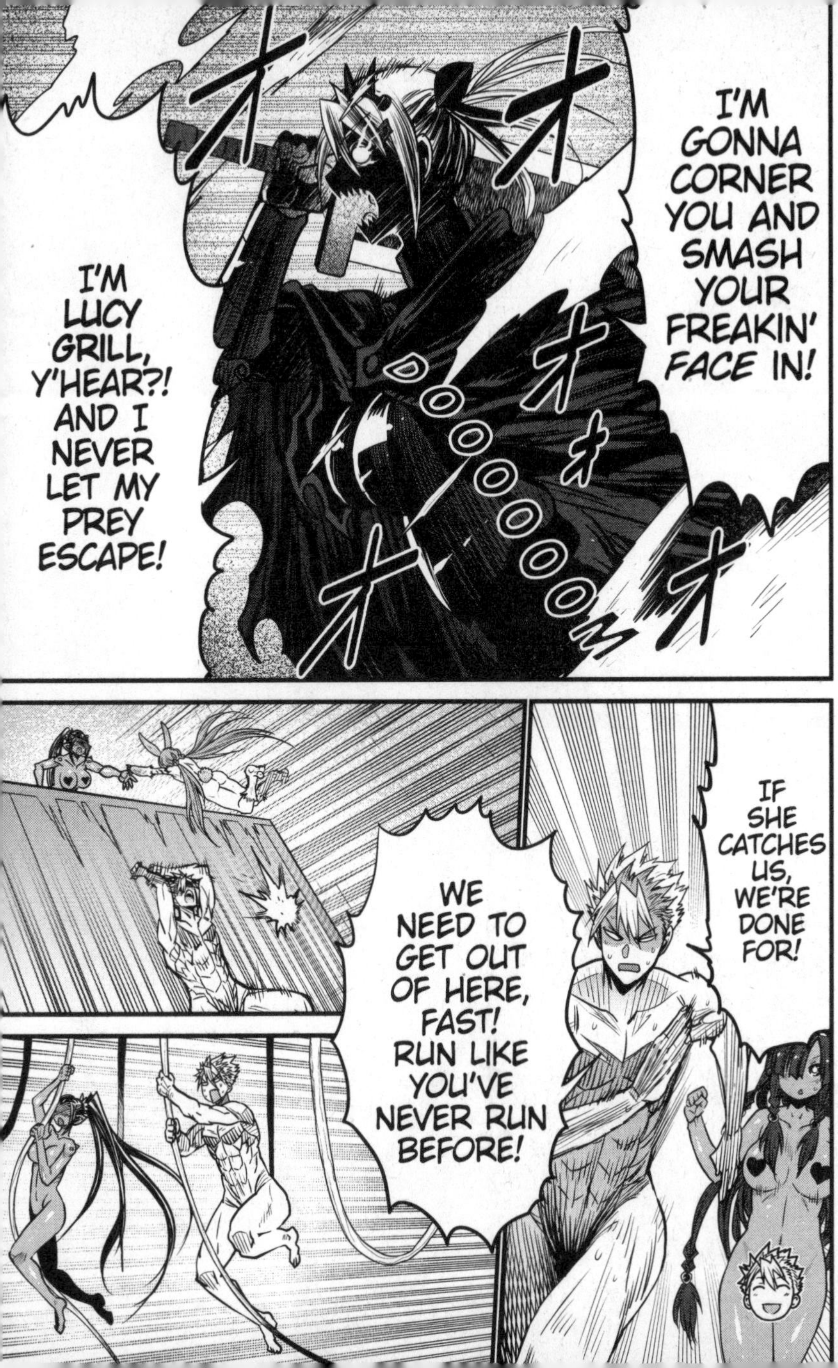
I'M GONNA CORNER YOU AND SMASH YOUR FREAKIN' FACE IN!
I'M LUCY GRILL, Y'HEAR?! AND I NEVER LET MY PREY ESCAPE!
DOOOOOOOOM
IF SHE CATCHES US, WE'RE DONE FOR!
WE NEED TO GET OUT OF HERE, FAST! RUN LIKE YOU'VE NEVER RUN BEFORE!

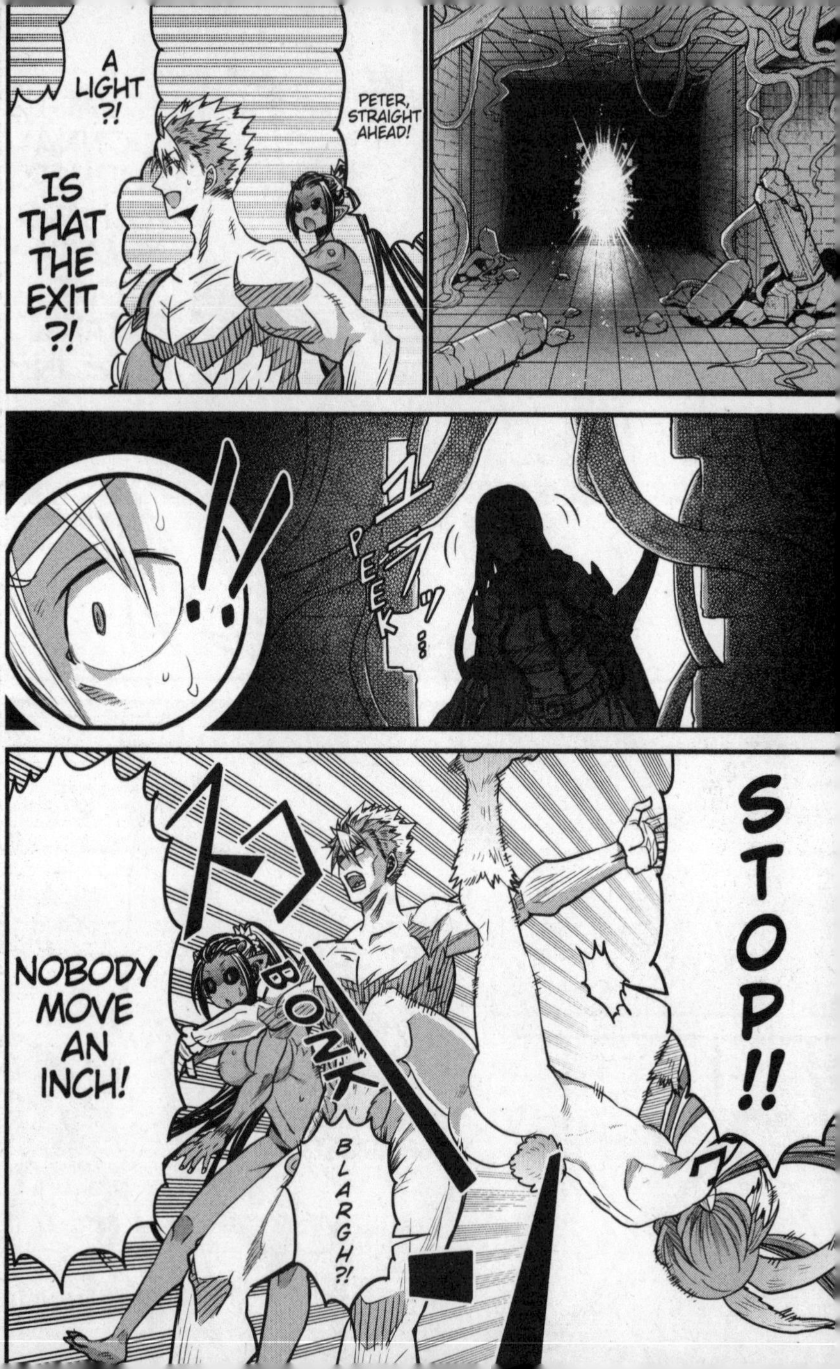
PETER, STRAIGHT AHEAD!
A LIGHT?!
IS THAT THE EXIT?!
PEEK
STOP!!
BONK
BLARGH?!
NOBODY MOVE AN INCH!

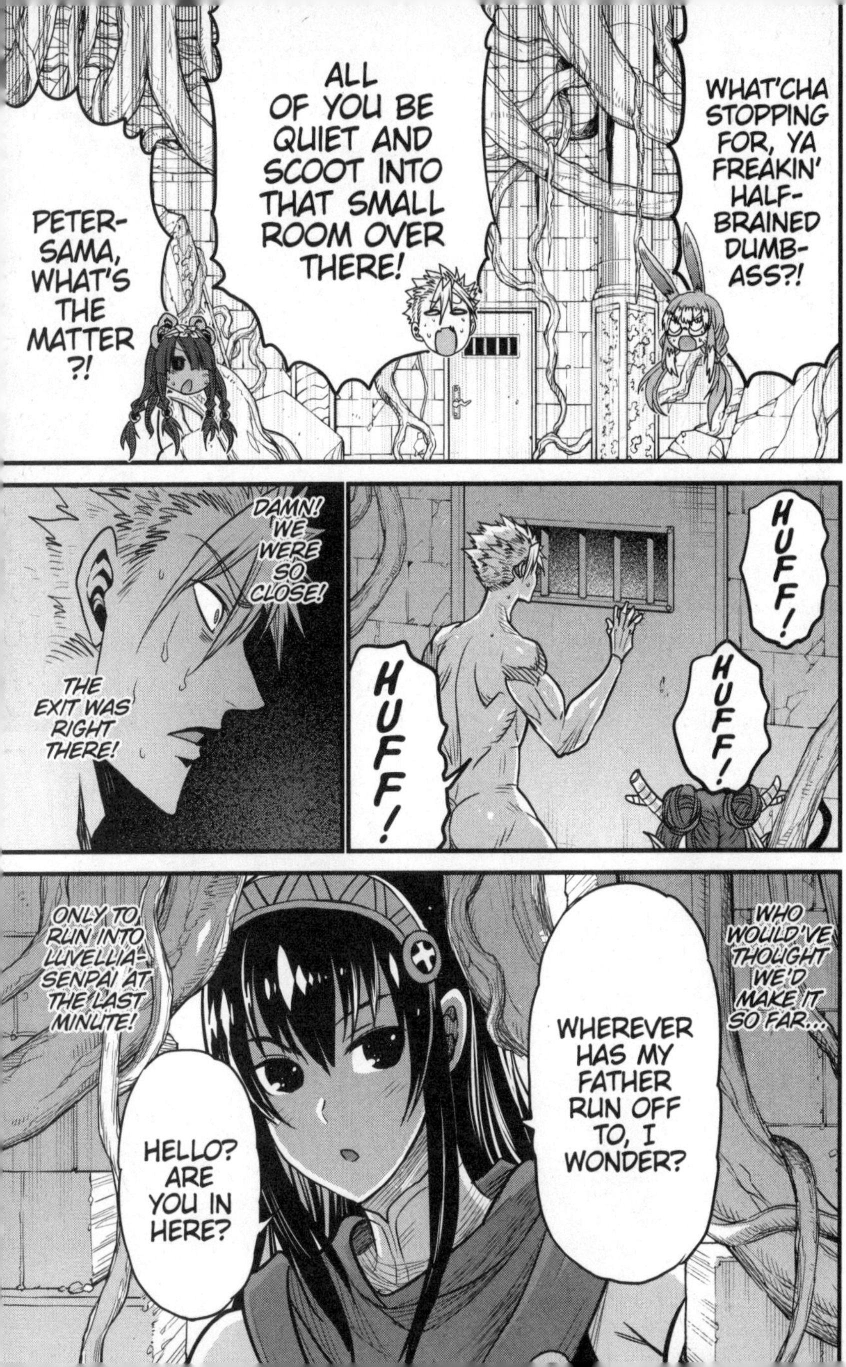
WHAT'CHA STOPPING FOR, YA FREAKIN' HALF-BRAINED DUMB-ASS?!
ALL OF YOU BE QUIET AND SCOOT INTO THAT SMALL ROOM OVER THERE!
PETER-SAMA, WHAT'S THE MATTER?!
HUFF!
HUFF!
HUFF!
DAMN! WE WERE SO CLOSE!
THE EXIT WAS RIGHT THERE!
WHO WOULD'VE THOUGHT WE'D MAKE IT SO FAR...
ONLY TO RUN INTO LUVELLIA-SENPAI AT THE LAST MINUTE!
WHEREVER HAS MY FATHER RUN OFF TO, I WONDER?
HELLO? ARE YOU IN HERE?

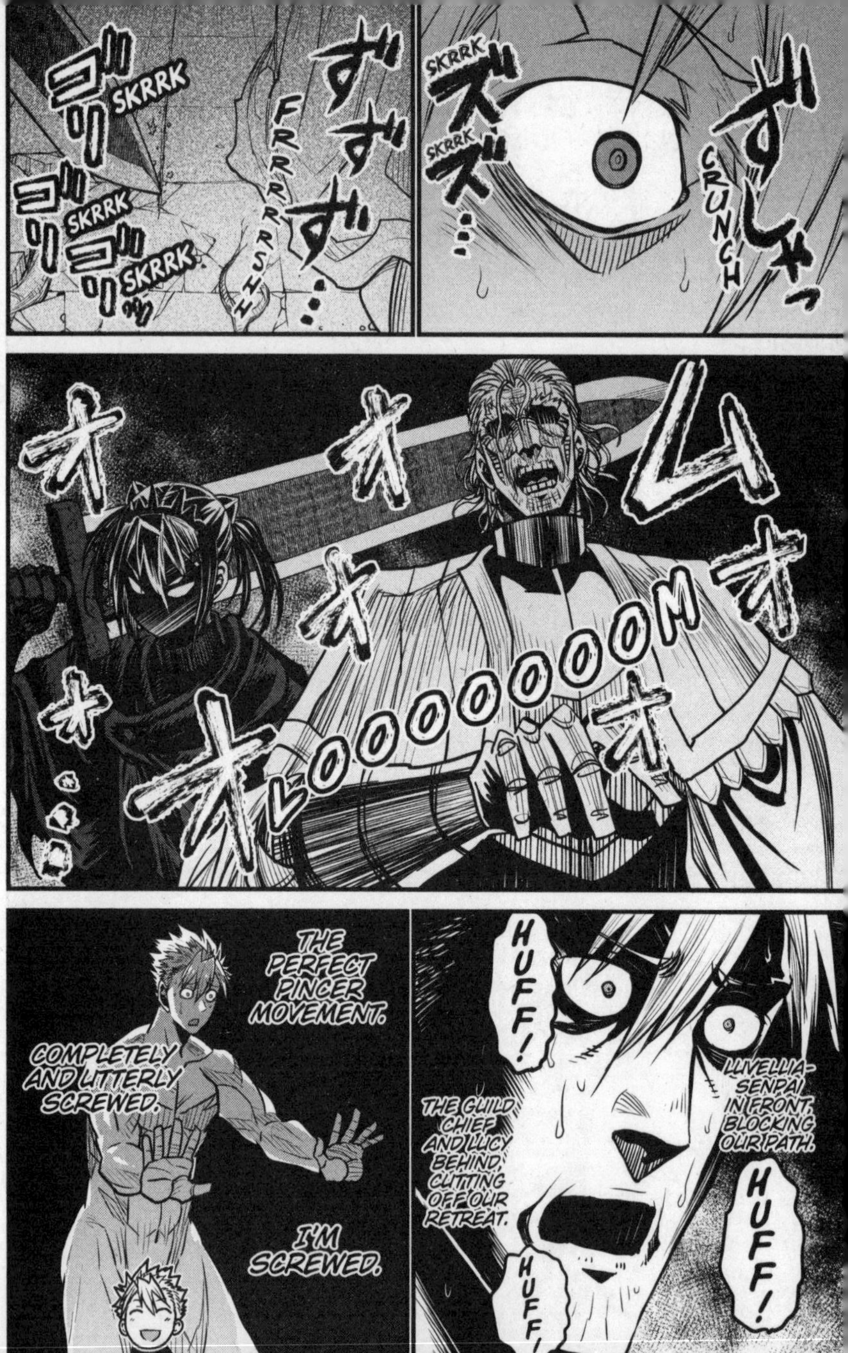
ずしゃっ
CRUNCH
ズズ…
SKRRK
SKRRK
ずずず…
FRRRRRSHH
SKRRK
SKRRK
SKRRK
SKRRK
LOOOOOOOOOM
HUFF!
LUVELLIA-SENPAI IN FRONT, BLOCKING OUR PATH.
THE GUILD CHIEF AND LUCY BEHIND, CUTTING OFF OUR RETREAT.
HUFF!
HUFF!
THE PERFECT PINCER MOVEMENT.
COMPLETELY AND UTTERLY SCREWED.
I'M SCREWED.

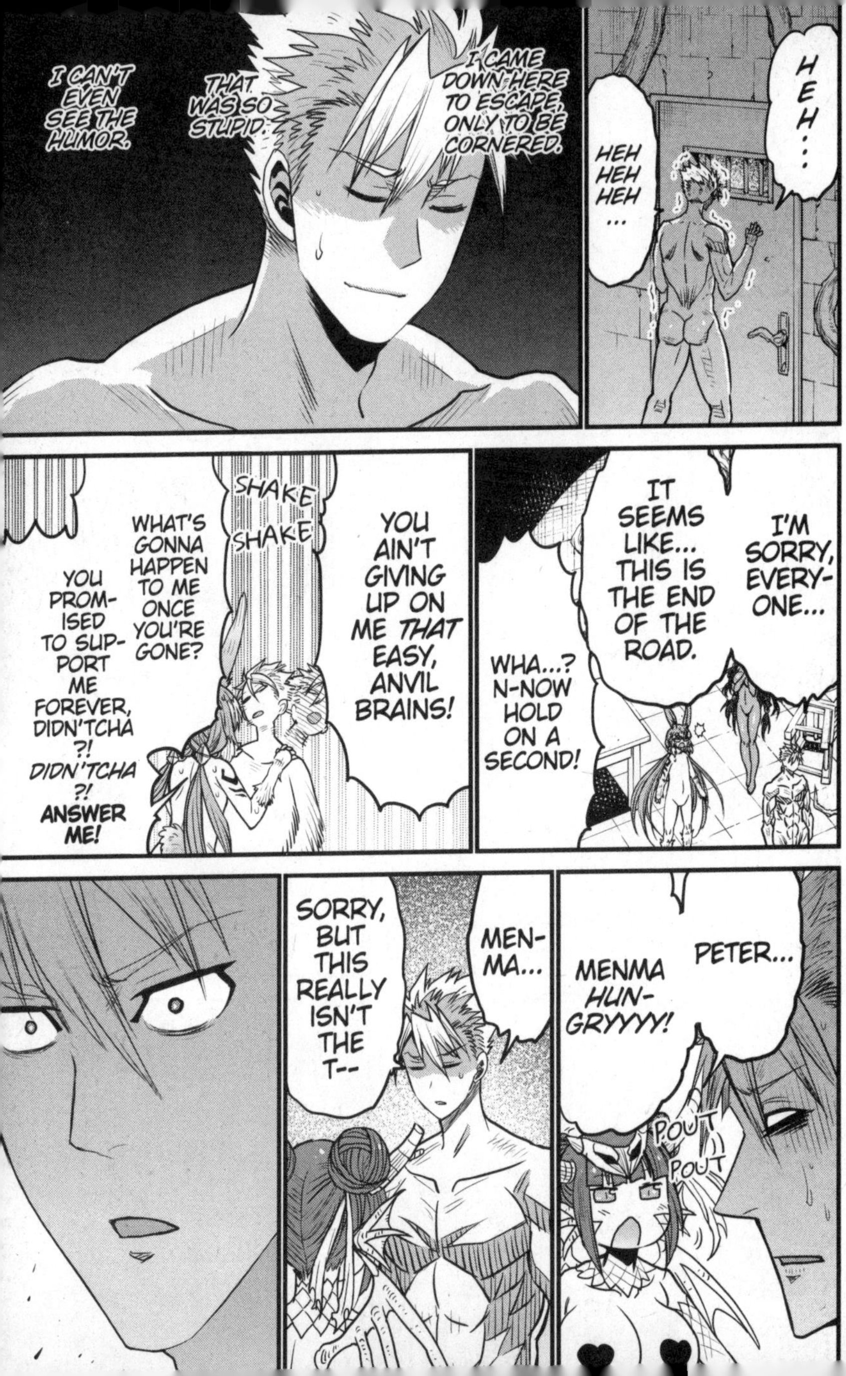
HEH...
HEH HEH HEH ...
I CAME DOWN HERE TO ESCAPE, ONLY TO BE CORNERED.
THAT WAS SO STUPID.
I CAN'T EVEN SEE THE HUMOR.
I'M SORRY, EVERYONE...
IT SEEMS LIKE... THIS IS THE END OF THE ROAD.
WHA...? N-NOW HOLD ON A SECOND!
YOU AIN'T GIVING UP ON ME *THAT* EASY, ANVIL BRAINS!
SHAKE SHAKE
WHAT'S GONNA HAPPEN TO ME ONCE YOU'RE GONE?
YOU PROMISED TO SUPPORT ME FOREVER, DIDN'TCHA?! DIDN'TCHA?! ANSWER ME!
PETER...
MENMA HUNGRYYYY!
POUT POUT
MENMA...
SORRY, BUT THIS REALLY ISN'T THE T--

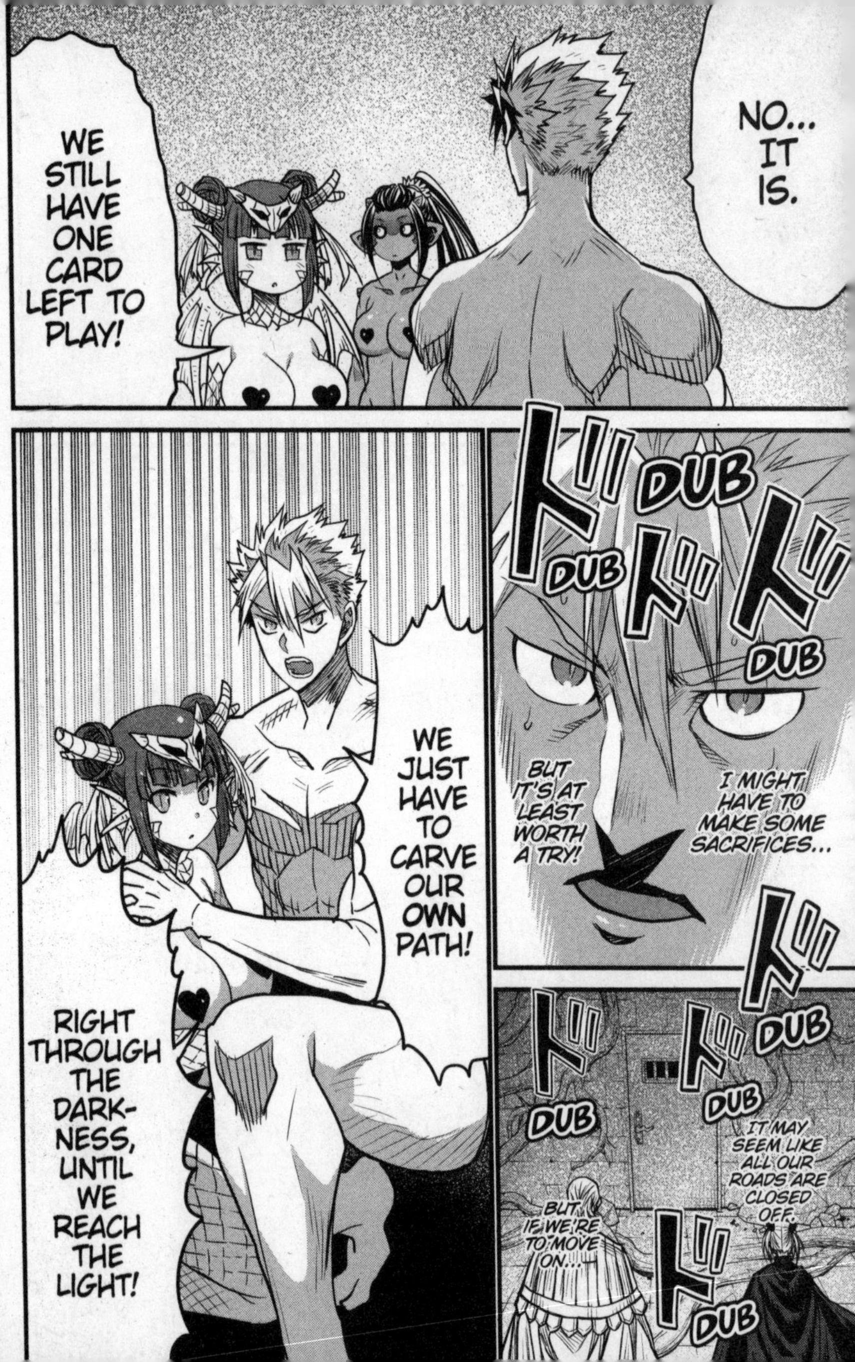
NO... IT IS.
WE STILL HAVE ONE CARD LEFT TO PLAY!
DUB
DUB
DUB
I MIGHT HAVE TO MAKE SOME SACRIFICES...
BUT IT'S AT LEAST WORTH A TRY!
DUB
DUB
DUB
IT MAY SEEM LIKE ALL OUR ROADS ARE CLOSED OFF.
BUT IF WE'RE TO MOVE ON...
DUB
WE JUST HAVE TO CARVE OUR OWN PATH!
RIGHT THROUGH THE DARKNESS, UNTIL WE REACH THE LIGHT!

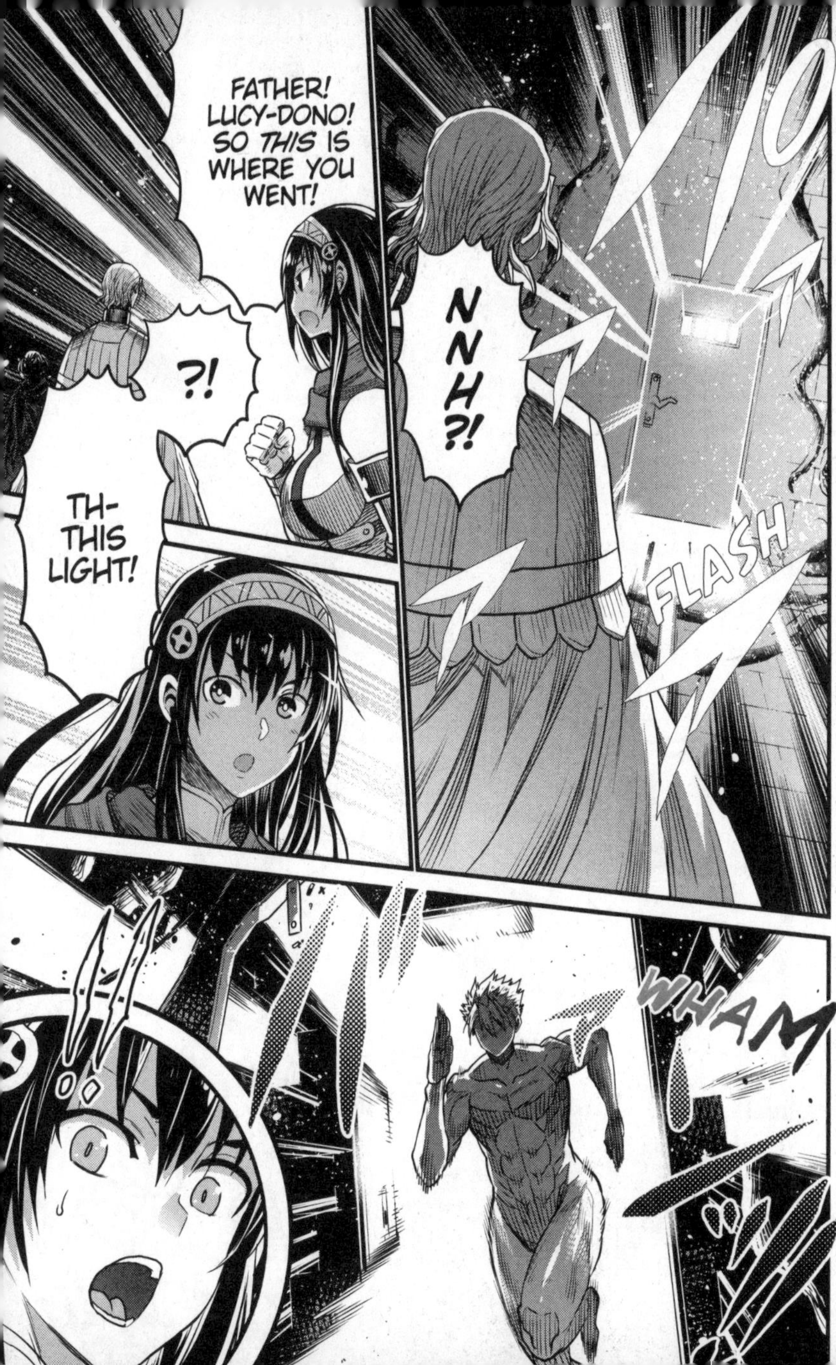
NNH?!
FLASH
FATHER! LUCY-DONO! SO THIS IS WHERE YOU WENT!
?!
TH- THIS LIGHT!
WHAM

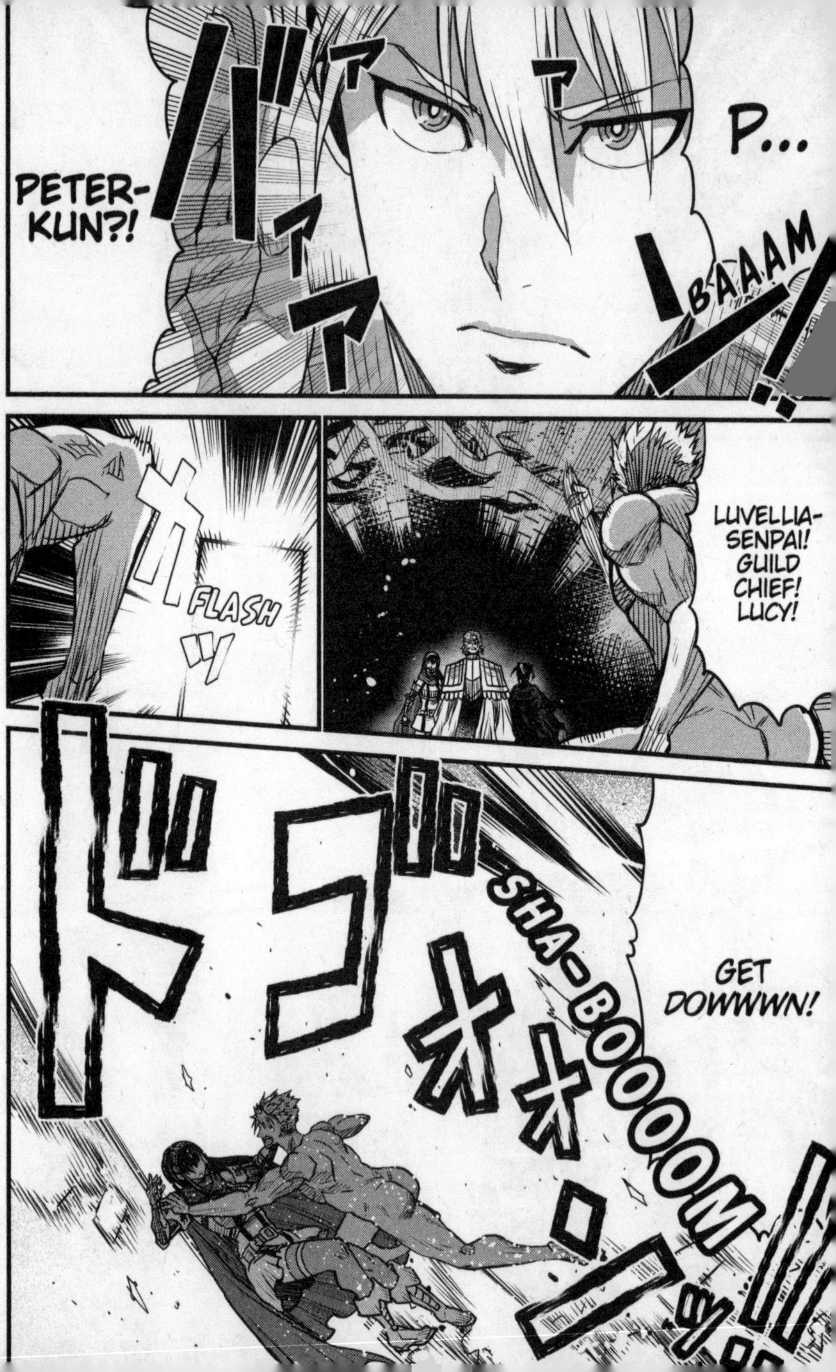
P...
BAAAM
PETER-KUN?!
LUVELLIA-SENPAI! GUILD CHIEF! LUCY!
FLASH
GET DOWWWN!
SHA-BOOOOOM

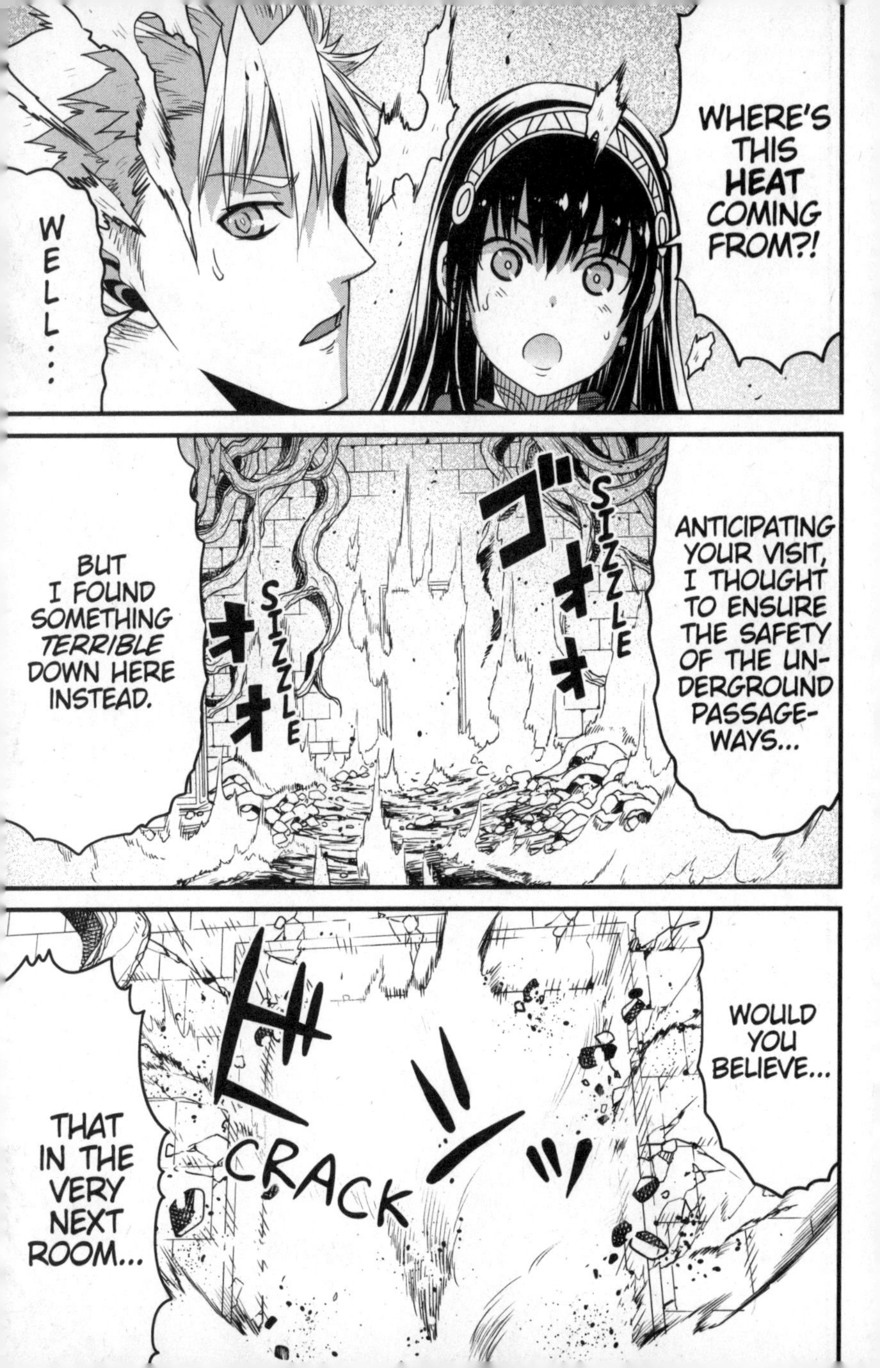
WHERE'S THIS HEAT COMING FROM?!
WELL...
ANTICIPATING YOUR VISIT, I THOUGHT TO ENSURE THE SAFETY OF THE UN-DERGROUND PASSAGE-WAYS...
SIZZLE
SIZZLE
BUT I FOUND SOMETHING *TERRIBLE* DOWN HERE INSTEAD.
WOULD YOU BELIEVE...
CRACK
THAT IN THE VERY NEXT ROOM...

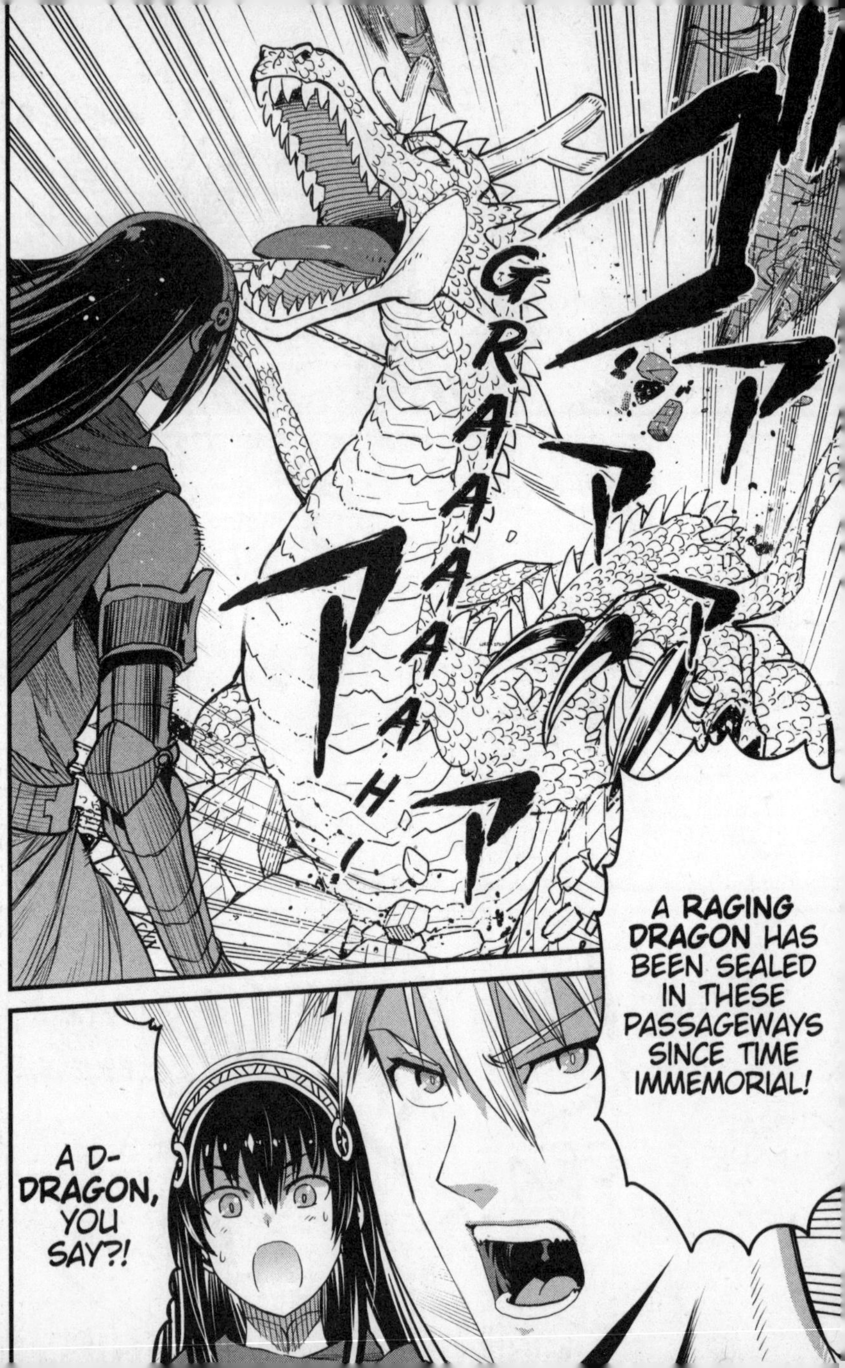
GRAAAAAAH!
A RAGING DRAGON HAS BEEN SEALED IN THESE PASSAGEWAYS SINCE TIME IMMEMORIAL!
A D-DRAGON, YOU SAY?!

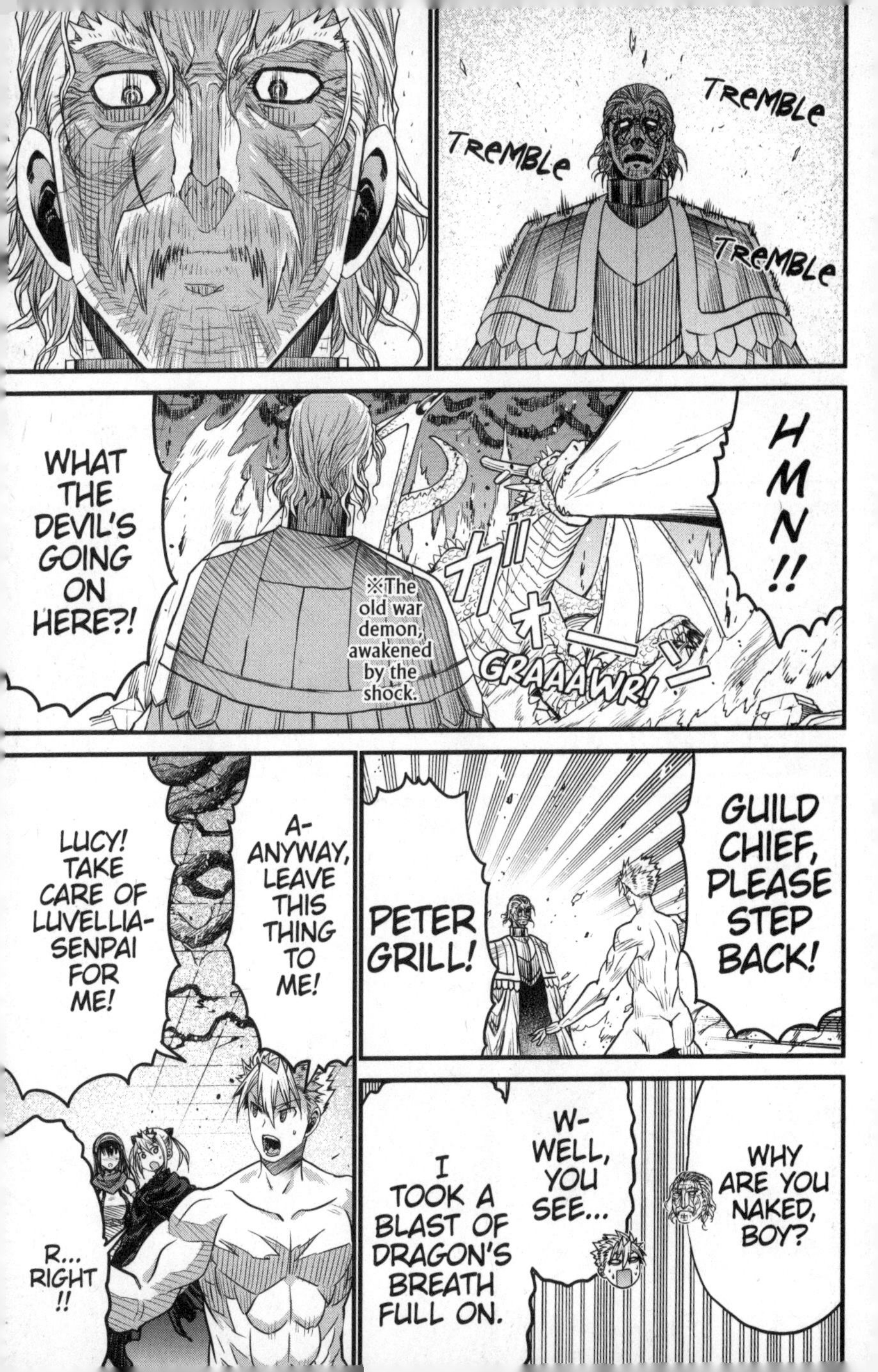

TREMBLE
TREMBLE
TREMBLE
HMN!!
ガオー
GRAAAWR!
※The old war demon, awakened by the shock.
WHAT THE DEVIL'S GOING ON HERE?!
GUILD CHIEF, PLEASE STEP BACK!
PETER GRILL!
WHY ARE YOU NAKED, BOY?
W-WELL, YOU SEE...
I TOOK A BLAST OF DRAGON'S BREATH FULL ON.
A-ANYWAY, LEAVE THIS THING TO ME!
LUCY! TAKE CARE OF LUVELLIA-SENPAI FOR ME!
R... RIGHT!!

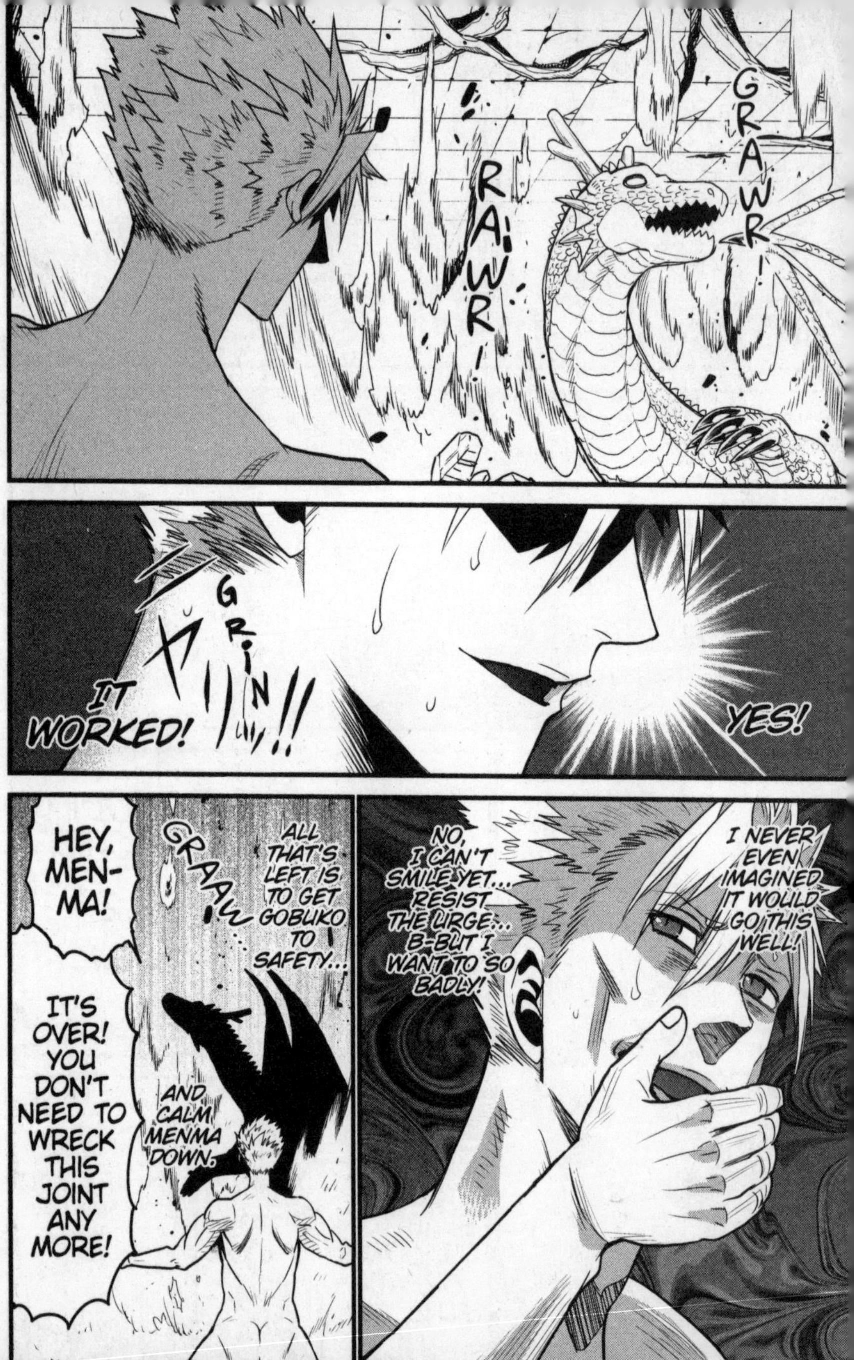
GRAWR!
RAWR!
YES!
GRIN!!
IT WORKED!
I NEVER EVEN IMAGINED IT WOULD GO THIS WELL!
NO, I CAN'T SMILE YET... RESIST THE URGE... B-BUT I WANT TO SO BADLY!
ALL THAT'S LEFT IS TO GET GOBUKO TO SAFETY...
AND CALM MENMA DOWN.
GRAAAW...
HEY, MENMA!
IT'S OVER! YOU DON'T NEED TO WRECK THIS JOINT ANY MORE!

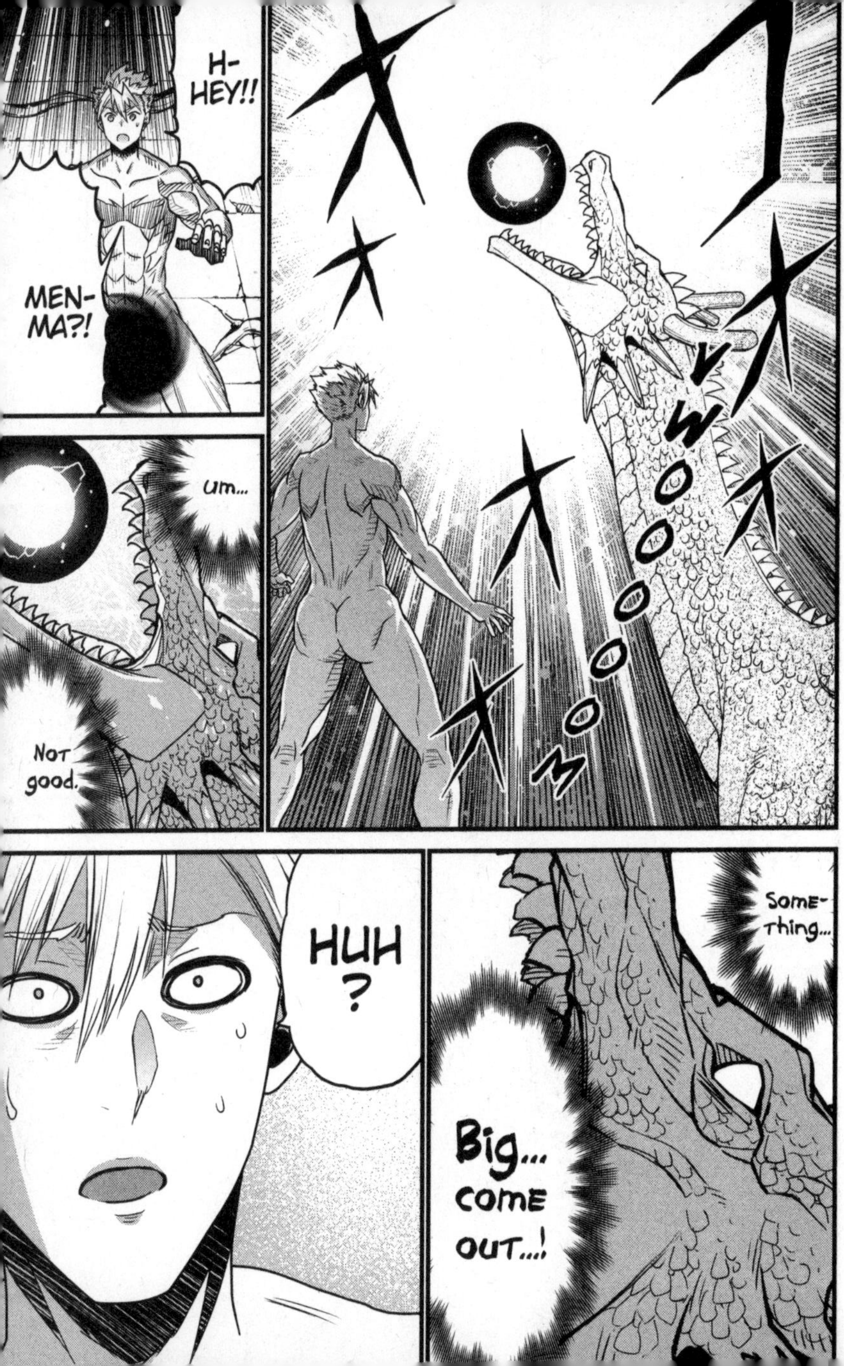
VWOOOOOOM
H-HEY!!
MEN-MA?!
um...
Not good.
Some-thing...
Big... come out...!
HUH?

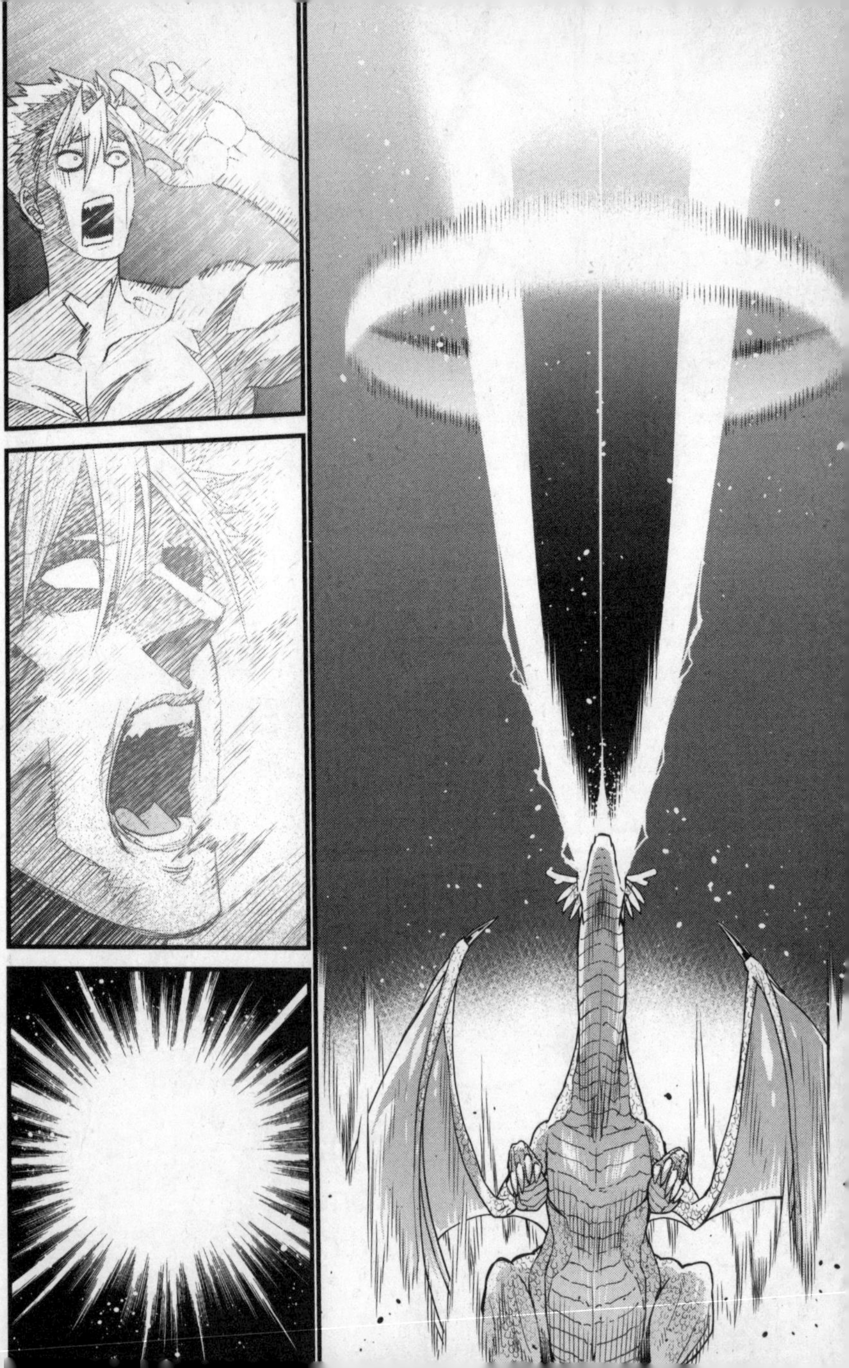

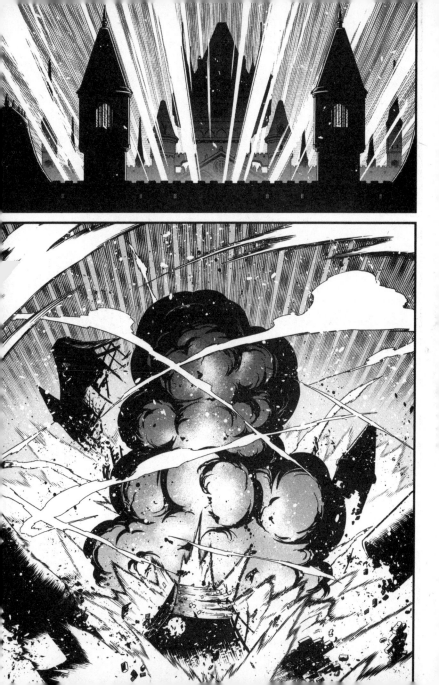

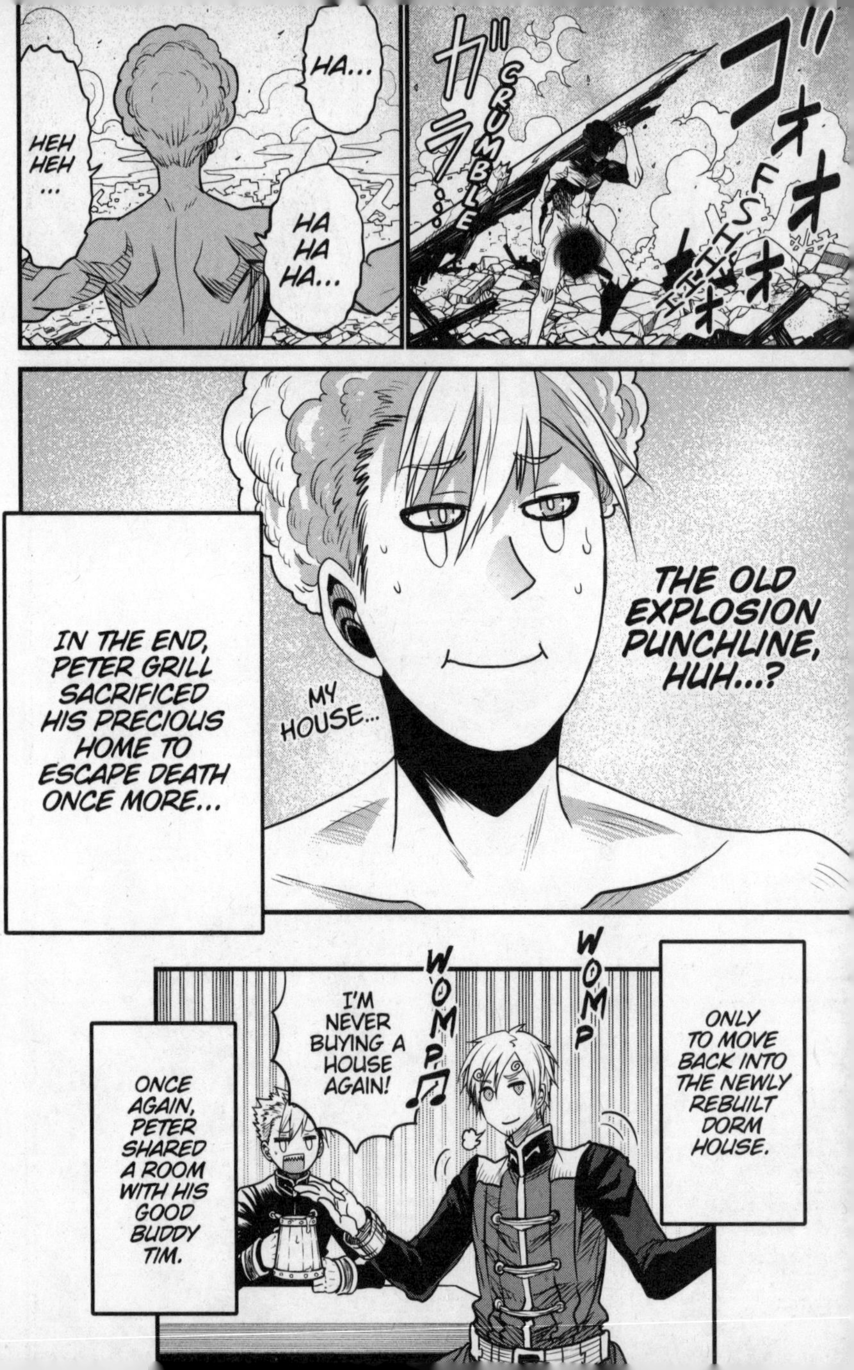
ゴォオオ
FSHHH
ガラ
CRUMBLE
HA...
HEH HEH...
HA HA HA...
THE OLD EXPLOSION PUNCHLINE, HUH...?
MY HOUSE...
IN THE END, PETER GRILL SACRIFICED HIS PRECIOUS HOME TO ESCAPE DEATH ONCE MORE...
ONLY TO MOVE BACK INTO THE NEWLY REBUILT DORM HOUSE.
WOMP
WOMP
I'M NEVER BUYING A HOUSE AGAIN!
ONCE AGAIN, PETER SHARED A ROOM WITH HIS GOOD BUDDY TIM.

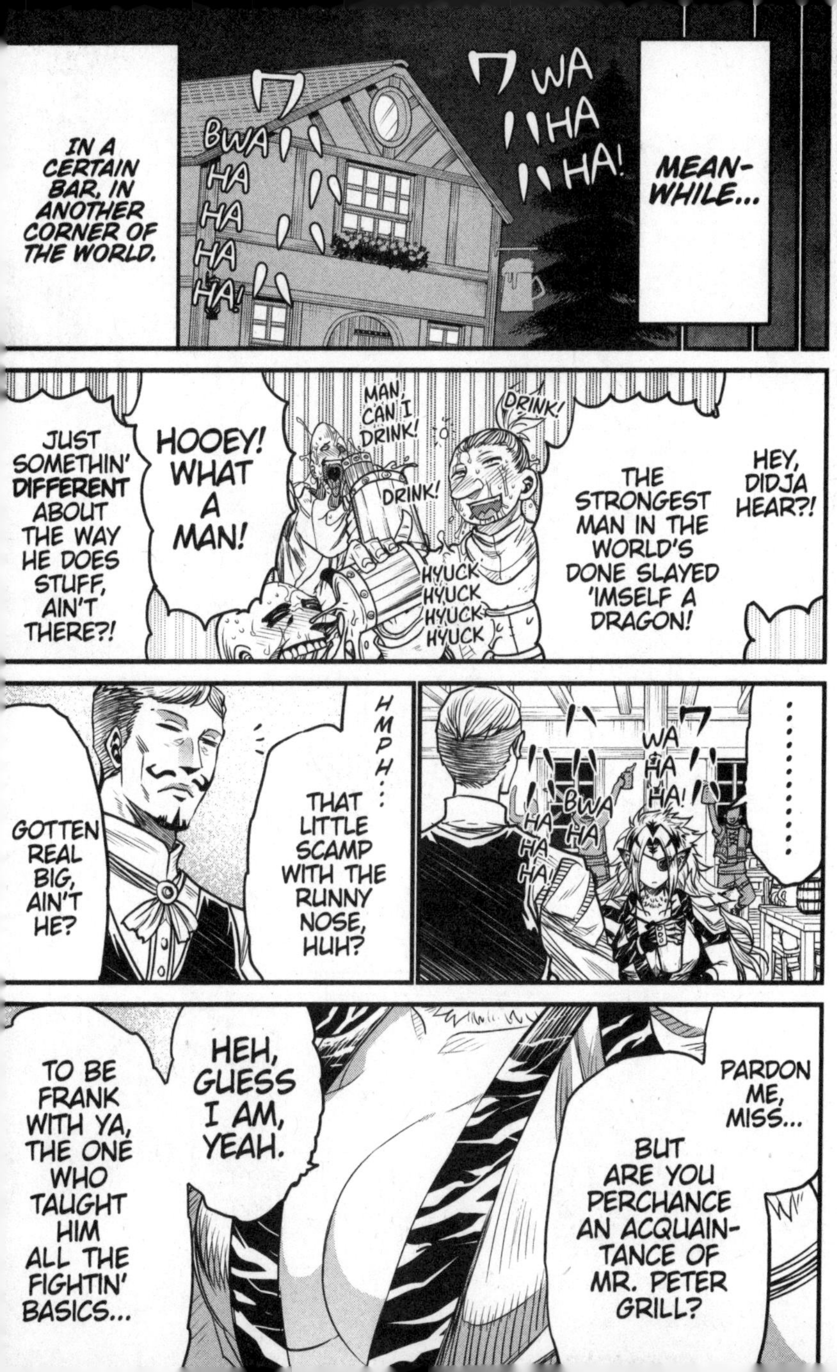
MEANWHILE...
WA HA HA!
BWA HA HA HA HA!
IN A CERTAIN BAR, IN ANOTHER CORNER OF THE WORLD.
HEY, DIDJA HEAR?!
THE STRONGEST MAN IN THE WORLD'S DONE SLAYED 'IMSELF A DRAGON!
DRINK!
DRINK!
MAN, CAN I DRINK!
HYUCK HYUCK HYUCK HYUCK
HOOEY! WHAT A MAN!
JUST SOMETHIN' DIFFERENT ABOUT THE WAY HE DOES STUFF, AIN'T THERE?!
......
WA HA HA!
BWA HA HA HA HA!
HMPH...
THAT LITTLE SCAMP WITH THE RUNNY NOSE, HUH?
GOTTEN REAL BIG, AIN'T HE?
PARDON ME, MISS...
BUT ARE YOU PERCHANCE AN ACQUAINTANCE OF MR. PETER GRILL?
HEH, GUESS I AM, YEAH.
TO BE FRANK WITH YA, THE ONE WHO TAUGHT HIM ALL THE FIGHTIN' BASICS...

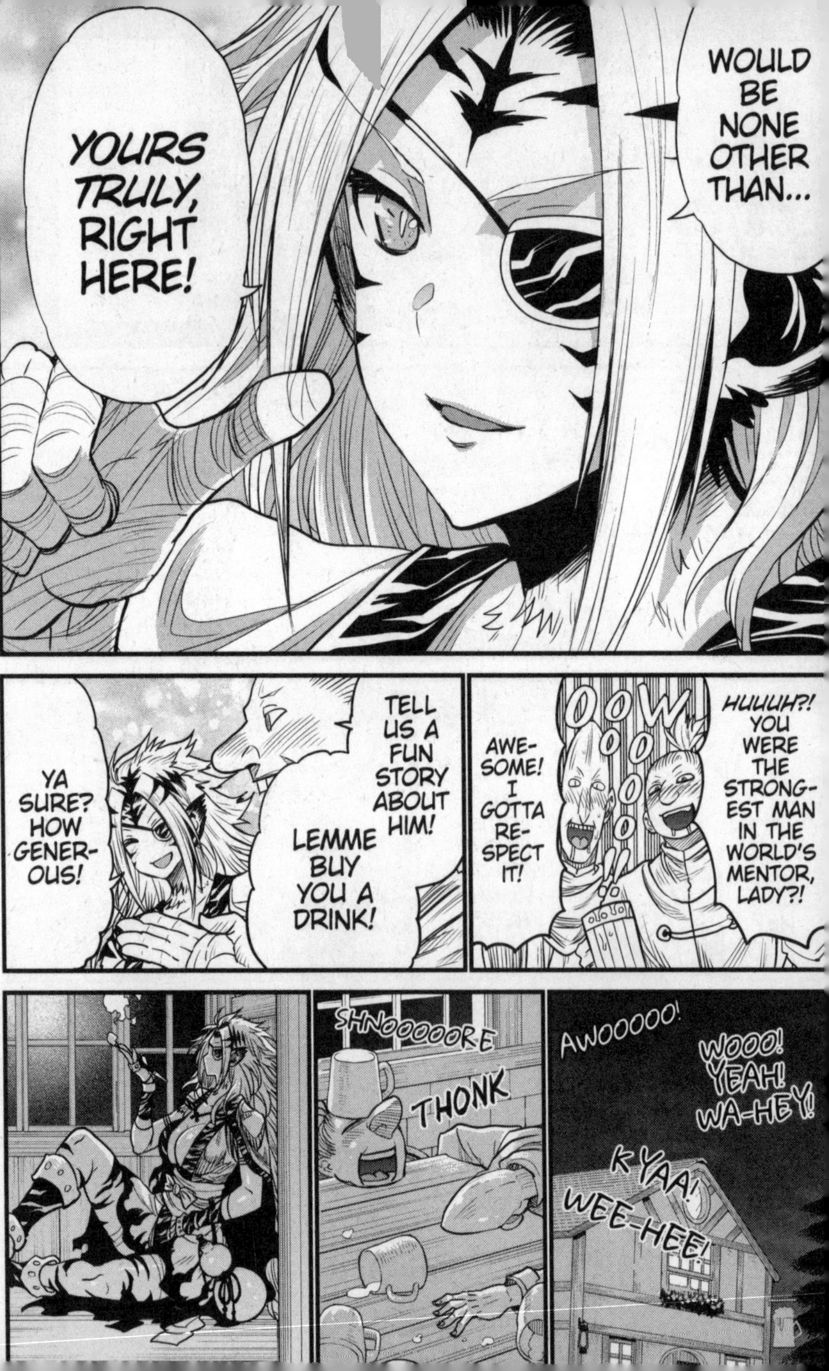
WOULD BE NONE OTHER THAN...
YOURS TRULY, RIGHT HERE!
HUUUH?! YOU WERE THE STRONG-EST MAN IN THE WORLD'S MENTOR, LADY?!
OOWOOOOO
AWE-SOME! I GOTTA RE-SPECT IT!
TELL US A FUN STORY ABOUT HIM!
LEMME BUY YOU A DRINK!
YA SURE? HOW GENER-OUS!
AWOOOOO!
WOOO! YEAH! WA-HEY!
KYAA! WEE-HEE!
SHNOOOOORE
THONK

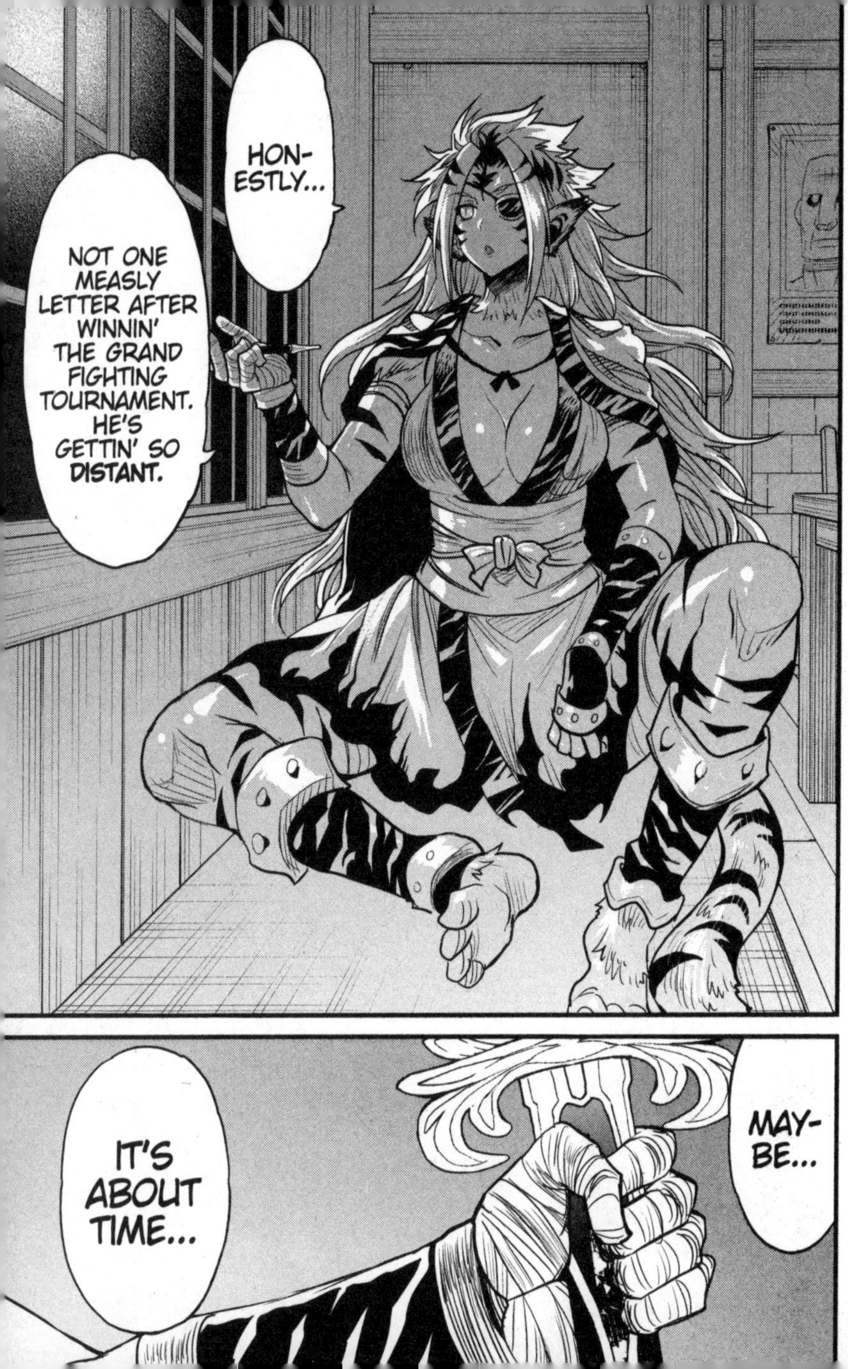
HON-ESTLY...
NOT ONE MEASLY LETTER AFTER WINNIN' THE GRAND FIGHTING TOURNAMENT. HE'S GETTIN' SO DISTANT.
MAY-BE...
IT'S ABOUT TIME...

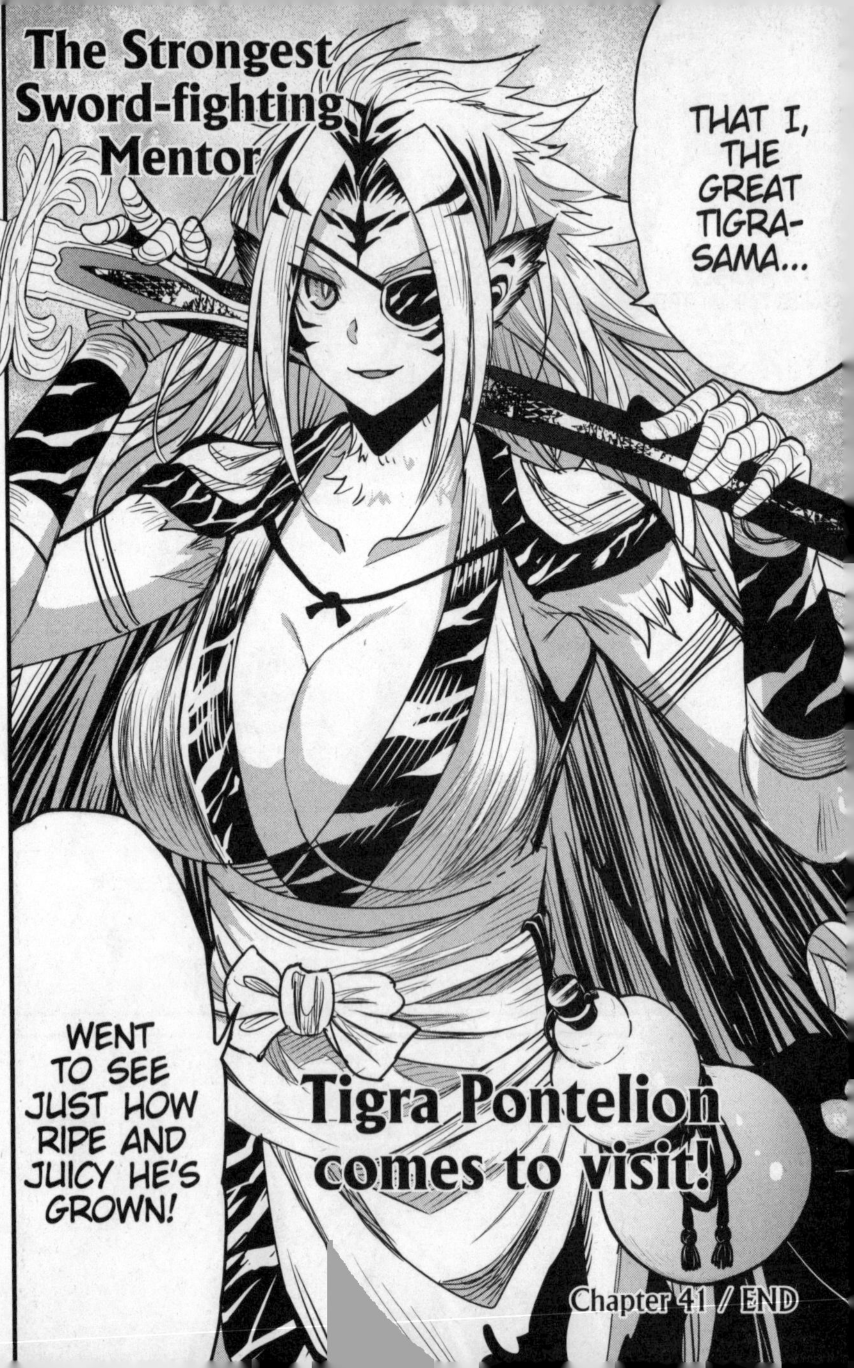
THAT I, THE GREAT TIGRA-SAMA...
The Strongest Sword-fighting Mentor
WENT TO SEE JUST HOW RIPE AND JUICY HE'S GROWN!
Tigra Pontelion comes to visit!
Chapter 41 / END

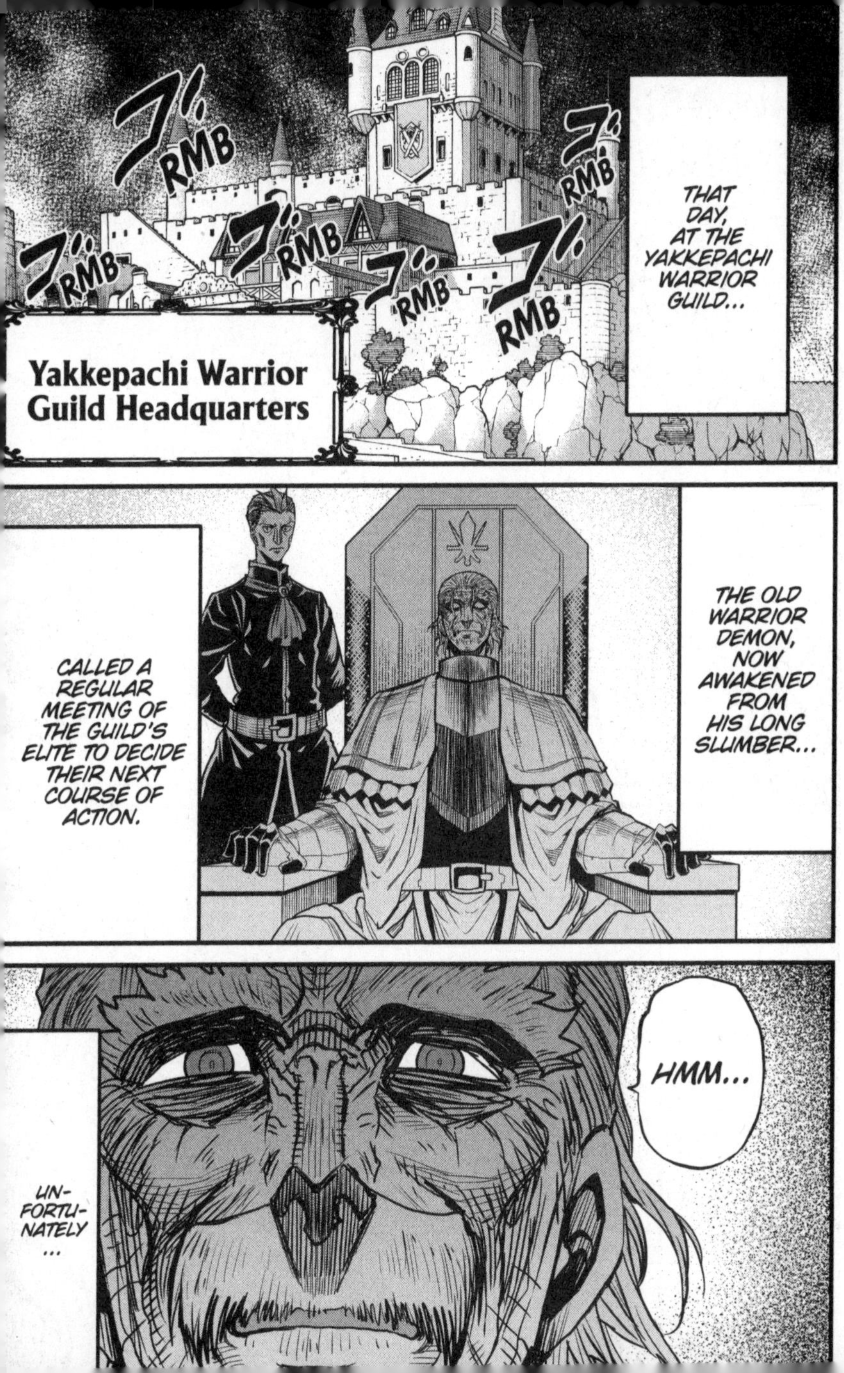
THAT DAY, AT THE YAKKEPACHI WARRIOR GUILD...
RMB RMB RMB RMB RMB RMB RMB
Yakkepachi Warrior Guild Headquarters
THE OLD WARRIOR DEMON, NOW AWAKENED FROM HIS LONG SLUMBER...
CALLED A REGULAR MEETING OF THE GUILD'S ELITE TO DECIDE THEIR NEXT COURSE OF ACTION.
HMM...
UN-FORTU-NATELY...

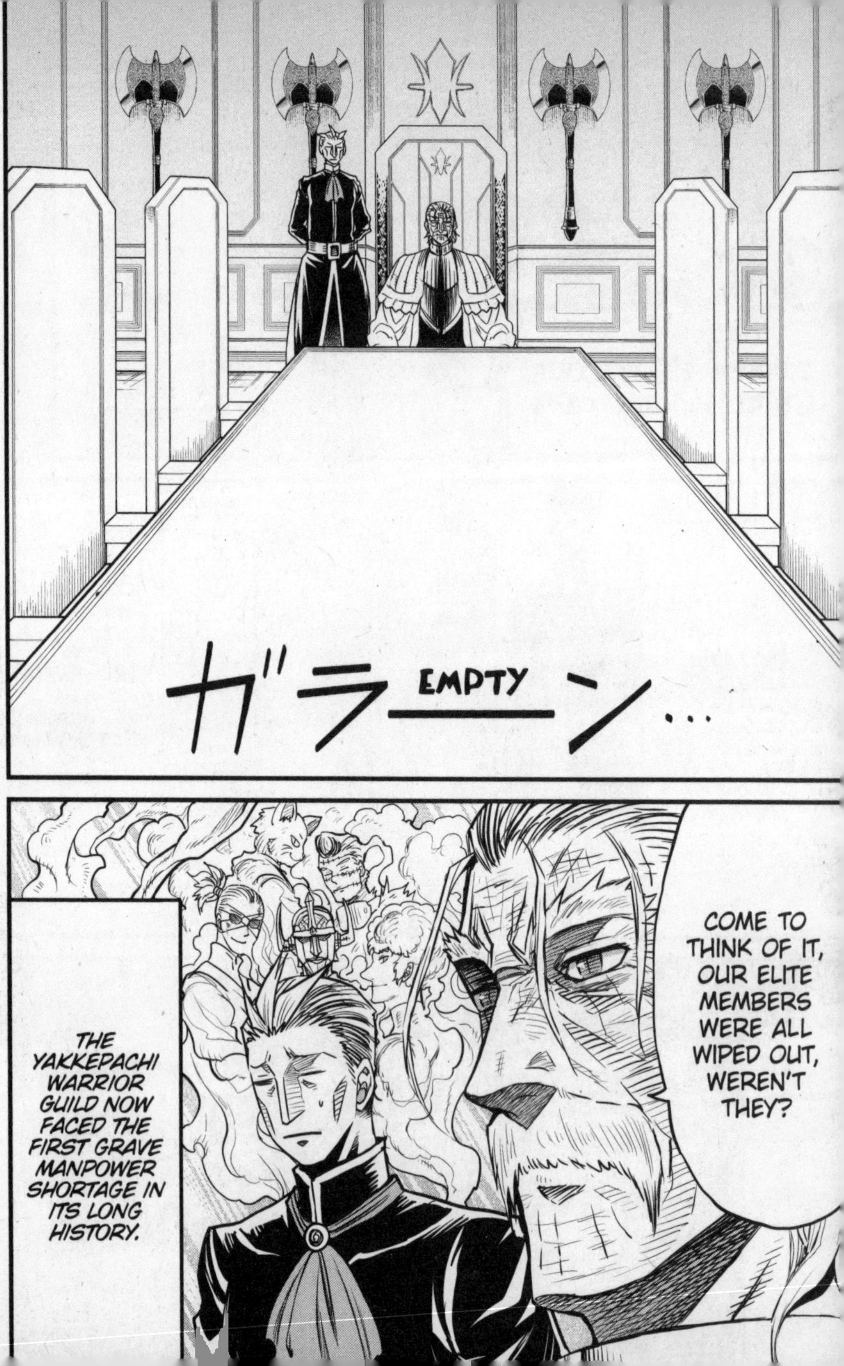
ガラーーン…
EMPTY
COME TO THINK OF IT, OUR ELITE MEMBERS WERE ALL WIPED OUT, WEREN'T THEY?
THE YAKKEPACHI WARRIOR GUILD NOW FACED THE FIRST GRAVE MANPOWER SHORTAGE IN ITS LONG HISTORY.

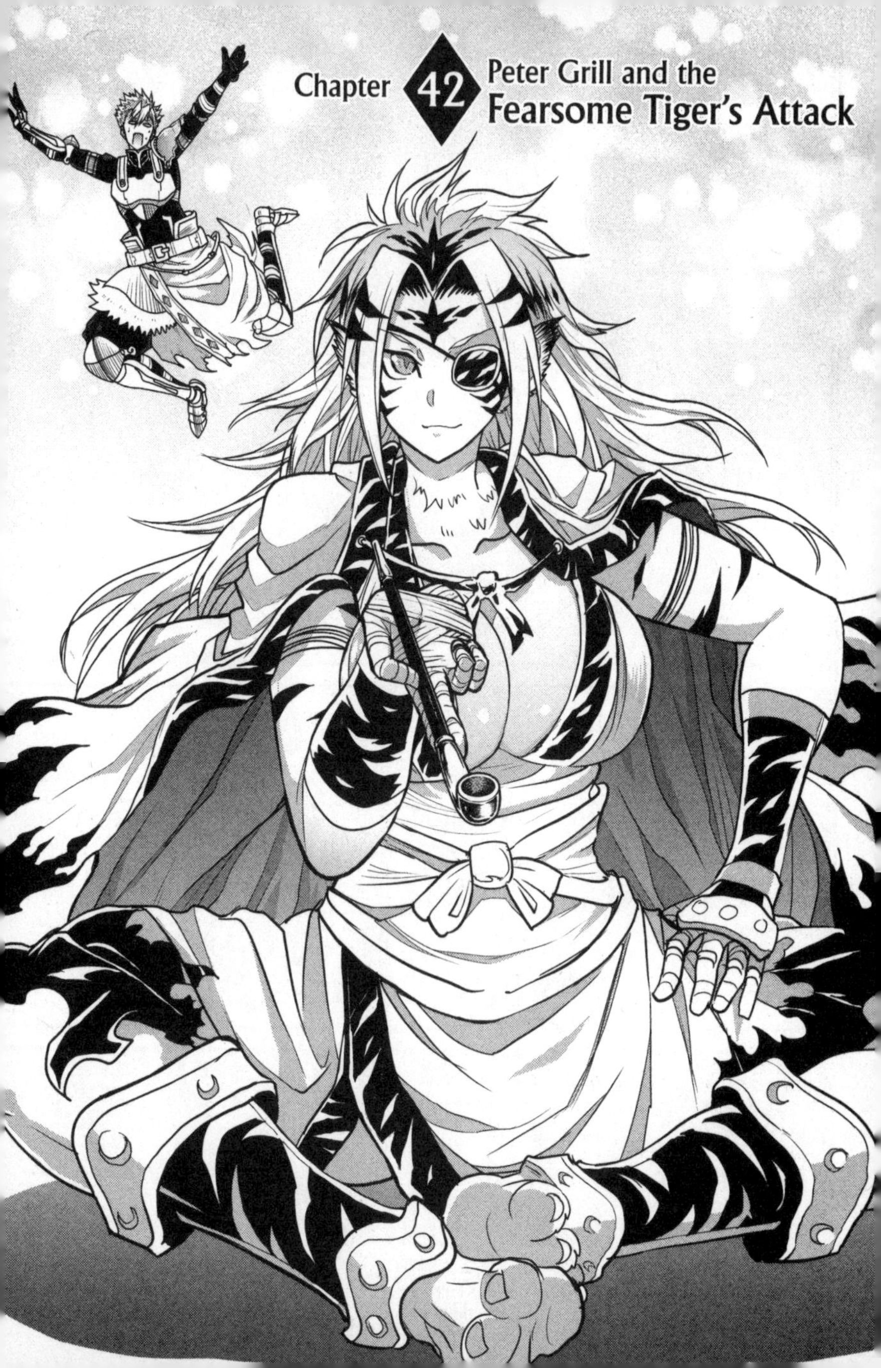
Chapter 42
Peter Grill and the
Fearsome Tiger's Attack

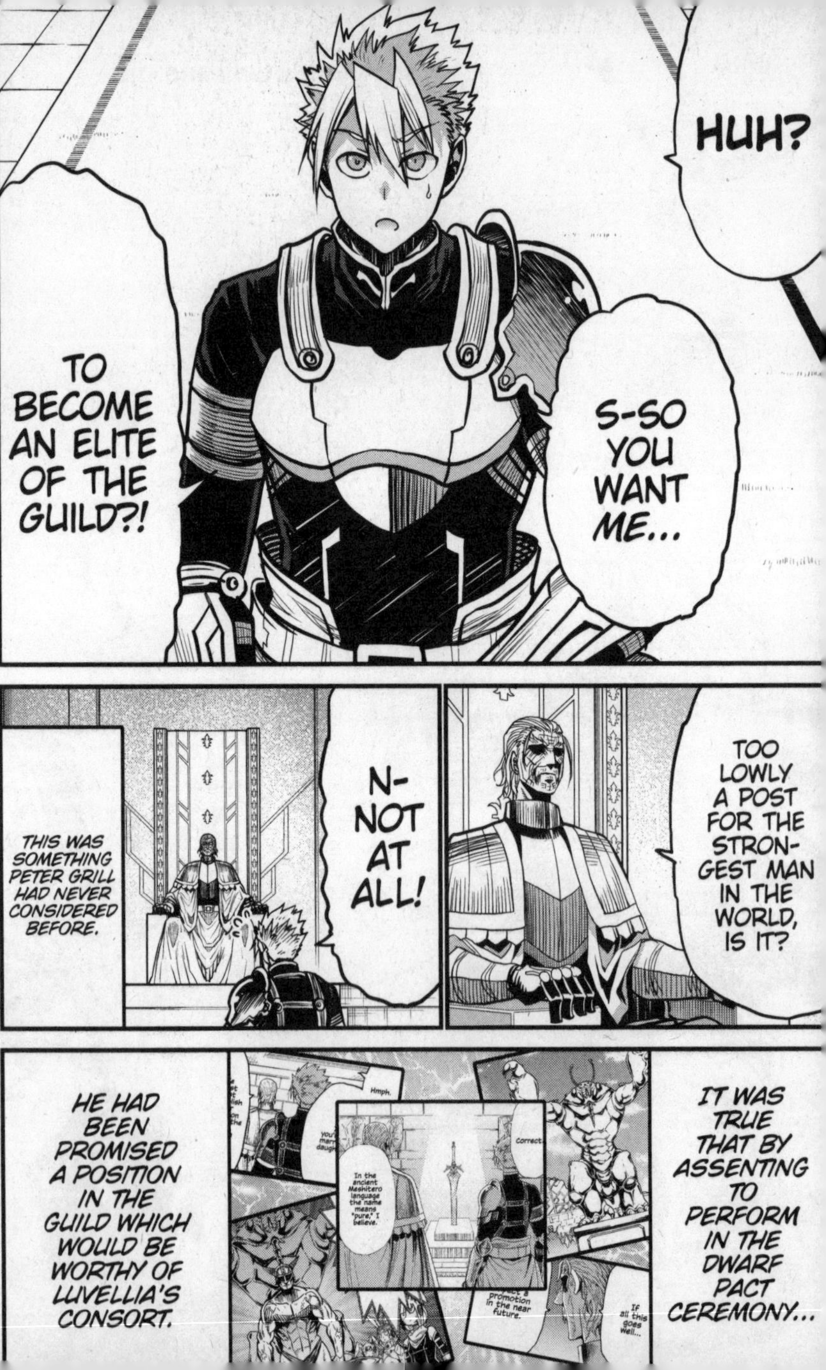
HUH?
S-SO YOU WANT ME...
TO BECOME AN ELITE OF THE GUILD?!
TOO LOWLY A POST FOR THE STRONG-GEST MAN IN THE WORLD, IS IT?
N-NOT AT ALL!
THIS WAS SOMETHING PETER GRILL HAD NEVER CONSIDERED BEFORE.
IT WAS TRUE THAT BY ASSENTING TO PERFORM IN THE DWARF PACT CEREMONY...
If all this goes well...
promotion in the near future.
Correct.
In the ancient Meshitero language the name means "pure," I believe.
Hmph.
HE HAD BEEN PROMISED A POSITION IN THE GUILD WHICH WOULD BE WORTHY OF LUVELLIA'S CONSORT.

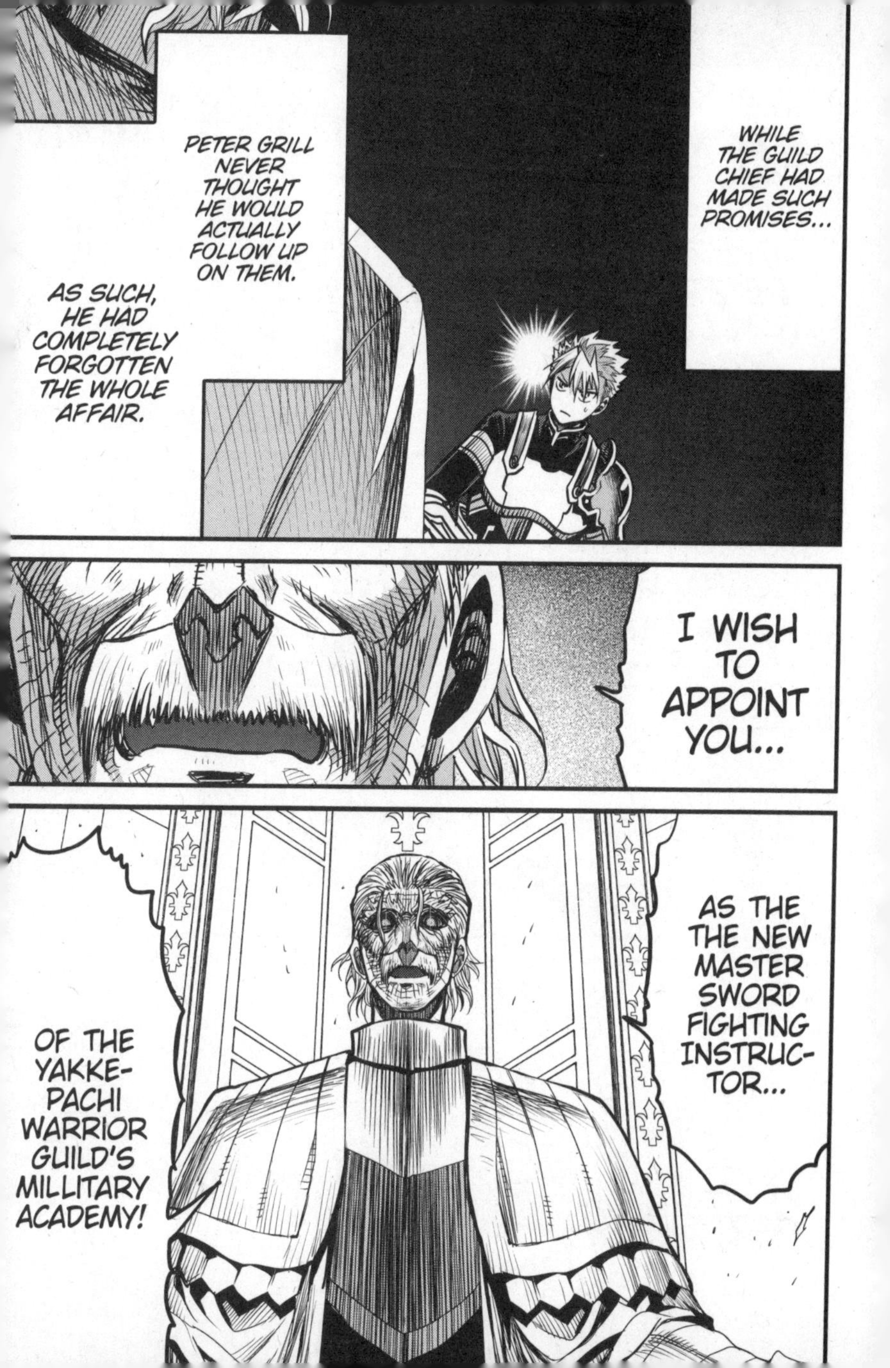
WHILE THE GUILD CHIEF HAD MADE SUCH PROMISES...
PETER GRILL NEVER THOUGHT HE WOULD ACTUALLY FOLLOW UP ON THEM.
AS SUCH, HE HAD COMPLETELY FORGOTTEN THE WHOLE AFFAIR.
I WISH TO APPOINT YOU...
AS THE THE NEW MASTER SWORD FIGHTING INSTRUC-TOR...
OF THE YAKKE-PACHI WARRIOR GUILD'S MILLITARY ACADEMY!

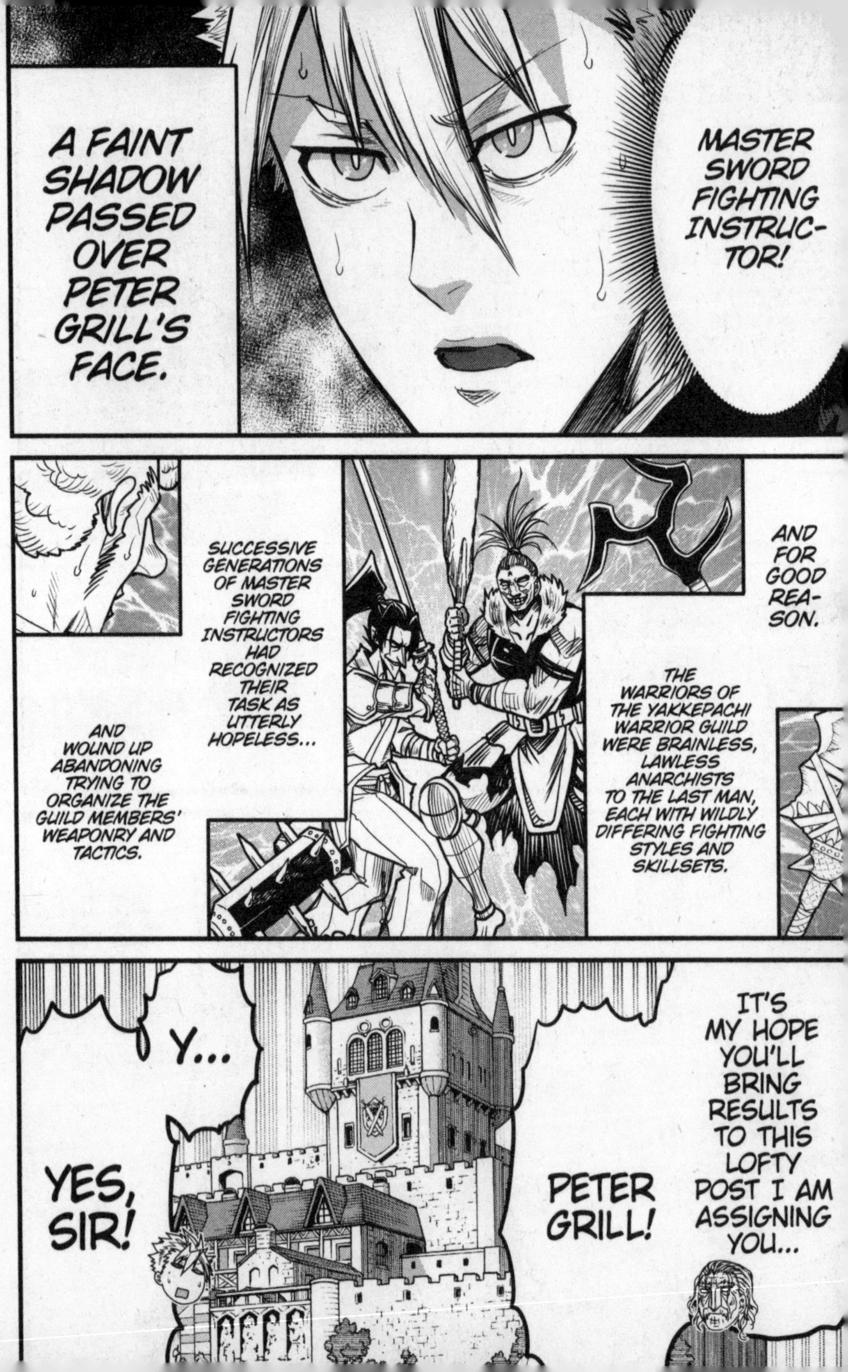
MASTER SWORD FIGHTING INSTRUCTOR!
A FAINT SHADOW PASSED OVER PETER GRILL'S FACE.
AND FOR GOOD REASON.
THE WARRIORS OF THE YAKKEPACHI WARRIOR GUILD WERE BRAINLESS, LAWLESS ANARCHISTS TO THE LAST MAN, EACH WITH WILDLY DIFFERING FIGHTING STYLES AND SKILLSETS.
SUCCESSIVE GENERATIONS OF MASTER SWORD FIGHTING INSTRUCTORS HAD RECOGNIZED THEIR TASK AS UTTERLY HOPELESS...
AND WOUND UP ABANDONING TRYING TO ORGANIZE THE GUILD MEMBERS' WEAPONRY AND TACTICS.
IT'S MY HOPE YOU'LL BRING RESULTS TO THIS LOFTY POST I AM ASSIGNING YOU...
PETER GRILL!
Y...
YES, SIR!

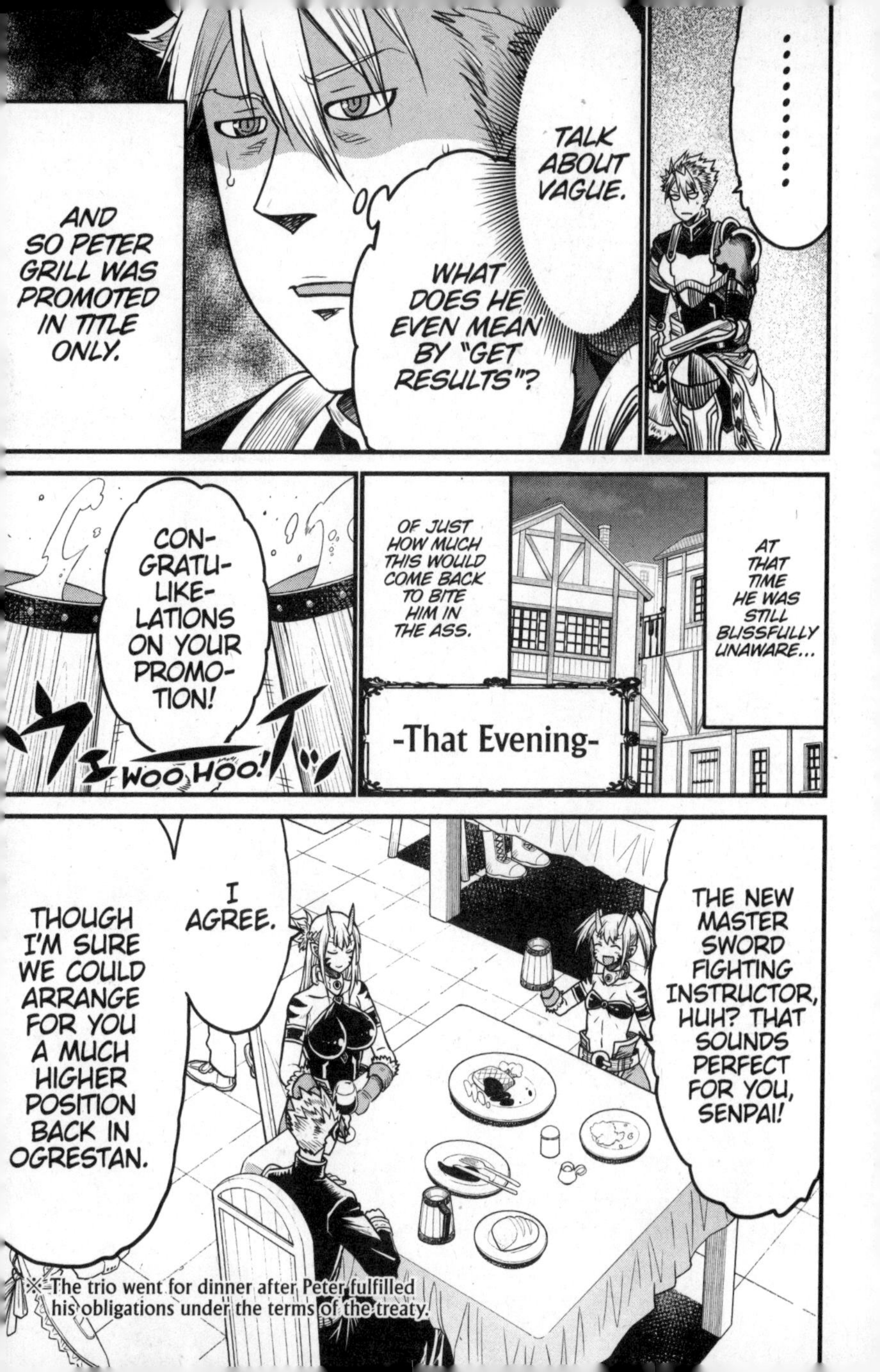
......
TALK ABOUT VAGUE.
WHAT DOES HE EVEN MEAN BY "GET RESULTS"?
AND SO PETER GRILL WAS PROMOTED IN TITLE ONLY.
AT THAT TIME HE WAS STILL BLISSFULLY UNAWARE...
OF JUST HOW MUCH THIS WOULD COME BACK TO BITE HIM IN THE ASS.
-That Evening-
CONGRATULIKELATIONS ON YOUR PROMOTION!
WOO HOO!
THE NEW MASTER SWORD FIGHTING INSTRUCTOR, HUH? THAT SOUNDS PERFECT FOR YOU, SENPAI!
I AGREE.
THOUGH I'M SURE WE COULD ARRANGE FOR YOU A MUCH HIGHER POSITION BACK IN OGRESTAN.
※The trio went for dinner after Peter fulfilled his obligations under the terms of the treaty.

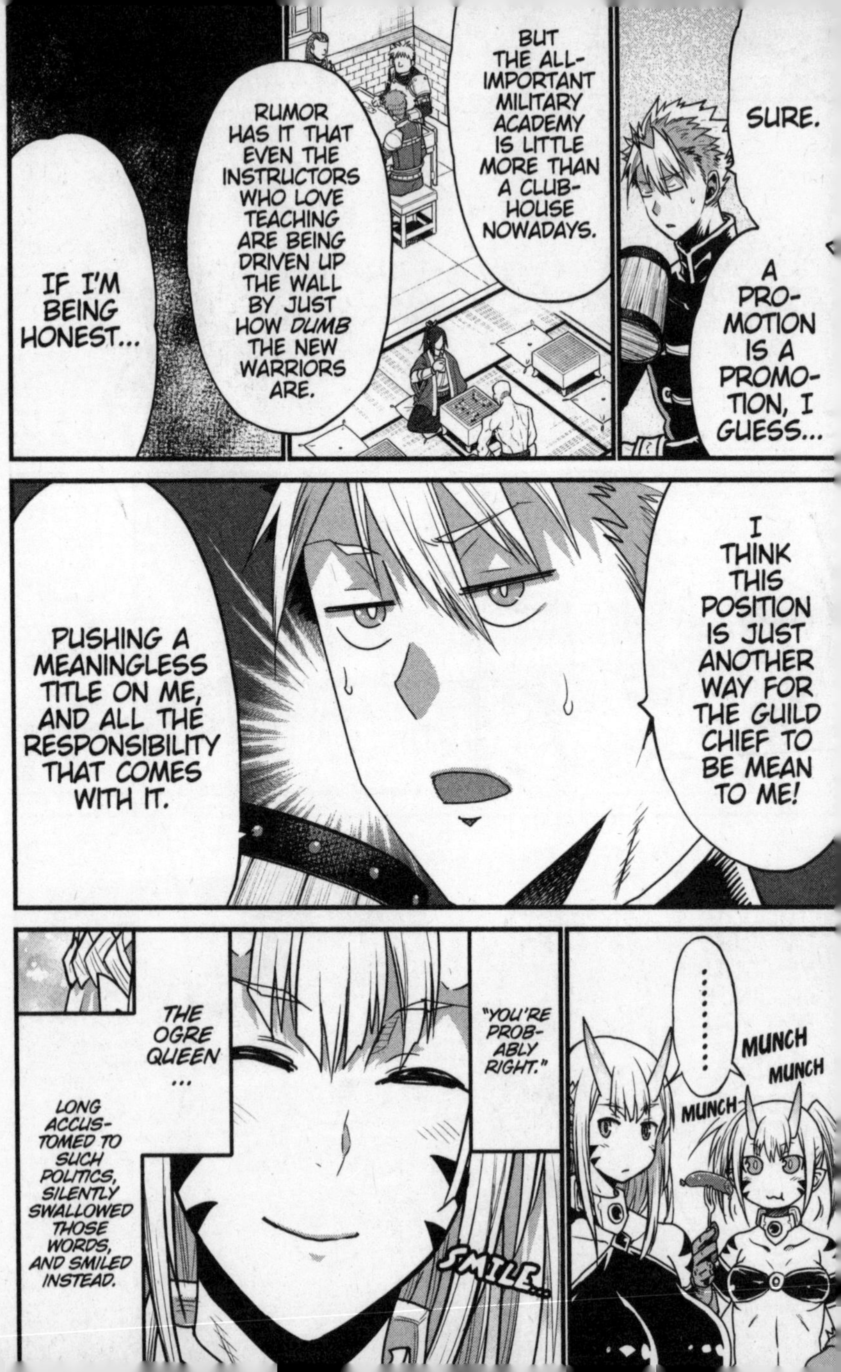
SURE.
A PROMOTION IS A PROMOTION, I GUESS...
BUT THE ALL-IMPORTANT MILITARY ACADEMY IS LITTLE MORE THAN A CLUBHOUSE NOWADAYS.
RUMOR HAS IT THAT EVEN THE INSTRUCTORS WHO LOVE TEACHING ARE BEING DRIVEN UP THE WALL BY JUST HOW *DUMB* THE NEW WARRIORS ARE.
IF I'M BEING HONEST...
I THINK THIS POSITION IS JUST ANOTHER WAY FOR THE GUILD CHIEF TO BE MEAN TO ME!
PUSHING A MEANINGLESS TITLE ON ME, AND ALL THE RESPONSIBILITY THAT COMES WITH IT.
......
MUNCH
MUNCH
MUNCH-
"YOU'RE PROBABLY RIGHT."
THE OGRE QUEEN...
LONG ACCUSTOMED TO SUCH POLITICS, SILENTLY SWALLOWED THOSE WORDS, AND SMILED INSTEAD.
SMILE...

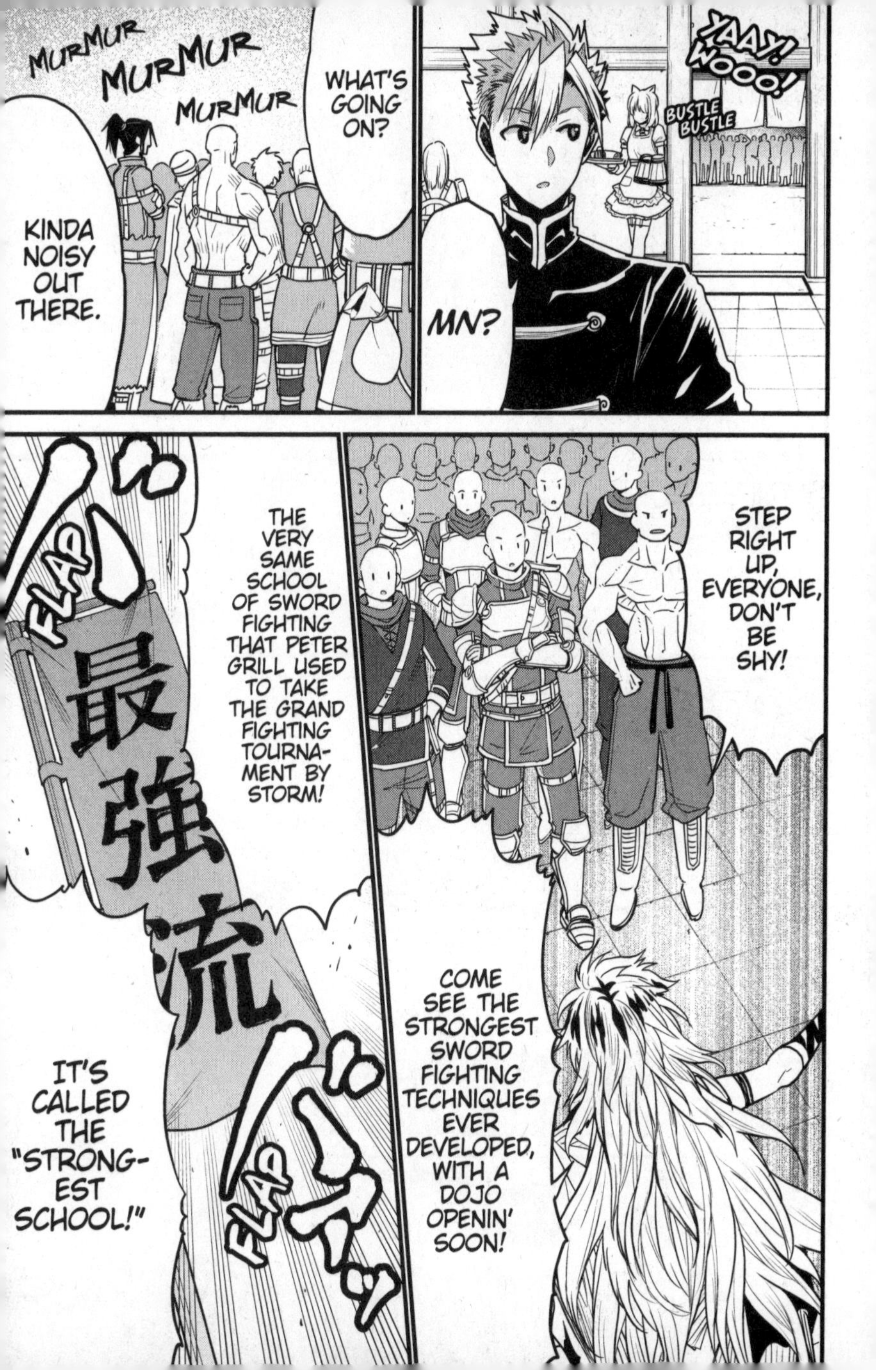
YAAY! WOOO!
BUSTLE BUSTLE
MN?
WHAT'S GOING ON?
MURMUR MURMUR MURMUR
KINDA NOISY OUT THERE.
STEP RIGHT UP, EVERYONE, DON'T BE SHY!
COME SEE THE STRONGEST SWORD FIGHTING TECHNIQUES EVER DEVELOPED, WITH A DOJO OPENIN' SOON!
THE VERY SAME SCHOOL OF SWORD FIGHTING THAT PETER GRILL USED TO TAKE THE GRAND FIGHTING TOURNA-MENT BY STORM!
FLAP
最強流
FLAP
IT'S CALLED THE "STRONG-EST SCHOOL!"

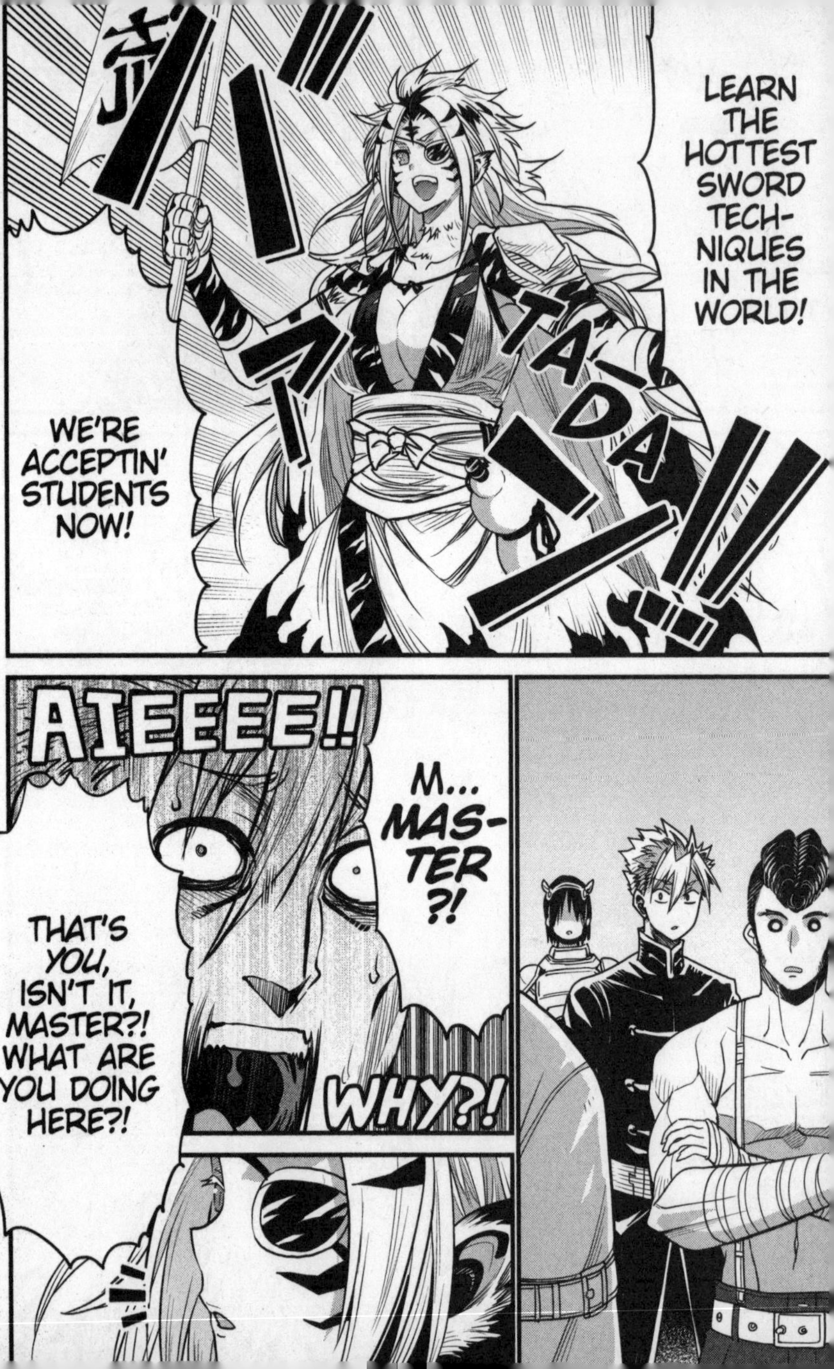
LEARN THE HOTTEST SWORD TECH-NIQUES IN THE WORLD!
WE'RE ACCEPTIN' STUDENTS NOW!
TA-DA
AIEEEE!!
M... MAS-TER?!
THAT'S YOU, ISN'T IT, MASTER?! WHAT ARE YOU DOING HERE?!
WHY?!

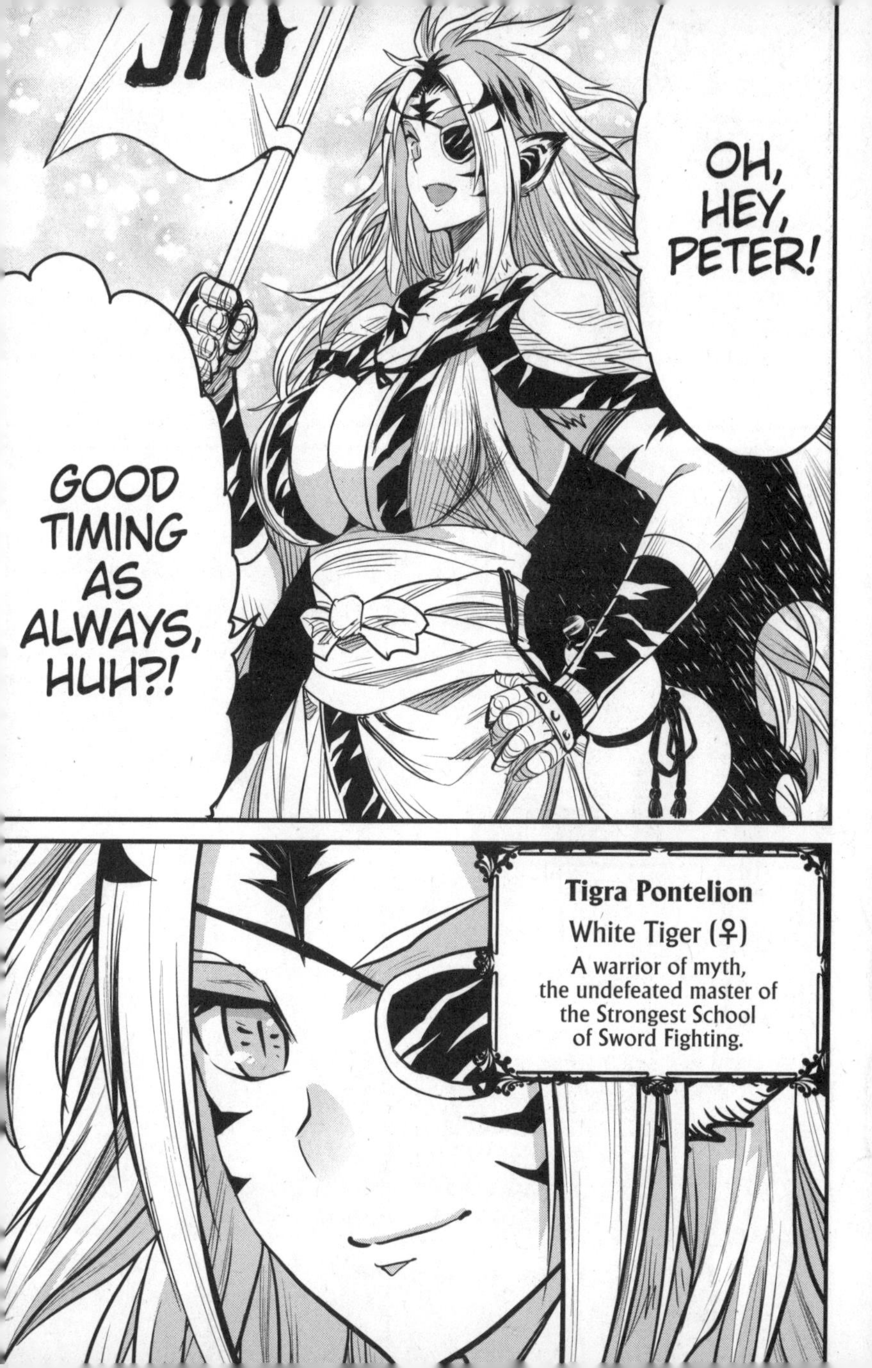
OH, HEY, PETER!
GOOD TIMING AS ALWAYS, HUH?!
Tigra Pontelion
White Tiger (♀)
A warrior of myth, the undefeated master of the Strongest School of Sword Fighting.

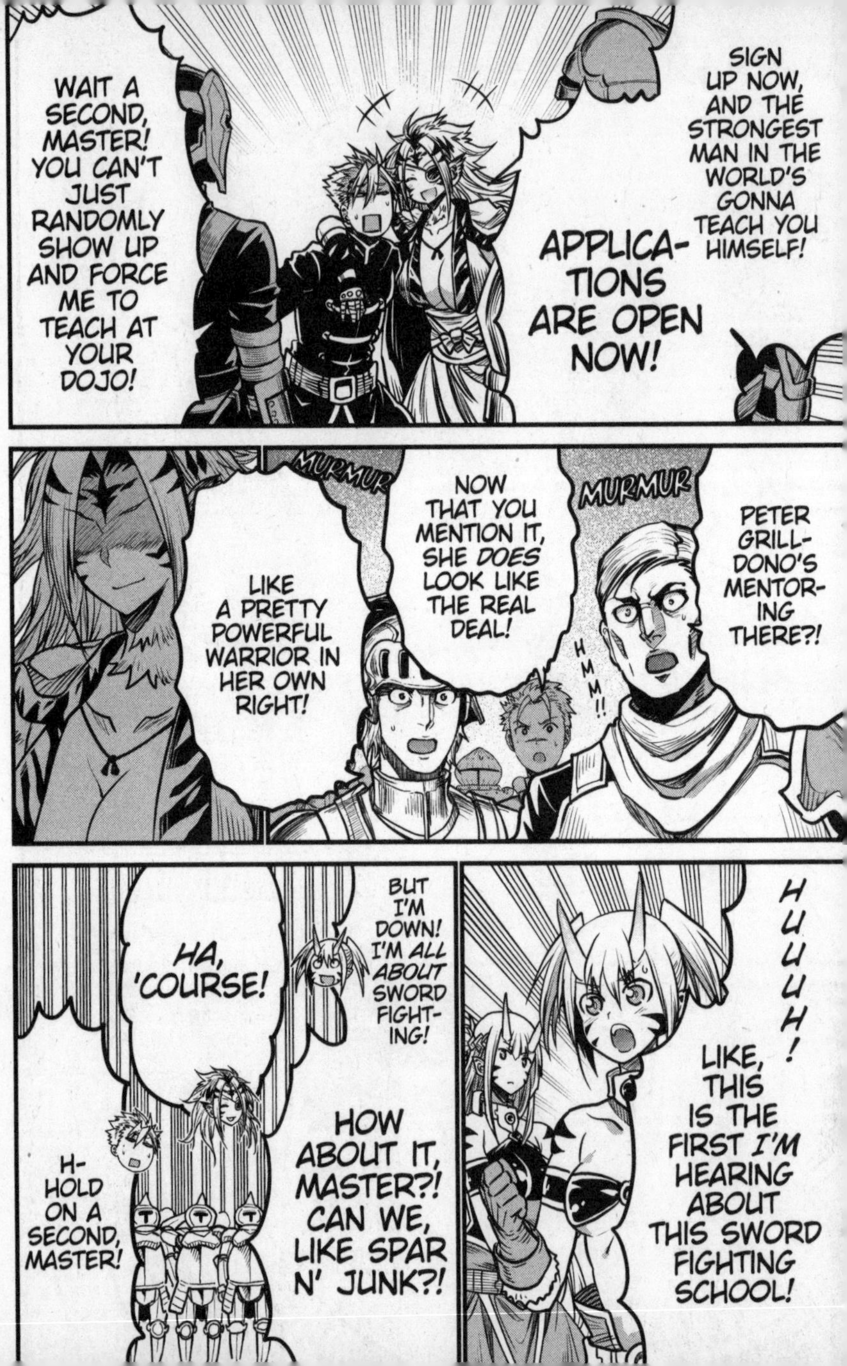
SIGN UP NOW, AND THE STRONGEST MAN IN THE WORLD'S GONNA TEACH YOU HIMSELF!
APPLICATIONS ARE OPEN NOW!
WAIT A SECOND, MASTER! YOU CAN'T JUST RANDOMLY SHOW UP AND FORCE ME TO TEACH AT YOUR DOJO!
PETER GRILL-DONO'S MENTORING THERE?!
MURMUR
HMMM!!
NOW THAT YOU MENTION IT, SHE *DOES* LOOK LIKE THE REAL DEAL!
MURMUR
LIKE A PRETTY POWERFUL WARRIOR IN HER OWN RIGHT!
HUUUH!
LIKE, THIS IS THE FIRST *I'M* HEARING ABOUT THIS SWORD FIGHTING SCHOOL!
BUT I'M DOWN! I'M *ALL ABOUT* SWORD FIGHTING!
HA, 'COURSE!
HOW ABOUT IT, MASTER?! CAN WE, LIKE SPAR N' JUNK?!
H-HOLD ON A SECOND, MASTER!

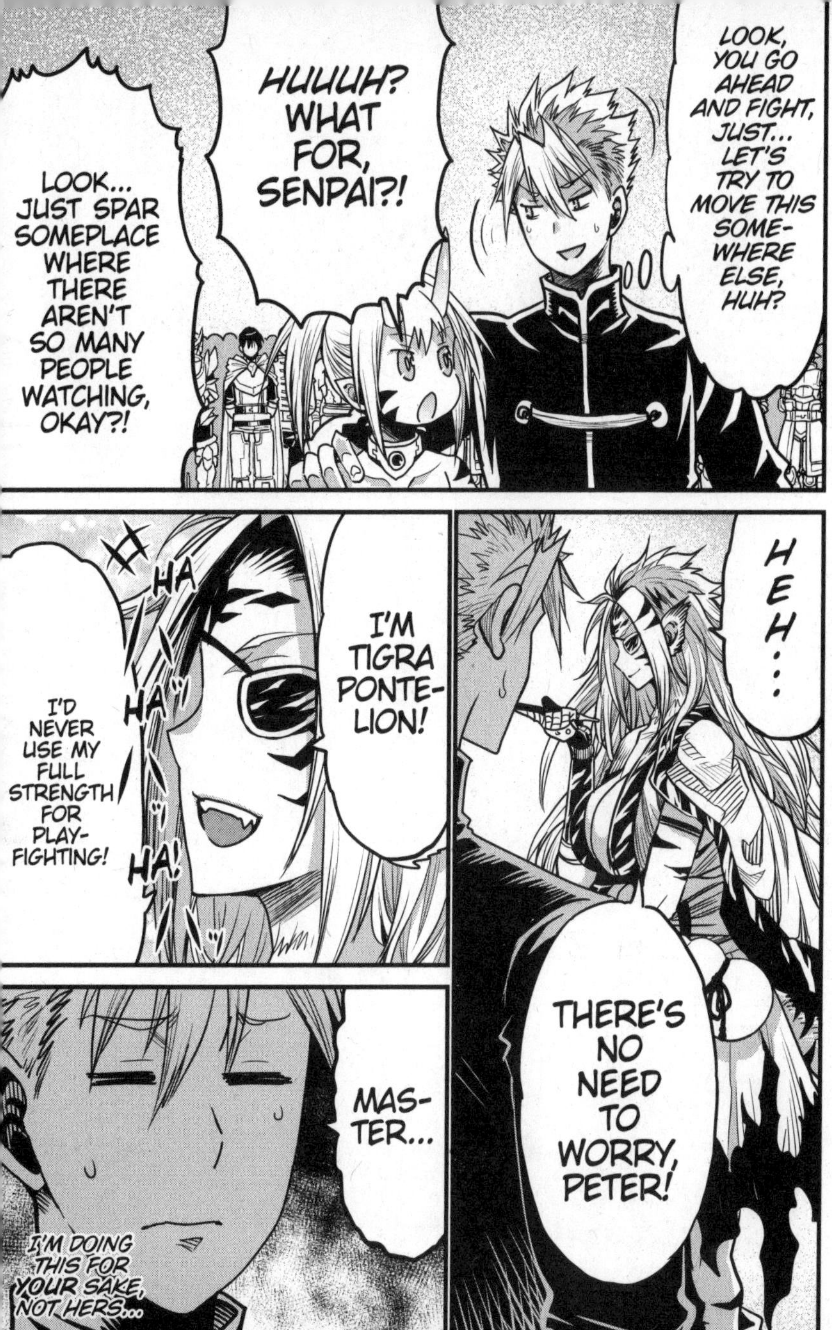
LOOK, YOU GO AHEAD AND FIGHT, JUST... LET'S TRY TO MOVE THIS SOME-WHERE ELSE, HUH?
HUUUH? WHAT FOR, SENPAI?!
LOOK... JUST SPAR SOMEPLACE WHERE THERE AREN'T SO MANY PEOPLE WATCHING, OKAY?!
HEH...
THERE'S NO NEED TO WORRY, PETER!
I'M TIGRA PONTE-LION!
HA HA HA!
I'D NEVER USE MY FULL STRENGTH FOR PLAY-FIGHTING!
MAS-TER...
I'M DOING THIS FOR YOUR SAKE, NOT HERS...

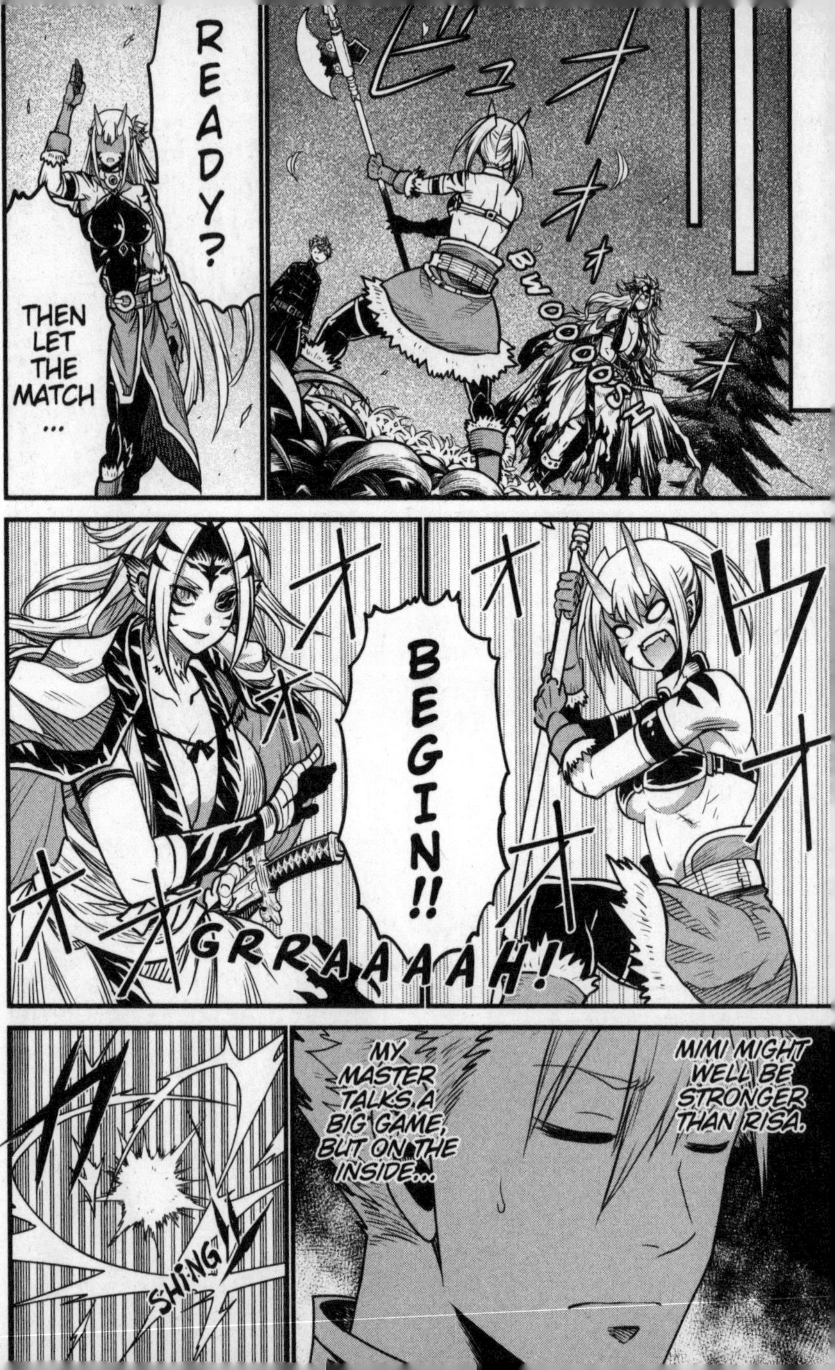
BWOOOOSH
READY?
THEN LET THE MATCH ...
BEGIN!!
GRRAAAAAH!
MIMI MIGHT WELL BE STRONGER THAN RISA.
MY MASTER TALKS A BIG GAME, BUT ON THE INSIDE...
SHING

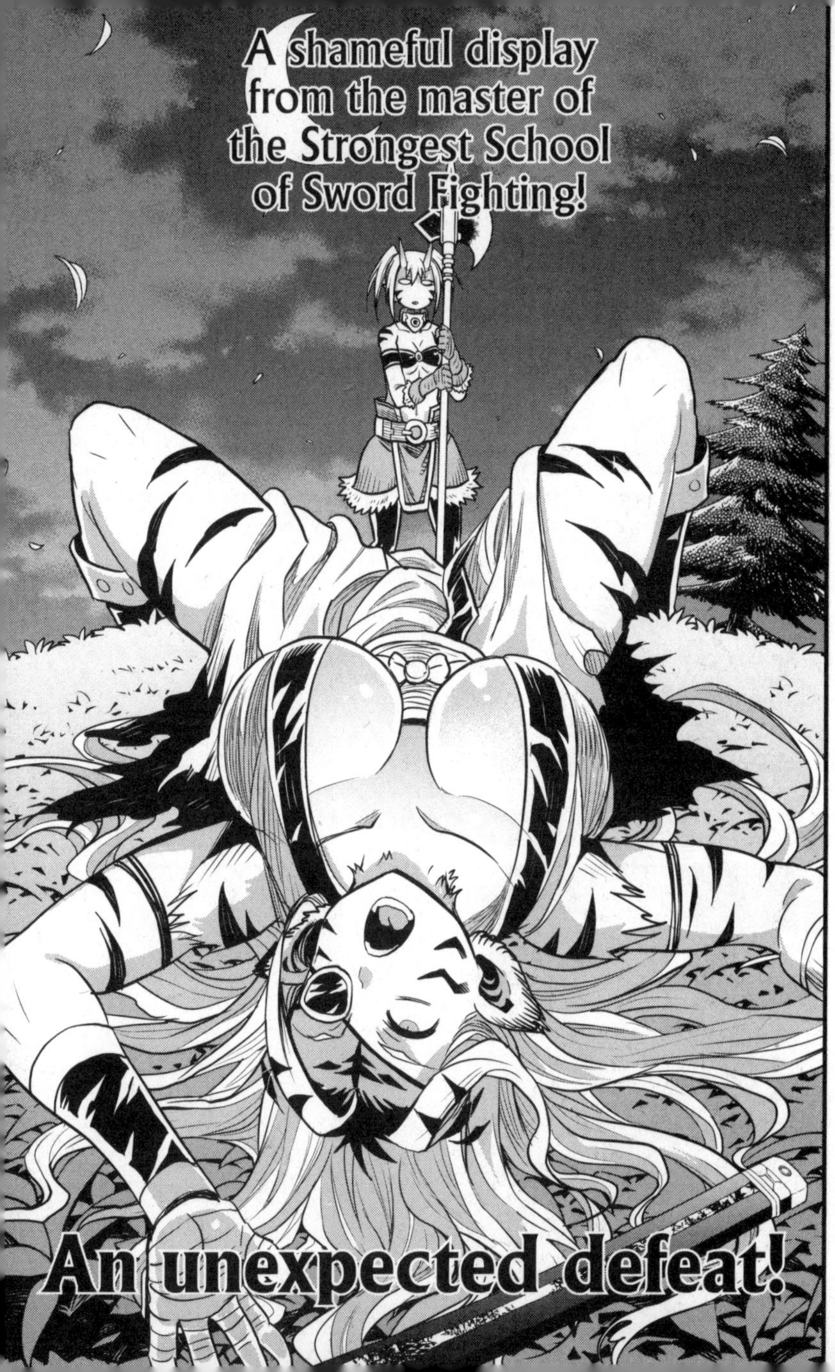
A shameful display from the master of the Strongest School of Sword Fighting!
An unexpected defeat!

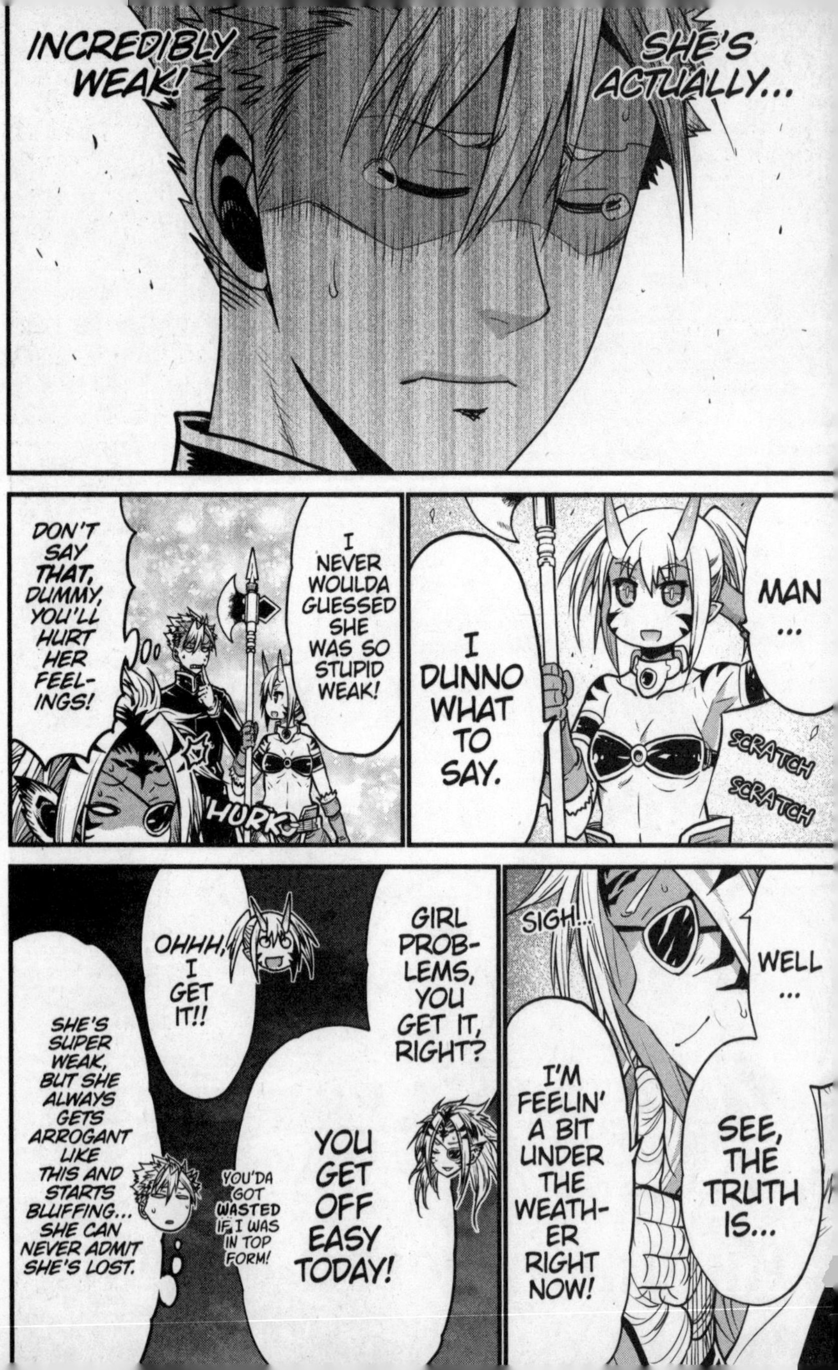
SHE'S ACTUALLY...
INCREDIBLY WEAK!
MAN ...
SCRATCH SCRATCH
I DUNNO WHAT TO SAY.
I NEVER WOULDA GUESSED SHE WAS SO STUPID WEAK!
DON'T SAY THAT, DUMMY, YOU'LL HURT HER FEEL-INGS!
HURK
WELL ...
SIGH...
SEE, THE TRUTH IS...
I'M FEELIN' A BIT UNDER THE WEATH-ER RIGHT NOW!
GIRL PROB-LEMS, YOU GET IT, RIGHT?
OHHH, I GET IT!!
YOU GET OFF EASY TODAY!
YOU'DA GOT WASTED IF I WAS IN TOP FORM!
SHE'S SUPER WEAK, BUT SHE ALWAYS GETS ARROGANT LIKE THIS AND STARTS BLUFFING... SHE CAN NEVER ADMIT SHE'S LOST.

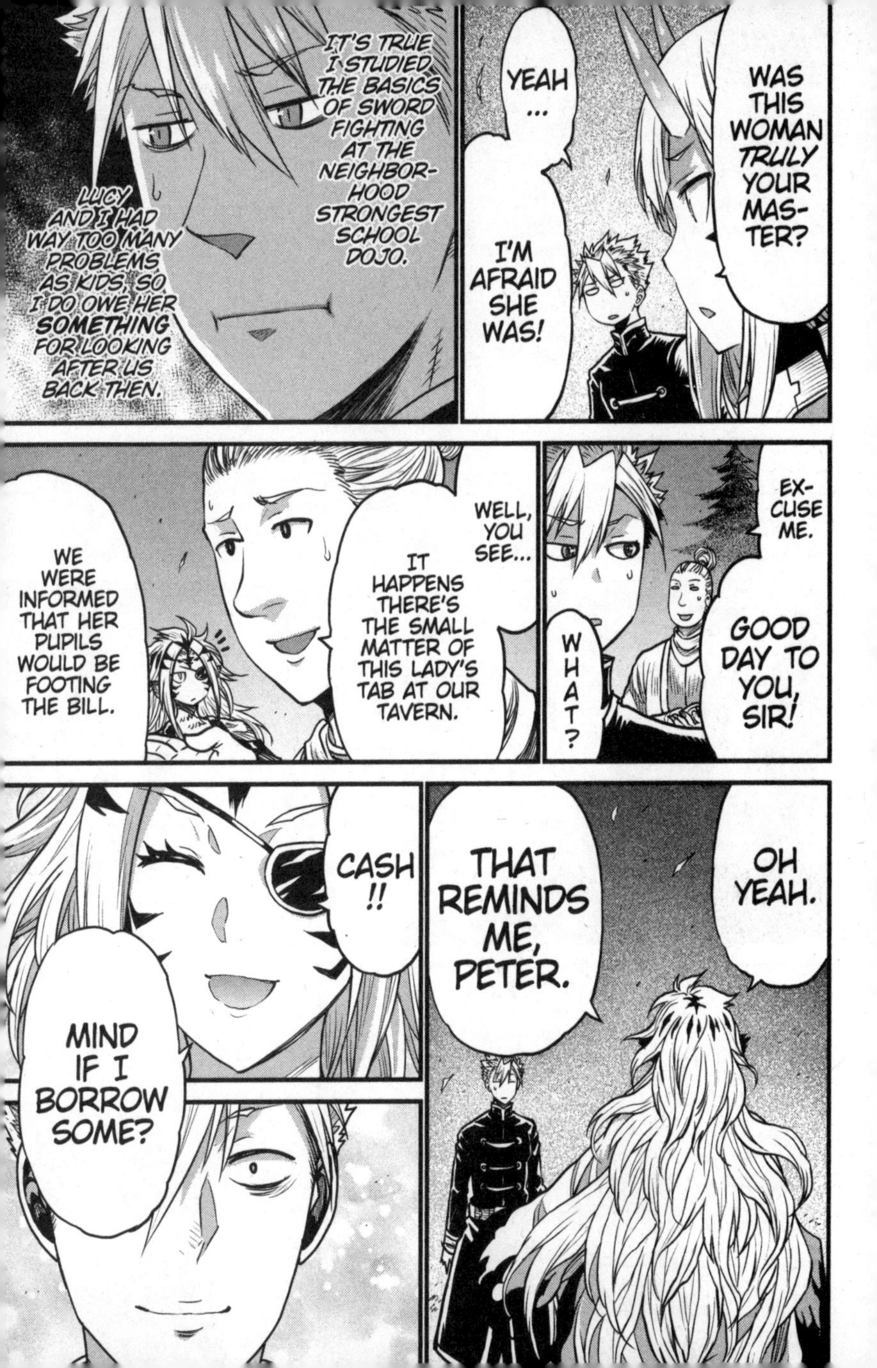
WAS THIS WOMAN TRULY YOUR MASTER?
YEAH ...
I'M AFRAID SHE WAS!
IT'S TRUE I STUDIED THE BASICS OF SWORD FIGHTING AT THE NEIGHBORHOOD STRONGEST SCHOOL DOJO.
LUCY AND I HAD WAY TOO MANY PROBLEMS AS KIDS, SO I DO OWE HER SOMETHING FOR LOOKING AFTER US BACK THEN.
EXCUSE ME.
GOOD DAY TO YOU, SIR!
WHAT?
WELL, YOU SEE...
IT HAPPENS THERE'S THE SMALL MATTER OF THIS LADY'S TAB AT OUR TAVERN.
WE WERE INFORMED THAT HER PUPILS WOULD BE FOOTING THE BILL.
OH YEAH.
THAT REMINDS ME, PETER.
CASH!!
MIND IF I BORROW SOME?

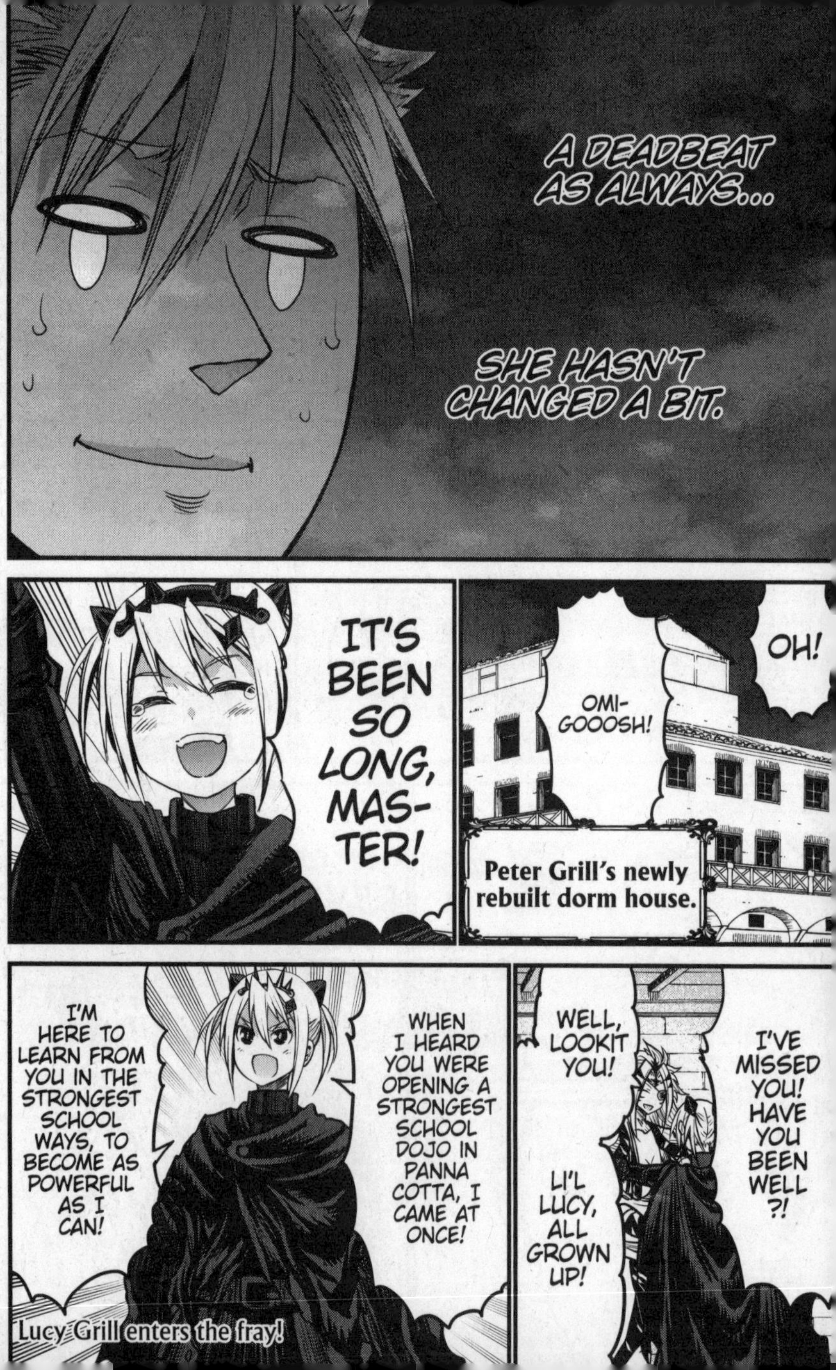
A DEADBEAT AS ALWAYS...
SHE HASN'T CHANGED A BIT.
OH!
OMI-GOOOSH!
Peter Grill's newly rebuilt dorm house.
IT'S BEEN SO LONG, MAS-TER!
I'VE MISSED YOU! HAVE YOU BEEN WELL?!
WELL, LOOKIT YOU!
LI'L LUCY, ALL GROWN UP!
WHEN I HEARD YOU WERE OPENING A STRONGEST SCHOOL DOJO IN PANNA COTTA, I CAME AT ONCE!
I'M HERE TO LEARN FROM YOU IN THE STRONGEST SCHOOL WAYS, TO BECOME AS POWERFUL AS I CAN!
Lucy Grill enters the fray!

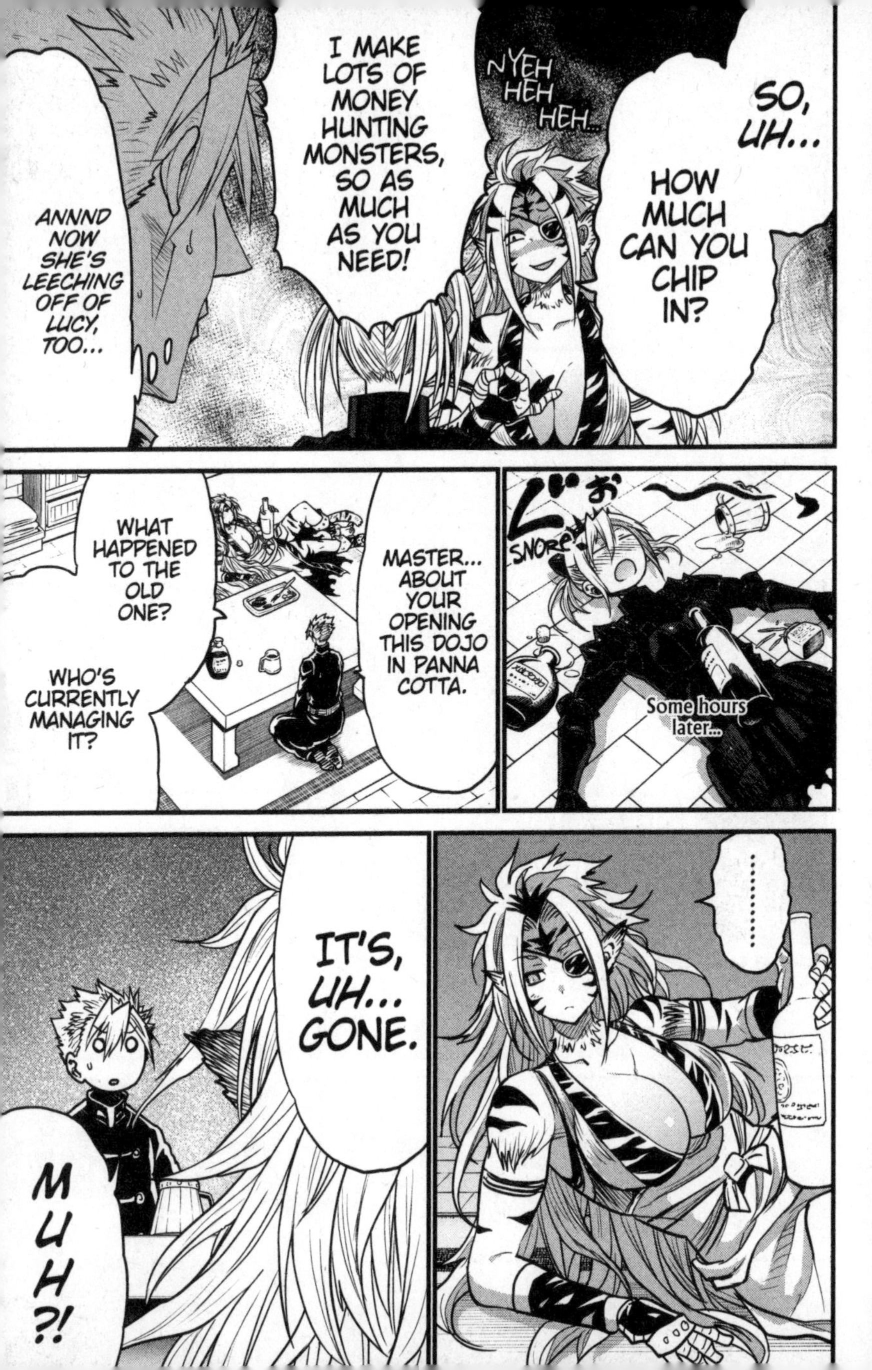
SO, UH...
HOW MUCH CAN YOU CHIP IN?
NYEH HEH HEH...
I MAKE LOTS OF MONEY HUNTING MONSTERS, SO AS MUCH AS YOU NEED!
ANNND NOW SHE'S LEECHING OFF OF LUCY, TOO...
ぐお
SNORE
Some hours later...
MASTER... ABOUT YOUR OPENING THIS DOJO IN PANNA COTTA.
WHAT HAPPENED TO THE OLD ONE?
WHO'S CURRENTLY MANAGING IT?
....
IT'S, UH... GONE.
MUH?!

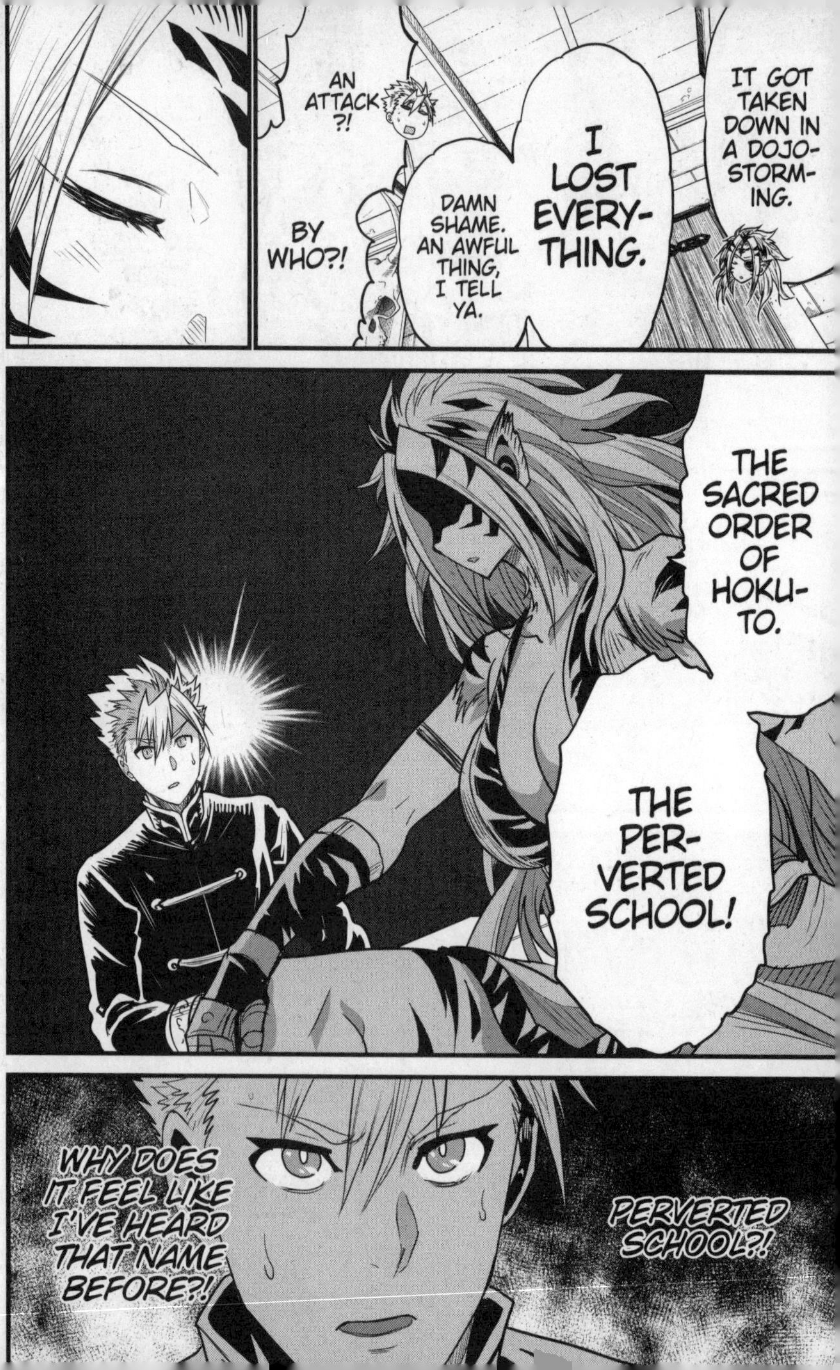
IT GOT TAKEN DOWN IN A DOJO-STORMING.
I LOST EVERYTHING.
DAMN SHAME. AN AWFUL THING, I TELL YA.
AN ATTACK?!
BY WHO?!
THE SACRED ORDER OF HOKUTO.
THE PERVERTED SCHOOL!
PERVERTED SCHOOL?!
WHY DOES IT FEEL LIKE I'VE HEARD THAT NAME BEFORE?!

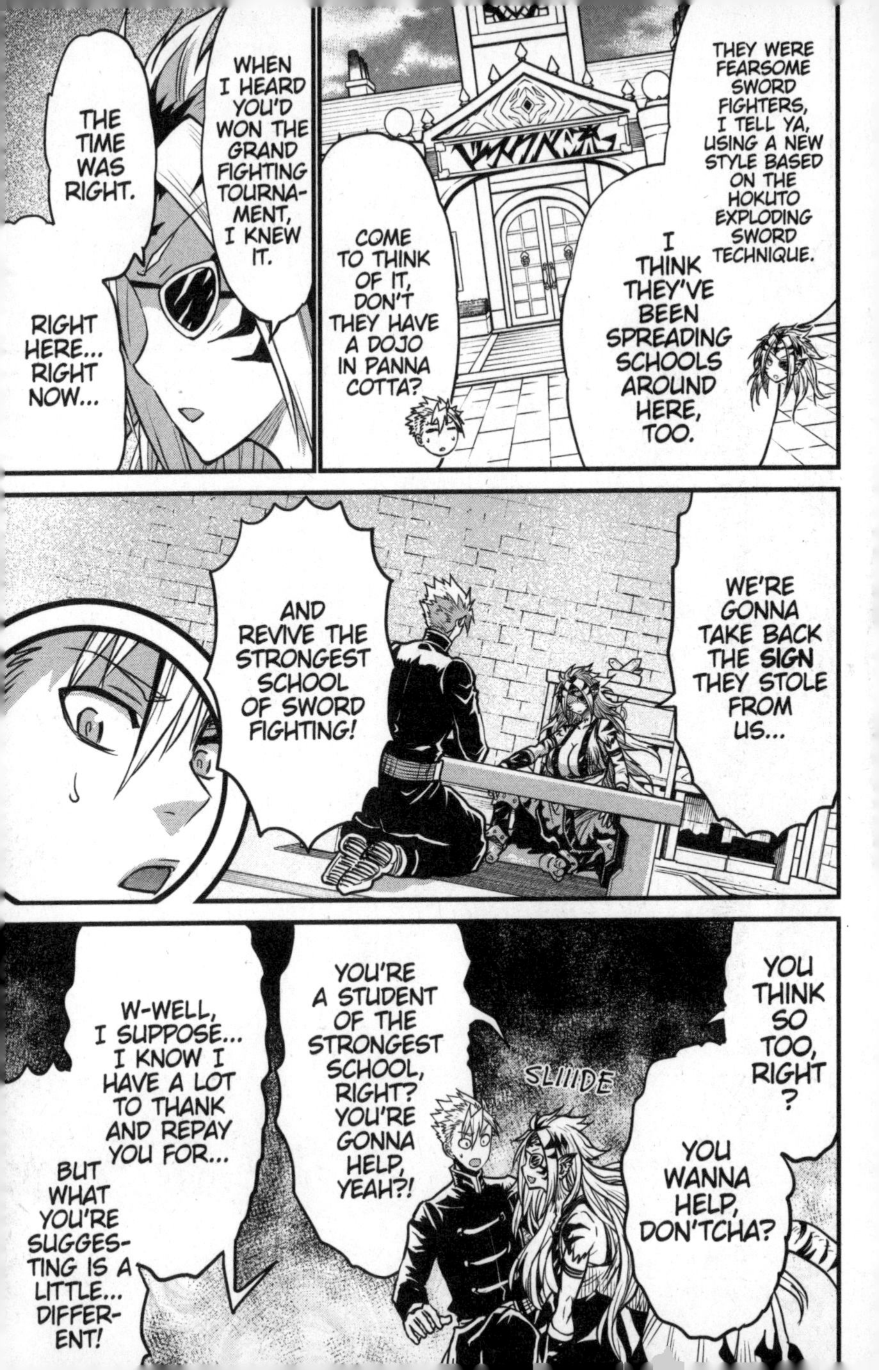
THEY WERE FEARSOME SWORD FIGHTERS, I TELL YA, USING A NEW STYLE BASED ON THE HOKUTO EXPLODING SWORD TECHNIQUE.
I THINK THEY'VE BEEN SPREADING SCHOOLS AROUND HERE, TOO.
COME TO THINK OF IT, DON'T THEY HAVE A DOJO IN PANNA COTTA?
WHEN I HEARD YOU'D WON THE GRAND FIGHTING TOURNAMENT, I KNEW IT.
THE TIME WAS RIGHT.
RIGHT HERE... RIGHT NOW...
WE'RE GONNA TAKE BACK THE SIGN THEY STOLE FROM US...
AND REVIVE THE STRONGEST SCHOOL OF SWORD FIGHTING!
YOU THINK SO TOO, RIGHT?
YOU WANNA HELP, DON'TCHA?
SLIIIDE
YOU'RE A STUDENT OF THE STRONGEST SCHOOL, RIGHT? YOU'RE GONNA HELP, YEAH?!
W-WELL, I SUPPOSE... I KNOW I HAVE A LOT TO THANK AND REPAY YOU FOR...
BUT WHAT YOU'RE SUGGESTING IS A LITTLE... DIFFERENT!

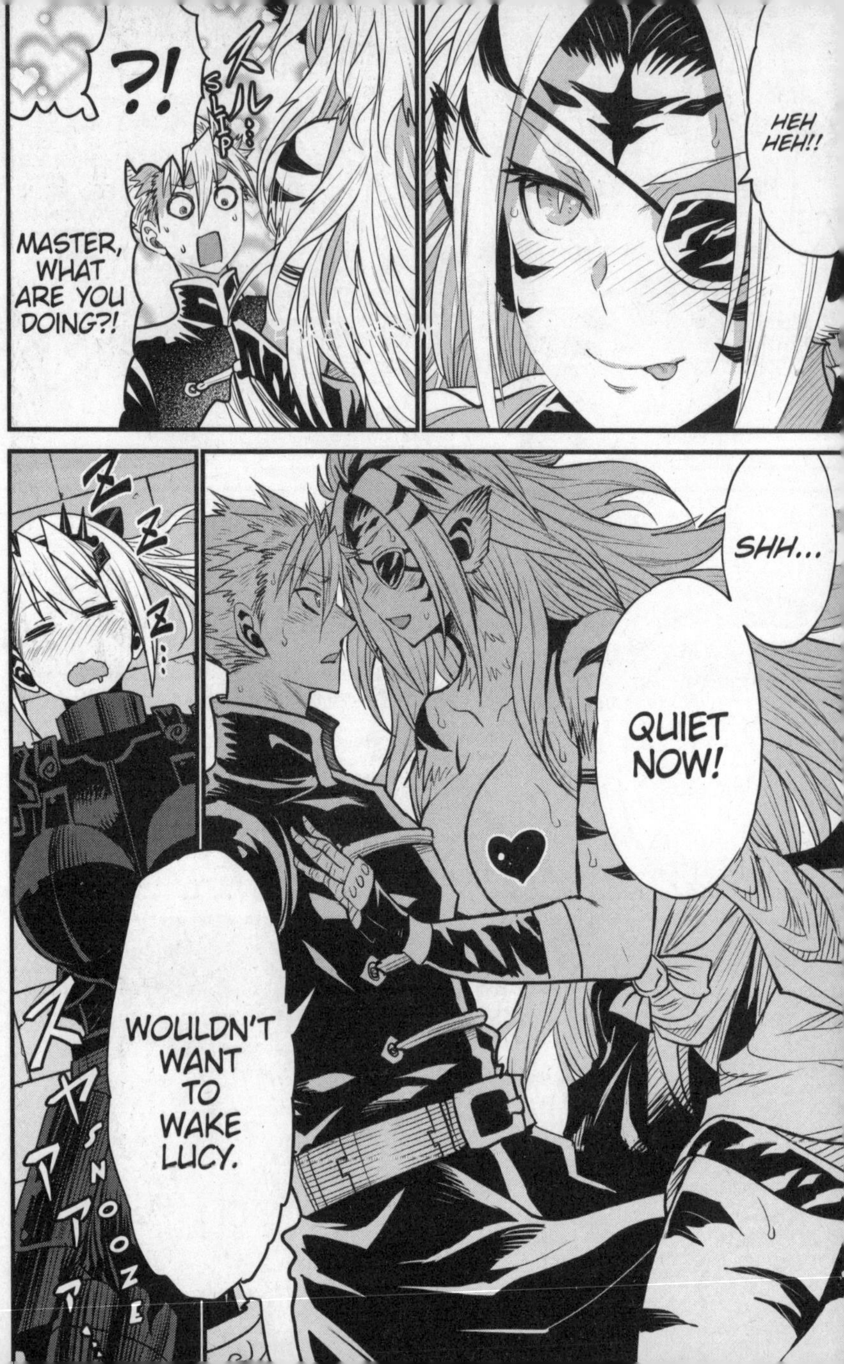
HEH HEH!!
SLIP
?!
MASTER, WHAT ARE YOU DOING?!
SHH...
QUIET NOW!
WOULDN'T WANT TO WAKE LUCY.
Z Z Z...
SNOOZE

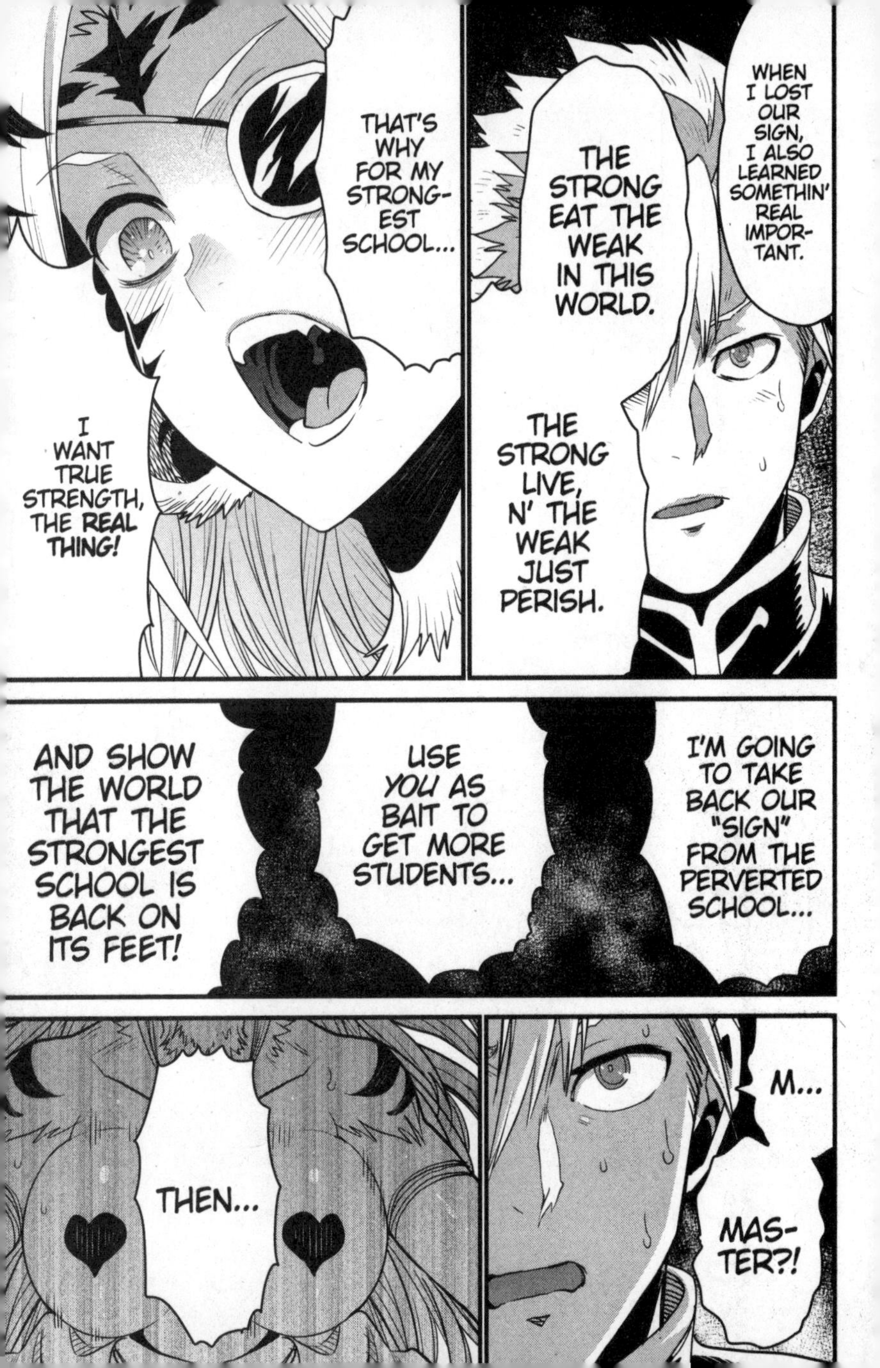
WHEN I LOST OUR SIGN, I ALSO LEARNED SOMETHIN' REAL IMPOR-TANT.
THE STRONG EAT THE WEAK IN THIS WORLD.
THE STRONG LIVE, N' THE WEAK JUST PERISH.
THAT'S WHY FOR MY STRONG-EST SCHOOL...
I WANT TRUE STRENGTH, THE REAL THING!
I'M GOING TO TAKE BACK OUR "SIGN" FROM THE PERVERTED SCHOOL...
USE *YOU* AS BAIT TO GET MORE STUDENTS...
AND SHOW THE WORLD THAT THE STRONGEST SCHOOL IS BACK ON ITS FEET!
M...
MAS-TER?!
THEN...

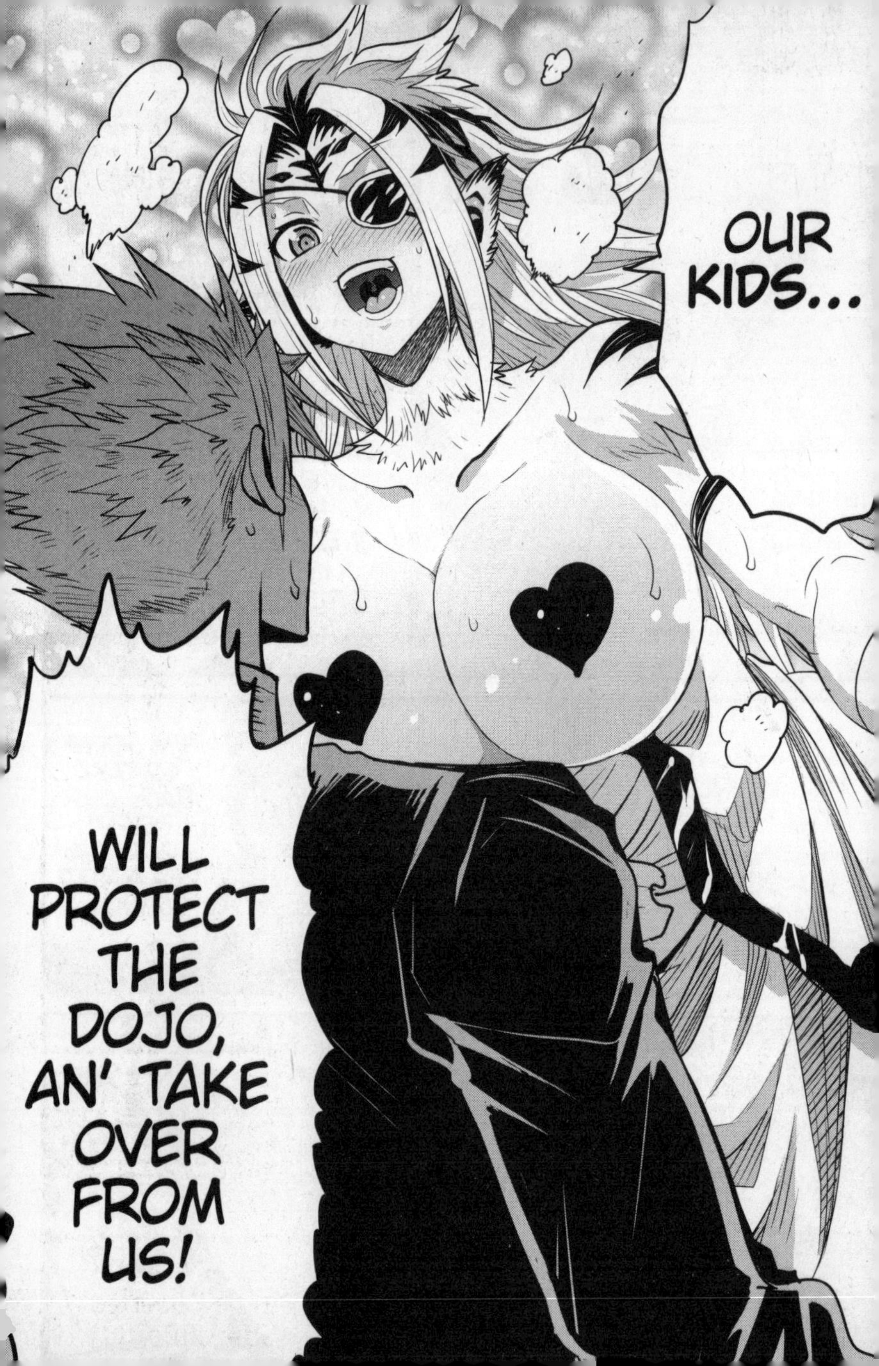
OUR KIDS...
WILL PROTECT THE DOJO, AN' TAKE OVER FROM US!

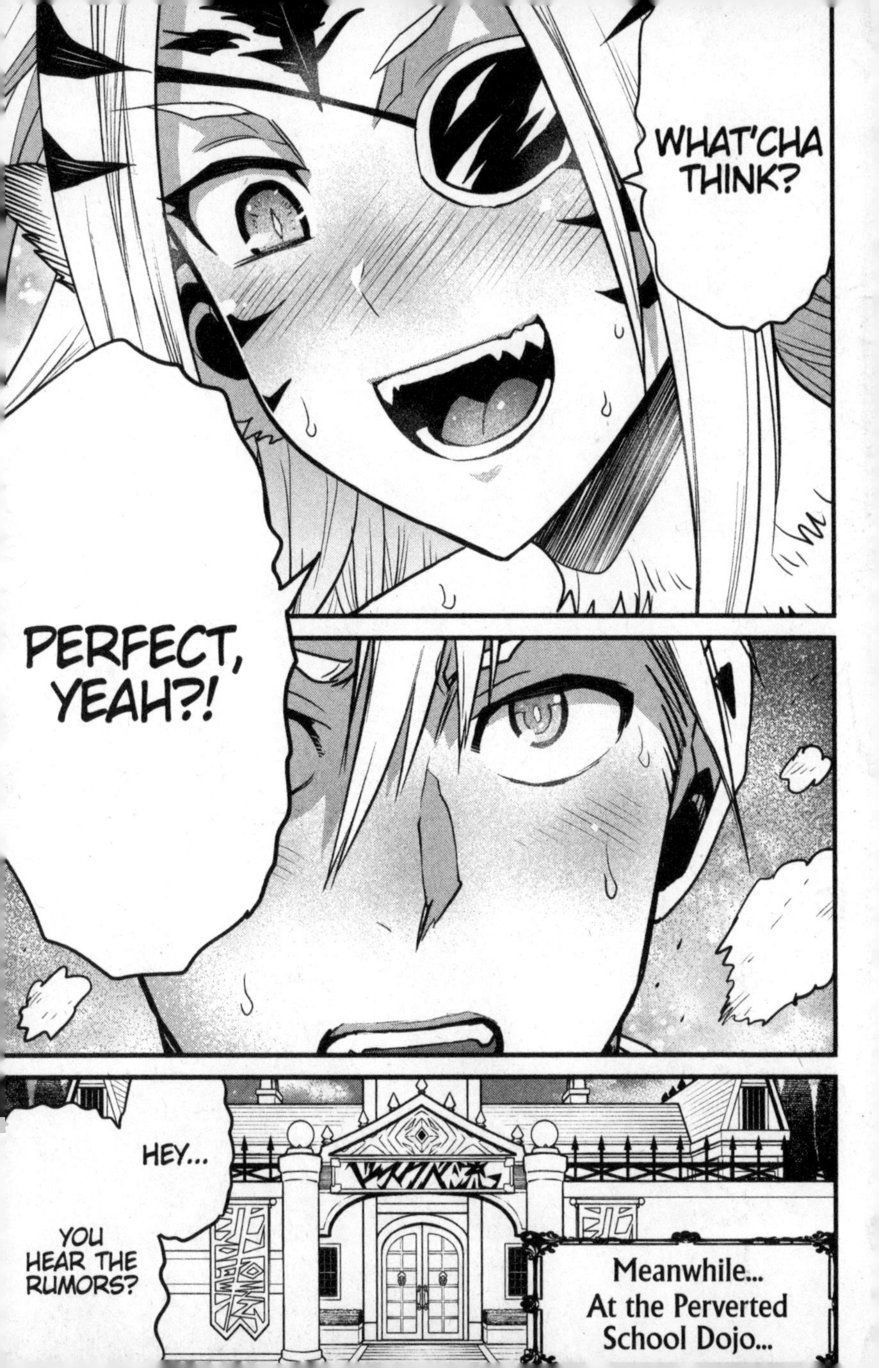
WHAT'CHA THINK?
PERFECT, YEAH?!
Meanwhile... At the Perverted School Dojo...
HEY...
YOU HEAR THE RUMORS?

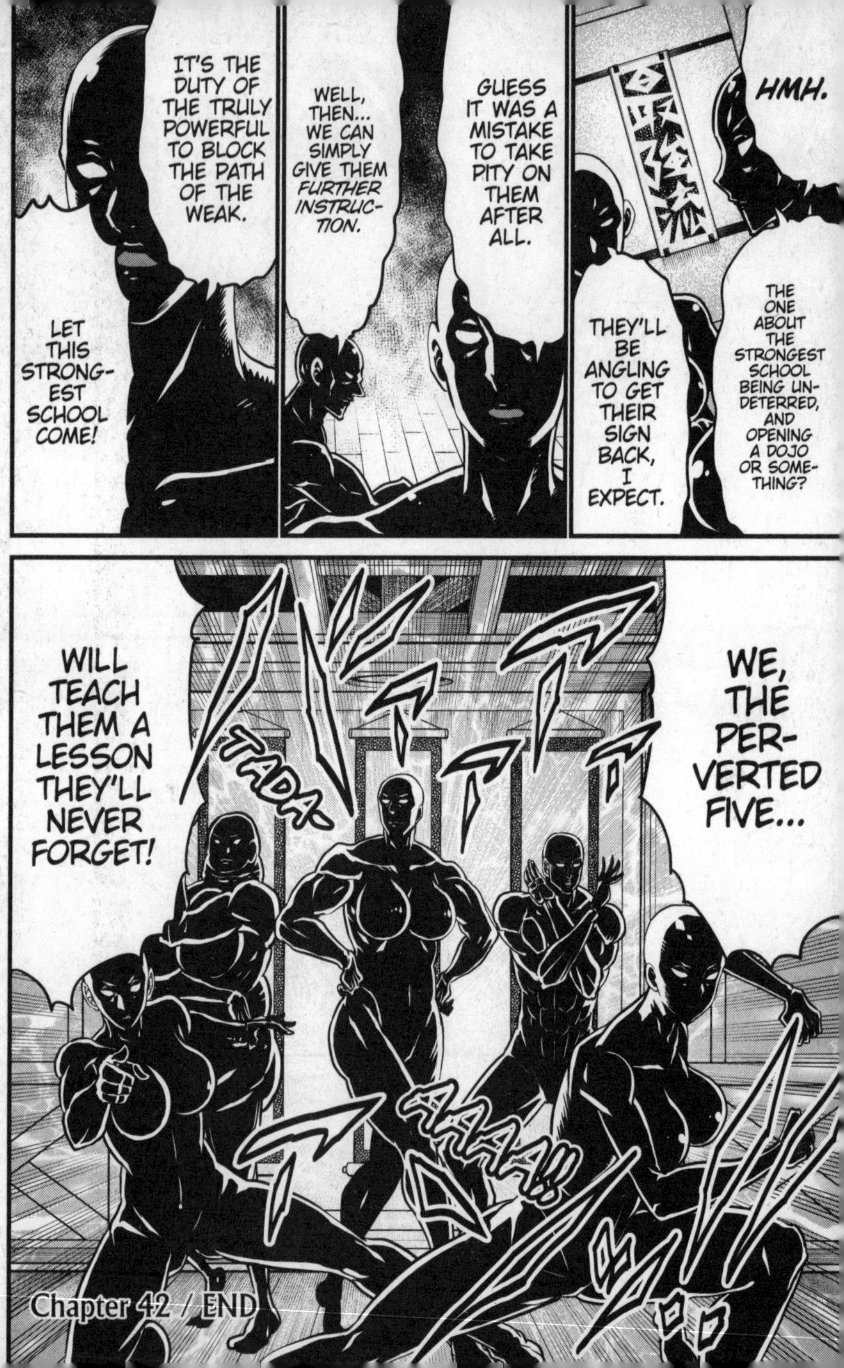
HMH.
THE ONE ABOUT THE STRONGEST SCHOOL BEING UN-DETERRED, AND OPENING A DOJO OR SOME-THING?
THEY'LL BE ANGLING TO GET THEIR SIGN BACK, I EXPECT.
GUESS IT WAS A MISTAKE TO TAKE PITY ON THEM AFTER ALL.
WELL, THEN... WE CAN SIMPLY GIVE THEM *FURTHER INSTRUC-TION.*
IT'S THE DUTY OF THE TRULY POWERFUL TO BLOCK THE PATH OF THE WEAK.
LET THIS STRONG-EST SCHOOL COME!
WE, THE PER-VERTED FIVE...
TADA
WILL TEACH THEM A LESSON THEY'LL NEVER FORGET!
AAAA!!

Chapter 42 / END

NEXT

The Perverted Five, whose faces I hadn't figured out by the end of this volume, make their debut!!

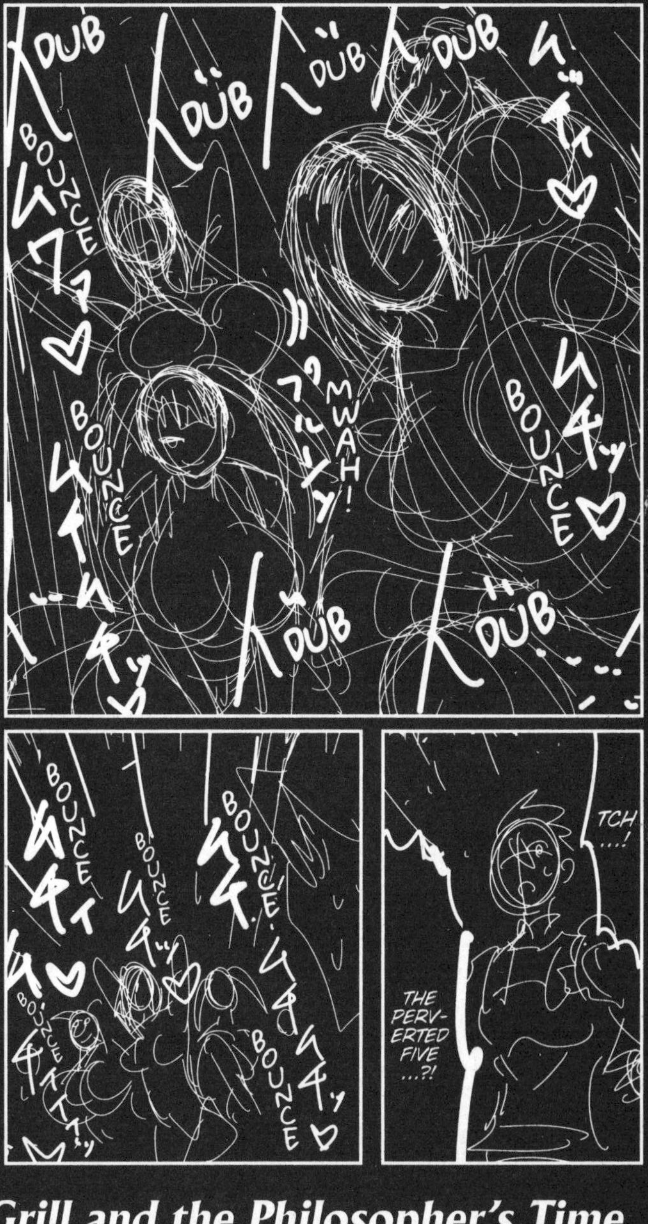
DUB
DUB
DUB
DUB
DUB
BOUNCE
BOUNCE
BOUNCE
MWAH!
DUB
DUB
TCH...!
THE PERVERTED FIVE...?!
BOUNCE
BOUNCE
BOUNCE
BOUNCE
BOUNCE

Peter Grill and the Philosopher's Time
Volume Ten—Coming soon!!!

SEVEN SEAS' GHOST SHIP PRESENTS

PETER GRILL
AND THE PHILOSOPHER'S TIME

story and art by **DAISUKE HIYAMA** **VOLUME 9**

TRANSLATION
Ben Trethewey

ADAPTATION
David Lumsdon

LETTERING
Mo Harrison

COVER DESIGN
Kris Aubin

SENIOR EDITOR
J.P. Sullivan

PRODUCTION DESIGNER
George Panella

PRODUCTION MANAGER
Lissa Pattillo

PREPRESS TECHNICIAN
Melanie Ujimori
Jules Valera

EDITOR-IN-CHIEF
Julie Davis

ASSOCIATE PUBLISHER
Adam Arnold

PUBLISHER
Jason DeAngelis

PETER GRILL AND THE PHILOSOPHER'S TIME VOL. 9

First published in Japan in 2021 by Futabasha Publishers, Ltd., Tokyo.
English version published by Seven Seas Entertainment, Inc.
Under license from Futasha Publishers Ltd.

Seven Seas press and purchase enquiries can be sent to Marketing Manager Lianne Sentar at press@gomanga.com. Information regarding the distribution and purchase of digital editions is available from Digital Manager CK Russell at digital@gomanga.com.

ISBN: 978-1-63858-802-3
Printed in Canada
First Printing: November 2022
10 9 8 7 6 5 4 3 2 1

READING DIRECTIONS

This book reads from ***right to left***, Japanese style. If this is your first time reading manga, you start reading from the top right panel on each page and take it from there. If you get lost, just follow the numbered diagram here. It may seem backwards at first, but you'll get the hang of it! Have fun!!

1
2
3
4
5
6
7
8
9

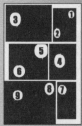